Planets in Youth

Other books by Robert Hand

Essays on Astrology

Horoscope Symbols

Planets in Composite: Analyzing Human Relationships

Planets in Transit: Life Cycles for Living

Robert Hand

Planets in Youth

Patterns of Early Development

A division of Schiffer Publishing, Ltd.
4880 Lower Valley Road
Atglen, PA 19310 USA

Planets in Youth: Patterns of Early Development
by Robert Hand

International Standard Book Number: 0-914918-26-5

Edited by Margaret E. Anderson
Typeset in 9 pt. Paladium on a Compugraphic ACM 9000
Composition by Hieratic Typesetting Co., Inc.
Printed by R. R. Donnelley & Sons Company on 55-pound SRT Paper
384 pages

Published by Whitford Press

Published by Whitford Press
A Division of Schiffer Publishing, Ltd.
4880 Lower Valley Road
Atglen, PA 19310 USA
Phone: (610) 593-1777 Fax: (610) 593-2002
E-mail: schifferbk@aol.com
Please visit our web site catalog at
www.schifferbooks.com
or write for a free catalog.
This book may be purchased from the publisher.
Please include $3.95 postage.
Try your bookstore first.

In Europe, Schiffer books are distributed by
Bushwood Books
6 Marksbury Avenue
Kew Gardens
Surrey TW9 4JF England
Phone: 44 (0) 20-8392-8585;
Fax: 44 (0) 20-8392-9876
E-mail: Bushwd@aol.com
Free postage in the UK. Europe: air mail at cost.

We are always looking for authors to write books on new
and related subjects. If you have an idea for a book
please contact us.

To Justine,
my own daughter

Contents

Foreword

The use of the sky as humanity's map and calendar, the primary means of orientation in space and time, dates back at least 5,000 years. But no period in recorded history can match the ferment in astrology today. The author of this volume is one of the leaders in the current exploration of new or long-neglected concepts and techniques. He is also one of a new breed of astrologers more concerned with the psychological sources of action than with the traditional attempts to predict precise results of psychological dynamics. When one successfully predicts precise action, it is a scientific triumph. When one helps a person understand why he or she acts in given ways, pointing out alternative expressions of the basic drives so that the individual learns to choose more effective ways of acting, it is a therapeutic triumph.

I must admit that with my scientific training, I would have been a bit more comfortable with the book if the statements had been more qualified: fewer flat assertions of "you are, you do, you feel," and more of the alternatives which I feel are always possible. Traditional scientific jargon is full of hedging qualifiers like, "there is a tendency, at times, other things being equal, subject to counter indications, provided the context of the chart supports it," and so on. But *Planets in Youth* comes far closer than most astrological productions to recognizing the complexity of the mind and the danger of statements that claim to be absolute and inevitable truth. The book discusses the growth of children, but is itself symbolic of the growth occurring in astrology.

It is especially encouraging that active research is now being done in this area. The human mind is still terra incognita to a greater degree than the depths of our oceans or the vast reaches of outer space. Astrology is shot through with controversy, as are psychology and psychiatry, which attempt to decipher the same complex subject, the human mind. You will receive very different concepts of human capacities from the followers of Freud, Jung, Adler, Rogers, Perls, Skinner, or the myriad of other presumed experts on psychology. In like vein, perhaps no astrologer ever completely agrees with any other astrologer. My own experience in working with psychological professionals has led me to see planets, signs and houses as all symbolic of the same twelve sides of life, as a kind of astrological alphabet. If this is true, the element and quality of houses must be taken into account in any weighting system to describe the relative power of fire, cardinality, etc. But I agree with Rob Hand that the basic nature of the planets is of greatest importance and that the aspects come next.

Only extensive research will settle such questions. In the meantime, all astrological theories are just that—theories to be tested. Astrology is a totally pragmatic study that has survived the test of time and the attacks of both religion and modern science. Those who have really worked with the subject know that a great truth lies half revealed and half concealed in the claims and counterclaims of its followers. There is a profound order in the cosmos shared by microcosm and macrocosm. Moreover, it is a meaningful and purposeful order. Astrology, the study of the correspondences between the patterns in the sky and the events of earth, offers a way to understand this order and to make our participation in the evolving cosmos more effective. It is not a religion demanding blind faith; it is a potential science in the process of being reborn. It is worthy of our best and most dedicated minds working together to purify and expand, to validate and use its incalculable potential value in helping our children grow and in creating a better world for them and for their children.

Since childhood is normally the time when a person is most flexible, when inner change occurs most readily, techniques that measure and evaluate children play a central role in psychology. If astrology is actually the most useful single diagnostic technique ever discovered or devised for understanding an individual's psychological dynamics, it is high time that it was applied to children. Yet almost nothing in the literature of astrology is specifically directed toward this goal. Rob Hand's book closes this gap and offers a helpful beginning in our search for deeper understanding of those who are too young to understand or to explain themselves. As with any collection of statements extracted from an understanding of the whole, the book must be used with discretion. All of us contain inner inconsistencies, so that one pattern may contradict another, leading to repression, projection, or pendulum swings until the individual is able to integrate the conflicting urges. Neither a book nor a computer can put the fragments together; only a human mind can integrate the ambivalences. But recognizing the conflicts is the first step toward solving them, and I hope that this book will help many concerned parents to take that first step.

Zipporah Dobyns

Chapter One

Parent and Child

The main text of this book is a complete set of natal delineations, much like those in other texts. The difference, however, is that this text is aimed at helping the student describe the basic psychological issues that confront children. If you are an adult reader, you can learn about the important developmental issues facing your children, or you can look back at your own childhood to discover the psychological energies behind your adult personality. The text is written in nontechnical English, but it is not intended to be a lightweight set of delineations. The matters that are discussed are important and can have a great effect upon the adult that the child grows into. There is some advice to parents about how to handle certain problems that may come up in childhood, so that they do not develop into serious problems in adulthood, when they are much more difficult to correct. A casual reader may be struck by the fact that the text is not written for children specifically. Although a reasonably mature young person could read it, the audience for this book is mostly adults.

The initial impetus for this book was the discovery that existing texts were totally inadequate for understanding children. All of them had one or more deficiencies. Most delineation texts are based on a fully formed personality, with very little thought to the kinds of energies that go into creating the adult personality. And since character is destiny, most texts discuss events and actions, which are the logical result of adult character traits. The problem is that all interpretations written for adults discuss the most probable manifestation of an astrological energy pattern. The writer has to assume that the adult handled the indications of his natal chart in a normal manner, but the reader often feels that he has been given a kind of cosmic judgment, especially since some writers take on a particularly lugubrious tone concerning the harder aspects. Although that is a serious problem with adult horoscopes, it is a disaster with children's charts, because their character is not fully formed. A change of parental tactics may help the child work out a potentially difficult energy pattern constructively or at least with the negative potential minimized.

This book is called *Planets in Youth*, but it is not restricted to young people. It emphasizes the dynamic growth potential of any natal horoscope, and in a very real sense, the text is just as good for adults as it is for children, if the adult wants to understand the energy patterns that have led to his or her present situation. Other texts, quite frankly, handle the fortune-telling dimension adequately. That is not the purpose of this text, nor is it an astrological "cookbook" in the usual sense, because the delineations give the reader a number of choices.

Also, most existing texts deal with issues that do not yet concern a young person, such as sexuality, career and money. These are potential issues in childhood, to be sure, and childhood events can have an enormous influence on adult attitudes about these issues. In this regard, the delineations here do consider such issues, even though there aren't any clear manifestations that have to be dealt with yet. There is ample information about situations that will affect the child when he or she grows up.

A characteristic of many texts, which is a problem for adults, and even more serious for children, is their moralistic tone; they pass judgment on an individual because of certain astrological indications without knowing the person. But the main purpose of astrology, especially for young people, is to help the individual learn who he or she really is and to accept it without being judgmental. Certain personality traits may be counterproductive in specific situations, and you may choose to modify or repress that trait, but only if you fully understand what and who you are. If you, either as a child or as an adult, have a clear mental picture of what you ought to be, but you also perceive that you do not live up to your image, then you will try to kid yourself and pretend to be what you are not. The usual result of this attempt is that you make a mess of being yourself, because the only person you can be adequately is yourself. You are doomed to be inadequate if you try to be anyone else. Astrological moralizing is contrary to the real purpose of astrology, especially with young people.

In this text, unpleasant indications are described as objectively as possible. Even if a delineation seems to take a moralizing tone, which I have tried to minimize, the reader should interpret my statements as indications of what *might* happen. In each case I try to suggest how one might correct any negative indications in the chart. A basic truth of astrology is that there is no such thing as an intrinsically bad horoscope; there are only poorly handled ones. And likewise, no chart is so positive that it can't be messed up in the course of your life, perhaps by inappropriate upbringing. Certainly some indications are more difficult than others, but most of the really difficult ones have to be reinforced by certain kinds of childhood events or relationships. If those negatively reinforcing events or patterns of relationship do not come about, then the negative quality can be not only minimized but even transformed into a positive indication. Astrology bears out the basic psychological dictum that the earliest years, roughly from one through four, have the greatest effect on a person's development and that our relationship with our parents is crucial.

The book contains a complete listing of astrological indications for the planets in the signs, in the houses and in aspect to each other. These are the ingredients for the analytical part of interpreting a chart. In addition, the introductory chapters present some approaches for putting the elements of the chart together into a coherent whole. Energy systems among the planets are discussed, as well as schemes for telling whether each planetary energy is strong, excessive or deficient. Other techniques of synthesis are also described. A more complete discussion of the main techniques of synthesizing and creating a complete psychological picture from the chart will be presented in a future text.

Definition of Childhood

Because this book deals with childhood, I feel it will be helpful to explain my idea of what childhood is, especially since this idea is implicit in all of the delineations.

First, we should understand that childhood is *not* a separate stage that people go through before becoming what they really are, that is, adults. Grown-ups too often think of children as completely alien entities from themselves. They believe that children's emotional drives, needs and desires are completely different from theirs. This is not true, and the only reason that most adults do not understand children is that they do not understand themselves. Most adults feel that their needs are reasonable and that they are motivated primarily by real needs, duties and responsibilities, whereas children are motivated by irrational drives and emotional impulses. Adults feel that they relate to the real world but that children do not. As a consequence, adults try to understand children by making up elaborate models of the reasons behind childhood behavior, and then they create a language to express fantasies they have generated. And in doing this, they try to impose on real children their pictures of what children are. The result is that the entity known as a child has been created by adults.

Most people treat children according to one of two basic models. Some believe that all children are naturally good and virtuous until made sick by a sick society, and that real education should get out of the way so that the child's natural virtue can assert itself. Others believe that children are naturally bestial, driven by irrational hungers that must be curbed by adults to create civilized members of society.

I prefer to assume, and my observations as a parent and teacher confirm this, that children have exactly the same needs and drives as adults, that they are neither virtuous nor bestial and that they do whatever will allow them to survive, both as biological entities and as personalities. A child reacts to a threat with exactly the same kind of energy as an adult. The only difference is that the child does not know as much about the so-called real world and cannot always manipulate it successfully to achieve a desired result. Because of this, a child often overreacts to a situation that an adult knows is not serious, which leads us to the real difference between children and adults. Children are adults in the process of becoming.

Because their personalities are much more in a state of flux, the astrological indications must be interpreted in terms of changing patterns of behavior and not as static patterns that are repeated over and over again. The psychological issues that a child confronts are not qualitatively different from an adult's, and in fact a child carries psychological baggage into adulthood without much change. In fact, one of the principal causes of neurotic behavior is that responses in childhood, *which were usually inappropriate even at the time*, are carried over into adulthood, where their inappropriateness is more obvious, although no more real. Transactional analysis teaches that each of us carries a child around inside ourselves. The psychological legacy of childhood becomes the basis of the adult personality, which means that any astrology of childhood must be an astrology of future adulthood as well. We only need to reinterpret the issues in terms of children's experiences. For example, they do not have jobs, but they do have school, and instead of bosses, they have teachers and parents. Clearly, their early experiences with teachers and parents directly affect their later relationships with bosses and other authority figures.

Although these statements are psychological truisms, they have been ignored by most astrological writers. What the child appears to be as a child is not very important. It may be fascinating to have an astrologer correctly describe a child's apparent personality, but it is not useful. It is much more important to view the child as a developing adult, to consider the kind of adult likely to arise out of the child's apparent personality. Most people spend much more time as an adult than as a child, and many persons whose childhoods were miserable have ultimately been very happy and self-fulfilled. The reverse is also true, and every other combination of miserable or happy childhood and adulthood as well.

Mother vs. Father

Obviously, one of the most important formative factors in a child's life is the relationship with his or her parents. No other people will ever have such a formative effect upon the child. Of course, this is true not just of biological parents, but also of any other persons who act as parents in the child's life. Therefore, in reading the chart of a child, one of the first things to do is to come to some sort of conclusion about the relationship with the parents and the probable effects on the child's development.

It is important to understand that a child's chart does not in fact describe what the parents *actually are*, objectively considered, but rather their relationship with the child and the way the child sees them. The charts of siblings can have very different descriptions of the same two parents, because each child sees their parents differently. In fact one way in which people can grow psychologically is to discover that their image of their parents was not accurate. This discovery liberates them from being slaves to their images of their parents and frees them from the effects of those images.

It may seem rather strange, but we should start by defining what a mother is and what a father is. These definitions may seem self-evident, but they are not. We tend to think that the father is always the biologically male parent, and the mother, the biologically female parent. Traditionally that would have been a safe assumption, but in this time of frequent sexual role reversals, it is no longer necessarily true. The father and mother roles can be played by literally anyone.

The mother's function, in brief, is to support and nurture the child in the earliest period of life, which is referred to elsewhere in the text as the lunar period. She is the parent who must welcome the child into the world and make it clear that the child is accepted for himself. Of course, in reality all mothers have to discipline their children even at a very early age, but they should not do it in such a way that the child feels rejected. The child psychologist Haim Ginott makes the very important point that when a child does something wrong, the parents must let the child know that it is the act that is wrong, not the child. Many parents spend much of their time chewing out their children for their transgressions in a way that calls into question the child's basic nature and integrity as a human being. This attitude activates the child's survival instinct, because from his or her point of view, being rejected by one's parents is an actual threat to survival. In such cases the child must either adapt and change his fundamental nature, which he cannot really do, or he must somehow cut himself off from that parent, psychologically at least. In either case the resulting psychological problem can be quite serious. It is the mother's function to prevent this situation by letting the child know that no matter how badly things go wrong, the child will be fundamentally accepted.

The mother also has the function of building up the child's inner nature, of putting the child in touch with his feelings, particularly love and affection. The child's ability to relate to others with love stems directly from the mother experience. Likewise, as the child learns to accept himself through the mother, he learns to accept others without forcing them to prove that they are all right through tests or demonstrations. The child should experience these feelings through the mother, and the emotions of empathy, sympathy and mercy, as well as the desire to protect and nurture, are all learned from her. In short, the mother establishes the basic inner stability of the child's psyche and makes the child believe that he is a worthwhile person, that his inner needs can and should be met by the world. Insofar as it is healthy to be concerned with one's inner self, the mother establishes this concern.

The father, on the other hand, has the function of initiating the child into the outer world, of pointing out what the world is and what the child must eventually do to fulfill its demands. Obviously this function complements the mother's function and is equally necessary. If the child does not experience the father's function to some degree, he will simply retreat into himself without ever confronting the world. He will always withdraw into the nice safe comfortable world of the womb. In fact, this is one of the more common psychological problems among human beings. The experience of the father role puts the child in touch with the external universe. And in astrological symbolism, the father and the concept of reality have the same symbol, Saturn.

The father archetype also has to do with consciousness and the development of the ego, as will be clear from the discussion in Chapter Two of the relationship of Saturn to the ego. The father teaches the child to make distinctions, to see things clearly and to think according to categories. Teaching the meanings of justice and law is another fatherly function, and an adult's sense of ethics is learned from the father, although it must be reiterated that this is not necessarily the biological father.

The father is also the archetypal authority figure, and throughout life, a person's relationship to authority is directly related to his father's attitude toward him as a child. Similarly, self-discipline develops from the father's training. As can be seen, the father is in many ways the archetype of adulthood itself.

From this discussion of the father and mother, it seems clear that the father should be connected with the tenth house and the mother with the fourth house, since these are the houses that relate to the archetypal patterns described. However, it is not that simple, because in every culture, especially ours, both parents play both roles to some extent, and the roles may even be switched completely. Sometimes one parent plays both roles, as is the case whenever the ruler of either the fourth or tenth is in the opposite house, with no other planet in that opposite house.

The only way I know to determine which house is which is to have the horoscopes of both parents. Then one can determine the dominant astrological symbolism of each parent. The dominant symbolism of one of the parents at least will be in the child's fourth or tenth house. Often it is as simple as the Sun sign or the ruler of the Sun sign on the cusp or in the fourth or the tenth. However, quite often the mother's or father's rising sign or its ruler is in the child's fourth or tenth.

But there are other symbols in a child's chart that tell about his relationship with the father or mother. Aspects to the Moon often relate to the mother, and afflictions to the

7

Moon may describe the mother's emotional state more accurately than the child's. However, if a child has an afflicted Moon, but the house of the mother is well situated, the Moon probably does not describe the mother.

Similarly, the Sun and Saturn describe the father, and an afflicted Sun can indicate a negative relationship with the father. But here again, if the house of the father is well aspected or situated, afflictions to the Sun refer to something other than the father. However, the fundamental meanings of an afflicted Sun are not altered. Refer to the delineations concerning the individual meanings of the various afflictions to the Sun and Moon. Sometimes Mars describes the child's relationship with the father, and Venus describes the relationship with the mother, but these are not as important.

We have noted that both the Sun and Saturn refer to the father. How are they distinguished? The Sun seems to symbolize an individual's experience of the father as a person, as an authority figure, as an archetype of masculinity. Saturn, on the other hand, seems to refer more to what the father teaches, that is, notions of reality, concepts of duty and responsibility and the general necessities of life. Like the Sun, the house of the father also seems to refer to the father as a person.

The relationship of the Sun to the Moon, as discussed in the Sun and Moon chapters, may also refer to the comparative effects of the father and mother on the child's development. Also see the section on Sun-Moon polarity in Chapter Two.

The Mother Complex

It is clear from the discussion of the mother's role in determining the child's emotional nature that her overall influence will have a great deal to do with the child's attitude, as an adult, toward himself and to the world around him. When this influence operates in an exaggerated or extreme manner, it is known psychologically as the *mother complex*. However, the mother complex does not always, or even usually, have a negative influence on the child's later life. Many of the most positive adult emotions and sentiments, including artistic ability, kindness and strong sentimentality, clearly are derived from one's relationship with the mother.

However, some very negative traits can arise when the symbolism of the mother is very strong and that of the father is weak or negative. The basic problem then is that the child is reluctant to grow beyond the early stage of ego development. This is the phenomenon of the child who doesn't want to leave the womb, who clings to his mother instead of going out and relating to his peers. He is shy and unwilling to leave home, needing to be taken care of to an inordinate degree and seemingly unable to stand by himself. Whenever the outer world offers a challenge in the form of simple competition with friends, an examination in school, or a demand that he perform some task consistently or fulfill some expectation, he regards it as a threat to his survival. Authority figures seem cruel and threatening, so the child tries to hide whenever one appears. Often this child feigns physical ailments in order to avoid going out and facing the world. All of these patterns are readily recognized in the child who is "tied to his mother's apron strings." Less familiar are the forms that this takes in adulthood.

Adults who suffer from a strong negative mother complex are extremely reluctant to compete against their peers or the larger society. Their parents may take care of them to an unusual degree, even after they have grown up. In more extreme cases, such a person will live with his parents much longer than normal.

Such persons are unusually passive, and when trouble comes in their lives, they try to make themselves out as victims of circumstances beyond their control. They may feel that no one understands them or appreciates them as the beautiful people they really are. They may really be beautiful people, as the qualities of gentleness and kindness are often very strong in them. But instead of showing the world their beauty, they expect the world to come to them. The current willingness of many middle-class young people to go on welfare and be taken care of by the state when it is not really necessary is a manifestation of this principle. The father archetype in our culture has been weakened by the fact that the father is usually absent from the home so much of the time.

But the mother complex can work out on another, more subtle level. As adults these people often seek some means to annihilate their adult personality instead of taking responsibility and developing themselves to their highest potential. They may do this through drugs, alcohol or psychological withdrawal, or it can be done more subtly. Many of these persons join movements that take care of them and do away with any need for individual responsibility. The teachings of these groups condemn the ego-consciousness itself, which arises more out of the father complex. Instead of recognizing ego-consciousness as an aspect of the self with a definite role to perform, they call it a life-destroying demon, all in the name of spirituality and higher consciousness. This is not to denigrate spiritual movements, but merely to point out that many people join them for neurotic reasons. However, it is my feeling that most of these individuals benefit from such groups, especially those that teach discipline.

As many of these individuals get older, a sense of world-weariness sets in, and their will to live weakens, for it has never been very strong. This tendency can be countered only by getting involved in something that gives them a very strong sense of meaning in life, which often means submerging their individuality in some higher purpose. This is exemplified by people who join mass movements, religious orders and the like. At its highest and healthiest, this principle can be expressed as an intense love of nature (mother nature!) and the ideal of the universe as an all-nurturing, protective entity that loves its children. This, of course is not a negative manifestation at all. Not only does it cure the neurotic patterns of many such persons, but also it corrects some of the disastrous consequences of the overdeveloped father complex, which characterizes society as a whole, as we shall discuss. The highest manifestation of the mother complex is the ideal of mystical union with God and the annihilation of the individual in the sea of cosmic consciousness. Keep in mind that some of the highest and most perfect ideals in human civilization result from people's struggles with major psychological problems. The fact that the symbolism of these high ideals is very closely related to the symbols of the conflict that gave them birth should never be interpreted as invalidating or trivializing the ideals. Psychologists sometimes try to explain away some of the highest principles of human culture as "merely" or "nothing but" a kind of childish neurotic symbolism.

However, another possible result of the mother complex is an attitude of nonaccep-tance of any kind of hierarchy in an organization. It is very difficult for such people to accept anyone else as having power or authority over them. They have a very strong belief that all people are equal in the most simple-minded, literal sense of the phrase.

This makes them natural egalitarians, politically and otherwise, which is not bad in itself. But it is bad when they will not recognize superiority of any kind whatsoever, even in ability or the real superiority of character of some people who work hard and carefully, with great integrity. When this egalitarian attitude is carried so far that all distinctions are leveled and no one can be considered an individual, the mother complex becomes perverse.

I am not arguing that everyone should accept authority unquestioningly, but that they should recognize the existence of authorities and the fact that many of them fulfill valid and necessary social functions. The integrated person who is not suffering from an overdeveloped mother or father complex can handle each encounter with authority on its own merits and evaluate it according to the immediate experience.

The Father Complex

An exaggerated father complex can be as difficult to handle as the mother complex and can result just as easily in a child who lacks self-confidence and the ability to assert himself. Like the mother complex, it has its positive side. However, the mechanism is different, and the problems associated with it are not likely to show up at such an early age. This is because the mother function is most influential in infancy, while the father function plays its most important role later on. If the mother function has gone wrong in the child's experience, it will be obvious by the time the child starts school. The problems that result from the father complex are more likely to be expressed during later childhood, adolescence and on into adulthood.

As with the mother-complex personality, the child has great difficulty coming out into the world. With the mother complex, it is because the environment created by the mother was so secure and warm, and the parents did little to build up the child's desire for independence. With the father complex, the child sees the world as a very difficult and forbidding place, because he has been taught that his whole worth as a human being depends upon his ability to perform and accomplish. The child concludes that tremendous demands are made of him even when they are not, and he develops a tremendous fear of failure. The antidote to this problem is for the parents to accept the child, especially when he fails, and to encourage the child to accept himself. The exaggeration of the importance of success versus failure leads the child to adopt a very conservative viewpoint. Because failure is seen as dangerous, the child will use only proven methods, which may kill his urge to experiment and experience life.

In some cases the child decides that the outer world is a threatening opponent that must constantly be challenged and overcome. It is difficult for such a child to cooperate with others, because every compromise, even in cooperating, is a loss of individuality and a serious threat. Such children adopt a very rigid stance toward life, either by establishing a position from which they can deal with the world as from an impregnable fortress, so that nothing can defeat them, or by trying to control and regulate their environment and the people in it until there is absolutely no spontaneity left. The worst part about the negative father complex is that while even the most difficult mother complex tends to be outgrown eventually, the father complex tends to be reinforced as one gets older. By middle age, the individual is extremely rigid and apprehensive about change. It is interesting that the extreme negative forms of both complexes cause the individual to become extremely conservative.

It is difficult for the father-complex personality to flow with the events of his life, because he is afraid that events will hurt him. So he tries desperately to control them. This is the origin of the overmanipulative, technical person whom we see so often today, who looks at an untamed river and instead of seeing the beauty of nature, sees only a potential source of electric power.

However, the greatest tragedy for this person is the effect on his emotions. Most people have wild and unpredictable emotions at some times in their life, which most of us learn to accept as part of being human. However, the father-complex person sees strong emotion as a threat to his control, so he tries to cut himself off from feelings in order to keep his universe neat and tidy. At the same time he exalts the principles of law, justice and morality at the expense of human understanding, compassion and mercy. His ideal is the God of the Old Testament, especially as described in the books of Judges and Kings. Once he decides on a course of action, he lets no human values stand in his way. Thus he can transform himself into an inhuman engine of righteousness, a threat to the humanity of all around him. Rigid ideas of justice and of right vs. wrong lead to thinking that everything in the world is either black or white. Nothing can be in between. This extreme is personified by the inquisitor who is willing to burn thousands in the name of righteousness for the slightest deviation.

These people cannot bear to be wrong, and when they realize that they are, they condemn themselves totally. They become unpersons in their own eyes and unworthy of living. At least they are consistent, in that they subject themselves to the same rigorous standards that they expect others to attain. In fact these people often apply their high standards only to themselves and are quite easy on others.

With this attitude they are likely to exhibit one of the more positive, but still self-punishing aspects of the father complex—the drive to succeed, to be a significant person. For these people, the point of succeeding is not to become better than others, but to be their equal, because self-acceptance is so difficult for them. Most people can accept a role in life and acknowledge that others are better at certain skills or have more talents. But father-complex people need to be supreme in some way, to excel all others just to feel adequate. The odd part is that once they have achieved this goal, they see the uselessness of the result. At that point, if they are sufficiently conscious to accept the worthlessness of their quest, they may give it up and move on to a more meaningful goal. This crisis often forces these people out of their difficulty.

As the highest spiritual manifestation of the mother complex is the mystical annihilation of the self in the ocean of godhood, so the highest spiritual manifestation of the father complex is the ideal of God the Father, as taught in the Judeo-Christian tradition, a transcendental God who is wholly other than the self. The philosophical counterpart of this is the ideal of the totally objective real universe in which truth exists completely independent of the individual, which is the basis of modern science. One can say that the scientific ideal of truth springs from the father complex, just as the mystical ideal springs from the mother complex.

Astrology, in fact, is the most curious mixture of the scientific and mystical that has ever existed, which is why it is attacked by both camps. However, this is also why astrology is so valuable, because only through a blending of these two ideals will the human race come to a balanced understanding of the universe and of itself.

From this discussion of the two important complexes within the self, it should be clear that the mother complex is lunar in nature and that the father complex is saturnine. The section on the Moon-Saturn polarity should make this even clearer. However, it is not quite sufficient to say that the mother complex springs from a strong Moon and the father complex from a strong Saturn. It is not even correct to classify people as being either one or the other. Most people whose charts indicate a problem with parental archetypes are a mixture of the two types. Usually one complex predominates, but the other is still present. After all, if a child's father experience has been difficult and negative, he will also retreat from the world, as signified by the mother complex. In fact, a child who has a tyrannical father and an indulgent mother usually exhibits quite a mixture of the two complexes, although in this case the mother complex is usually the stronger. However, quite often the absence of a father results in a negative father complex, as the child tries to piece together a *modus operandi* in the world by himself.

No single astrological indication can prove conclusively that either of these complexes will occur. The basic and obvious reason for this is that even when all the astrological indications are present, the environmental conditions that give rise to the complex may not be present. Also, a person with either of these complexes is as likely to show its positive traits as the negative ones, given the proper chart indications. However, keeping those points in mind, here are some indications that can tell whether these problems might develop.

However, keeping those points in mind, here are some indications that can tell whether these problems might develop.

For the negative mother complex, look for a strongly placed Moon and Neptune, especially if Neptune afflicts the Sun. Also look for a debilitated Mars, such as Mars afflicted by Neptune. The Sun should be weakly placed but not afflicted by Saturn, for that is more likely to indicate a strong father complex. Further indications are a fourth-house Sun, a fourth-house Moon, or a heavy emphasis on Cancer, but only if the masculine planets are weakly placed or afflicted by Neptune.

A negative father complex usually comes about if Saturn is placed in affliction to the Sun or Mars or is itself afflicted in the fourth house. Saturn rising or in the tenth is more likely to grant a positive father complex, unless there are some seriously debilitating afflictions to the Sun or Mars. Generally speaking, the stronger the power of Saturn in the chart, the stronger the tendency toward a father complex of some sort.

When a strong Saturn is combined with weakness in the self-assertive planets (the Sun and Mars) and a strong or heavily aspected Moon, there is likely to be a combination of these complexes. That child will find it difficult to handle his life.

One last point. A difficult relationship with either parent will not necessarily create the kinds of problems described here. What will create problems is a relationship that does not reinforce the child's basic self-confidence, so that the child feels unloved. Often a turbulent relationship with the parents conceals a strongly loving bond between parents and child. Likewise, a relationship that seems very smooth may in fact undermine the child's strength if he does not receive a basic feeling of love from his parents, or if the parents—especially the mother—are unwilling to let go of each phase of the child's development, so that the child can progress to the next phase of growth.

Chapter Two

Planetary Energies

Certain planetary energies operate as systems, usually in pairs. This is so even when these planets are not all related in the horoscope by aspect, sign or house. The planetary energies have certain complementary functions with respect to each other in the development of the psyche and in life in general. Certain planets belong to more than one pair or group, and in one instance at least, there is a rather large grouping of planets in one large complex. This is because the energies represented by the planets are not simple ones. Each planet represents a complex of symbolic patterns, and particular facets of one planet interact with particular facets of the others.

For example, the Moon represents, on one hand, the irrational part of the mind that is largely controlled by emotions. In this respect it is a polar complement to Mercury, which represents logic and rational thinking. But on another level the Moon is related to the mother complex, a pattern of energies within the psyche that is in contrast to the Sun and Saturn, which are associated with the father complex. These two planetary groupings represent two different facets of the Moon.

Another point to remember is that the astrological symbolism is not really exhaustive; that is, certain principles and ideas are not clearly spelled out by any planetary combination. This is why astrology is totally incompetent in many areas. In recent years, several tests have been conducted in which astrologers have been asked to distinguish between suicides and nonsuicide controls, for example, or between mentally retarded and gifted children. In these studies, astrology as it is presently constituted did not succeed. Even though astrologers can comment meaningfully upon certain attributes of the mind, we do not seem to be able to predict intelligence with any degree of reliability. This may be because of an inherent limitation in astrological symbolism, or it may simply be that we haven't yet discovered the correct technique. The same is true for prediction of suicides, which is complicated further by the general reluctance of modern astrologers to deal with death, since past predictions of death have given the art such a bad name.

However, certain astrological energy systems are very important for understanding the development of the young personality. The beginning of each chapter in the text of delineations gives the basic meaning of that planetary symbol. The individual delineations are necessarily analytical in nature; that is, they cannot take into consideration other factors than those involved in that particular combination. The purpose of this section is to help the reader consider all the factors by discussing each of the planets in relation to another or to a group of planets. The following planetary complexes are discussed: the Sun-Moon polarity; the Moon-Saturn polarity; the Mars-Venus polarity; the Jupiter-Saturn polarity; and the components of the ego complex—the Midheaven, Sun, Mars and Saturn. From these discussions the reader should be able to evaluate how the energy systems are working in the horoscope.

Sun-Moon Polarity

This is an extremely important relationship. The delineations of the several Sun-Moon aspects make it clear that these bodies have a fundamental effect on the equilibrium of the personality. The relationship of the Sun to the Moon can be understood if we regard the Sun as the basic energy of the self, while the Moon is the medium in which that energy operates. For example, the Sun is our basic will, our physical and psychological energy, representing our conscious intentions in life and our basic style of being and acting. The Moon represents the emotional context in which this process takes place, our sense of emotional security, unconscious attitudes, habits and psychological complexes built up during our earliest years.

If both the Sun and Moon are strong and function in a compatible manner, the child can face every problem in life with a sense of wholeness. He won't have the sensation that there are two persons struggling for mastery of himself. He believes that his intentions are right and appropriate, both intellectually and emotionally. His intuition and feelings provide reliable clues on which to act, knowing that he will be reasonably correct. Similarly the child's conscious mind is in tune with his emotional needs and can satisfy them without violating its integrity. Children who have a strong and compatible Sun and Moon also have little or no difficulty making friends, and as adults they get along easily with the opposite sex (unless there is some difficulty with Mars or Venus, which are also important in this regard).

A proper Sun-Moon balance also is a sign that the child experiences the influence of both mother and father in a harmonious manner and that both parents reinforce the child's positive qualities and work to minimize the negative characteristics. This does not necessarily mean that the parents get along with each other, although they usually do. What this really indicates is that the parents agree to respect each other's views in bringing up the child. It is important to realize that even with a difficult Sun-Moon balance in the child's chart, the parents can minimize problems by agreeing to respect each other and to present a united influence to the child. If the parents do not respect each other's positions and do not try to work in harmony in bringing up the child, even a favorable Sun-Moon balance will be weakened. And it is also important that both parents take an active part in bringing up the child. If one parent, usually the father, assigns the whole task to the other, the Sun-Moon balance may be disturbed.

Curiously enough, certain kinds of Sun-Moon imbalance can be extremely productive, because by having to confront a fundamental difficulty, the developing personality develops a great deal of inner strength. Also, certain Sun-Moon imbalances create a lot of energy that the personality can draw upon. These situations are noted below.

What does one look for in a chart to decide whether there is a favorable Sun-Moon balance? First of all, there should be no serious afflictions to either the Sun or the Moon. Mars and Pluto afflictions to either the Sun or Moon may indicate a serious conflict with the parent indicated by that body, which may weaken the parent-child relationship and create uncertainty in the child's mind about that sexual aspect of himself or herself. (Both sexes always have aspects of the opposite sex within themselves.) Thus Mars or Pluto afflictions to the Moon may disturb the child's relationship with the mother and make the child feel uncertain about his or her feminine aspect. Saturn afflictions to the Moon may have a similar effect, and in the case of boys, this may lead to difficulty with women when older. A girl will experience the difficulty directly within herself, which will seriously affect her self-esteem as a woman.

Afflictions from these same planets to the Sun may create difficulties in the child's relationship with the father, which in turn will affect the child's masculine aspect. These problems will affect not only a boy's relationship with authority figures, but also his sense of self-esteem as a male. In a girl's chart these afflictions will affect relationships with males in later life and also may create problems with authority figures.

Usually, of course, the Sun symbolizes the father while the Moon symbolizes the mother, but this is not rigid. Sometimes the parents' roles are reversed, and quite often the Sun and Moon roles are played by persons other than the biological parents. Saturn afflictions in particular may indicate a serious foul-up concerning the father or mother role, such that the parent symbolized by the afflicted Sun or Moon is not able to fulfill the role properly. This results in underdevelopment of the child's personality. Usually the problem arises when that parent is physically absent or emotionally distant from the child or there is such conflict between parent and child that the parent is not able to make an impact on the child's development. This does not always make the child hate that parent; instead it can make the child idealize his father or mother instead of dealing with him or her as a real human being. Of course all children idealize their parents to some extent, but in this case the idealization continues even into adulthood, long after most children have learned to deal with their parents as ordinary people.

In addition to the need for an unafflicted Sun and Moon, the relationship between the bodies themselves is important. Traditionally it is considered favorable if the Sun and Moon are in signs of the same element (both in water signs or both in air signs), or at least the same polarity (positive or negative). Even better, according to tradition, they should be in favorable aspect to each other, as sextile or trine. And it is true that this usually does promote an inner sense of equilibrium and balance. Assuming that other parts of the chart do not contradict this, the child will have a sense of ease and natural flow in his life.

However, the more difficult aspects between the Sun and Moon—opposition, square, semisquare and sesquiquadrate—or the more difficult sign relationships need not create that much difficulty. In some cases they give the personality a dynamic quality that may enable the child to achieve more than would be possible with an easier Sun-Moon relationship. But this dynamic quality is accompanied by inner tensions that make the child's early life more difficult. If the Sun and Moon are weakly placed in the chart or afflicted, it is even more difficult for the child to work out the problems.

Another factor to be considered, but the least important of those discussed thus far, is the sign placement of the Sun and the Moon. Both the Sun and the Moon are more favorable when they are in signs that agree with their nature. The Sun is at its best in the fire and air signs, even though traditionally it has been considered to be debilitated in Aquarius and Libra, the signs of its detriment and fall, respectively. True, the Sun may be somewhat less solar in these signs, because both Aquarius and Libra stress relationships rather than self alone, but it actually operates quite effectively in these signs. The only signs that seem to be difficult are Capricorn and Virgo for both sexes and the water signs for males. Capricorn and Virgo are not really that much of a problem, but many people with the Sun in Virgo or Capricorn feel that there is something wrong with the sign. If they do not feel that way, there is no problem. Water signs are difficult for males only because these signs are very sensitive and feminine, and in this culture it is difficult for boys to contend with a strong internal feminine streak. For adults this influence is not so much of a problem.

Traditionally the Moon is at its best in Cancer and Taurus and at its worst in Capricorn and Scorpio. There is some basis for this belief, but if the Moon is otherwise all right, Capricorn and Scorpio are not serious problems. Actually, in some respects the Moon is least lunar in Gemini. This does not create as much of a problem for the child, however, as for the people around that child, because it usually indicates a certain emotional insensitivity.

If, after evaluating the Sun and Moon by the above criteria, you find that the Sun is stronger than the Moon, certain effects are indicated.

First of all, the relationship with the parent who acts as the father is likely to be somewhat better than the relationship with the mother parent. The child, while still very young, becomes aware that there are other people in the world who must be taken seriously. Superficially, the child matures more rapidly, but only superficially, because his emotional development is slower. Often the child becomes very serious and takes himself too seriously, lacking a sense of humor, and finding it very difficult to be wrong. He can be quite insensitive to others' feelings, even rather pushy and domineering, and often not very gentle. Girls with this pattern may become tomboys, which is not an especially serious problem, but as adults, they may find it difficult to assume the traditional female roles in society. Boys do not have much of a problem with a strong Sun in childhood, but they do not become aware of the finer and gentler aspects of life. As children, they try to become independent of their mothers, not wanting to be tied to their apron strings. As adults they may be very hard on the women in their lives.

If the Moon is much stronger than the Sun, these patterns are reversed to some extent. Here the mother figure is the more influential, and the child's emotional development may be more rapid, although it is often characterized by excessive dependency, needing to be taken care of and led about. Although the child's emotional development is more rapid than it would be with the Sun dominant, it is not necessarily more successful. The dependency patterns of these children can cause them to be arrested in a very infantile stage of development, and early childhood habits are very numerous and difficult to correct. However, their emotions are very dominant in their personalities, and they express them freely.

Sun-dominant children should be encouraged to develop their finer sensitivities and to get in touch with their feelings. But Moon-dominant children should be encouraged to become independent and self-determining. Otherwise they will always seek out a strong person to run their life for them.

Moon-Saturn Polarity

Many of the same issues are important here as were important for the Sun-Moon polarity. This is because the Sun and Saturn are both related to the experience of the father archetype. However, the emphases are different here.

In relationship with Saturn, the Moon describes the aspect of consciousness that involves feeling, emotion, one's personal needs, caring for and being cared for by the mother and, later on, others, and early habit patterns. This pattern operates in a relatively unconscious manner. The Moon aspect of a child does not make clear distinctions, and in an adult it operates whenever one gets tired of splitting hairs and decides to go ahead on the basis of "gut feelings." It makes an adult feel merciful and compassionate even toward those who have done wrong. The symbol of the Virgin Mary in the Catholic Church gives an idea of the positive lunar archetype. The intensely personal Moon puts subjective considerations ahead of objective considerations. Even more important, the Moon is often the energy that enables us to love and accept ourselves for what we are and in turn to accept and love others.

The Moon is strongly connected to the sense of a personal past, the sense of roots and heritage. It often describes the behavior patterns that we go through when we are tired, exhausted and looking for someplace, someone or something that will help us relax and pull ourselves back together again.

Saturn represents the opposite of all this. It denies personal feeling in favor of what must be done from an objective point of view, Saturn is always looking outward. It is concerned with society rather than the self. Strongly saturnine persons usually do what they feel is right in a nonpersonal frame of reference, even if it works against their emotional needs. Obviously Saturn provides the energy of discipline, which is necessary to counter the self-indulgent tendencies of the Moon. Saturn is also very serious and strong. Unwilling to put up with simple human frailty, it demands that weakness be punished, which often makes a person condemn himself for his own weakness and constantly try to live up to criteria that seem to come from within but actually come from outside himself.

As Saturn works to clarify distinctions, it also works to create a sense of separation, which is closely related to distinction. Thus Saturn can lead to feelings of loneliness and alienation, which must be healed by the Moon's energy. But the influence of Saturn is very important if an individual is to progress and mature. Unlike the Moon, it is future oriented, rather than past oriented. In general it can be said that Saturn is oriented to adulthood and maturity, while the Moon is more related to early childhood.

Obviously a proper balance between these two bodies is necessary if the child is to be happy. It should be clear that a weak Moon or one that is overwhelmed by Saturn will create more problems in early childhood, while a weak or deficient Saturn will create more problems later. Aspects between the Moon and Saturn often indicate conflicts between infantile needs and adult criteria. The Moon in hard aspect to Saturn often means that adult responsibilities were thrust upon the child at an early age and that he or she was never really permitted to be a child. For further information see the delineations for the individual Moon-Saturn aspects.

In general, a person with a weak Moon is out of touch with his or her feelings, and if Saturn is strong in the chart, it usually means that the child was forced to grow up too fast, just as with an actual Moon-Saturn affliction. As with a strong Sun chart, the child is very concerned with being right and takes any criticism as a serious personal defeat. Such children must be made aware that they are loved for themselves, not because they are "good" boys or girls. If that is not made clear, they will really fear that if they do something that adults disapprove of, they will be rejected entirely and cut off from all love and care. To a child, this is tantamount to a threat of abandonment and death, and it can create severe trauma, as has been amply demonstrated by psychologists. In fact, one of the most important reasons for an adult not being true to his or her own inner being is a strong Saturn coupled with a weak Moon and/or Sun.

Astrological indications of this and other Saturn problems are the following: Saturn in the first; Saturn in the Midheaven or tenth house; Saturn afflicting the Moon, or afflicting the Sun with an unaspected Moon; an afflicted Moon; and strong combinations of Moon and Neptune. If both the Moon and Saturn are strong and well aspected, the child is likely to have a very decisive and strong personality, without the problems just described. Sign placements do not seem to make much difference here. We are more concerned with the quality of the lunar and saturnine energies and the degree to which they are integrated in the chart than with the quality conferred on them by the signs.

A strong Moon and a weak Saturn indicates an overly dependent personality, a person who cannot get away from parental influence. Such children are hypersensitive and unwilling to go out into the world and face the challenges offered by relationships with one's peers. Such children may be undisciplined and self-indulgent, concerned only with their own self-interest and unwilling to keep agreements or commitments.

While the strong Saturn type is out of touch with the feelings, the lunar type is likely to be dominated by them and to act compulsively and irrationally, often out of habit. In general, a strong Moon and weak Saturn is similar to a strong Moon and a weak Sun. A strong-Moon, weak-Saturn type is likely with an angular Moon, especially rising or in the Midheaven, with hard aspects between the Moon and Jupiter and an unaspected Saturn. Often it occurs when a strong Moon is combined with Mars-Saturn or Sun-Saturn hard aspects. In this case Saturn is not weak so much as turbulent, which increases the child's feeling of insecurity and makes him try harder to hold onto the lunar energies in his life. The issues associated with a strong Moon may also be found in persons with a strong emphasis on Cancer and a weak Saturn.

It must be said that when strongly lunar types overcome their problems, they have a great ability to understand others intuitively and are able to make others like them very much. These people are often the publicity agents and promoters of the world. Remember that none of the above patterns will necessarily be expressed in the negative ways described here. That will happen only if the parents make no effort to de-emphasize the child's negative traits and reinforce the positive ones. All children need the proper mixture of love, reinforcement, support and discipline. It is just that the children discussed here need more reinforcement than others—the saturnine child needing more love and emotional support, and the lunar child needing more independence and strengthening.

Mars-Venus Polarity

Astrologers have not generally paid enough attention to these two planets as a pair. They are linked as closely as the Sun and Moon, and although they are not quite so central to the personality, they have an extremely important role. Also, these two planets are so obviously connected with sexuality that their larger role in the psychological structure of an individual has usually been overlooked.

Everyone needs to strike a balance between being self-assertive and aggressive, on one hand, and getting along with people, on the other. A person who continually acts in a hostile and self-assertive manner, who constantly challenges others and tries to score victories over others, will not have many friends. But a person who is so afraid of losing a friend or of making a bad impression that he always gives way before another's demands or accedes to another's wishes, no matter how destructive it is to his personal integrity, will also not have many friends, because no one will respect him. This is the psychological dimension of the Venus-Mars polarity, apart from the issue of sex, although this polarity is closely related to sexuality. When it functions best, sexuality is the most perfect balance between self-expression and getting one's own way (Mars), and successfully relating to another in a process of give and take (Venus). Two people in a sexual relationship are presumably having a good time both for themselves and for each other. Anyone with a favorable Venus-Mars balance can create this kind of balance in every aspect of their lives. They are fun to be with, but they do not seem to compromise themselves in order to get along. As adults, such people usually have a rather erotic air, but in childhood this is usually not so apparent.

A person who has a strong Mars combined with a weak Venus does not pay enough attention to getting along with others. Such a child is extremely involved in finding himself, learning his own strengths and testing himself against others. They constantly challenge and goad people into responding. Often they seem to be asking for punishment, but really they are only trying to discover the limits of their strength. They can be extremely hard on weaker and more docile children, and they fight constantly with those who are their equals. They also enjoy testing and challenging the physical universe and may take wild risks just to see what they can get away with. It probably does no good to restrict these children in an effort to keep them out of trouble, for they will create trouble despite the parents' best efforts. Children have as much power to create trouble as adults; it is only when we believe that children are less creative because they are physically weaker that we are astounded when they do something remarkable.

Instead of punishing them, parents should help these children find outlets for their abundant energy through athletics, work or exercise. And parents must be resigned to a few accidents, which probably won't be fatal or permanently damaging. The main problem for the strong Mars child is that he can cut himself off from love, because people do not enjoy someone—child or adult—constantly beating others over the head. Such a child can become isolated and alone and what is worse, in his overriding concern with being strong, he will not even admit that something is wrong. But this child's life will indeed be impoverished unless the situation is corrected.

There are many indications of a strong Mars pattern, and in this instance a sign often shows the pattern. A strong Aries, such as Aries rising, Sun in Aries or a number of planets in Aries, can indicate this trait. More important, however, are an angular Mars, Mars-Sun hard aspects, or Mars-Moon hard aspects. These indications will not result in the negative effects discussed above, however, unless combined with a weak Venus, such as an unaspected Venus with little emphasis on Libra or the seventh house. Mars strongly aspected by Pluto, especially in hard aspect, can produce an extremely aggressive nature, and this combination can be one of the most difficult for the people around the child. On the other hand, it can mean that the child is subjected to another person's harshness and overassertiveness. A child with this or another strong Mars combination should not be treated harshly or roughly, because that only makes the potential problems more serious. However, the parents should be very firm, because a strongly Mars child respects firmness, and they should be as fair as possible.

A strong Venus with a weak Mars may indicate a child who is extremely charming, but not very capable of taking care of himself. Such a child may be too accommodating and may allow others to take advantage of him rather than cause unpleasantness or get involved in a fight. They are good peacemakers but are easily victimized.

Another problem with strong Venus children is that they may not be very energetic, preferring peace and quiet to any kind of vigorous activity. Indeed they may be genuinely lazy and self-indulgent. More than anything else, they need discipline. And it is sometimes difficult for parents to provide this, because such children are so good at wrapping adults around their little fingers.

Boys who have a strong Venus and a weak Mars may have even more difficulties, because boys are traditionally expected to be self-assertive and tough. But these boys, while young, may prefer activities that are usually considered girlish, and certainly they will be more interested in developing the aesthetic aspects of their personality than in following more traditional masculine pursuits. Such boys may have difficulty getting along with their peers, who will kid them a bit or even beat them up for being "sissies." These boys really need strong support from both parents. Many parents, especially fathers, get very upset by sons who show strongly developed feminine aspects. Under normal circumstances they are no more likely than other boys to become homosexuals when they get older, but certainly this is more likely if as children they are made to feel ashamed of the "feminine" sides of their beings. The important thing for all children is to be who they are, to be real, and not to have to deny what they are for the sake of getting along with others. This is especially true with strong-Venus, weak-Mars boys.

Girls with a weak Mars and a strong Venus obviously will have less trouble with regard to traditional sex roles, but they can have some problems. If not encouraged to develop some self-assertiveness, they will become dependent upon others and play super-feminine roles to get others to do everything for them. When they grow up they may become the classic "clinging vine" stereotype, which no one enjoys or respects.

A strong Venus and a weak Mars usually occurs when Venus is strongly aspected but not afflicted and when Mars is weakened, usually by hard aspects to Saturn or Neptune. These aspects also may denote a difficult relationship with the father, which is one of the experiential sources of the strong-Venus weak-Mars imbalance. Merely being strongly Libran will not have this effect, nor will any other strong Venus indication by itself, unless Mars is clearly in trouble in the chart.

The important thing to realize is that the difficulties discussed here can arise only if one of these two planets is quite weak. The weakness of one is more important than the strength of the other. It takes a good Mars to make Venus really work, and vice versa.

Jupiter-Saturn Polarity

Jupiter and Saturn form another pair of interacting energies, and as with the other pairs, the important point is not the aspect between these two bodies but their total strength or weakness in the chart. Jupiter signifies the ability of the individual personality to reach out and embrace the world, to have a wide range of experiences and a large field of action. Jupiter signifies the processes of growth and maturation. It also signifies the individual's ability to view the world or any large system as a whole.

Saturn, on the other hand, is the principle of limitation and order. It represents the rules of any game one is playing, in this case the game of life, including what must be done and what cannot be done. It also signifies a person's understanding that he is separate from all other selves in a fundamental metaphysical way. Jupiter tends to see the world in terms of togetherness and connection.

Together, these two bodies create the form of one's life, the sum total of what is done and what is not done, the limitations and opportunities, the growth and the restrictions placed upon it. When they are in balance, a person can accept limitation and at the same time have the drive to go around that limitation and even take advantage of it to advance further. Persons with these two planets in balance are able to plan cautiously and yet take every reasonable chance. In fact, even when these two planets are in hard aspect to each other, there is the opportunity to strike such a balance. Many millionaires have rather serious Jupiter-Saturn afflictions, which have forced them to focus on attaining this balance, just to keep from failing totally. The most difficult situation occurs when the two planets are totally unconnected to each other, with one very strong and the other very weak.

A strong-Jupiter, weak-Saturn person is usually very undisciplined, has sloppy habits and never knows when to quit, going to extremes in every activity. While they are children, the effects are not usually so bad, but it can seriously affect their adult lives. The habit of taking a sloppy, slipshod approach to every task can be corrected while a person is young. The problem, as with Venus, is that adults and other children find Jupiterian children quite enjoyable and are inclined to be easy on them. But to discover whether this problem exists, one only has to see whether the child's love of freedom and eagerness for new experience is turning into irresponsibility and superficiality.

Another problem that sometimes arises with a strong-Jupiter, weak-Saturn combination is that of arrogance, especially toward other children. Jupiter sometimes leads a child to brag and pretend to be better than he is. A child with this pattern often finds it difficult to accept the fact that he is only a child and therefore at the bottom of the social pecking order. These children may be unwilling to accept their place and to spend time preparing to be competent adults. They prefer to pretend that they are already adults, which they cannot be.

The strong-Saturn, weak-Jupiter child usually has a rougher time than the other type. This child often thinks that the world is ganging up on him, and in fact the world may make very heavy demands on his maturity before he is ready to handle it. (Note that this is the opposite of the strong-Jupiter, weak-Saturn child, who wants to be acknowledged as an adult but does not actually want the responsibilities.) If Jupiter is weak, the strong-Saturn child often does not have the resources, either spiritually or otherwise, to handle adult demands while he is still a child. Consequently these children develop a very negative self-image and approach life from a very discouraged point of view, often feeling that they do not deserve much and that they must settle for very little in life. They may develop patterns of repeated failure, which they may blame on circumstances or on themselves. Many of these children even take responsibility for failure and difficulties that are not their fault. Others try to portray themselves as victims of circumstances or of someone else's malevolence.

The father's influence is especially important to these children, and he or another adult male can do the most to minimize the effects of this pattern by encouraging and supporting the child at every turn. He must teach the child not to view the world from a dark and gloomy point of view, but to look at the bright side of life for the opportunities it can offer. Above all, when the child does fail in some way, the parents should not condemn him harshly, for that will make him feel even worse. These children carry inside them a strong parent figure who reprimands them continually.

If this pattern is not checked early in life, these children can develop into narrow suspicious adults whose lives are ultimately motivated more by fear than by anything else. They may become extremely conservative and selfish, being unable to share for fear that they will never have enough. Above all, these children have great difficulty relating to and sharing themselves with others.

The strong-Jupiter, weak-Saturn type can be seen in any chart in which Jupiter is angular or strongly aspected, while Saturn is distant from the angles and relatively weakly aspected. However, a strong Capricorn influence can compensate for a weak Saturn. Jupiter is likely to be difficult in hard aspect to the Sun, Moon or Mars.

A strong Saturn and weak Jupiter comes about when the above relation between Jupiter and Saturn is reversed. Here a strong Sagittarius can correct the balance somewhat. When Saturn and Jupiter aspect each other, especially by hard aspect, the child may alternate between the two patterns before reaching some kind of equilibrium. Reaching an equilibrium is the single greatest problem for these children, and usually they do not achieve it before their Saturn-Saturn conjunction by transit at the age of twenty-nine.

The Ego Complex

All the planets in this group have been discussed under other headings, but their roles with respect to each other and to the Midheaven have not been touched on. The ego complex of chart factors consists of the Midheaven, the Sun, Mars and Saturn. As a group they are the most important determining factor in what a person is, what he does and how he is distinguished from other people. The Moon is also extremely important, but its influence is felt before the ego principle is formed. The nature of this important process has already been discussed in the sections on the Sun-Moon and the Moon-Saturn polarities. The Ascendant-Descendant axis is also important to this discussion, even though it is not an integral part of the ego complex.

Briefly, from an astrological point of view, which does not correspond totally to any one system of psychology, the ego complex consists of these psychological factors:

1. An individual's sense that his life has a unique orientation and that what he does and experiences is different from what others do and experience. Each person has a unique role to play. This correlates with the Midheaven and to a lesser extent with the I.C.

2. One's sense of being clearly distinct from others, the belief that I am not my neighbor, no matter how much I have in common with him. This sense of separation and differentness is the result of Saturn, but the actual boundary line between oneself and others is the horizon, the Ascendant-Descendant axis. Saturn signifies the sense of separateness, while the horizon indicates the exact form it takes and how it is experienced.

3. The need to survive and maintain one's individuality in the face of pressures from people and circumstances. This is signified jointly by the Sun and Mars. I call it simply the will-to-be or the ego-drive. This function of the Sun and Mars should be clear from the discussions in the individual chapters on those planets.

Childhood is the early phase of ego development. At birth the senses described above are not clearly developed. One is fed, clothed, cared for and accepted without having to fulfill many demands, which is as it should be. In fact this period of infancy, which I call the lunar period, is absolutely fundamental for the development of a secure ego later on. It is the foundation.

As the ego begins to develop, the child learns not only that he is separate from others, especially the mother, but that his interests are not the same as other people's. His own needs and wants are sometimes necessarily at variance with those of the people around him. One of the great challenges of growing up is learning to balance one's own and others' needs. Far too many children are not taught how to do this, so they either feel that they come first in every way, that no one else counts for anything, or they feel that their own needs and wants are less important, so that they always give in to others.

We have discussed under other headings the problems that arise when Mars, the Sun and Saturn become too strong too soon. There is no need to go over this again except to note that those problems are in fact problems of ego development.

But the planetary energy of Neptune, which can be very powerful for good or ill, becomes a very important consideration at this point. The energy of Neptune opposes the development of a normal ego, and when it is strong in a child's chart, certain problems should be watched for. But in order to understand how this can work, we have to understand something that is not usually recognized about the ego complex, that its total combined energy is closely related to one's experience of reality.

Philosophers have long debated the nature of an objectively real universe and the individual's relationship to it. One of the principal issues in this debate has been the extent to which an individual makes his or her own reality. An extreme position on this issue is the radical view held by some Eastern schools that our experience of reality is totally an illusion created by our minds, and that there is no reality apart from that. The other extreme is the dominant Western view that there is an absolute reality out there that we can experience, but our minds tend to distort reality somewhat if we are not taught to look at it properly. In both cases, oddly enough, it is the mind that is the source of distortion of what is actual, real or true about the universe.

Fortunately we do not have to resolve this debate. But we do have to recognize that the way we experience reality depends on several factors operating simultaneously. First of all, whatever is truly real out there impinges upon our senses in some way to produce valid data about the physical world. We call this direct experience. Second, we are taught a structure of concepts, a culturally imposed belief system, by which to interpret direct experience. Third, an intense experience provokes emotional responses that futher color the direct experience. When this happens, the experience is often incorrectly interpreted by the mind, and we are often confused about whether the energy we feel as part of an experience actually exists out there in the world or whether it exists entirely as emotions within ourselves. This problem is especially acute when we believe that our physical survival is threatened. Children jump to conclusions in this area more quickly than adults, because they know they are more vulnerable.

The chief point is that only a small portion of what we think we know really comes from direct experience through our senses. Most of our knowledge of reality results from concept structures taught by parents and other authority figures, as symbolized by the Midheaven, and by peculiarities of our individual emotional conditioning, particularly concerning survival, and the will-to-be, as symbolized by the Sun and Mars. Saturn, of course, also relates to what we are taught and how we fit into our culture.

There are literally thousands of ways of interpreting raw, direct experience, a fact that is easily verified by studying the wide variety of cultural viewpoints that the human race has taken throughout history. Each culture has been convinced that its view of the world is the only accurate one, and I think no one could deny that this is true of our culture as well. Much of our reality structure is derived from our relationship to the larger culture, which is directly related to the energies of the ego complex as described by the symbols of the planets of the ego and the Midheaven. Saturn is especially important in determining an individual's view of reality.

A key point here is that Neptune denies and threatens this structure, but not because it is a nasty malefic sent by the creator to afflict us. Neptune, too, has a creative role to play in our personal development, namely by helping us transcend the narrow ego consciousness, a process that should occur late in life. Theoretically one grows in wisdom and perspective as one gets older and becomes less attached to matters that concern just oneself. I say "theoretically" because most people's development is arrested, and they do not advance to this stage. Neptune plays a creative and very spiritual role in this process. However, just as Saturn can be destructive if its demands are made too early in life, so Neptune can have a destructive effect if its energies are felt before the ego has had time to develop. And since the ego is so closely related to one's experience of reality, Neptune can even threaten a person's reality system.

In a child this can be very serious. The ego must develop properly if the child is to confront the world in a healthy manner. When a strong Neptune is in conflict with the ego, the child may want to withdraw from the confrontation, not merely by fantasizing and daydreaming, which is normal and rather healthy, but through a more active, fearful withdrawal from the world. Saturn can create this effect as well, but with Neptune the withdrawal is accompanied by a negative use of fantasy or make-believe, such that the child refuses to deal with reality. He may be dishonest or self-deluding, or he may run off and hide, either literally or metaphorically. Often, in confrontations with other children, these children cannot stand up for themselves except by resorting to devious tactics. They believe that in a fair fight they will lose for certain. You must understand that such a child is not lying in the usual sense. In many cases they are genuinely unaware of the dichotomy of truth and falsehood. They create their own reality, which constantly changes to fit the needs of the moment. Even a child knows that he must survive, and he will change reality, or at least his concept of reality, in order to survive.

In a more common expression of Neptune's energy, the child doesn't lie necessarily, but he is easily led around and influenced by stronger children in ways that are quite unhealthy for him. Often he makes himself a victim of someone else's strength and even uses the victim role as a way of acting out his aggression toward stronger people. The childish ploy of holding one's breath until suffocation threatens is a common example of this tactic. The victim pattern can also be seen in adults, especially in women who have been taught that they cannot succeed in a direct confrontation with a man, because they believe he is more powerful.

A closely related pattern is that of being confused and never having a clear idea about what is going on. Such children appear weak and indecisive, even more than other children. They can't seem to find a direction in life while they are young, and in fact they may never do so. They seem to have no special will-to-be and find it very difficult to establish a career or any other life purpose when they are older.

In later life, this Neptune syndrome may be expressed through using drugs or alcohol to excess or by withdrawing from the world into some strange spiritual cult. Some people go into the Church, which is a more positive use of this pattern. Nuns and monks, not only in Christianity but in all other religions, manifest this type of pattern. The main problem with the Neptune syndrome is that it short-circuits the ego development. Both as a child and as an adult, the person tries to either transcend or escape from the world before the ego has developed.

I want to stress very strongly that the patterns described here represent *extreme* Neptune problems. In most children these patterns are evident only in certain well-defined areas of life, even if they have the indications of a strong Neptune, that is, weak ego development. But wherever Neptune is strong in a child's chart, you should look for some feeling of inadequacy or weakness. Even in early life, Neptune may be expressed creatively, through imagination, creativity in art or music, or even strong sensitivity and compassion for the needs and wants of others. These traits also are the result of an ego that is not so strong as to block out concerns coming from others. However, to be safe, a parent should try to reinforce the child in the areas of weakness indicated by the placement of Neptune. The individual readings in the text tell more about these areas.

Ego problems because of Neptune are likely to occur with the following indications: a strong hard aspect between Neptune and the Sun or Mars, sometimes Neptune in hard aspect to the Moon, or Neptune rising or on the Midheaven. Saturn in hard aspect to

Neptune can also signify serious difficulties if the aspect affects an angle, the Sun or the Moon. Again, the nature of these difficulties is explained in the individual delineations.

Mercury, Uranus and Pluto

Several planets, namely Mercury, Uranus and Pluto, have not been covered in this description. It is not that they are less important than the others, but that they do not fit so easily into these systems. However, each of these planets has a place in the development of the child's personality, which we will discuss briefly.

The general significance of Mercury is covered in the chapter on that planet. Mercury plays a very important role in childhood, and in fact in ancient astrology it was considered the ruler of youth. This is because the issues indicated by Mercury—communication, education, movement and learning to think—are all extremely important aspects of being young. In fact for most people these issues are never as important later in life as when they are young. Thus the aspects and house placement of Mercury are likely to have the greatest influence upon a child's development at this time. For example, a hard aspect between Mercury and Saturn is likely to indicate a rigid pattern of thinking that develops very early and continues throughout life, so that the person has great difficulty adapting or changing. It usually means that some aspect of the mind has been closed off because adult demands or restrictions have been placed on the child. Or the closing off may be caused by fear or insecurity.

A properly functioning Mercury is also very important to the development of the ego complex, because Mercury confers the power to think and to clearly perceive distinctions and categories, which are so important in developing a sense of oneself. Thus Neptune in hard aspect to Mercury may indicate unclear thinking that does not reinforce a well defined self-image and self-knowledge. Mercury-Jupiter aspects represent an effort to encompass as much of the universe as possible through the mind and communication and even through travel. See the individual delineations for the effects of other planets in combinations with Mercury.

Uranus plays its most important role in life in middle to late adulthood. In childhood its role is rather upsetting, for it usually induces a feeling that some aspect of the outer world cannot be relied upon. This throws the child back upon himself and forces him to take greater control of his life. Thus Uranus often indicates a high degree of independence, because the child has decided that he cannot rely on adults to do what has to be done, so he does it himself. For further information on Uranus, see the chapter on that planet (pages 309-326).

Pluto has to do with all major, intense psychological and environmental transformations, both for children and for adults. Children whose charts show a very active Pluto (strongly aspected and/or angular) undergo changes that are unusually intense, and they seem to thrive on encountering and overcoming difficulties. Even though they are often hurt by these difficulties, they seem to place themselves in situations that invite such encounters. Often their lives are very dramatic and intense. For further information, see the chapter on Pluto (pages 345-358).

Chapter Three

Elements and Crosses

As any student of basic astrology knows, in addition to the planets, signs, houses and aspects, there are two larger groupings of symbols, which are at the same time simpler and more comprehensive than any of the other symbols. By evaluating the strengths and weaknesses of these symbols in the chart, the reader can learn much about what behavior patterns to look for in a young person. These symbol groups are the four elements—fire, air, earth and water—and the quadruplicites or crosses—cardinal, fixed and mutable. The elements relate to signs and to planets, but the crosses usually relate only to signs. Some astrologers also apply the element principle to houses, but I am not in favor of this because it takes the parallels between the signs and houses too far, resulting in some furious bending of the symbolism. Each of the elements and crosses will be discussed in turn, along with the probable effects on a child's chart.

Before getting into a description of elements and crosses, however, we should examine the method for telling which ones are dominant and deficient in a chart. The following explanation is not intended to be absolutely rigorous, but it does provide a systematic approach to the problem.

To determine elemental dominance, give two points to the elements of the signs occupied by the Sun, Moon, Midheaven and Ascendant, and one point to the elements of the signs of the other planets. This will give a rough idea of relative elemental strength. Below is a table based on Figure 1, the chart of a six-year-old child. It is a tabulation of the point score for each element, based on the chart factors therein.

		Score
Fire:	Sun (2), Mercury (1), Venus (1), Neptune (1)	5
Earth:	Mars (1), Saturn (1), Pluto (1)	3
Air:	Ascendant (2), Midheaven (2), Uranus (1)	5
Water:	Moon (2), Jupiter (1)	3

These are preliminary values, which must be checked by seeing if any planets are near the angles (±5°), or are in aspect to the Sun (±5° orb). Many of the planets have strong qualities of one of the elements, and this affinity can affect the overall balance of the chart. Any planet that is near the Ascendant or Midheaven gives three points to its element. A planet near the Descendant or I.C. gives two points to its element. A planet in square, opposition or conjunction to the Sun gives three points to its element, while trines and sextiles give two. In this case, we are referring to the element that the planet has the greatest intrinsic affinity for, not the element that the planet is in by sign. For handy reference, the planets are listed below according to their dominant element, although Uranus and Pluto are not entirely clear. See the following sections on each element for further clarification.

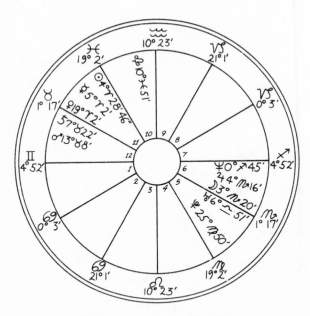

Figure 1. Natal chart of a six-year-old child

Fire:	Sun, Mars and possibly Jupiter
Earth:	Saturn, possibly Venus
Air:	Mercury, Uranus and possibly Venus
Water:	Moon, Neptune and Pluto

In our sample chart, the Sun is opposite Uranus, which gives us three additional points for air, although Uranus also has a fiery quality. The Sun is trine Neptune, which gives a definite water factor of two, and Neptune is also near the Descendant, which gives another water factor of two. Water has a final score of seven, and air has a score of eight.

This chart is a fire-water-air dominant type, but none of the elements is sufficiently strong or weak to give us a classic type. That would require a score of no more than two for the weakness and nine or more points in a single element for the strength.

We evaluate cross strength in the same way, except that we do not count the planets near the angles or aspecting the Sun. We count only the factors in signs, using the same scoring as for the elements. Again we make up a table.

		Score
Cardinal:	Sun (2), Mercury (1), Venus (1), Uranus (1)	5
Fixed:	Midheaven (2), Moon (2), Mars (1), Jupiter (1), Saturn (1)	7
Mutable:	Ascendant (2), Neptune (1), Pluto (1)	4

This chart is weakest in mutable, but not weak enough to suggest a deficiency. Actually, in many respects this chart is unusually well balanced.

Again I repeat that this technique is only a guide to help the student early in the evalua-tion. As a complete measure, it has certain drawbacks, such as the fact that the orb of aspect of an elemental planet to the Sun is not taken into consideration in the score. In a finer analysis this would be considered. Astrologers do not usually determine elemental dominance by this method but rather by looking at the whole chart, weighing various factors, and getting an overall impression. But that is very difficult for a student to do, and thus this guideline is provided.

Fire

The element of fire is associated with the signs Aries, Leo and Sagittarius. The difference among these three signs is that they are of different crosses. In fact many of the changes from sign to sign can be attributed to the relationship of the elements to the crosses. Fire is also strong in the Sun, Mars and probably Uranus, although not so clearly.

Fire represents will, spirit, freedom, consciousness and energy. In a child whose chart shows a strong emphasis on fire, these qualities will be very evident. A fire child needs plenty of growing space and should not be severely limited or disciplined unrea-sonably. Although it is probably not a good idea to always explain to a child in detail why he should do a particular thing at a given time, especially if time is a factor, a fire child should eventually be given such an explanation. After a heavily emotional confrontation with a fire child, when the energies have cooled down, is the best time to discuss the situation. If you give a fire child the feeling that adults always use power arbitrarily and without rules, that child will later use his power in the same way, often against the kinds of people who seemed arbitrary in the past. Because of their spirited nature, such children may rebel against authority and show a strong self-assertive drive while quite young. Fire children are likely to lose their temper easily, which is good in that it releases the energy instead of holding it in. Fire children do not usually hold a grudge unless the abuse or seeming abuse is repeated over and over again. They are more open and forthright than most children, preferring to act out front where the world can see them. If you encourage honesty in such a child, you will get it, although it may be coupled with a brutal frankness, especially in Sagittarians.

Fire children are very emotional, but in a passionate and strong-spirited manner rather than quietly brooding and deep. They like to release energy, and indeed they often seem to be channels for a kind of cosmic energy that does not even seem to belong to them.

Fire children try to get away from dependency as early as possible, wanting to go off and do what they choose rather than stay at home and be affectionate. This is not to say that fire children are lacking in affection but that they don't want to be tied down or limited in their freedom of movement by bonds of love.

Certain problems are likely to arise with a strong fire child, including rebelliousness, as has been stated, which can be dealt with by explaining the reasons for your actions. But these children may also be rather insensitive and thus hurt the feelings of children who are more sensitive. Sometimes they are excessively aggressive and try to dominate other children. They are no more likely to be bullies, but they often try to run the show. The problem of anger and outbursts of temper has already been mentioned.

Fire children are also quite unconcerned with anything practical. They want to be allowed to do whatever they want, whether or not it is useful or even possible. Often a strong fire person overestimates his abilities and energies. You may have trouble getting a fire child to rest, but in my opinion they are no more likely to be hyperkinetic than children of any other element. We do not yet know where that characteristic comes from. On the positive side, however, their lack of concern with practicality makes fire children potentially good at abstract studies that have no immediate, obvious use. However, it may not be easy to keep a fire child at that kind of study because of the energetic nature of the element. In this area, Leo is the most stable of the fire signs.

Fire children may also have an emotional problem resulting from the very masculine nature of the element. It may be hard for them to cry or show emotions that they consider weak or "mushy." Such a child hates to admit that something is wrong, because he so needs to be strong and independent. Even if they need their mothers very much, they may not admit it until the situation is hard to correct. It is not that fire is secretive, but that these children do not want to appear weak.

A chart that is deficient in fire presents some problems in that the child may lack will, independence and personal vigor. In general, the lack of fire indicates that the qualities described above will be deemphasized. Such persons tend to have difficulty asserting themselves and acting independently of others. However, you should check not only the signs but also the planets that are emphasized. Saturn strongly aspecting the Sun or Moon or near the M.C. or Ascendant will greatly tone down a fire chart.

Earth

This is the element of reality and practicality. Taurus, Virgo and Capricorn are the earth signs, while Saturn is the most strongly earthy planet. Venus also has an earthy side, which shows its relationship to Taurus. Traditionally, Mercury was assigned to Virgo as well as to Gemini, which could give it some earthy characteristics, but modern experience suggests that Mercury is almost purely airy in nature. Astrologers who have been researching the asteroids feel that some of them are quite earthy, but they are beyond the scope of this book.

Earth children are usually quieter and more placid than fire children, with the possible exception of Capricorn. They are practical, always wanting to know what good something is. They are not particularly interested in abstractions, but they are very good at making other people's idealistic dreams real, if it can be done at all. Obviously, earth people are rather conservative, preferring to deal with the tried and true. However, you can talk an earth person into anything, once he or she has seen that it works.

When earth people get into a project that is rather involved and abstract, they are very good at organizing it and making up a system. Earth children need order in their lives, and if they do not have it, they may feel very insecure. They also need a sense of discipline, although they are not weak willed, with the possible exception of Virgo. They will resist very strongly, even though they are not usually the ones to initiate an attack. And they hold on to any position they take until the opposition is worn down, unless you can make them see the usefulness of changing their stand.

One of the greatest strengths of earth children is their ability to stay in control of themselves no matter how strange and difficult their environment becomes. They develop a solid sense of reality at a very early age and do not easily lose track of what is important and what is not. Their excellent sense of proportion prevents them from taking unimportant matters too seriously. However, one exception to this is that some earth children get too carried away with organizing situations and running them efficiently. As adults, earth persons are quite likely to dismiss aesthetic and artistic considerations in favor of purely practical solutions. Certainly earth children should be encouraged to develop their imaginations, because the combination of imagination and solid practicality can be extremely effective, and it counters their tendency to become dull and unimaginative, which can result from overemphasis on the earthy qualities.

Another serious problem among earth children is one of self-image. Very often they feel that they are dull, uninteresting to others and easily overlooked. They may feel this way even when it is clearly not true. Capricorn and Virgo are most likely to do this, while Taurus is more contented with himself. Also, earth children view the world very seriously and feel that it is necessary to really struggle to accomplish anything or attract other people's attention. This is one of the reasons why Capricorn in particular is so driven to succeed. Again, this is less true of Taurus than of the others.

While earth children can be as intelligent as children of the other elements, their concern with the practical often turns into anti-intellectualism and mistrust of abstract reasoning. Earth persons often feel that others are trying to put something over on them, and they are immediately mistrustful of smooth talkers, unless they are totally sure of their own knowledge or ability in the area under discussion. The best cure for this is to encourage the earth child's imagination and as much competence as possible in some area of activity. The earth child's sense of self-esteem is strongly focused on being able to do something well. Taurus in particular, but also Virgo and Capricorn, often are able to make objects of considerable beauty and craftsmanship because they have the patience to do a good job. Children of other elements may lack the persistence to truly finish a job.

In a very real sense, earthy persons are the "salt of the earth," the people who act as the backbone of a culture. In many ways they are the most reliable people, and any earth child should be encouraged to be reliable rather than be like those who are more flashy but less productive.

A child whose chart lacks an earth emphasis may be rather impractical, although the most common manifestation of a lack of earth is not so easy to define. It is a strange sense of not being rooted in the physical universe. The earthy type enjoys the pleasures of the senses and relates very well to his or her physical body. A child who is low in earth may not have a very well-developed body sense and may even regard his or her body negatively. In later life, non-earth types find it hard to keep their sense of reality straight, and they may lose all sense of proportion in situations of stress.

A lack of earth means that the child should be kept in touch not only with his or her body but also with the physical universe. They should be encouraged to be outdoors with nature, to make real objects and to avoid situations in which people behave in an unreal manner with no thought for practical concerns. Although strongly earthy people are not attracted to such situations, they can handle them very well, because they always know where truth and reality lie.

Air

Air is the element of intellect and reason, objectivity and ideas. Gemini, Libra and Aquarius are the air signs, and the planet Mercury is almost purely air. Uranus also has a strong air component, as does Venus, but it has an earthy component as well.

Air children are very quick and active mentally. They enjoy getting around and having new experiences. Unlike earth but like fire, air children are not very conservative, finding old ways somewhat dull and stultifying. They need constant activity, at least in their minds, for they tend to get bored quite easily. But this is compensated for by their ability to find amusement in almost any situation, making up games, getting interested in studying some matter or, if all else fails, reading or talking. Like fire children, air children may need a lot of room to move around in. However, once they have traced out the area where they live, their neighborhood for example, they do not have such an urgent need to continue roaming about for new experiences. As long as their immediate environment gives them enough to do, they don't need to go farther afield.

The air child's strongest talent is the ability to think and reason clearly and objectively. They do not let their emotions take control and distort their thinking. Thus they make excellent students of intellectual subjects, arbiters in human disputes (especially Libra) and counselors in any situation that requires clarity and objectivity. They excel at abstract subjects such as science and math, but they are also good at mechanical skills, especially if earth is strong as well. They are fascinated by problems and will spend much time working out the answers.

The greatest deficiency of this element is that air persons can be rather out of touch with their own and other people's feelings and emotions. They simply do not think emotional considerations are important and cannot understand why other people are always showing their emotions—crying or losing their temper. This leads air children to an insensitivity that is somewhat different from the fire insensitivity. The latter results from the individual's need to exert his will without hindrance from anyone else.

The air insensitivity comes from not understanding emotions. Much of the sterility and intellectualism of modern academic thought comes from the excessively airy flavor of these studies. If something cannot be understood according to an intellectual rationale, it is unimportant. In this regard, Libra is a bit different in that it may substitute considerations of harmony and aesthetic beauty for reason and logic, but even here the rationale is more important than the feeling.

For this reason, air signs may be out of touch with themselves as well. They may try to live according to their rational beliefs about what is right and correct, paying no attention to their feelings. They may turn themselves into intellectual problems to be solved instead of simply experiencing their emotions and dealing with them. It is vital that the parents of air children let them express their feelings and emotions freely. Also they should be encouraged to appreciate values other than the rational and orderly, such as imagination and fantasy.

Air people are very good at communicating with others, because their ability to understand matters rationally makes them good at explaining things to others. They are also good at influencing others' opinions, and a parent should be aware of an air child's ability to sway people, because he can make his point of view seem so convincing. Air types are good at playing with ideas as objects, totally independent of their own point of view.

Air children are usually liked by others. They know how to create a favorable impression and are usually willing to make compromises in order to seem more attractive to others, with the possible exception of Aquarius. They are entertaining to be with, often the life of the party. Libra in particular will spend a great deal of time trying to be attractive to others. But in spite of their adaptability, air types don't lose track of themselves. They remain real people, because what they give and compromise is not usually a part of themselves that they consider important.

A deficiency of air can mean an inability to think clearly or reasonably. Particularly if there is also a strong emphasis on water, such people may be unable to detach themselves from their own point of view. Air gives the ability to see someone else's point of view, and a lack of air means that ability is lacking. Also a deficiency of air makes it difficult to communicate with and relate to others.

Water

Water is the element of soul, feeling, emotion and compassion. Its signs are Cancer, Scorpio and Pisces. Strongly watery planets include the Moon, Neptune and possibly Pluto, although that is not yet entirely clear. Venus and Jupiter also have some watery characteristics.

Water children are the most sensitive and emotional of all, and they can often feel not only their own emotions but also those of the people around them. When a water person meets someone for the first time, he is often able to evaluate very quickly and accurately who and what that person is. It is very important that the parents handle this ability carefully and not permit water children to associate with people who are turbulent or disruptive or who have very strong negative feelings. All of these negative vibrations will become part of the water child. For this same reason, it is not necessary to reprimand water children harshly, for they get the picture of anger with very few words. In fact it is less important to reprimand water children when they have done wrong than to reassure them afterward. Always be sure to give the water child an opportunity to make up for what he has done. Do not hold in your anger or irritation against them, because they will feel this, and their sense of security will be undermined.

This brings us to another point. It is vital that a water child have as secure a childhood as possible, because their emotional impressions of childhood do not fade. They hold onto their past with great tenacity, because the impressions remain so vivid. Scorpio is tougher than the other two signs, but even in a Scorpio, an emotionally insecure childhood will leave serious scars. With Scorpio, and to a lesser extent with the other water signs and planets, this can result in irrationally compulsive behavior as an adult, which is very difficult to overcome. They may be suspicious of people they don't know.

Like earth, water is conservative, unless the experiences of the past were not very secure. An insecure childhood will make a water person spend his whole adult life looking for the peace and serenity that he lacked in childhood, and in doing so he will avoid anything that reminds him of the past. However, water persons normally prefer familiar and reassuring situations. For this reason they make friends slowly and may appear withdrawn. However, the friends they do have remain important to them for a long time.

It is very important to help water children get away from themselves because they tend to get very involved in their internal worlds. On the positive side, this can result in a vivid and creative imagination, but negatively, it can cause them to lose touch with reality. Water people may get lost in dreams and idealism, even if they do not show it outwardly.

If water children are brought up to feel secure in themselves, they can be marvelous people. Their sensitivity gives them enormous concern for others and a desire to help those who are less well off. They bring out in everyone they meet the emotional richness of life, because they encounter so much of the world through their feelings. With their rich imaginations, they can be extremely artistic, and they have a great understanding of the gut level of human existence. A water person would almost rather feel bad than feel nothing.

Another great need for water children is to learn to look at life from a detached perspective, to see the world from another's point of view. Their logical and rational intellect should be developed, so they can at least communicate their feelings to others and thereby get some release from emotional tension. Emotions may dominate their thinking so much that it is hard to reason with them.

A lack of water in a chart indicates that the characteristics described here are absent. Such a person has difficulty empathizing with others. Although their emotions may be active, they are not central to the individual's consciousness. Such persons may neglect their own inner needs in favor of practical or intellectual considerations, to the extent that their inner selves cry out for expression without the conscious personality really being aware of it. Such persons begin to act coldly and without feeling until they finally realize that something is wrong, although they don't know what.

Cardinal

The cardinal signs are the first signs of each of the four seasons: Aries, Cancer, Libra and Capricorn. They are rather assertive, although not always in obvious ways (Cancer for example), and they like to take the initiative. They hate to sit by and wait for someone else to begin an activity that should be started now. They want to start every project and be the first to do anything. For this reason it is sometimes difficult for cardinal-sign people to cooperate, with the possible exception of Librans, who are so involved in relationships that they take the initiative in starting them.

Unfortunately, the other side of the coin is that cardinal signs may not sustain the effort to finish what they have started. Most people have a mixture of the three crosses, so this isn't a common problem. However, if a child has a large amount of cardinality and is weak in fixed signs, the parents will have to make a great effort to train him to complete projects or to not start them at all. Otherwise they will be surrounded by a mass of unfinished projects.

Cardinal children enjoy being leaders, even though they do not always have the necessary self-assertiveness. This can create an internal conflict if a cardinal child is forced to assume a secondary or passive role while a stronger person takes the initiative. For this reason these children may avoid group activities rather than endure watching someone else run the show.

In a difficult situation, cardinal children usually prefer a direct approach and will charge directly into the situation to resolve it as quickly as possible. Their main problem in dealing with adversity is lack of persistence. They get discouraged easily and need a great deal of support to help them stay with a problem.

A deficiency of cardinality in a chart leads to certain other problems, most commonly, difficulty in getting started on projects. Once they do start, however, such people are able to keep on moving. Often persons who are deficient in cardinality will wait for others to start something before they get involved. However, this does not mean that they are passive necessarily. A strong emphasis on Mars or the Sun in the chart will go a long way to make up for a lack of cardinal signs.

Fixed

If people with cardinal signs are good at providing the initial leadership, those with fixed signs are the ones who sustain an effort over the long haul and who bring about the real accomplishment. The fixed signs are Taurus, Leo, Scorpio and Aquarius. Persons with strong fixed-sign emphasis are very persistent and stubborn, and once they are moving in a certain direction, it is very difficult to get them to stop or change course. If a child has this kind of emphasis and a weakness in mutable signs, he will be very resistant and stubborn, but in a curious way. Often the fixed child, instead of actively resisting, simply does not move or goes away for a while, hoping that you will forget what you have demanded. The fixed-sign type has a very long memory, and you have to be as persistent as he is to make an impact.

As the term "fixed" suggests, these children are not very adaptable and do best in a very stable environment where they can rather slowly adapt to the status quo. In this kind of environment they can become extremely effective. And when changes do threaten, the fixed-sign type can be extremely secure and able to face the change, if he or she has enough stability and a solid sense of self. A secure fixed-sign child will often be totally unflappable in a crisis, although he or she still doesn't really change but merely persists.

Unlike the cardinal signs, the fixed-sign type has the ability to stick to something, and these two crosses can be very complementary. They will stay with a project to the end, although they may have trouble recognizing that an activity is finished. They may want to keep on working forever, without really coming to a conclusion. When a project is concluded, it's time to start another one, and here again we encounter the central problem of this sign type, that is, difficulty in getting started.

Children who are deficient in fixed signs lack both persistence and resistance. They always yield in the face of adversity, because they try to adapt to the crisis. They may even try to become someone else in order to win approval so that the problem will go away. Or, like those with cardinal signs, they may try to bulldoze through the situation, until they recognize that they cannot make an impact, at which time they will run away. Children with a lack of the fixed quality should be encouraged to persist and to realize their own inner strength so that they will hang on and not give up.

Mutable

The mutable signs are Gemini, Virgo, Sagittarius and Pisces. These are the signs of change, and their key attribute is adaptability. The cardinal signs charge directly into a confrontation with adversity, and the fixed signs simply resist it and maintain themselves. But the mutable signs either try to find a way around the problem or they give way in the face of the attack to make it lose force. This attribute of mutability is not a weakness, because although they bend like a reed in the wind, they do manage to survive and persist. They believe in flowing with the energies of the surrounding environment, and they may actually take on different characteristics with different groups of people. Nevertheless, these children have a core of inner truth that enables them to make quite a subtle impact on those around them. By appearing to give way, they sometimes get others to accept their way of doing things. All the mutable signs except Virgo are known as dual or two-bodied signs (meaning that they have two distinct sides), which reflects the mutable person's ability to have more than one facet.

These children thrive in unstable and changing circumstances. They are able to grab what they need on the fly and adapt very quickly to new conditions. In fact they often get bored if the situation is not constantly changing.

With all of this adaptability, however, mutable children can be very devious at times. It is hard to pin them down to a definite course of action or a definite commitment. They feel that such commitment limits their freedom to do whatever seems necessary in a particular situation. Not being forthright can be a major problem, except possibly with Sagittarius, in which the element of fire demands a certain honesty and integrity. However, the Sagittarian child may state that he cannot make a commitment.

The function of mutable-sign people is to finish what others have started and transform it into something else. Without the mutable signs, activities and situations that had outlived their usefulness would simply continue, and new activities would have to begin right on top of them. The mutable signs guarantee change and the sweeping away or transformation of the old.

The most negative trait of the mutable signs is the lack of persistence, which it shares with the cardinal signs. Given any kind of resistance at all, the mutable-sign type simply changes direction and takes the line of least resistance, even if inappropriate.

Persons who are deficient in mutable signs do not adapt very well, and will stay on an obviously wrong course of action just to be stubborn, or they will give up in despair and take no action at all. In a rough situation it is mutable signs who adapt and continue to the end when the other two types have either given up or been defeated.

Chapter Four
Case Studies

Judy Garland

I have chosen Judy Garland as a case study to illustrate some of the principles set forth in the introductory chapters of this book, because her childhood was quite unusual by everyday standards—she started playing in vaudeville at a very early age—and because the consequences of that childhood were expressed in her adult personality in very unfortunate ways, including the self-destructive use of drugs and alcohol. We will examine the natal indications and trace how the energies in her personality, as symbolized by the planets, led to those problems and how this might have been prevented.

The chart is erected for June 10, 1922 at 6:00 A.M. C.S.T., in Grand Rapids, Minn. The cusps are given according to the birthplace system of Walter Koch.

First let us examine the balance of elements and crosses in Garland's chart according to the techniques that we have already discussed in Chapter Three (see pages 32-40).

		Score
Fire:	Moon (2), Mars (1), Neptune (1)	4
Air:	Sun (2), Jupiter (1), Saturn (1), N. Node (1)	5
Earth:	Empty	0
Water:	Ascendant (2), M.C. (2), Mercury (1), Venus (1), Uranus (1), Pluto (1)	8
Cardinal:	Ascendant (2), Mercury (1), Venus (1), Jupiter (1), Saturn (1), Pluto (1)	7
Fixed:	Neptune (1)	1
Mutable:	M.C. (2), Sun (2), Moon (2), Mars (1), Uranus (1)	8

To the values in this table we add additional points for angular planets and planets that are in aspect to the Sun. The only two planets that are within five degrees of the angles are Pluto and Uranus, which are next to the Ascendant and the Midheaven, respectively. Pluto gives an additional three points, probably for water, although its elemental nature is not completely clear. Uranus gives an additional three points for air and might increase the fiery nature of the chart as well. There are also several aspects to the Sun, although two of them are too far out of orb to affect this matter very much. But Sun opposition Mars definitely gives an additional three points to fire, the semisextile to Venus might give an additional point to air and perhaps one point to earth, although that would not change the lack of earth in her chart. Sun square Uranus and Sun sextile Neptune may have an effect on the chart, certainly, but they

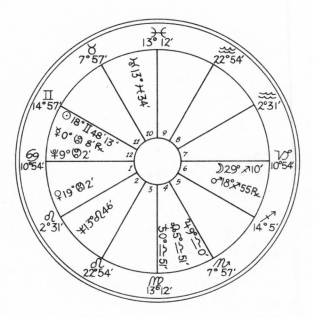

Figure 2. Natal chart of Judy Garland

would not change the elemental balance very much. The final total, therefore, is fire, seven, not including the angular Uranus; air, eight; earth, zero unless we give it the one point for Venus; and water, eleven.

This analysis immediately brings out two important facts. Garland was very weak in earth and in the fixed signs. Weaknesses in crosses and elements are by no means fatal, but they are indications that should be noted. The lack of earth is a sign that she lacked grounding in the physical universe. Persons with little or no earth may or may not be practical in some way, but they do lack the usual inherent ability to distinguish between concerns that have a real, immediate and practical effect on their lives and those ones that do not. They tend to inflate trivial issues out of all proportion to their actual significance, and at the same time to neglect the issues that really do have immediate importance. A person who has no earth easily loses track of herself and becomes totally wrapped up in a world of illusions. If the chart shows other indications of a possibly unstable personality, this can become quite a serious problem. Needless to say, the theatrical world was in many respects the wrong place to bring up such a child.

The weakness in fixed signs and the emphasis on cardinal and mutable signs indicates a person who has the energy to get into new situations and adapt to change, but without great staying power. This is also an indication of instability.

The strongest element in Garland's chart is water, indicating her acute emotional sensitivity and the ability to sense what was happening in the people and circumstances around her as well as in herself, but not necessarily clearly. It was her water quality that made her music so emotionally powerful to many of her fans. They felt that she really lived the emotions she was singing about, and indeed, she probably did. Water is very useful in show business, but it increases one's sensitivity to pain to an inordinate degree.

When we turn to more specific indications, several factors in this chart immediately strike us as unusual. First, Pluto is conjunct the Ascendant in Cancer, along with Venus, and Uranus is close to the Midheaven. It is unusual to have so many planets so close to the angles, and these planets will have unusual significance. Venus, in particular, is an indication of Garland's considerable artistic ability, although by itself, it could simply mean a person who is very attractive to others, as she was. Venus is discussed further later in this chapter.

The Sun is in Gemini in the twelfth house and in close opposition to Mars in the sixth in Sagittarius. We also have a T-square of Mercury in Cancer opposite Moon in Sagittarius, squared by Saturn in the fourth in Libra. Even in a superficial examination of the horoscope, these indications stand out so clearly that we should start here to find out the main issues in Garland's life. In general, I recommend that students start reading a chart by looking at the most powerful activity in terms of angularity and major aspects to the lights. After that, it is a good idea to examine any other major configurations.

This chart gives us a great deal of material to work with. First of all, there is Cancer rising, which tells us how she projects her personality into the environment, that is, how she appears to others, how she affects them and how she relates to them. Eventually this response feeds back from others to the self and further conditions the way in which she relates to the world.

Cancer rising makes her extremely sensitive to the environment, a person who picks up vibrations from others very intensely and clearly. For this reason a person with a Cancer Ascendant needs a great deal of peace, security and stability in early life so that sensitivity does not become an overwhelming factor. Also, since Cancer is the sign of the home and mother, the mother figure is very important in her life. Normally a Cancer Ascendant child should not be moved around much in early childhood unless the family life is very secure. Such a child needs a solid base on which to grow.

Pluto is conjunct the Ascendant, which indicates an unusually intense approach to life, even for a Cancer Ascendant. Even as children, people with this placement are extremely powerful personalities, whom others may find too intense to be around for any length of time. They need to make a tremendous impact on the world around them and will not leave any situation in life the way they found it. As children, they are very willful and do not accept frustration gracefully. I do not personally know this about Garland, but I would expect her to have an intense and brooding temper. She might not lose her temper very often, but when she did it would be quite spectacular. Often such a person tries to have great power over the people around them and may be unable to refrain from meddling in their lives. This trait is hard to curb in a child, but the parents could help by instilling in the child a respect for the rights of others.

Another attribute of this placement is a need for very intense experiences. This person likes to live at the cutting edge, so she tends to get involved in very risky or dangerous activities just to feel more intensely alive. She is fond of staring death in the face. As a child, she may seek out activities that frighten adults and that may be quite dangerous. Unfortunately, unlike some other indications of daring, this one confers no particular luck and may result in accidents. But all of her life she will probably go to daring extremes in everything. Right from the beginning, she assumes a dramatic posture in every situation.

Added to this is the square from the fourth-house Jupiter in Libra, an indication of Garland's extremely strong will to succeed. Since Jupiter is in the fourth house of one or the other parent, we have an indication that she felt that her parents would accept her as a human being only if she did well. This attitude can be a source of considerable difficulty, because it is very important for the child to understand that even if a parent is angry with her, that parent basically loves her. This square raises the possibility that Garland did not really believe this about one of her parents. Normally the chart would not clearly show which parent belongs to the tenth house and which belongs to the fourth house. However, there are indications that in her case the mother is the fourth-house parent. However, we must look further before concluding that Garland did have a serious problem with her perception of her mother's love. By itself, the Jupiter-Pluto square is not quite enough, so let us turn to the fourth-house Saturn.

The crowning difficulty of this chart is the Moon-Saturn-Mercury T-square from the sixth to the twelfth and the fourth. This combination of symbols immediately tells any competent astrologer that the person has a very strong alienation pattern. The fourth-house Saturn is the focus of the problem. At best, it is a difficult placement, signifying the need for a great deal of nurture and support. It also means that in infancy, when an infant needs to be accepted, fed and cared for unconditionally, adult demands get in the way. The obvious manifestation of this pattern in Garland's life is that she became part of the family vaudeville act at a very early age. It could also indicate that her parents were too busy trying to survive in show business to pay adequate attention to their child. Even with plenty of emotional support, a person with this placement tends to think of herself as alone in the world. Often this placement coincides with feelings of internal emptiness, unworthiness and even weakness.

By itself, Saturn in the fourth does not present insuperable difficulties, but it is made worse by the fact that the theme is repeated with the square to the Moon. This indicates that the child is likely to have problems with her mother or mother substitute. Because she is female, her own self-esteem will be weakened considerably. Only total attention and loving support from her mother can mitigate such powerful symbolism, especially with the added effect of a Cancer Ascendant. At best, this child is somewhat out of touch with her emotions and when older will avoid close intimate emotional situations for fear of getting hurt, even though she has a strong need for emotional contacts with others. At worst, and I think one can say that Garland got the worst, such a person is extremely lacking in self-confidence, with a sense of loneliness and isolation from others. There is a very strong tendency toward depression and melancholy, which she may try to alleviate through drugs, particularly depressant drugs such as alcohol and barbiturates.

When Mercury in the twelfth house is added to this T-square, we can see that her whole way of thinking about the world is colored by this aspect. Very early in life she tends to set up rather rigid thought patterns, which in this case are probably depressive. As an adult, even if someone shows her a way out of her problems, she will be unable to see it or accept it. She will tend to get locked into dysfunctional behavior and emotional patterns that are very difficult to change.

Added to these configurations is the sesquiquadrate from Neptune to the Moon, which is quite close, indicating a classic pattern of alcoholism and drug abuse. This pattern is also associated with other extreme forms of mental instability. Unless this person has an idyllic childhood, mental breakdown as an adult is extremely likely.

Neptune is also within orb, although by my own standards a bit wide of sextiling the Sun and trining Mars. As has been discussed, Neptune is associated with weakening of the reality structure and the will-to-be. You might think that the trine and sextile aspects would mitigate the influence of Neptune, which would be true if any effort were made to improve the conditions of her childhood. In fact, the twelfth-house Sun opposition the sixth-house Mars implies a very strong but turbulent will-to-be, to the point of having trouble getting along with others. This is partly because of the house placement of these two bodies, for both the sixth and the twelfth are houses of ego-denial rather than gratification. Although the drive for self-assertion is very strong, it does not operate with confidence and conviction. To want your own way very badly but not feel that you have the right to get it is extremely unpleasant. While the trine-sextile to Mars and the Sun from Neptune probably indicates a very spiritual and sensitive nature, it also has the effect of weakening her self-confidence further.

Recent research, using the positions of the planets in relation to the Sun rather than to the Earth, as is the usual practice in astrology, suggests that trines and sextiles connected to hard aspect patterns like this Sun-Moon position actually intensify the negative effects of the pattern. It is reasonable to assume that the same effect occurs from the earth-centered point of view as well.

Note that Uranus is in close quincunx to Neptune as well and forms a slightly wide-orbed T-square with the Sun-Mars opposition. This suggests a strong drive toward nonconformity and rebelliousness. The Midheaven in a child's chart is the symbol of authority figures and those who guide the child into the external world. These persons serve as role models, and they have more influence than anyone else on the objectives that the child pursues in life.

The role of the Midheaven is closely related to the father's role, but in many cases the mother plays that role, which is why astrologers are unsure whether the fourth is the house of the mother and the tenth the house of the father, or vice versa. In Garland's chart we can assume that the father is the tenth-house parent, because the Moon-Saturn square seems to tie the fourth house to the mother. Thus the symbol of Uranus on the Midheaven indicates that her paternal role model is unconventional and unusual, to say the least. This is not bad in itself, but it does introduce another element of instability in a chart that cannot afford any more.

Uranus quincunx Neptune, which symbolizes altered states of consciousness, normally has more to do with the generation than the individual. But her Uranus on her Midheaven and Neptune so strongly tied to the Moon are strong indications that the Uranus-Neptune aspect is affecting her personally. The phrase "altered states of consciousness" refers to any state—sleep, meditation, drug-altered state, higher awareness—other than the consciousness with which most people face the real world. In Garland's case this aspect suggests that her basic consciousness is not securely tied to the reality that most people accept. Given the overall instability of her chart, this is another weakening factor.

Another element in the chart that should be mentioned at this time is the quincunx between Venus in the first house and Mars in the sixth, along with the semisextile from Venus to the Sun. Since the Sun and Mars are somewhat repressed by their placement in the twelfth and sixth houses, the Venus provides an outlet for the energy. As we have already mentioned, this placement of Venus might confer artistic talent. Any aspect between Venus and Mars can indicate work of an artistic and creative nature, and this aspect is a sign that the work is carried out with great vigor and vitality. The very close semisextile to the Sun ties the Venus energy to the Sun's basic energy drives in the personality. Thus creativity or art becomes an important mode of self-expression. The Sun in the twelfth means that it is difficult for her to express her total personality before the world, but the Sun-Venus connection indicates that she can do this through art or entertainment.

The aspects among the Sun, Venus and Mars also affect relationships. In general, Venus quincunx Mars suggests some tension between the desire for relationships (Venus) and the need to assert oneself (Sun and Mars). Because of this quincunx, she asserts herself covertly, which hinders the action of Venus and makes relationships more difficult. Children with Venus rising often try to manipulate those around them by being cute and charming, a device she used all her life. Also the Cancer Venus indicates that she is possessive of others in relationships, which is reinforced by the many indications of insecurity in her chart. Yet the Sun-Mars opposition in the freedom-loving signs of Gemini and Sagittarius give her a strong desire for personal freedom. Any Mars-Venus aspect makes a person very attractive, but the quincunx means that this attractiveness is difficult for her to handle.

We have not yet come to the real point of this analysis, that is, to ask whether anything could have been done to change this seemingly irrevocable pattern in her life? Could she have been brought up to lead a healthy and happy life? And another interesting question, could she have been as creative if her personal life had not been such a mess? I will start with the last question and answer yes. She was extremely talented, and she approached her work like a craftsperson. Her neuroses were not the basis of her appeal, and astrologically, the aspects indicating creativity had little to do with the Moon-Mercury-Saturn T-square that seems to lie at the heart of her problems. In fact her life was considerably less productive because she spent so much time breaking down and pulling herself together, losing time that should have been spent creatively. And her problems with drugs and alcohol shortened her life considerably. Many people carry the idea of mental instability as the necessary source of creativity too far. Judy Garland's sicknesses ultimately destroyed her creativity.

The other two questions are more difficult to answer. Even a child quickly learns to use her weaknesses as well as her strengths to define herself in the world. Many people are afraid to lose their problems because they feel that those problems are such an important part of their identity. An adult can get in touch with the fact that she is not her problems, but this is harder for a child, although a child is less rigid in other respects.

I have already referred to several ways in which better upbringing would have minimized the potential negative effects of an aspect. Given the environmental conditions of her childhood, it clearly would have been difficult to correct her problems, but as an exercise in what might be called astrological therapy, I shall describe the proper course.

First of all, many different areas of the chart indicate her need for a stable home life and a secure relationship with her parents. This is seen from the fourth-house Saturn square the Moon, the Cancer Ascendant and Uranus on the Midheaven. Of course, all children need stability, but this chart shows a greater need than most, because with Saturn in the fourth she might not feel reinforced even when she was given plenty of emotional support.

The twelfth-house Sun means that she must be encouraged at every turn and helped to feel fundamentally all right as a human being. A twelfth-house Sun is often a sign of an early childhood incident that makes a person feel that she can't show her true self to others without being rejected. Such a person is likely to hold herself in instead of simply being herself with others. Only a great deal of parental encouragement can overcome this tendency.

The strong Neptune aspects require very careful handling. Such a child should not be told that her fantasies are worthless, because that is not true. But her fantasies must not become a substitute for objective reality, either. Such a child must be encouraged to use her fantasies as a source of creative self-expression. In adult life, all really strong creativity comes from Neptune.

At the same time she should be encouraged to face up to the demands of the external world and helped to believe that she can handle it. It is very important to isolate her from psychologically unstable and turbulent people because a Neptunian child is extremely sensitive, as is Cancer rising. Such a person feels other persons' problems as her own and finds it very hard to shut out negativity from others. Around negative people, she becomes negative, at least until she establishes a strong enough self-image to stand on her own against such people. Unfortunately this would require a more stable home life than she had.

Garland's powerful drive for success would not be a problem in a more stable personality, but with the Jupiter-Pluto and Moon-Saturn squares she needed constant reassurance of her worth. This pair of squares would tend to make her feel worthwhile only insofar as she accomplished something great. People can be happy only by accepting what they are, not what they can become.

One fact that should be pointed out is that many people with charts as spectacularly difficult as this are living quite decent and satisfactory lives. They are usually intense, and in some ways very extraordinary, individuals, with strong energies lying just beneath the surface of their personalities. Often these people accomplish more and have more productive lives than anyone else.

The kind of reinforcement that a child is given early in life does have an extremely important effect upon later development. In its present form at least, a chart is not a complete indication of how the child will develop. The chart can give some clues about the kind of childhood environment that a child is likely to encounter, but it cannot tell the whole story. If it did tell us everything, there would be little point in doing astrology for children, except to forecast the inevitable.

The fact that the chart is not a complete indication is a strength rather than a weakness, for it enables us to use the chart to pinpoint possible future problems and then work to prevent or minimize them. If one's life course were really inevitable, I for one would prefer not to know.

We should look at Judy Garland not as someone who was cursed by destiny, but as someone with a particular set of traits who fell into the worst possible environment for developing her strengths and minimizing her weaknesses, except for her creative ability. She would have had problems in any environment, but it was not inevitable that she would be so overwhelmed by them.

Yet the fault was not totally in her environment. Shirley Temple, whom we discuss in the next section, had many of the same obstacles to a normal and happy childhood that Judy Garland had. There were differences between their childhoods, but mainly they differed in their inner personalities. Shirley Temple was better equipped intrinsically to handle the challenges of being a child in show business. Problems are created by the encounter between the child, as symbolized by the horoscope, and his or her environmental conditions, not by the child or the environment alone.

There is one last factor to consider also. My experience as an astrologer seems to indicate that the awareness of the person has a great deal to do with how the situation turns out. If a person blunders through, not really understanding the energies involved, the situation will usually have the worst possible results. But if the person knows what he or she is up against, the energies or their manifestations can be modified enough to avoid the worst effects and even make the energies constructive. Ultimately astrology is useful because if properly done it can raise people's consciousness, but only if the client is shown that there is a possibility of creative change in difficult times. I think we can assume that Judy Garland never got the benefit of such understanding, which would have assisted her in handling her problems.

Shirley Temple

In this instance we study a chart of someone whose childhood was unusual but reasonably successful. From the public point of view, of course, she had an *extraordinarily* successful childhood, but I mean that she became a reasonably well-balanced adult, which in view of her childhood success is quite amazing. This is Shirley Temple, the child movie star of the thirties and forties.

The most unusual fact about her life is that the pinnacle of success came so early. She did not follow the usual pattern of having the primary career peak in mid-adulthood. Through politics she has managed to come back into the limelight as an adult, but not as much as when she was a child. In her horoscope, we will look for answers to two questions. First, how did she come to be successful so early in life? And second, how did it happen that her early success and her later relative obscurity did so little damage psychologically?

The first question can be only partially answered. Fame is very difficult to see in a chart and certainly cannot be detected with the relatively basic techniques described in this book. In fact, according to many of the criteria of traditional astrology, she shouldn't have been famous. (By traditional, I mean the fortune-telling astrology that one finds in nineteenth-century books.) For example, Saturn in the first house is square Mars—widely by my standards, although not by the standards of oldtime astrology. Saturn is retrograde, and as if that were not enough, Saturn is square the Midheaven itself. In addition, the tenth house is empty, with most of her planets below the horizon. This chart, along with many others that I have examined, has taught me to disregard many of the old criteria that were supposed to indicate success.

In my opinion, the techniques of the Uranian system of astrology provide the most useful indices of success. For those who are familiar with Uranian astrology, the method is simply to examine the Aries axis and see what midpoints are attached to it, as well as what planets are standing at 0° of the cardinal signs. Shirley Temple has the Moon within one degree of 0° Cancer. For more details, the reader is referred to books on the Uranian system, especially *The Language of Uranian Astrology* by Roger Jacobson (Uranian Publications, Franksville, Wisconsin, 1975).

Even the most advanced techniques, however, can only indicate the form of a person's fame if it does happen. They cannot predict whether or not the person will actually be famous. Certain factors must be present, but they are not a guarantee.

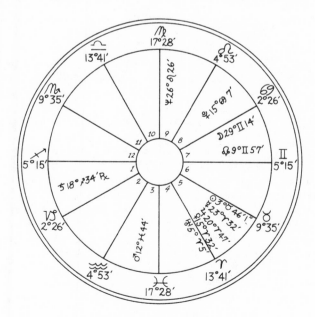

Figure 3. Natal chart of Shirley Temple

Now, given that Shirley Temple was famous at an early age, which we know without astrology, what enabled her to handle it well as she grew older? Oddly enough, the answer lies in some of the "afflictions" mentioned above, particularly the first-house Saturn. This placement indicates that adult demands intruded into her life at an early age, which made her take a serious view of life while very young. She had no childhood in the usual sense of the word, which need not be bad if the child is given plenty of reinforcement to withstand the demands of premature adulthood.

It is also interesting that her first-house Saturn is in Sagittarius, which is also on the Ascendant. The fire nature of this sign enabled her to project an image of herself as a gay, carefree child full of enthusiasm and energy. Most people find Sagittarians likable because of their positive and simple, buoyant approach to life. The presence of Saturn tells us that she was not as fun-loving and cheerful as she appeared on the screen, however. Now that she is an adult, the more realistic side of her personality has come out, and she has revealed herself as a very conservative and serious person. Strong conservatism is one common adult manifestation of a rising Saturn.

What indications do we have that she was given the necessary reinforcement to survive the adult demands that were thrust upon her from a very early age? The tenth and fourth houses are nearly empty except for Uranus at the far end of the fourth. This indicates the irregular nature of her childhood home. She obviously could not count on her home and family environment to provide the usual support and stability that a child needs. Mars, however, is so near the end of the third that it has begun to influence the fourth house. It is trine Pluto, which suggests that her relationship with one of her parents caused her to become quite strong willed and very ambitious at an early age.

On the other hand, Mars is in Pisces, where it cannot easily develop its full energy potential. She probably had periods of lassitude and discouragement, although the trine from Pluto in the eighth house lent strength. The eighth-house Pluto indicates that her will and energy had a very intense quality. Many children have strong impulses to do something significant or to engage in a serious project, but their impulses lack staying power. With the trine from Pluto to Mars, one would expect her to be quite persistent in pursuing an objective.

Neptune, the ruler of her fourth-house cusp, is in decent shape—sextile the Moon and trine Mercury. This indicates that the fourth-house parent encouraged her sensitivity and made her imagination more acute. In fact this is an immediate sign of her acting ability. As a child she was probably able to get directly into the fantasy of making a movie almost as if it were reality, just the way other imaginative children make their fantasies so real for themselves. Mercury is also in the fifth house, which we will discuss further on. For the moment we will just note that the Neptune placement does not indicate any severe problems with the fourth-house parent.

The fact that Saturn is square the Midheaven and the fourth-house cusp is significant. Basically it means that the parents did not allow her to be just a child and that they were the immediate reason why she had to assume the essentially adult role of earning a living while still a child. This could be a disastrous indication if there were not several counterindications, a few of which we have already explored. In any case, the parents of a child with this aspect should be careful not to make too many adult demands on the child. If they do, the child may become a cold, narrow and fearful adult, someone who constantly suspects that the world is out to get him or her. A little of this may be evident in Shirley Temple Black's adult personality, but she seems to have withstood the pressure fairly well.

The tenth house we find empty. Mercury, its ruler according to traditional astrology, is also well placed in the fifth house. It is conjunct Jupiter, the ruler of Temple's rising sign, which indicates that her tenth-house calling was in a fifth-house area, as movie acting certainly is. But Mercury also indicates that her parent of the tenth house had a broadening influence upon her mind and encouraged her to express herself, which she did and continues to do. Nevertheless, the Virgo influence on her Midheaven made her believe that it was important to take a careful, craftsmanlike approach to everything she did. Note also that Pluto is sextile the Midheaven, another indication of ambition, although it applies to any age.

In addition to positive, or at least non-negative, influences from the parents, there are several indications of strength that not only help to overcome any negative factors in the chart, but even may transform them into positive ones. A certain number of so-called difficult aspects are necessary in the chart of anyone who is at all successful in life.

First of all, the rising Saturn is trined by both the fifth-house Venus and the fifth-house Jupiter, which is her chart ruler. The Jupiter-Saturn trine indicates patience and persistence, the ability to hold up under difficult circumstances. This gave her the personal strength to withstand her very unchildlike childhood. Venus in this chart rules the sixth house, which along with the tenth is a house of occupation. Venus trining Saturn in the first indicates work in an area of amusement, recreation and self-expression, for example, movies. It also indicates that she used her creative talent to make money and in general capitalized on her personal appeal for practical, in this case professional, ends. A Venus-Saturn combination is often a sign of a commercial artist, either in graphic or performing arts.

Note, by the way, that the fifth house is the most crowded, which helped overcome any negative effects from the first-house Saturn. It indicates that even though she was exposed so early to the practical demands of adult life, she also had a strong drive for self-expression and self-gratification. This means that any activity she was involved in had to be fun as well as work. Fifth-house people have an extraordinary ability to make play out of what others consider work. Also, of course, at a simpler level of astrology, the fifth house is the house of theater and performing.

Venus is also square Pluto, which in most astrological textbooks is interpreted in purely sexual terms. It is often considered, quite luridly, as an indication of insatiable sex drive and the desire for every kind of perverted sexual expression, especially with Pluto in the eighth. That could be true, of course, but the true essence of this aspect is seeking in love relations of *all kinds* a very high order of intensity, and seeking relationships that totally transform one's life. In a child this usually means extraordinary emotional intensity and a tendency to form very strong attachments or dislikes. It can also indicate that the person uses other people's love to manipulate them and control what they do. Or someone else does this to them. At any rate, parents should watch a child who has this configuration so they can prevent the child from going too far with this tendency. And under no circumstances should the parents manipulate the child in this manner. The child has to be taught that people give and receive love purely for each other and that love should never be subjected to manipulation.

The wide Mars-Saturn square has been discussed briefly. To comment further, this is a potentially negative aspect, which must be handled with great care. It is an indication that the child felt that very strong demands were made upon her and that she did not have the energy to fulfill them. Often this aspect undermines a child's self-confidence, because she cannot live up to the demands. But it can increase self-discipline enormously and help the child focus her energy, especially when the aspect is so wide. The lack of exactness makes hard aspects easier to deal with and more easily transformed into positive ones, especially in a chart that has as much strength as this one. Note that both Mars and Saturn receive trines from other planets—Mars from Pluto and Saturn from Venus and Jupiter. This also helps, because the stability of the trines overcomes the danger of any instability indicated by a square.

Another aspect that helps to create strength, especially at the innermost psychological level, is the sextile between the Sun and Moon. It is out of sign, but not very wide in orb. This is an indication that her parents had a harmonious and reinforcing effect on her. (See the section on Sun-Moon polarity in Chapter Two, pages 16-18.) This aspect helps to minimize conflict between the two most basic parts of the personality, the inner emotional and largely unconscious side (the Moon), and the outer, active, will-directed side (the Sun).

The influence of Uranus also helped prevent Saturn from gaining the upper hand over the chart. We have already mentioned the possible disruptive effects of a fourth-house Uranus, but this one is trine the Ascendant, indicating independent strength and a desire to set her own course.

We have not yet paid much attention to the signs. They do have an influence, of course, and we should take them into consideration, with the proviso that whenever a sign and a planet contradict each other, the planet takes precedence over the sign. Other astrologers might disagree on this point, but the weight of the evidence is definitely on the side of my position. For example, astrologers have arrived at almost universal agreement about the meanings of the planets and their precise location in the heavens, with the possible exception of Pluto, the newest planet to our knowledge. Astrologers also seem to agree on the meanings of the signs, but they do not agree about their location. Some place the signs with respect to the vernal point, the so-called tropical zodiac. Others place them with respect to the constellations as they were in antiquity, the sidereal zodiac. For purposes of psychological interpretation, I personally find the tropical zodiac more useful, but I realize that the question is by no means closed, and for that reason, I give the symbolism of the planets precedence over that of the signs whenever I delineate a chart. With that in mind, let us proceed.

Her Sun is in Taurus, which certainly helped her to be resistant and tough in the face of a pretty unconventional childhood, but exactly how Taurean is she? To answer this question, we examine the element and cross emphases. Here is the breakdown.

Fire:	Ascendant, Mercury, Venus, Jupiter, Saturn, Uranus, Neptune	Score 8
Air:	Moon, North Node	3
Earth:	Midheaven, Sun	4
Water:	Mars, Pluto	2
Cardinal:	Mercury, Venus, Jupiter, Uranus, Pluto	5
Fixed:	Sun, Neptune	3
Mutable:	Midheaven, Ascendant, Moon, Mars, Saturn, North Node	9

Also, Mars is near the I.C., which gives an additional two points to fire. As we can see from this tally, she is not at all balanced in terms of elements and crosses. Her deficiencies, however, are not so striking as the dominances of mutable and fire. As a mutable-fire person, she showed the qualities of her Ascendant, Sagittarius, more strongly than those of the Sun sign, Taurus. This signifies that although she had the toughness granted by Taurus, she did not have the Taurean resistance to change. An enormously flexible child, she nevertheless had the strong will of a Sagittarian. This indication confirms the effect of the Uranus-Ascendant trine. At the same time, the number of factors in the cardinal signs kept her from being totally passive and submissive. She is perfectly capable of taking the initiative in life.

Here we have an example of stress factors that in some charts would produce great difficulties. But here they worked out very positively. Without the balance between premature adulthood, indicated by the first-house Saturn, and the drive for pure childish self-expression, which is characteristic of both the fifth house and fire, the dominant element, she would have been a very serious and lonely child who felt that the world is only an obstacle to be overcome, not an experience to be enjoyed.

A Friend's Child

This case study is quite different from the others. Instead of taking a well-known person, we will examine the chart of a newborn child about whom we know nothing directly. We do know something about the parents. The data is withheld for reasons of privacy, but the birthtime is quite accurate, because an astrology student of mine was present at the birth and checked the time very accurately. Of course, since there is some uncertainty among astrologers as to what precise moment should be considered the birthtime, there may be some small error. In fact there are indications in the chart that the actual time of birth was a bit earlier, something less than five minutes.

The child, a boy, was born during the Saturn-Uranus square of 1975-1977. Normally a square such as this would affect only the whole generation, but in this case the square is solidly tied into a personal point in the chart, namely the Sun, which makes it clear that it will affect this chart. The Sun-Saturn aspect indicates great sensitivity concerning the child's relationship with the father. That is, the relationship will have to be quite good in order to avoid some of the classic Sun-Saturn father difficulties, which we shall describe later.

Other outstanding features of this chart are the Moon in Cancer sextile the twelfth-house Jupiter, Mars square Neptune from the fourth to the sixth, Venus in the third conjunct Mercury and sextile Neptune, and Mercury the Ascendant ruler as Gemini is rising.

The first step is to examine the relationship with the parents. It is easy to establish which house represents which parent, because the degree of the mother's Sun is on the child's Midheaven. Therefore she is the tenth-house parent, while the father is the fourth-house parent. As we have shown in Chapter One, the mother symbolized by the tenth rather than the fourth suggests that the parents' roles are reversed, so we should see whether the chart corroborates that possibility in other respects. We find that the indicators of the father are poorly placed in this chart, which supports the idea of role reversal. First of all, in the fourth house, which we now know to be the house of the father, we see a Mars square Neptune in the sixth. This is an indication that the father, if he is not careful, could undermine the child's basic self-confidence and make him feel insecure about the safety and reliability of the home environment as a basis for emotional support. By itself, Mars suggests conflict in the home, but the square from Neptune indicates that it might not always come out into the open. This aspect is a call to the parents to make sure that all the emotional energies within the family structure are brought out into the open and dealt with. No one's emotions should be permitted to simmer beneath the surface and create feelings of nervousness and instability.

In the past the father has had a bit of a drinking problem, and the Mars square Neptune could be an indication of this. Certainly any further manifestation of the father's drinking problem would have a very serious effect on the child's self-confidence because it would deprive him of the masculine role model that he needs to develop into a healthy adult. Incidentally, children of both sexes need both a masculine and feminine role model.

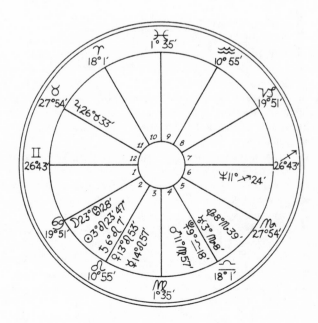

Figure 4. Natal chart of a young boy

56

Another important indication is the Sun conjunct Saturn square Uranus, which could mean considerable tension with the father. As described in the delineations, Sun-Saturn afflictions indicate either emotional distance from the father, his physical absence, or excessive idealization of the father. Given the Mars square Neptune, we can probably eliminate the last possibility. And of course the negative manifestation of these aspects is not at all inevitable.

The Uranus square Sun and Saturn indicates that the child's image of his father will be quite unusual and eccentric, which in itself is not bad. We can expect that the child will have a strong desire to be individualistic and nonconforming, but this will be inhibited by Saturn. If the father is not particularly careful, the child will develop extremely ambiguous love-hate feelings about him, which could be very destructive of the child's self-image. Incidentally, by equating the arc between the Sun and Saturn to age according to the time it takes the progressed Sun to move that distance (a technique called solar arc directions), we can see that the tension would reach a maximum at about two and three quarters years. However, if Uranus is solar arc directed to the Sun, we can see another tense period at about three months.

At the very least, this aspect grouping of the Sun, Saturn and Uranus indicates that the child will be rather tense in several ways, not knowing whether to be disciplined and strict or to break loose and become free. The parents should watch for psychosomatic illnesses caused by tensions and should do everything possible to ensure a reasonably tranquil childhood environment. It should be stressed, by the way, that when the child grows up, this aspect could mean a very powerful and resistant personality, someone who can persist through great tension and stress and accomplish a great deal in the process. However, this can happen only if the family minimizes stresses during childhood.

The Gemini Ascendant indicates that this child will be quite flexible in handling others, which would help to counter the natural inflexibility of his fixed-sign Leo. However, it is clear for several reasons that this child will not be a typical Leo. First, the conjunction between the Sun and Saturn will quiet down the normal exuberance of Leo and make the child considerably more subdued. In fact, probably no one would guess that this child is a Leo. Also the Moon in Cancer is an indication of greater emotional sensitivity than is usual with Leos. It is also a sign that the mother will be more important than usual in this child's development.

In fact the Moon is the first in a series of indications that the child's relationship with his mother will be much easier than that with his father. The Moon in Cancer is sextile Jupiter—a twelfth-house Jupiter to be sure—but it indicates a kind and unselfish side to the child's personality. Venus is conjunct Mercury, the Ascendant ruler, and both are trine Neptune. This is a strong indication of great sensitivity and of a creative and even artistic imagination. The child is likely to be an idealist and a romantic at a very early age. Along with the Cancer Moon, this group of aspects is a sign that for maximum mental stability the child should have a very quiet and stable childhood. He should not spend much time with strongly negative people, because he will pick up the negative vibrations, and with Mars square Neptune, his sense of security may be undermined.

The overall indications in this chart suggest that the feminine planets are in much better shape than the masculine, and that throughout childhood, this boy may show more clearly developed feminine characteristics. This is not a problem in itself, but his male peers may give him some trouble over it. This could be the type of child whom other boys call a "sissy," and it is very important that his parents give him enough self-confidence to resist the pressures. If he tries to deny his strong femininity, as many boys in this situation do, he will suppress his strongest personal resources, such as creativity, compassion, the ability to feel strong emotions clearly and the ability to bounce back after emotional crises.

This child should be encouraged to read and write, because the third house is very strong, with the Venus-Mercury conjunction very near the cusp and with Saturn in the second but close to the third-house cusp. These indications would not come to much, however, if his family did not respect reading, artistic sensitivity and creativity. Both the father is extremely bright and very musical, and the mother, although not educated beyond high school, is quite bright and interested in learning. She is also rather heavily involved in astrology and mystical thinking.

The Saturn near the cusp of the third is extremely important, because a planet in the last degrees of a house affects the next house. Mercury conjunct Venus in the third indicates creative imagination, especially in sextile to Neptune, but Saturn helps to ensure that he will have enough discipline to apply his skills and talents concretely. Also the Sun-Saturn conjunction indicates discipline and the ability to make something real out of his talents, if his childhood is stable. If it is not, as an adult he could be so wrapped up in his neuroses that he will have no time for creativity.

It can be important and useful to look up the first aspects occurring after birth, because they indicate the first progressed aspects that will influence the child's life. Checking an aspectarian for the child's birthdate, we find that the first aspect to become exact after birth is the parallel aspect of Venus and Mercury (having an effect similar to that of the conjunction), which was also very close at the moment of birth. This tells us that the Venus-Mercury conjunction will be even more important than we thought. The idea of looking up the first aspect is based on sound psychology, namely, that the earliest influence in a child's life will be the most important in his development. Thus the artistic influence will affect him at a very early age, although it is hard to say how it will be felt.

The next aspects after birth are the almost simultaneous Moon sesquiquadrate Neptune and Moon sextile Jupiter, which will be influential when the child is about three months old. This will affect his relationship with his mother, presumably positively. However, the parents should be careful of certain things. Children are especially sensitive to feelings of abandonment under Moon- or Sun-Neptune aspects in the progressed aspects. This does not usually mean that the child is in fact abandoned, but that he interprets some experience as abandonment. It will be quite important in this child's future development to receive considerable support and care during the third month, when this aspect becomes operative. However, the almost simultaneous Moon sextile Jupiter means that this crisis is not likely to be very serious. It is interesting to note that this progression coincides with transiting Uranus going forward to square natal Saturn, which can be an aspect of sudden separation and tension. Also remember Uranus coming by solar arc to a square of the Sun at three months, a further suggestion that the parents should be careful with the child at this time. The child will be unusually sensitive to disturbances. Also the symbolism as a whole suggests that if the father is not careful, events during this period will ultimately lead to deterioration of the father-son relationship and strengthening of the mother-son relationship.

There are some other early transits to watch. Not only does Uranus square Saturn shortly after birth, but also Saturn will transit over the Venus-Mercury conjunction several times in the first year of life, which further suggests some kind of emotional crisis, possibly caused by an interruption in a relationship.

Another factor to be noted is that except for Jupiter in the twelfth house, the chart is below the horizon. This suggests that the child's inner life will be more important than his relations with the outer world. If he is given enough self-confidence, he will be able to determine his own inner values. However, along with this there is a danger that the child will spend too much time in his own private world, especially with the aforementioned Neptune aspects. He must be encouraged to come out of himself at least far enough to develop normal relations with his peer group.

Last but not least, we look at the dominant elements and crosses, as described in Chapter Three. Doing a tally of the planets in the elements, we find that the Sun, Mercury, Venus, Saturn and Neptune are in fire signs; Mars and Jupiter are earth; air contains the Ascendant and Pluto; and the Midheaven, the Moon, the north node of the Moon and Uranus are water. Using the point system, we come up with the following scores (recall that the Sun, Moon, Midheaven and Ascendant are given a score of two while the other factors are given a score of one): fire, 6; earth, 2; air, 3; and water, 6. Earth is the weakest element, suggesting that the child's mental ties with the real physical universe are not very strong, that he can easily lose touch with reality. He may encounter experiences in which he loses perspective and certain factors are blown up out of all proportion to reality. He needs to be constantly grounded in the real and the material. Fortunately, a score of two is not as difficult as a score of zero. Also the Sun is near conjunction with Saturn, which could help quite a bit, giving three more points to earth.

The strength of fire suggests a strong will, but the afflictions that we have noted may undermine that. Certainly, as he grows older, he will have a strong desire to encounter the spiritual dimension of existence and that may make him more reluctant to be limited by the physical world. Concretely this indicates a strong desire to transcend the limitations of normal reality and to encounter the basic energies of the universe. It is very hard to describe this in more concrete terms, I am afraid, but in general strong fire indicates an unwillingness to accept the universe as it is. The strong water suggests that he will be very sensitive, as other sources have also indicated, and his emotions will be very powerful and important to him. Along with the preponderance of planets below the horizon, it also suggests that he will react to the world rather subjectively. However, the Sun-Saturn conjunction may mitigate that considerably.

We go through a similar procedure for the crosses or quadruplicities. In the cardinal signs we have the Moon and Pluto; in the fixed signs, the Sun, Mercury, Venus, Jupiter, Saturn, Uranus and the north node; in the mutables, the Midheaven, Ascendant, Mars and Neptune. The score works out to: cardinal, 3; fixed, 8; mutable, 6. Cardinal is weak, indicating that this child will not be one to start projects, but he will be a sustainer. When others take the initiative, he will keep the activity going. He is also likely to be quite stubborn and persistent, but because of the strength in mutable signs, he can adapt. These are both good indications for being able to withstand any problems that may result from insecurity and instability in childhood. This will help make his personal security and stability less dependent on a totally stable home life, although this will still be more important to him than to most children.

It is interesting to note that the mutable side of his personality will be more obvious than his fixed side when people first meet him. This is because of his mutable Ascendant, which determines the kind of first impression one makes on others.

For those who like the idea of signatures obtained from integrating the dominant cross with the dominant element, this child has either a fixed fire (Leo) or a fixed water signature (Scorpio). Since the Leo signature is confirmed by the Sun and other planets in Leo, I would go along with that signature. However, Leo does not sit well with the quantity of Neptune and the probable personal insecurity that we have been talking about. The answer is very simple; a Leo can be as insecure as any other sign. If this child is not carefully brought up as described, he could become a person who tries to assert his individuality in various ways because he does not believe in it himself. On the plus side, however, he could become an adult who, unlike most Leos, is more concerned with the good of those around him than with himself. These two manifestations are equally probable. Environment will make the difference.

Chapter Five

Sun

The Sun in the Chart

The Sun in your chart represents your basic personality drives and behavior patterns, the kinds of activities you prefer, and the way you assert yourself toward others. The sign occupied by your Sun at birth describes the nature of these basic drives and patterns. However, in any sign, the Sun always represents your desire to be important to the people you know and your ability to be independent and self-reliant.

If the Sun has good aspects from other planets, it is a good indication that you can stand on your own, be self-confident and maintain yourself against pressure from others. It is also an indication of sound health and physical vitality. Difficult aspects to the Sun usually indicate major psychological problems, which will have a profound effect upon your life. But keep in mind that people usually achieve greatness through dealing with these difficult patterns in their lives rather than because of the easier aspects alone. So you should view any difficult aspects to your natal Sun as areas that require work, but realize that the work can be very successful.

It is important to note that if the Sun is strongly aspected by Saturn, the whole nature of your Sun sign will be suppressed somewhat, and you will be quieter and more reserved than you would be otherwise.

Sometimes a poorly situated or aspected Sun will signify that you try to overcompensate by acting arrogant or overly prideful toward others. Such behavior is not usually an indication of a well-aspected Sun. On occasion, difficult aspects to the Sun mean lowered physical vitality and health problems.

Sun in Aries

You are very energetic and spirited. It is difficult for you to wait for other people, even your parents, and you tend to be impatient if events don't move as quickly as you would like. For this reason you prefer to work by yourself, if you find that others aren't moving as quickly as you do. This may cause you to become totally wrapped up in yourself, simply because you aren't relating to others enough and not paying enough attention when you do. You have a mind of your own, and you do not care if anyone else agrees with you. You resent it fiercely when people try to impose their thinking or their methods on you.

You like to be the first to do everything, and often you take risks that others consider unwise, because you want to be known for doing something that no one else will do.

Just be careful to avoid real trouble, and try to listen to what others have to say. They are not always trying to get in your way; in fact they may be trying to help you.

You are rather quick to anger, but you do not hold grudges. As soon as your angry mood passes, which is usually quite quickly, you are willing to forget and forgive. However, while you are angry you act rashly and may say things that you will regret.

In talking with other people, you prefer to be simple and direct, and whenever possible you are honest, simply because it makes life easier and simpler. Just be careful not to be so blunt that you hurt people's feelings, since some people are emotionally hurt more easily than others. You may also be rather competitive, which may alienate some people, but most will realize that your competitiveness is good natured and not intended to harm.

Sun in Taurus

You are very patient and like to do things slowly so that you can see what is really happening. You want to make every moment last, so you try to work carefully and slowly. Others may criticize you for being slow, but that may mean only that they are not as careful as you are.

You like to be comfortable. You enjoy sitting in a comfortable chair in warm surroundings, taking it easy. Also you may tend to overeat, and you should be especially careful about sweets and fatty foods, because you could gain too much weight. With your love of comfort and ease, you may try to avoid strenuous situations, but you really need such experiences to help you mature. You may feel quite lazy at times, and you will have to push yourself to do the tasks that have to be done.

On the other hand, people will probably like you because you are affectionate; you give and receive love easily. Basically you are even-tempered and slow to anger. However, if others try to take advantage of your placidity, they will quickly discover that when you are roused to anger, you don't calm down easily. On those rare occasions when you do get angry, be careful not to lose your temper so completely that you do something you will regret later.

In any kind of work that you do, you want to be able to point to practical, real results. You find it difficult to work for abstract goals. You don't mind working a long time for the results you want, but you have to understand and relate to those results.

Sun in Gemini

Your mind is very quick and agile, and you are curious to know the answer to every question as quickly as possible. Unfortunately, if the answer is difficult or takes a long time to figure out, you may lose interest and turn your attention to some other matter. As you get older it is very important to lengthen your attention span, or your very good mind will not be used properly.

You like to travel and see new sights. You quickly get tired of whatever you are used to and want to trade it for something different. You don't particularly care whether something is long lasting, as long as it is exciting while you have it.

You enjoy games, especially ones that require you to match wits with someone else, such as a question and answer game. A very playful person, you sometimes like to play tricks on other people. Just be careful that your tricks don't hurt anyone.

Your moods change very quickly, and you don't spend a great deal of time being unhappy or sad. All it takes to make you feel better is to have something new and interesting to do. In fact, boredom may be one of your worst problems.

You may become very fond of books and reading, or you may prefer to learn by talking with others. You are very much attracted to people who seem intelligent and who can teach you about new subjects.

Sun in Cancer

You are an emotional person who is sensitive to the subtle ways that people communicate with each other. If there are bad feelings in the air, you know it.

You very much need to have emotional support and to know that your loved ones love you, especially your mother. It is important to know that you will be taken care of and that no matter what happens, you will always have a secure place to come home to. When these needs are fulfilled, you are a very generous and giving person. You like to take care of people and give them the love and comfort that you need so much. You like to know that others feel free to come to you for help and reassurance at any time.

However, if your own basic needs are not provided for, you will withdraw into yourself and act very insecure, as if there were only a limited quantity of love and attention in the world and you were afraid of losing your share. An insecure Cancer can be very selfish, just as a secure one can be very generous.

You are attached to the old familiar things that you have had since earliest childhood. You may keep an old toy long after you have stopped playing with such things. You probably have a secret, quiet place that is all your own, where you can go and be alone with your thoughts. Wherever you go in life, one of your first objectives in new surroundings will be to find such a place for yourself.

Your home and family will always be important to you, both the home you are growing up in and the one you will have later on. It is important to you that both of these be secure.

Sun in Leo

You are spirited and strong willed and like to be the center of attention. Sometimes you may be a show-off, which others may find annoying. Nevertheless, other people like you because you are basically warm and affectionate. You work very hard to get your way with others. You should be careful of carrying this trait too far, however, because it may turn away people who would otherwise be your friends. You are proud and consider yourself important. The positive side of this is that you are reluctant to compromise yourself or lose other people's respect. Being respected by others is very important to you, and for this reason you are less likely than others to tell lies. You feel that everything should be out in the open.

Once you have made up your mind about a particular course of action, you are very persistent. You select a goal and follow it through to the bitter end. When you are older, you will want to be a person of some importance and, if possible, a leader. Even while you are young you will play this role whenever possible, which should work out very well, because you also want to be worthy of being a leader. For you, self-respect is as important as the respect of others.

Sun in Virgo

You are very careful in everything you do, and you put a high value on neatness. When you aren't neat, you lose respect for yourself, because you have very high standards in that as well as in other areas, which you want to come up to as much as possible. You expect others to live up to those same high standards, and you are easily disappointed if they do not. When you see something wrong in someone or something, you don't hesitate to point it out. But you will have to learn to be considerate when you do this, because criticizing others creates bad feelings.

You are very interested in learning as much as possible about the world, particularly about how to use various kinds of tools. Since you want to learn practical skills, it would be a very good idea to have a hobby in which you use your hands. In whatever you make or do, you apply the same standards of perfection that you want other people to live up to. As a consequence, your work is far more careful than other people's. If you know you can't do something right, you won't do it at all.

You tend to worry about your health, but you don't need to. Your health is as good as anyone else's; you are just more concerned about it. Probably you will follow good rules of health.

You like to help others because being useful makes you feel good. You are able to put off what you want for yourself in order to help someone you love do what he or she wants. Others will respect you for this.

Sun in Libra

You are warm and affectionate, and you enjoy being with people. You don't like to be left out of the crowd for any reason, and you will work very hard to make sure that you are liked by people of all ages. Yet you are not retiring, in fact, you are quite strong willed and often the person in a group who makes things happen. It is just that you feel the need to be with others in order to express yourself.

You like beautiful things and dislike anything ugly. You are more conscious of nice clothing than most young people and always try to look your best. But your love of beauty does not apply just to yourself. You prefer attractive homes and furnishings, pleasant scenery, and even art and music, in which your tastes may be well developed.

Very often when you have to make a decision, you have great difficulty making up your mind. This is because you see both sides very clearly, and it is hard to choose between them. Consequently you may waver back and forth and not reach a decision until it is too late. On the other hand, your ability to see both sides makes you a very good peacemaker when other people are having an argument, for you can make them see both views also. Besides, you hate to see people arguing. You like peace and harmony in relationships.

Some people who have the Sun in Libra show a different side of the sign. They like to engage in contests and arguments and enjoy being pitted against someone else in one-to-one encounters. According to researchers, more generals are born under this sign than any other.

Sun in Scorpio

You are very intense and have extremely strong feelings, which you find difficult to talk about because they are also very complicated. As a result, you are likely to be a quiet person who spends a great deal of time brooding and thinking about your feelings. When you lose your temper, you get extremely angry; fortunately, that doesn't happen very often. And when you are angry, you don't easily forgive the person who caused your fury, even if it is someone whom you like very much. For this reason you have ambivalent feelings about many people. On the other hand, if you do love someone, your feeling is very intense. You don't commit your emotions lightly. And you have no respect for anyone who plays with other people's feelings.

You are very sensitive and your feelings are easily hurt, but you won't run off and hide if someone hurts you. Instead, you strike back and fight hard. Scorpio is one of the hardest fighters of the zodiac.

You have a great love of the mysterious and hidden. You may be attracted to the super-natural and have a great love of horror stories, crime novels and suspenseful TV programs. You also want to know what is going on in people's minds, so you make an effort to learn as much as possible about human nature.

Sometimes other people have difficulty understanding you, and for this reason you may not make friends easily. But the friends you do have will be very good ones who will probably last for your whole life.

Sun in Sagittarius

You are a fun-loving person who enjoys games. You are very spirited and energetic and need to spend a lot of time outdoors to release all your energy. Because of your strong need to feel free, you may find it difficult to put up with the restrictions that adults want to impose on you. However, you have quite a bit of self-control. So you shouldn't need as much discipline as some young people.

While you are friendly to others, you dislike anyone who tries to tie you down emotionally or who acts jealous of your relationships with other people. You want freedom to be friends with anyone, and you won't let others dictate to you about this.

You are very curious and want to know the answer to every question that comes to mind. To satisfy your curiosity, you hang around the people who can answer your questions. Quite possibly you will turn to books for the answers you seek. As you grow older, you will become interested in finding out how the universe works in the broadest terms.

However, coupled with this interest in the universe is a tendency to be sloppy and careless about details. Because of this, you may jump to conclusions about a situation before you have enough information. Also you may not be very neat about yourself. You feel that picking up and cleaning are not important enough to waste your time on. However, you are cheerful and positive, and people enjoy having you around.

Sun in Capricorn

You are much more serious than others your age. Even adults notice that you act older than you are. After a while they may expect this of you and ask you to take on responsibilities beyond what is required of other young people. You have two kinds of feelings about this. On the one hand, you like being taken seriously and enjoy having responsibility, but on the other hand you see that other young people aren't saddled with such responsibilities, and you tend to envy them. You feel that everyone should work to get what they want, and it annoys you when others get something they don't deserve.

You may develop a rather odd and unusual sense of humor. Through jokes and humor, you show that you recognize the seriousness of life, but you also escape from its overwhelming effects. Often your jokes are aimed at yourself.

When you grow up, you want to be important and achieve something real that everyone can point to as yours. You are ambitious in everything you do and will work very hard to excel over others. But you will not take credit for anything that you have not done yourself, to make sure that all your achievements are real.

You are very practical and always ask what good something is. In school you do best at studies that obviously have some practical application. You are very concerned with what is real and what is not and are less interested in fantasy and pretending than others. Whatever is not real has little value for you.

Sun in Aquarius

You like new things and new ideas and are bored by old ways of thinking and acting. The friends you choose are people who feel the same way. You are an individualist and a free spirit, but at the same time you need to work and share your life with other people. Friends are very important to you, although if they try to hold you back or make you conform to their ideas, you will rebel and go your own way.

However, even though you are attracted to new ideas, you don't readily change your thinking once you have made up your mind. Actually you are quite stubborn, which may confuse other people, who interpret your interest in everything new and different as evidence of a very changeable mind.

Because of your fondness for new ideas, you enjoy studying science, technology and other subjects that enable people to control the world in some way. As you get older, you may be attracted to more offbeat studies, such as astrology and the occult.

When you are with a group of friends, you think about the group as a whole rather than just about yourself. You try to do what is best for everyone, without at the same time going against your personal needs. This can cause problems for you if your needs conflict with the needs of the rest of the group. But basically you are fair, and you try to make sure that everyone gets the same deal. You will stand up for anyone who is not being treated fairly.

Sun in Pisces

You are a very sensitive and emotional person who quickly picks up moods and emotions from other people and makes them part of your own. As a result, you find it difficult to be around people who are feeling angry, sad, or unhappy in any way, because you begin to feel that way, too. This trait makes it very easy for others to hurt your feelings. You are much more likely to cry than people with other Sun signs, although you may try to hold back your tears. But this sensitivity is not bad, although you may not always like it. Because you have the ability to put yourself in someone else's place, you have an exceptional understanding of other people's needs. You don't like to hurt anyone, because you know how it feels to be hurt. Whenever possible, you try to help others, because it makes you feel good about yourself.

Very often you like to go into your own private fantasy world and think about ideas that mean something only to you. You don't usually talk to other people about your private world, because you feel that they would not understand, and you are probably right. Just don't spend so much time there that you lose track of what is happening outside in the real world.

You may be somewhat shy, because you feel you have to trust people before you can really open up to them. With your sensitive feelings, you want to make sure that others won't hurt you before you really accept them as a friend. But even though you are shy, you do need other people, for without them you feel lonely, even in your own world.

Sun in the First House

You have a strong personality that immediately makes an impression on other people. When you enter the room, everyone knows it. You are very strong willed and energetic. The problem with this is that you may not let the people around you be themselves. Your own energies are so strong that you try to impress your will upon others, and you are very impatient when people try to assert themselves with you. Nevertheless, they have the right to assert themselves, and you should give them the chance, even though you may find it irritating.

Your high level of self-confidence can be very useful, as long as you know your limitations and avoid being cocksure. Don't try to do more than you can, and when you are unable to do something, don't take it as a personal defeat. It's hard for you to realize that no one can do everything.

You are physically strong and should enjoy good health. If you can learn to accept your limitations and control your energy properly, you will be able to do a great deal. People with the Sun in this house who learn how to get along with others and let them have their way now and then are very well liked. But if you do not learn these lessons, you will not be liked.

Sun in the Second House

You love security, which for you means being surrounded by comfortable and familiar objects. You like to own things—toys, books, whatever—because it makes you feel good. The only problem is that you may try to own more things than you really need, so that your life is cluttered with material possessions. You are likely to be a collector of some sort, and since you have an excellent sense of value, your collection will probably be quite valuable, as long as you are systematic. Otherwise you will be surrounded with vast quantities of junk.

It is difficult for you to part with your possessions, and you may find it difficult to share, but if you want to have good friendships, you will have to learn how. You are even possessive of your friends, and don't like to share them with anyone else. If a friend pays too much attention to someone else while you are together, you are likely to feel jealous. But you have to learn to share that person with others. Your friend can like someone else and still like you.

As you get older, you will have a strong sense of values, which you will not compromise. Just be sure that your values go beyond material objects and that what you value is worthwhile. You have the ability to preserve a strong sense of integrity and security in this changing world.

Sun in the Third House

Your mind is active, quick and quite curious. You are fond of talking and asking questions, although you sometimes speak when you have nothing to say, just for the fun of it. Other people may find this annoying, however, You are restless, and to be happy you need constant change. You like to travel around, perhaps by taking long walks or by bicycling around town. The more you can experience, the happier you are.

Your curiosity and your quick mind will help you in school, but you will have to learn to discipline yourself, because you won't want to spend much time on any one subject. You like to do a little bit in many areas, but that is not the way to learn. Also it would be good to develop your mind through reading and writing, which you may be very skillful at, but only if you work at it. When you are older, communications may be an important part of your career.

You like to match wits with others, as in arguments, both friendly or unfriendly, and in word games or puzzle solving.

Your brothers and sisters, if you have any, as well as relatives and neighbors, will be important in your life. You may learn much from one of them.

Sun in the Fourth House

The warmth and security of your home are very important, for you need to know that you have a place to withdraw to. When you are feeling bad or the going is tough in the outside world, you want a family you can depend upon for comfort and protection. If you do not have this support, you may become very nervous and fearful. Your parents are very important people in your life, even more than ordinarily, and their attitudes and ways of doing things will have a tremendous impact on you.

You are likely to be a quiet person with strong feelings and emotions, and you keep to yourself a lot. If you are around loud or domineering people, your natural tendency is to withdraw into yourself. But you aren't really weak or retiring, because by going into yourself, you gain strength. In fact, no one can force you to do something that you don't want to do.

Although you may be quite successful when you grow up, you will not care much for being famous or in the limelight. You are much more concerned with living up to your own inner standards and having a rewarding personal life.

When you feel good and secure about yourself, you like to bring people into your home and share your good feelings with them. In fact, all of your life you will try to protect and shelter those who need it. You will not keep what you have to yourself, unless you are afraid for some reason.

Sun in the Fifth House

Above all, you want to be yourself, and you will resist anyone or anything that tries to make you conform to a standard that you can't accept. You may even be a bit of a show-off who enjoys performing for people in athletic competitions, plays or other such presentations. In a way, you are always on stage. You are quite competitive and have a lot of energy, and you enjoy all kinds of games and amusements.

It may seem that you don't take anything seriously, but this is not really true. You take life itself seriously, and you want your life to be a successful performance. Because of your strong sense of pride, you get very angry when someone insults you. You have a strong sense of honesty and are very direct with people. It doesn't seem necessary to hide any fact about yourself or anyone else; consequently you can be quite blunt.

Since you enjoy being the center of attention, you can be domineering as you try to grab center stage. If you try to be the outstanding person in every group, you may get into serious conflicts with others who have the same drive. Only one person can be the leader at a time, and that one shouldn't always be you.

Nevertheless, because you are very forthright and open, other people will respect you. And as soon as you get over the more childish kinds of showing off, they will like you, too, because you are warm and emotionally demonstrative.

Sun in the Sixth House

You are somewhat shy, so it is difficult for you to be out in the open in the center of attention. You prefer to work quietly on the sidelines. But whatever you do, you want to do very well. You have high standards and want all your work to be as nearly perfect as possible. You enjoy learning how to use tools, and you may spend quite a bit of time learning techniques and making models or something similar. Along with crafts, however, you enjoy mastering and perfecting mental skills. And in this area also you will be extremely painstaking and careful.

You may find it hard to stand up to aggressive people. But unless you learn to do this, they may try to run your life, which you would not like at all. You need to be more self-confident and less self-critical. It isn't that you aren't as good as others; it is only that you have higher standards.

One of your great strengths, which will develop as you get older, is that you are able to put off fun and good times for the moment if you know that something is coming up later on that is worth waiting for. You are very concerned with long-range goals and more disciplined about staying with them than most people your age.

At times your health may be delicate. Therefore you should learn as much as possible about how to take good care of yourself through proper health and hygiene habits. With good care, your health can be as good as anyone else's.

Sun in the Seventh House

You are at your best with another person, either working or just having a good time. You are able to adjust your own needs to someone else's so that together you make a pair that works better than either of you would separately. By yourself you don't feel that you can do as much.

You are very social, and you have learned early in life to get along with others. For this reason, you are able to help others patch up an argument, because you see both sides of the controversy. Very likely, friends will come to you for advice on how to handle the problems they are having with other people. When you grow up, you may be very good at a profession that involves counseling and advice-giving.

Some people express another side of the seventh-house Sun. You may really feel like arguing and fighting with others, instead of trying to get along. You seem to feel that if you can't join them, you will fight them. This may be necessary at times, but don't make a habit of it, because everyone gets tired of fighting eventually.

You should learn to be more independent. With another person, you are capable of being the stronger partner, but your need to be with someone else may make it impossible for you to act alone when you have to. Also avoid making compromises that require you to give up something essential just to keep a friend. Sometimes you have to let the person go.

Sun in the Eighth House

A serious person, you know that you will have to go through many important changes as you grow. Your life is going to have many phases of development, each of which will be interesting in itself. And this is how you want it to happen, because part of you realizes that if you stand still, your life will be empty and dull. You are attracted to mysteries and to finding out about the deepest aspects of life. You will ask questions that are far more searching than those asked by others of your age. Sometimes your seriousness and intentness will disturb others, but they will get used to it and realize that you are a deeper person than most. You do everything thoroughly and as if it is very important to you. If a task doesn't seem important, you won't bother with it.

You will have to spend some time learning about possessions and money, because while you are young you may not be able to distinguish between what is yours and what belongs to others. You must learn to leave other people's possessions alone and keep to your own things. As an adult, however, you will probably make a career of handling other people's property or money; if you learned the lessons of your youth, you will be unusually responsible about handling possessions—yours as well as others'.

Sun in the Ninth House

You have a strong sense of curiosity, and you want all your questions answered as soon as possible. But you are also willing to work to get the answers, if you know they are forthcoming. You are interested in studies that reveal the most about the world around you on a broad scale, such as astronomy, world history, geography and even philosophy to some extent. When you are older, you may be interested in law.

Your restlessness is not limited to ideas, however. You are fascinated by anything concerning foreign and distant places; you want to travel to see the world. Unlike many people of your age, you are not bothered by homesickness when you are away.

More than most, you are tolerant of people's faults and willing to ignore the bad side, as long as there is sufficient good in someone. You do not like people who are too critical or who see only the bad side of things.

Fortunately for your future, you will learn early to plan ahead and prepare for tomorrow. You never put off doing something until the situation is too far gone to save. You act immediately or as soon as you can, even in planning for your future, which you will do earlier than most people.

Sun in the Tenth House

You are a person who wants to make great achievements in the world and to be in control of your own destiny. You find it difficult to follow someone else's orders unless you really respect that person. As you grow older, you should train for an occupation in which you can be your own boss or at least have quite a bit of independent authority. If you apply yourself to your work, you will accomplish a great deal.

However, while you are young, these traits will make it difficult for you to accept other people's authority. You are inclined to talk back to someone who tries to discipline you, because even now you believe you know better than most other people.

Your relationship with your father is very important, because he can teach you what the world is about. If your real father is not with you, another adult will be important in a fatherly way. You will be greatly influenced by his ways, although you will occasionally disagree with him and try to rebel. But the respect you have for each other is very important to you.

You want to know what the world is about, what is important in the public eye and what is generally considered significant. You are not particularly interested in the dreams and fantasies that fascinate other young people. You feel that if you are ever going to be known for your accomplishments, you must find out now what is important. Among people of your own age, you will try to be a leader, and your peers will look up to you.

Sun in the Eleventh House

You are very social and enjoy being with friends rather than by yourself. With others, you are accommodating. You try to find out and emphasize what you and someone else have in common, instead of getting caught up in differences. You are also at your best when working or playing with others, a team player who knows how to make the best possible contribution to the workings of the group. But this does not mean that you are a follower. You are quite capable of being a leader, because you understand what is best for all of you, not just yourself, and you are able to get others to work with you for group goals.

You are also an idealist with high hopes for your life. You are not willing to be satisfied with small achievements and accomplishments, yet you are not totally impractical, either. Your sense of reality is strong, and especially as you get older, you will understand the limits of what is possible.

Your most positive trait is your concern for those who are close to you, as well as for people in general. Your sense of justice is strong, and you want to make sure that everyone gets a fair shake. Generally unselfish, you are willing to work for causes that will help everyone, not just yourself.

Sun in the Twelfth House

A shy person, you prefer to stay in the background if possible; in fact, you like to hide. Because you don't like to be watched, you find it difficult to meet new people or to get up in front of a group. It's hard for you to be open and direct, even when you know there is nothing to be afraid of.

You have more compassion for others than most young people do. You love mysteries and secrets, imagination and fantasy. When you were younger you probably played with imaginary friends, but you know the difference between real life and fantasy.

You may have had an extremely painful experience when you were very young. If so, you may think it was a punishment for something that you did, and you may be afraid that it will happen again. Perhaps you wonder whether there is something wrong with you. In fact, whatever happened was an accident for which nobody is to blame. You are not a bad person, and there is no reason why it should happen again.

When you grow up, you will probably have an unusual understanding of the supernatural. You will always be a compassionate person. Getting up in front of an audience will probably never be easy, although you can learn to do it if you really want to. But you would rather be the one who works behind the scenes and really makes things happen. You'll take pride in true accomplishment rather than empty show.

Sun Conjunct Moon

You were born near the time of a new Moon, which means that your Sun and Moon are in the same sign, and that sign is especially important in your chart. Be sure to read those pages very carefully.

The new Moon is a time of new beginnings. You like to start projects, which may eventually become quite important, perhaps long after you have gone on to something else. You may even set events in motion without being aware that you are doing it. This is because the new Moon is a time of spontaneous action, without much self-awareness, and this is reflected in everything you do. You must learn to think of the consequences of your actions, to see how they fit into the larger scheme.

Also you should be more aware of the impression you make on others. You don't necessarily impress people badly, but you should know what effect you do have. Even though you seem to be unaware of what you are doing, you may be very effective. You often feel that you have a lot of energy inside that has to come out, and many times you will do something simply to release that energy.

As you get older, you will become more self-aware, but you will grow faster if you make an intentional effort to do so. Relationships are very important for your development, more because of what you will learn about yourself than because of what you will learn about others.

One great advantage of this aspect is that since the Sun and Moon are in the same sign, your feelings and emotions are not usually in conflict with your conscious personality. This enables you to act with singleminded purpose.

Sun Sextile Moon

You have an inner sense of peace and harmony, which usually is the result of a harmonious childhood. But even if your early home life has not been peaceful, you will come through the experience with a sense of balance. A sociable person, you enjoy meeting people and making friends, and when you are older you will have fairly easy relations with the opposite sex.

You are good at getting along with others, for you can see how your desires fit in with others' goals. When working with other people, you are able to make the necessary compromises. You feel that you are stronger as part of a group than by yourself.

In general your early life will prepare you for adulthood quite well. The habits that you acquire now will reinforce the goals you want to reach in life. You will not approach life with divided feelings. However, there is one possible problem. Since you are usually able to make situations work pretty well, it is somewhat difficult for you to change. You get comfortable with the situation as it is and will not change it unless it becomes totally intolerable, which is not likely to happen. Therefore there is some danger that you will settle for whatever way of life comes along rather than what is most suitable for you in the long run. This may not make you unhappy, but it can limit your choices in life unnecessarily. Keep this in mind and try to be more open to change and improvement.

Sun Square Moon

You probably feel as though your personality has two sides working at cross purposes, each with its own goals and ways to reach those goals. This aspect is often a sign of inner emotional conflict, which is not all bad, however. You have the capacity to challenge yourself from within, to question and examine yourself. Thus, as you go through life and meet various challenges, you will be used to the idea of making changes. In fact in a real sense you will never stand still, but must constantly evolve and grow. Although your early life may be rather emotionally stormy, you will probably come out ahead in the long run. There is one danger, however. Probably you will feel that there is some tension between your parents. They may or may not get along with each other, but you will see them as being quite different, and their influences will seem to pull you in two different directions. This is probably the source of your feeling that your personality has two different sides.

When you are older, it may be difficult to have easy relationships with the opposite sex, another reflection of your inner tensions. You attract persons of the opposite sex who symbolize the side of your personality that you are less aware of. As a result the people you attract may seem to not accept you as you are. The real problem is your lack of self-acceptance, however. And this is the lesson you will face throughout life—to accept yourself. The only thing wrong with you is that you think something is wrong.

Sun Trine Moon

Your inner emotional balance gives you fewer psychological problems at the outset than many other people have. You have the feeling that you can approach any difficulty in life with complete strength and unity of purpose. Once you have made up your mind on any issue, you go ahead without further question. Your childhood home prepared you well for what you have to do in life. Your habits and unconscious feelings will work for your intentions rather than against them. You have an easy approach to life, making it unnecessary to strain yourself in anything you do. In fact, you will probably find that if you leave matters alone, everything will work out for the best. You have an ability to flow with events without offering much resistance. You are willing to accept and enjoy the world as it is.

Whenever you have to deal with serious tensions in your life, you can devote all your energy to resolving them without having to worry about fighting battles with yourself.

As you get older, your relationships with the opposite sex should be quite good. Others will sense your emotional balance and be attracted to you.

Sun Inconjunct Moon

This aspect suggests that there is a subtle conflict going on inside you that may sometimes create emotional problems. The Sun signifies your conscious personality, the way in which you act and the kinds of activities that you like to get involved in. The Moon signifies the emotional and less conscious side of you. It indicates the habits that take over when you are not acting consciously and feelings that come up from deep inside you. The inconjunct aspect between the Sun and Moon means that the Sun part of your personality is quite different from the Moon part, and it may be hard for you to relate them to each other. It is as if you are divided in two, so that whenever you have to make an important decision, especially one that involves your feelings, the different sides of your personality want to go in opposite directions. You sometimes find it difficult to decide if you like something or if you want to take part in some activity.

But a much more difficult problem arises if you decide that one of these personalities is good and the other bad, so that you try to repress and hold down any behavior from the "bad" side. Unfortunately, that only makes it more difficult to handle that side, so that you have intense urges to do things that you think you should not do. You begin to act in ways that betray the image of yourself that you are trying to build up.

The only solution is to accept both sides of your personality, for they are both you, and it is important to express them both. It is only your attitude of rejection that makes one side good and the other side bad.

Sun Opposition Moon

You will learn to understand yourself through opposition to the world and other people, perhaps in good-natured competition with friends, perhaps through fighting. The form of your opposition is up to you. You are likely to ask friends what they think of you or of something you have done, because you want to get outside your own personal point of view and see what others see. This does not mean, however, that you are always willing to make your ideas agree with other people's. On the contrary, you usually fight for what you believe to be right. But you want to know what others feel, because it gives you a necessary perspective.

You want to know the objective truth about the world, the truth that exists independently of yourself. For this reason you will read mostly nonfiction, especially writings on scientific subjects, because these teach you about what is really "out there" in the world. At the same time you are not likely to give your own emotional reactions the attention they deserve; since they are personal, you feel they are less important. And you treat people's personal feelings this way too.

As you get older, you will respect people who make solid worldly achievements that have concrete, observable results, such as successful businessmen or builders, people who complete large-scale projects that everyone can point to.

Sun Conjunct Mercury

You have a good mind, and you enjoy talking with people. A good conversation means more to you than many other things, but you may have one problem. This aspect indicates that you like to take the active role in any discussion; that is, you are a better talker than a listener. Even when you make a real effort to listen, your mind tends to wander to another topic or to your next remark. To a certain extent you can't help this, but if you are conscious of it, you can prevent it from becoming a difficult problem. It may mean, however, that you can gain information more readily from reading than from listening to someone.

Your mind may or may not be fast, but it is working constantly. You have a great need to express your opinions, and you can't stand it when people don't take your ideas seriously. On the other hand, you probably take time to organize your ideas so that others will be forced to take you seriously, because what you say makes sense.

Sometimes this aspect means that you have a lot of ability to work with your hands. Certainly such activities as building things or working with gadgets are good for you as a way to release nervous energy that would otherwise build up. Without such an outlet you will probably develop nervous habits such as fingernail biting. You like to learn about new techniques in whatever you study. Anything new is somehow more interesting than what is old, and you particularly enjoy making innovations yourself.

Sun Conjunct Venus

This is a very favorable influence, which should be of great assistance throughout your life. You have the ability to make others like you. When you want, you can be very agreeable and charming and can even win enemies over to your side simply by being friendly. And this is not just appearance; you are truly a very affectionate person who enjoys giving and receiving love. However, unless you get proper reinforcement from your loved ones, you may not be especially demonstrative. You are sociable and like to be with friends.

You may have to work out one problem. It is almost too easy for you to find your way through life by being friendly and warm. You tend to compromise to keep the peace, even when there is a serious issue to be worked out. At times it is necessary to confront people directly and forcefully; otherwise people may not take you seriously, or they may try to walk all over you. This is about the only difficulty presented by this aspect.

You are fond of beautiful things and may have some ability in the arts. At the least you will appreciate the arts and will be able to make artistic judgments without relying on the opinions of others. In fact others may come to you for your opinions on questions of art and good taste.

You also enjoy good food and drink, which may be a problem unless you are careful not to overdo it.

Sun Conjunct Mars

You are very strong willed and rather aggressive. You may or may not try to start fights, but you will certainly never run away from one. This has both a good and a bad side. On one hand you are tougher than most and harder to defeat in any kind of contest. You are very competitive and do not give up easily. You enjoy pitting yourself against others in contests, both friendly and unfriendly. You do not give in easily, and you will live up to your standards at all times, regardless of obstacles. Once you have decided that you are right, you are not afraid to go it alone if necessary, and you will dig in your heels against pressure from others to change.

The bad side of this is obvious. Your reluctance to compromise may result from pigheadedness rather than from a sure sense of what and who you are. You may express your competitiveness by provoking fights where no real disagreement exists, and you may also attract others who want to fight even when you don't feel like it. But the greatest problem is that once you have committed yourself to something and made it part of yourself, you will not give up on it, no matter how wrong you are. It becomes too personal, and a defeat on some matter becomes a defeat of yourself as a person. You must learn to detach yourself somewhat from the things you believe in.

Physical activity, especially athletics, should provide a good outlet for your abundant physical energy. If you keep this energy bottled up, you will get angry very easily and provoke a violent showdown between yourself and others.

Sun Sextile Mars

You have a great deal of physical energy as well as a vigorous mind. Everything that you do, you do positively and assertively without any great effort. You are not especially conscious of being strong and assertive. It just comes out naturally.

You do not like to keep still or stay cooped up for any length of time, because you need to release energy continually. However, you are not terribly impatient, and you can control your energies as long as necessary. You have a strong sense of fairness and justice, and you will stand up for what you believe. If a friend is unjustly attacked, you will defend him. In a way, you regard your friends as being part of you, so that an attack on them is an attack on you, to which you react accordingly. For this reason you are a good team worker and player, although you can work by yourself if need be. You don't especially need others in order to be effective, but you can work in harmony with them. However, it isn't easy for you to adjust your goals to match other people's, so it would be better to seek out those who agree with you on important matters.

You have good health and need to be active. Try to engage in some physical activity as often as possible; otherwise you will begin to feel itchy and restless, as the energy within you tries to find release.

Sun Square Mars

There is an element of rash and impulsive aggression in your life, which can work out in either of two ways.

First of all, you may be very self-assertive with regard to others and even look for fights. Persons with this aspect are often too quick to see a challenge in a situation that is really quite innocent. You must learn to be slower on the draw and find out what others really intend before you act defensively. Also you will have to learn to control your aggressiveness. You do not always have to run the show or even participate in it. Learn to accept an equal role with others in some activities, for someone else may know better how to do that particular thing. The leader of a group should be the one who is best, not the one who is most aggressive.

Sometimes this aspect can be more subtle, however. You may not be aware of your own aggressiveness, but you may attract others who respond to it anyway. If you find that you are continually being attacked without warning or provocation, this may be your problem. You may provoke people without even knowing it. A very subtle tone of voice or a hint that you are unwilling to compromise may trigger off strong reactions in other people.

Another way that this aspect can emerge is that you may suddenly feel very angry at the slightest frustration, even though you had been feeling very peaceful. This aspect may be a sign of a quick temper that flares suddenly and without warning.

Sun Trine Mars

You are quite vigorous and self-assertive, with an abundance of physical energy, which you should express through physical activity. Otherwise you will feel cooped up and restless. You also have a strong need to be yourself and to do things in your own way. You will listen to someone else's advice and if it seems correct, you will follow it, but you make it clear that this is your own decision. Even while you are young you must be given as much responsibility as possible for your own life. It is essential that you develop a strong sense of who and what you are.

Athletic activities are good for you, because you enjoy competing with others. However some people with this aspect do not enjoy sports but like to compete in games of mental skill.

You can work very hard, if necessary, but you prefer to approach any activity like a game. Thus you are very good at what you like to do, but not so good at what you do not like. You need more self-discipline, because you can't do only what you enjoy.

In group activities, you are at your best either as a leader or working independently. You do not particularly want power over others, but you need to have power over yourself. You may act rashly at first and use responsibility unwisely, but you will quickly learn to handle it better. In general you admire strength, courage and self-confidence, and you will try to develop these qualities as you grow older.

Sun Inconjunct Mars

You have a rather strong will, which may be difficult to control. This is because your way of doing something tends to interfere with what you want to gain by doing it. Your actions in some situations may surprise people by contradicting what they have learned about you as a person. Inside of yourself, you may even begin to feel that you can't approve of the way you act, or you may feel that you can't deal comfortably with the results of your actions. In other words, you get yourself into real jams.

The only real cure for these problems is to think before you act. Most of them come about because you act impulsively and hastily or out of anger and frusttation. Such actions will usually work against you, not because those impulses are wrong, but because they don't work out as you expect. Your angry style is different from your usual style of acting, when you are more in control of yourself.

If you can learn to handle this problem, you can gain quite a bit of power over your life, because you are able to attack problems and situations in two rather different ways. When one approach cannot solve it, the other may be able to. Any connection between the Sun and Mars helps you stand up and assert yourself. You can fight successfully, but only if you learn to control your energies.

However, it is not good for you to hold your angry feelings in. When you feel angry or resentful, your feelings are quite strong, and if you hold them in, they can turn into sickness or infection. In some cases your feelings can become self-destructive and bring about an accident. If you can focus your anger, express it and let it go, you will never remain angry for very long.

Sun Opposition Mars

You will come to understand yourself best by pitting yourself against others. But the problem you have to face is how to do this. For example, you could simply be a fighter who stirs up trouble and discord wherever you go, someone who gets angry at the drop of a hat and is very touchy about getting your own way. In this case your life will turn into an endless struggle with those who oppose you, which would eventually be almost everyone, because they want to get their way too.

On the other hand, you could be simply a competitive person who enjoys a good contest with others through games or other competitions to see who is best at some activity. It isn't necessary to go into each contest as if it were for blood, but you can still play seriously. The main idea is to respect your opponent and play against him fairly. If you can expand the idea of playing competitive games, as in sports, to all activities in which you are being compared to someone else, you will do very well.

Probably you have plenty of courage and confidence in yourself. As long as you can keep from becoming rash and self-centered you will be all right. Others will admire your strength and determination, if not always your sense. Your basic task is to learn to channel this energy, not suppress it. You actually need contests with others to help you find yourself. If you suppress this need and hold the energy down, you will feel a sense of repressed rage that will spring out at the worst possible moments.

Sun Conjunct Jupiter

This is a very favorable influence, but you should know something about it to make the best of it in your life. Most people with this aspect have a very warm, outgoing and happy personality. You are likely to be generous and to enjoy doing things for people. In fact, the more you do, the better you feel about yourself. But you tend to have a very high opinion of yourself anyway, which can present problems, for you may become arrogant and conceited if you aren't careful. Probably you are a good person, but you do not have to prove it constantly to others. Your positive traits and abilities will come through by themselves.

Also be careful of a tendency to overdo everything, to be extravagant and careless. This results from an overconfident feeling that you will always have whatever you need and that you can do anything. Try to find out what you really are and what you aren't; in this way the favorable side of this aspect will come out strongly.

You also want to be concerned only with important matters, so you strive to learn as much about the world as possible. As you get older you may move about a lot so that you can experience as much of the world as possible. You don't like to be caught up in silly little problems. You are broad-minded and tolerant of unfamiliar or offbeat ways.

Basically you are optimistic, and by thinking positively you often cause matters to work out positively for yourself. Others may think that you are lucky, but there is much more to it than that. Your optimistic, positive attitude affects both you and those around you by making everyone more willing to make an extra effort.

Sun Sextile Jupiter

This is a very favorable influence, which should help you overcome many problems that may crop up in your life. You have the ability to act when the time is right. As you get older, this sense of timing will be very useful, for it can help you succeed in business. Almost everything you do and everyone around you will be affected by your ability to see life on a grand scale and to put it all into proper perspective. You know what is important and what is not.

The only problem with this aspect is that you may be inclined to take life too easily. At times success will seem to fall into your lap without any special effort, which may cause you to think that the world owes you a living. But you can't depend on the world to provide everything you need. If you take that attitude, you will find that you are unable to make your own way. However, the slightest effort on your part will bring rewards out of all proportion to the effort, so that you seem to be flowing along easily through life.

Usually people like you because you always try to be friendly and warm. You trust people and are quite open, but you hate to see someone taking advantage of others, for you have a strong sense of fairness and justice. You are quite idealistic and will work hard to bring your ideals into reality.

Sun Square Jupiter

This can be a very useful aspect if you learn to control its exuberance. Throughout your life the world will test you to see if you can overcome your tendency to overdo everything you get involved in. Learn to act more moderately and not take on more than you can handle. If you learn to understand your own limitations, you will discover that you have the ability to act at the right time. This is not because you are lucky, but because you know what you are doing and when to do it. An excellent sense of timing is one of the rewards of learning to live with reality. Even so, you enjoy taking a risk or making a definite move when more cautious people are standing still. If you know yourself well, you will be successful. If you do not, you will act before you should and go off half-cocked, under the foolish belief that nothing could go wrong.

Sometimes this aspect may make you overconfident in other ways, so that you pretend to be much more than you are and act arrogantly toward others. If you do this, others will dislike you and begin to work against you. Come down off your high horse and be a friend to those who want to slow you down. If you choose, you can be very friendly and charming and win people over with your honesty and generosity.

You like everything around you to be big and grand, which is fine if you know your limitations and what you can handle. If you do not, you will spend too much money and waste what you have. Avoid living more richly than you can afford.

Sun Trine Jupiter

This is one of the most favorable aspects in a natal chart for most people. It means you have a good disposition and a cheerful nature, and usually you have good relations with others. You are likely to have good luck and fortune as well, although by itself this is not a sign of wealth. However, your optimism can create wealth simply because you think and act positively. Usually someone with this aspect has no feeling of not having enough; even if you have only a little, that is all you want.

However, this is not a very dynamic aspect. If something goes wrong in your life, you may not take the necessary steps to make things right again. You may be tempted to sit back and hope that everything will work out all right by itself, since it always has in the past. This kind of passive attitude, the only real negative side of this aspect, may even result in laziness.

You want to be free to experience as much of life as possible. You have always been aware that there is a great deal to be seen and explored in this world, and you want to see as much of it as you can. In later life, you may travel quite a bit.

Others will like you and offer to help you when you need it. There may be an important person who will show you what direction to take in life. Take advantage of such people and learn what they have to teach, but do not depend on others to bail you out of every difficulty that you encounter, Eventually you will have to find your own way, and if you make an effort, you will probably do very well.

Sun Inconjunct Jupiter

This can be an extremely useful aspect, if you learn to have more self-control in what you do. Jupiter is always high-spirited, wanting to do and encounter everything and enjoy life thoroughly. Yet in some combinations, it means that you are unwilling to work for what you want. You may feel that you are such a fine person that you deserve to have everything done for you. Certainly you are worthwhile in your own way, but that doesn't give you a right to be taken care of without contributing your share. As with all Sun-Jupiter energies, if you learn to support others, to make them feel good and happy in your presence, you will get their support as well. Then there will always be someone to help you when you need it. But if you act arrogant toward others, they may not stay around to support you.

It is also important to discipline your habits and try not to do anything to excess, as you may tend to do. You may gain a great deal of weight, for example, or damage your health in other ways. Laziness and physical softness are very great dangers with this aspect. You may tend to be sloppy in the way you dress and take care of yourself.

Nevertheless, this aspect has possibilities for positive and helpful energy. You may be a very optimistic person who helps people in need at the critical moment. If so, others will help you when you need it. If you can control yourself and keep from going overboard, you will find that you can be quite lucky. But don't assume that luck will always carry you through. Work as hard as you can to get what you want and act fairly and honestly with others; then the luck will be there.

Sun Opposition Jupiter

This is usually quite a good aspect, but you will have to learn to be more restrained and cautious. You are likely to be rather careless and get involved in so many different activities that you cannot handle all of them at once. Also you may take foolish risks, because you feel that no matter what, you won't lose. Unfortunately, this is not true. If you are careful, however, you will do quite well.

In relationships you want to be totally free. You do not want others to fence you in at all. If someone tries to hold you back, you may run away or try to break free. Because of this, you may resent teachers, parents and other authority figures.

However, for the most part you like people and they like you, because you are cheerful and good natured. You have enormous energy, which must be expressed. You are often the ringleader of a group that plays jokes on others, although you aren't mean.

As you get older, the main danger is that you will have too high an opinion of yourself and think you can do anything. This can cause trouble with others, who won't appreciate your bragging or showing off. But if you can avoid this problem, you will continue to be well liked.

If you can learn to plan carefully and realistically without overextending yourself, you will do very well indeed. As long as you don't overdo, you can act very effectively with an excellent sense of timing.

Sun Conjunct Saturn

You are very serious and have difficulty playing the kinds of games that other young people like to play. You will always seem older than you are. Even while you are young, you want to do meaningful work that will continue to be important as you grow older. You want to be with adults as much as possible and learn their ways. You try to learn as much as you can from them.

However, you are likely to be very hard on yourself, either demanding too much of yourself or feeling that others demand too much. You aren't willing to simply enjoy being young. You may hold yourself in so much that it is hard to let go and have a good time. Or you may hold back because you feel that others will not let you be yourself.

As you get older, this can be a real problem. It may become more difficult to express your emotions to others, and you may begin to feel lonely and cut off from people. But this doesn't have to be. It is only that you are unwilling to express yourself, even to those who might really like you. This side of your personality will probably cause the most difficulty when you are a young adult. As you grow into middle age, you will begin to feel easier about yourself. Then your sense of discipline and your ability to work hard and long will stand you in good stead with others. Also you will be tougher than most people and able to withstand pressure and hard times when others give up. While you are young, however, you may not appreciate these traits.

Sun Sextile Saturn

You are quite reserved, and people may think you are shy because you do not like to make a display of yourself, preferring to observe others quietly. You may impress people as emotionally cool, but probably you feel much more than you show on the surface. You are patient and self-disciplined, and adults can depend on you to be reliable. You often appear older than you are, for you are quite serious and not given to childish behavior, like so many people your age.

You like to be either alone or with serious persons like yourself. You want to be involved in activities that seem important. In your work, you approach every task carefully and with forethought, not wanting to rush anything, for that might prevent you from doing a good job. In your surroundings, you dislike sloppiness and disorder.

Your only real problem is that you won't let yourself be young. There are things to be learned while you are young that you cannot learn by being a "little adult." Learn to let go a bit more; no one will disapprove, which is what you may fear. The inner voice that tells you to be prim and proper is your own and nobody else's.

Sun Square Saturn

This aspect can be difficult to deal with. You may feel that the world is always working against you, preventing you from doing what you would like to do. You have particular trouble with authority figures. For example, you may feel that your father and other adults are too strict with you or that you do not see enough of your father. At the same time you probably feel that the outer world is a cold, hard place in which there is no room for feelings such as yours. Some people in your life may be hard on you, but your real problem is that you are hard on yourself. You are too self-critical, too likely to judge your own performance harshly. Other people only reinforce your own negative feelings.

However, there is a very real positive side of this aspect. You have a strong sense of what should be done in any situation. If you can stop judging yourself and start looking at your life with more detachment, you will always be able to see what needs to be done and do it. You have a strong sense of discipline, and you consider reality very important. You have very high standards of achievement and perfection, which you want others to live up to as well as yourself. If you strive to achieve those standards without condemning yourself for not getting immediate results, you will be able to go far. Even if you never achieve your goal, you will have gone farther than most. Look at what you have accomplished rather than at what you haven't.

Sun Trine Saturn

A rather quiet person, you may act quite a bit older than you are. You are serious and very much concerned with doing what is right rather than doing just what you want to do. Adults will notice this and will give you more responsibility than most people your age have, which you will probably enjoy. You are patient and willing to work a long time to reach a goal. The promise of future reward is enough to keep you going.

In everything you do, your standards are very high, and you haven't much patience with people who do things the quick, sloppy way. You insist on a very strict code of behavior, both for yourself and for others.

You are likely to be quite tough physically, which you may not be aware of while you are young, but it will become apparent as you get older. Many people with this aspect have a small but wiry build, although other factors in your chart may signify otherwise. You are not likely to be the muscle-man type, but you are probably more physically resistant than most.

You like to learn, but only in a very structured setting, and you are interested only in practical and useful subjects. If you cannot see the usefulness of something, you are not likely to see much value in it. You will have to learn that knowledge that does not have any immediate use may be helpful later in unexpected situations. So don't let narrow ideas about usefulness keep you from studying abstract subjects.

Sun Inconjunct Saturn

You will have to learn the difference between having self-control and discipline, on the one hand, and totally denying yourself any self-expression, on the other. This aspect can mean that you feel extremely unworthy, which undermines your self-confidence and makes it hard to face obstacles in life with confidence and determination.

You may even feel that persons, forces or circumstances are conspiring to prevent you from doing what you want. You may be limited by fear or by the belief that you don't deserve to get what you want. With this aspect there is a danger that your frustrated energies will turn into physical ailments that further limit your freedom of action.

Sometimes you may be afraid to get the freedom to do what you want, for the rigid structure and rules that you are forced to live under seem to give you a feeling of security. At the same time, however, part of you does want to be free.

You will always require structure in your life, and you will always be happier with some kind of discipline. But you should also try out new kinds of experiences, do new and different things and expand the structure of your life. Instead of always staying home, go out and see new places, meet new people. This is the only way that you can learn to overcome your shyness and lack of confidence. And occasionally you must let yourself go and express your real wishes and desires, no matter how immature, wild or crazy they seem. You are still a young person, which is a fact that you and those around you must keep in mind. You can't be expected to grow up too quickly.

Sun Opposition Saturn

This aspect can have a very inhibiting effect, which you may spend a good deal of your life learning to handle properly. In a very real sense, you will never be young in this life. From the beginning, you will be more serious and more concerned with adult affairs than most young people. You will prefer to spend time with older people and to have them think well of you.

The problem is, however, that you are your harshest critic, often feeling that you have so little to offer that no one can love you. You feel that people will not accept you as you really are, that you have to earn their love. This isn't true, and your only real problem is thinking that it is. People who do like you will try to make you realize that fact, but it won't be easy. You take criticism far more seriously than praise, even though the praise may be just as deserved. It is very bad for you to be around persons who don't support you, because you will take it much harder than you should.

Your father will be very important to you, although you may feel that he is too distant. With this aspect your father may not live with you at all. In that case you will use others to find out how you are doing, and you will do this in such a way that people will be critical of you, thinking that that is what you want.

Although this aspect may be difficult while you are young, it is often found in the charts of people who accomplish a great deal.

Sun Conjunct Uranus

You are quite impulsive and like to do everything your own way, when and how you want. If you do not get your own way, you may feel quite frustrated and angry, although you are not likely to lose your temper. Instead you will be disruptive and rebellious in subtle ways. If someone tries to make you move in a certain direction, you will probably move in the opposite direction. You hate to be restricted in your movements or subjected to any kind of force. Your need for freedom is very strong, but unless you learn some self-discipline, you will never finish any project you start. You will do everything halfway. However, if you build your own system of discipline instead of trying to work with the discipline imposed by others, you will do quite well. You are not opposed to acting in an orderly manner, only to doing what someone else dictates.

You are quite innovative and creative and can see new ways of doing things before other people do. For this reason you may be attracted to scientific and technical studies. If someone points out a new approach, you are perfectly willing to accept it, as long as no one tries to force you into it. If you can control your tendency to act rashly and impulsively, you will be able to accomplish a great deal.

You may act as a goad to others, because you like to rile people up a bit and make them see the world differently. You are very annoyed by people who seem to be stuck in the mud, and you want to do something to change them. Just remember that they have the right to be left alone if they prefer.

Sun Sextile Uranus

You like ideas that are different and new; in fact, you are bored rather quickly by anything that is not interesting or exciting. Nevertheless, you are capable of persisting in a task until you finish it, but you probably won't get involved in the same kind of task again, unless you found it particularly interesting. In school you have a definite bent for technical subjects, such as math and science. You enjoy tinkering with machinery and want to know as much as possible about how every gadget works. Once you understand how it works, you try to make it work even better. This aspect usually confers some sort of inventive talent.

You have a quick mind in most subjects, but you should watch out for your tendency to jump to conclusions hastily. You may be more interested in coming up with a new procedure than in doing something the right way.

You have a strong sense of fairness and cannot bear to see anyone getting the short end of the stick. While you are young, you may not be able to do much about this, although you can fight to make sure that people your age are treated fairly. And as you get older, you can work with other people for large-scale social reform.

Sun Square Uranus

This aspect indicates that you are likely to behave rashly and impulsively. You are inclined to rebel against authority figures of any kind, and such persons may resent you. However, you don't intend to do harm, you just want to be allowed to do things your way. But you will often have to prove that your way is best. You can't expect that others will just let you be. You have to recognize that because of the way you act and project yourself, other people will think you are throwing out a challenge, even when you are not trying to. Don't be surprised when others try to prevent you from having your way, even when it is quite reasonable.

You probably enjoy consciously prodding others to get out of their rut and move in new directions. You might express this by playing practical jokes on people. If so, remember to be careful of their feelings, for you may not be as sensitive to being hurt as others are. If you aren't careful, you may be disliked with good reason.

One result of your impetuousness, which you should watch out for, may be a tendency to have accidents. This is most likely to happen when your energies are frustrated and you act suddenly and impulsively. If you are feeling nervous and jumpy for any reason, be very careful around machines or anything else that could cause an accident. Even if an accident doesn't occur, you may provoke an incident or sudden encounter with another that leads to an angry blow-up. Often you may not even understand how you contributed to this.

Sun Trine Uranus

You are fond of anything new and want to live just the way you want, with plenty of excitement and interest. You want your life to be filled with change. The idea of spending a lifetime in one place doing one thing is very unpleasant, and you will do everything you can to prevent it. As you get older, you will probably break away from your family and your past and move out in a totally new direction. You may remain on friendly terms with your family and birthplace, but you won't be tied down by them.

Also you won't be tied to the standards of behavior that have come down from the past. Even while quite young, you will work out your own code. You will always be tolerant of persons who are quite different from yourself; in fact, you may even be attracted to them because of that. You want to see as many aspects of life as possible.

You will enjoy new and stimulating kinds of recreation, such as hang-gliding, sky-diving or other wild pastimes, even if others consider them quite risky or terrifying. You enjoy the excitement, however, and are bored by the tamer games that most people play. Although by itself this aspect does not create much danger from accidents, you should be careful that your desire for excitement does not get you into truly dangerous situations.

Sun Inconjunct Uranus

There is a side of your personality that is very restless and impatient with rules, even when you know they are for your own good. You want very much to go your own way and do your own thing, even when you aren't entirely sure that it is the right direction for you. So you rebel in subtle ways by having sudden fits of obstinacy and moods of feeling very contrary, especially to your parents or other authority figures.

Sometimes the energy of this aspect comes out in other ways as well. At times sudden upsets may occur in your life that totally alter your plans, so that you have to change course entirely. When this happens, you must learn to yield to the pressure and flow with the change. It may be difficult for you to realize it, but such an upset occurs because you have blocked much-needed changes in your life, or they have been denied you. However upsetting these changes are at first, they will give you the freedom you need to grow as an individual. Unfortunately, if you always wait for changes to come in this manner, they are likely to be very startling and unsettling. If you learn to assert your individuality more directly, the changes will not seem so upsetting.

As with many other inconjuncts, astrologers have found that if you suppress your need and desire for freedom in your life, this energy may be expressed through illness or accident. While you are young, you may have accidents because you suddenly make unpredictable, rash movements. Later in life this aspect can signify cardiac problems, but only if you suppress your natural need for self-expression.

Sun Opposition Uranus

You have a strong need to do everything your own way, and the more that other people try to get you to do something their way, the more you resist. You are likely to be rather rebellious toward authority figures or anyone else who tries to restrict your freedom of movement.

The friends you choose are likely to be quite unusual, and if your parents or someone else tries to prevent you from seeing these people, you will be even more powerfully attracted to them. It is important that you decide on your own course of action, because then you are less likely to act rashly and foolishly. Pressure from others brings out the most negative aspects of your personality.

You really need excitement in your life, so eventually you will adopt a lifestyle that is different from normal, and that reflects what you are as a person. You will want to live at a very fast tempo, for you are easily bored when the pace gets too slow. Sometimes you play jokes on others and try to stir things up among the people you are with, just to make the situation interesting. But be careful of this, because you are denying others the freedom to go their own way, which you demand for yourself.

You may be fond of taking risks, but you must learn to estimate these risks carefully, or you could get into trouble because of accidents or disruptions that no one wants to put up with. If you are not careful, you may disrupt others so much that they no longer leave you alone and will try to restrain you.

Sun Conjunct Neptune

You are very sensitive and inclined to withdraw from fights with others. It is not that you are especially afraid, but that you are very bothered by turbulent and aggressive feelings. When you are around people who have negative feelings, you can feel them immediately, and they make you feel bad. But this trait can help you become a kind and compassionate person, because you so easily feel what others feel.

You like to pretend and create worlds in your mind in which you can do anything you want. But it is very important to learn the great difference between the world that you create in your mind and the one outside that you share with others. Many people with this aspect have a great deal of trouble recognizing reality for what it is. Don't lie when it is convenient to do so, because eventually you will become as confused as the people you lie to. If you train your creative mind properly, your fondness for fantasy can help you produce significant poetry, art or music. But without training you may simply be unable to deal with reality.

Be careful about the food you eat and the kinds of medicines you take. You may be more subject to allergies than others and sensitive to certain kinds of foods. When you are really ill, even a doctor may be unable to find out what is bothering you, so you should learn for yourself what is good for you and what is not.

Sun Sextile Neptune

You are likely to be very imaginative and to spend a great deal of time in your own fantasy world. This can be very useful, as long as you learn to recognize what is real and what is not. In almost any kind of creative activity—art, music or poetry—you can see and express ideas that others cannot visualize. Also you are very sensitive to others' feelings, and you understand aspects of people that even they cannot express.

But this sensitivity can be a problem at times. You may be easily hurt by people's remarks, even when no hurt is intended. You are quite thin-skinned, which may make it hard to assert yourself against people who are more aggressive and domineering. You may pretend to be patient and pleasant even when you are quite angry about a situation that you feel can't be changed. You must learn to be more forthright about your own feelings, for you have as much right as anyone to be yourself. If you are angry, come right out and show it and don't become the victim of another's energies.

You are also an idealist, who would very much like to see a more beautiful and perfect world. But this vision may lead you to ignore the positive and good features of the world as it is. Learn to see the beautiful side of reality, as well as the harsher facts. Do not abandon your ideas in a misguided effort to be practical, but don't let them poison your relationship to the real world either.

Sun Square Neptune

With this aspect you may have to face a number of problems. First, you may be subject to feelings of inferiority and self-doubt, even when they are not justified. You must learn that, in your own way, you are as good as anyone else. There is no need for you to be so shy and self-deprecating. Sometimes your fear of defeat and feelings of weakness may lead you to avoid a fight, even when the issue is important enough to fight for. Therefore you may lose battles unnecessarily, or you may resort to devious tactics, which will make others mistrust you. Occasionally someone with this aspect will develop habits of lying and deception.

You pick up impressions from other people very easily. Without even realizing it, you may perceive something about someone or receive a feeling or emotion without knowing where it has come from. Sometimes this can produce real confusion, making it difficult to figure out what you should do in a particular situation. Being indecisive is a problem that you must overcome. Don't worry so much about taking the wrong direction when you have to make a decision. Everyone makes errors, and you are no worse than anyone else, although you may think you are.

It is important to take good care of your health, because you are likely to be very sensitive to certain substances and subject to allergies and minor infections. Avoid drugs and all medications, unless absolutely necessary. Usually your health will not be a serious issue, but if you are not careful about it, your constitution may be weakened.

Sun Trine Neptune

You are quite creative, but you tend to withdraw into fantasies and daydreams, especially when you have a problem. You must learn to overcome this problem and face the truth before you can benefit from this aspect. There is nothing wrong with fantasies, but it can be very destructive to confuse fantasy and reality.

At your best you are very sensitive to other people's needs. You are able to put yourself into another's position and feel what he feels, which makes you reluctant to hurt anyone, since you are easily hurt yourself. Also you tend to identify with an underdog or anyone who is in trouble of some kind.

As you get older, your creative imagination can be very useful in the arts, music or poetry. You are able to see and feel aspects of life that others cannot, and even as a youth you will be more insightful than others. However, especially while you are young, you may have trouble understanding exactly what your insights mean. As with all Neptune-Sun aspects, you are very likely to be confused in situations that demand strong action. But as you get older this problem will clear up.

You are attracted to mystical, even supernatural ideas and dreamy, fantastic subjects. You feel a great need to see something in the world besides the material facts that are taught in school. And because you are unusually sensitive to anything mystical, you may very well find it. However, do not expect others to understand you in this regard, unless you develop the ability to communicate very clearly and effectively.

Sun Inconjunct Neptune

You are very sensitive to your environment and to the people around you. On one level of your being, you feel what is going on very acutely. Unfortunately your understanding often comes in terms that are very difficult to communicate to others, because their meaning is not clear in your own mind. Your greatest danger is in being exposed to negative people who are full of anger or depression or who act very harshly toward you and undermine your self-confidence. Your self-confidence has to be boosted at every conceivable opportunity, and it would be very destructive for you to be criticized sharply, unless the person has made it very clear that he or she loves you.

If you do develop a bad self-image because of such negative influences, you will assert yourself in unhealthy ways. Instead of standing up for your own rights, you will give in to another's will, but in such a way as to make that person feel guilty. Often you will refuse to tell someone what you really want, thereby allowing him or her to hurt you without meaning to. You may begin to see yourself as a helpless victim of circumstances.

On the other hand, you can develop into a compassionate and understanding person who instinctively knows what others need and how to serve them. True selfless service to others, giving of yourself voluntarily rather than because you feel there is no choice, will make you feel good, just as the negative behavior described above will make you and everyone else feel bad.

Sun Opposition Neptune

You must be more direct and forthright in your actions and not be afraid of losing whenever you are faced with a conflict. You will have to learn to handle conflict, because it is a normal part of life. You are a sensitive person who is easily hurt by what others say, and you may very well have to develop a thicker skin and discover that people's remarks cannot really hurt you.

But you are also an idealist who wants the world to be quite different, although you may delude yourself into thinking that it already is different. When dealing with others, you have to be especially careful that you are seeing them as they really are and not idealizing them. Learn to accept and appreciate people as they are, for they are all right as they are.

You tend to get discouraged too easily when circumstances turn against you. Because of this, you may avoid dealing with people directly, preferring to work behind the scenes where no one can see what you are doing. You may even become quite dishonest in your relations with others, not because you want to be a liar, but because you are afraid that you cannot win in a direct encounter.

Be careful of what you eat and drink, and limit your use of all drugs, even prescriptions, to those that are absolutely necessary. You are likely to suffer from allergies and adverse reactions to some drugs, and you may become dependent on others. Your body is as sensitive as your mind and should be treated with care.

Sun Conjunct Pluto

You are more likely to go to extremes than most people because you don't like to do anything halfway. You want every experience to be complete and intense. For this reason you are more serious than most persons of your age, so you get involved only in activities that seem important.

You are strong willed and like to get your own way, so you may find it difficult to make compromises with others in order to get along. But that is precisely what you must learn to do; otherwise you will be alone and cut off from people who won't want to associate with you. You have a strong desire to be a leader, which you can do quite well, as long as you keep other people's needs in mind along with your own. You are particularly good at leading others in carrying out an important task. You like to take on ambitious projects that test your abilities.

If someone keeps you from getting what you want, you don't respond right away. Instead, you carefully look for the best way to get around the obstacles and wait for the best time to act. This kind of planning gives people the impression that you are secretive, which may bother them. In fact you do enjoy being mysterious. You must learn to be a bit more open so that people will trust you. If you insist on being mysterious, people may imagine things about you that aren't true.

Sun Sextile Pluto

You are quite strong willed, perhaps stubborn, but you do not try to push anyone around. You simply demand to be allowed to do things your way. In a situation in which you must work hard and apply yourself, you are among the best, because you feel that anything you do should be done well.

You are likely to influence those around you, not because you try to, but simply because your personality has a drive that impresses others. For this reason it is very important to become aware of yourself and of your effect on others, so you will not be a negative influence on them.

You are very curious, wanting to know the answer to every question that occurs to you. To get the answers, you are willing to work and to study very hard, which can be useful in school if you are interested in your subjects. As you get older, this may lead to an interest in studying human nature through psychology, psychiatry or healing, or you might study a more occult subject, such as yoga.

You are psychologically rugged, a person who can withstand change without getting upset. As long as you have some basic security in the world, you will be able to hold your head high, even at times that are quite rough for the people around you.

Sun Square Pluto

You must learn to be very careful how you deal with others, especially people in positions of authority. You tend to get involved in personality conflicts in which you have to prove your strength or suffer defeat. These conflicts often arise without your understanding how they came about. Others often misunderstand your actions, which puts them on their guard. You know that you do not intend any harm, but others may not realize this. Another problem is that when you are angry, you are likely to be extremely angry, and you may seem rather violent. Even if you cool off quickly and never carry out any of your threats, you may scare others into protecting themselves.

As you get older, you will probably be quite ambitious, and you will work very hard to get ahead. Do not expect to have an easy time, however. Others will continually force you to prove that you are good at what you do. This opposition from others could make you so strong that you will triumph over it, or it could make you give up in defeat. If you can keep trying against all odds, you will probably achieve quite a bit in life. You should know that in spite of the obstacles you may encounter, if you try as hard as possible, the results will be worth it.

Sun Trine Pluto

You are the kind of person who affects the people around you even if you make no special effort to do so. You may not even be aware of it. But your influence is not likely to be disruptive, so you have little to worry about. But you should learn to be aware of the impression you make and take responsibility for being an influence on others.

You do not like to have everything around you completely settled. You enjoy making changes, for it helps you understand a situation better. And you have a great need to understand everything you do and to experience everything fully. You may be inclined to carry your activities to such extremes that other people get scared. But you do not scare easily, and you don't want to miss a thing.

Your life may go through quite a few changes, but this will not bother you, because you want to grow. You want to understand yourself as much as possible. You look into yourself quite a bit, and as you get older, you will have a better knowledge of yourself and your potentials than most people have. You will also come to know other people deep inside, which you can use to control them, if you choose. But you should be very careful how you do this. Unless you work for their good, people will fight you and your influence.

Sun Inconjunct Pluto

There will be many changes in your life, and you will be affected by deep psychological forces that may be difficult to understand at times, as well as confusing to the people around you. You approach people with great intensity, and your emotional involvements are seldom casual. Either you like people very much or you dislike them intensely. Possibly your attitudes on other matters will be extreme also. One of the most important lessons that you will have to learn is to be more moderate.

You have a very strong will and can be quite stubborn, even when you don't have any particular reason to be. It is as if you automatically resist any pressure to act in a particular way, even if you know it is good for you. This may arise from a fear of being controlled, helpless or manipulated by anyone else. As you get older, this fear may lead you to manipulate others so that they cannot manipulate you. It is very important to develop confidence in yourself, so that you will not behave this way very frequently. Your relationship with your father will be particularly important, for his actions and his opinions of you will strongly affect your sense of well-being.

You are very serious for your age, perhaps too much so, for taking everything very seriously can destroy much of the joy in life. Not all encounters are important and require you to put yourself on the line, although you may try to live that way.

Sun Opposition Pluto

Your strong will and stubbornness may get you into conflicts with others, because you are never willing to let anyone else have their way. You should admit to yourself that you enjoy a good battle, because it enables you to experience your own strength, assuming, of course, that you know you can win. The trouble is that even if you get tired of fighting, you cannot turn off the conflicts. You will have to learn to get along with others and save your energy for times when it is really important to get your way.

You will be strongly affected by the people whom you encounter. In order to see yourself clearly, you need others as a mirror. Sometimes you will learn through conflicts and sometimes through working with people, but the better you understand how others work, the better you will understand yourself. This means that unless you work especially hard to get along with people, your life will not develop as fast as it should.

You should work with others to bring about changes in your own life and in the lives of those around you. You are not the kind of person who can live with a set pattern for the rest of your life. Without change and growth, you will begin to feel so restless that you will tear things down just for the sake of change. You will break up old relationships and form new ones, pull up stakes in one place and go somewhere else. This need for change is part of what you are, and you should accept this.

Sun Conjunct Ascendant

You have a very strong personality, and when you enter a room, everyone knows it. As you get older, this will happen because of your impressive bearing, but while you are young it may just be that you are a show-off who has to be the center of attention. You want to be the leader of the group, the person whom all the activity revolves around. While you can be very charming and winning, your attitudes can make people very angry. Also you may have too good an opinion of yourself. You should concentrate on getting to know yourself and your limitations as accurately as possible. Then you can make the most effective use of your energy.

You may have difficulty getting along with authority figures, because even while you are young you want to be your own boss. You will handle this problem either by fighting the authorities or by allying yourself with them to gain authority.

Your best trait is your basic honesty; you respect real merit in others and are willing to develop it in yourself. Not satisfied just to impress people with empty show, you will want to have real significance in the world. You have integrity and will not treat others badly if they are reasonable.

Even if you are inclined to show off, people see that you are really good-hearted, and they will not usually dislike you. And your striving for genuine success will eventually win their respect as well.

Sun Sextile Ascendant

You are quite sociable and outgoing, fond of getting around and meeting people. You get along easily with others and can have satisfying friendships without giving up being yourself. You prefer to work or play with others rather than by yourself.

Your personality is strong, and others will appreciate your energy, for you enliven any activity that you are involved in. Yet you do not take over, you simply add your own energy to the energy of the group. You know what it means to share and exchange with others, not only your energy but also your ideas. You enjoy a good conversation, listening and then adding your own observations.

However, you are somewhat restless and don't like staying in one place for long. Even while you are quite young, you will enjoy traveling. You want to maintain an active tempo, so you are likely to get bored if events do not go quickly enough. And it is important that others not try to confine you. If you are allowed to get around on your own, you will develop adequate self-discipline without being unduly restricted.

Sun Square Ascendant

The problem you will have to resolve is that if you pursue what you want in life, you may not be able to get along with others. Others may seem to resist your every effort, so that to get ahead you have to cut yourself off from relationships. You may either withdraw into yourself or strive to have a significant career. Either way, you will have some difficulty relating your personal needs to those of others.

But this is only a test, through which you can learn to be yourself honestly with others. If you compromise yourself just to get along with people, you will only feel dissatisfied. And you won't gain the true respect of others, which will be very important if you hope to succeed at anything in life.

Even if you make a lot of mistakes early in life, as your life goes on you will develop a strong personality and learn to set your own goals. It will be more important to know who you are and what you can do than to have others know it. And by pursuing your own goals, you will win people's respect.

Sun Trine Ascendant

As you get older, you will develop considerable self-confidence and a need to live exactly as you want. You also have a strong desire to perform in front of others, perhaps just as a show-off or as an actor or performer in games or other situations that demonstrate your talents. You enjoy games and playing, but work is a different problem. You see little reason to do anything you don't enjoy. You will have to learn to do things that are distasteful at first. The positive side of this is that when you are older you will probably find an occupation that you enjoy because you are unwilling to make the usual kinds of compromises in choosing a career. Thus you have a good chance to be happy and successful in your work.

You have pride and a sense of your own worth, which will be seen and respected by others if you deal with them fairly, as you probably will. You are usually honest because you feel that the direct approach to people and situations is best. The only problem is that you may be rather blunt, not taking time to be diplomatic when you feel you have something important to say.

You like to learn about anything that increases your understanding of the world, but you are not very patient with detailed information that seems unimportant. You want to understand on a grand scale, but you may not be so clear about the details.

Sun Inconjunct Ascendant

Your relationships with other people can be very intense. While you are young, they may be quite difficult, because you feel that others will accept you only if you deny yourself in some way. Or you may constantly feel you should put off doing what you want in order to do what you have to do. Usually your ideas about what you have to do come from the people around you. Also, contacts with other people will frequently force you to make serious, major psychological changes. Difficulties in your relationships with friends and family are signs of profound internal changes.

You may find that no matter how hard you try to show others who you really are, they misunderstand you somehow. This is because the angular relationship between your rising sign and Sun sign indicates that your internal energies are quite different from the energies that you show to the world. You are not intentionally dishonest with the world, you simply present a confusing complex of energies. As you get older, you will learn more about your effect on people, which will enable you to put the two sides of your personality together so that they work smoothly. Be patient and do not hurry. Look at each relationship as an opportunity to learn more about yourself through your effects upon others. You will know you have learned this when you no longer attract people who are psychologically difficult to deal with.

Sun Opposition Ascendant

You have a great need to interact closely with other people. By yourself, you are not at your best. The question is, what kind of interaction will you have? You can work closely with others as partners, or you can work against them as opponents. And if you work against them as opponents, will it be a friendly competition, or will you fight them as if they were enemies? Many persons with this aspect like to pick fights and get into arguments, as if they can find themselves only through conflicts with others. This may be your choice, but it is a rather stormy way to live. You could choose to compete less fiercely and still learn to know yourself by what you can withstand in another.

It is more likely that you will prefer to work closely with another person in a partnership. Since you express yourself more clearly when you are with someone else, you are unusually sociable and enjoy being around other people. When you get older you will want to have close relationships with the opposite sex, and when one affair ends you will soon seek out another partner. When you are an adult, some kind of marriage partnership will be very important to you.

Sun Conjunct Midheaven

Even while you are young, personal success and achievement will be very important. You will want to shine among your friends and be someone whom they can look up to. You will measure your success in life not so much by your inner sense of values, but by the impact you make on other people. This aspect often means that you will be socially successful, but you must work for it; such success is not automatic.

You have a great need to be in control of your life. As you get older, you will try to work in a business in which you can be your own boss. You are very independent and do not like working under someone, which can create problems while you are young. Thinking that you know better than your elders, you may rebel against their power over you. If you establish a pattern of rebellion, personal success will be hard to come by. You need help from others to get anywhere. So you must avoid being arrogant, for that will alienate people.

However, if you are willing to learn from others while you are young and put all your energies into developing skills that will be useful later, you will probably achieve something important in your own terms. In that case you will know what you want to do and how to guide others. You can enable others to fulfill their destiny as you fulfill yours.

During childhood, the influence of your father or of a similar guide figure is especially important to you.

Sun Sextile Midheaven

Throughout your life you will probably have a clear idea of where you are headed and what your objectives are. And in finding your way, you will get help from authority figures, such as parents and teachers. You are able to avoid serious conflict with others as you pursue your life goals, because you are willing to make compromises and to work with others so that all of you can achieve your goals. Although you are interested in getting ahead in life, you are not so caught up in yourself that you cannot help others. If necessary, you will even make real sacrifices for someone whom you believe in. Also you are able to use other people's help in such a way that everyone benefits.

You are able to be independent and get along with others at the same time. Although you are not a follower, you don't need to dominate others either. Your objective is to make your life worthwhile, but you can feel successful without having great popular acclaim. You have your own standards and goals, and you have enough self-awareness to know when you are on the right track.

While you are young, you may not understand fully what you are doing with your life, but do not be impatient, for this understanding will come. You may have a number of different interests, but each of them will probably help you understand what you eventually should do.

Sun Square Midheaven

You have a great deal of self-assertive energy, and you will want to get ahead in life, to be well known and highly regarded by others. But in order to get where you want to go, you must learn to make some compromises. Your relationships may be difficult, especially early in life, because others may sense that you are interested only in yourself, which puts them off and keeps them from wanting to help you. Adults may resent your know-it-all attitude, for they feel you aren't old enough to know much of anything. While you are young you may have a lot of conflicts with authority figures, but eventually you will learn how important they can be to you.

Another possibility is that you will attract people who are very dominant, who will not let you do what you wish. A friend like that is more of a rival than a real friend. But you can gain something by testing yourself against such people. You can gain a greater understanding of your strengths and limitations, which will make you more effective. On the other hand, domineering people can be a real barrier to your getting ahead. In any case the main thing is to understand yourself and the kind of effect you have on other people. Then you will always know what you are doing and how you influence the course of events through your own energies.

Sometimes this aspect signifies conflicts with your father. However, even though you may resent him now, he is the most important person in your development.

Sun Trine Midheaven

This can be a strong indication of personal success. You have a strongly developed notion of who you are, and even while you are young you will want to be an achiever. You want a great deal out of life in terms of goals and material possessions, but you are willing to work for them. Although you are quite young, you see the necessity of putting off today's pleasure to reach tomorrow's goals. At the same time, you can get others to work with and for you, so that all of you can achieve your goals.

You are probably a very practical person. You may have very strong ideals, but you are not likely to be carried away by them, unless the planetary energies in your chart are very idealistic. Even then your ideals are likely to be about matters that affect everyone in the real world. You have a strong sense of your own values, and you will not get along well with people whose values are very different.

Authority figures, starting with your father, will be very important in your life. If your father is absent from the scene, your mother may play a fatherly role. The first people in your life who act as authorities will strongly influence your ideas of success and the kind of success you will pursue. Generally speaking, you should have a very good experience with these people, and they will give you a great deal of self-confidence so that you can stand up for yourself. Eventually you will be able to make independent decisions and govern your own life as well as the lives of others.

Sun Inconjunct Midheaven

While you are young, you will find it difficult to decide what to do with your life. The demands of the world may sometimes be hard to handle, because they don't seem to take advantage of your natural abilities and instincts. Also, much of your time will be taken up with learning routine skills that do not seem at first to have much connection with reality. But don't try to rush your life. Even if you can't see why you should learn a skill, try it out anyway. Later on, its purpose may become clear. Also you tend to rush through your tasks, because you are impatient to get to something else, but in that way you don't learn anything very thoroughly. Or you may try to live entirely for what you think is most pleasurable at the moment rather than for your long-range goals. Certainly you have a right to be young and happy, but don't overdo it; the lessons you do not learn well now will create problems when you try to pursue a future course of action.

This aspect can mean some tension with one of your parents, although it is not likely to be serious or destructive. In fact it may play a very positive role later on by forcing you to confront certain issues that you would otherwise have ignored. However, while you are young, you may resent this parent quite a bit. Do not take this too seriously, unless some other area of your chart indicates a more negative relationship.

Sun Opposition Midheaven

You are very concerned with your inner personal world and less influenced by others' ideals and expectations than most people. You are "inner directed" to an unusual extent, and you rate the importance of matters in your world according to very personal reactions. All of your life, you will be more subjective than most people.

You are not principally concerned with achieving anything that others would consider great or significant. For you, it is important to have your personal world—your home, parents and family—operating smoothly. You may always be attached to the place where you grew up, and even if you move away, you will have strong emotional and psychological ties to this place. As you grow up, the ideal home situation is one in which there is very little turmoil; you need a more secure and stable home life than most. Without it, your self-confidence and ability to be independent will be severely hampered. You might even become dependent on someone else for the rest of your life. However, if you are allowed to develop in a secure environment, you will become a very strong person upon whom others can always lean. Your success will come through self-understanding rather than through playing the games of the outside world. Self-esteem is more important to you than the esteem of others.

Chapter Six

Moon

The Moon in the Chart

The Moon signifies your basic emotional patterns, your habits, unconscious attitudes and feelings and whether or not you feel supported within the universe. The Moon also tells a great deal about your attitude toward your own past and the historical past. The placement of the Moon often describes your relationship with your mother.

The Moon sign, which is the most important sign after those of the Sun and the Ascendant, describes how you express your emotions and how well you deal with them. Some signs are easier for the Moon to be in than others, but none are truly bad. Like the other planets, the Moon has strong and weak points in any sign, and you should try to develop the strong points.

A real problem comes up if your Moon sign and Sun sign are very different. This creates a split between your conscious personality, as signified by the Sun, and your feelings and emotions, signified by the Moon. It is then difficult to feel completely at peace with yourself in anything you do. You feel that you want to do one thing, but you know that you must do something else.

If the Moon is well aspected, you express your emotions very easily. Even more important, you are sensitive to other people's needs and emotions, feeling that you belong with them and that they belong with you. A very badly aspected Moon may mean that you are lonely and have difficulty expressing your feelings toward others. Often this causes you to think that the past is holding you back and that basically the universe does not support you.

Moon in Aries

You are very high spirited and quite courageous, although other people may not realize this until they have made you angry. Even if you are ordinarily quite shy and retiring, when your feelings are aroused, you are a fighter for what you think is right for others as well as yourself. The force and energy you display may sometimes come as a surprise to people. You are quite independent, and you don't follow along with what others do unless you have concluded that they are right. And you do not care if anyone agrees with you.

However, there is another side to this. When your feelings are aroused, you are impulsive and careless. You may act before you think and regret it later when you have calmed down a bit. You may have quite a temper, and when you are provoked your anger takes over and makes you say things that you don't really mean. However, when you settle down, you forget your anger very quickly and don't hold a grudge. As you grow older, you must learn to be more in control of yourself. You may hurt the feelings of those who are very sensitive to the anger you display when aroused. Others may not understand that you aren't as angry as you seem and that your mood will pass quickly.

Moon in Taurus

You like warmth, comfort and the security of familiar surroundings. You like to be near a fire or in a favorite chair, and you enjoy good food. A very loving and affectionate person, you also need love and affection from the people around you. It is important for you to know that everything around you is going on as usual. You are not very fond of changes, especially in your own little world.

But you are very patient and do not get upset easily. When other people are angry and emotional, you can keep calm and make everything all right again. Even while you are young, others may come to you for help and advice because you are supportive.

Sometimes you find it hard to get going. You may be reluctant to leave a comfortable situation and go out to get some work done, or you may have trouble getting up in the morning. And when you do get going, you move a bit more slowly than most people, which may be rather annoying to others, but that is just your way.

Emotionally you are very stubborn. It is hard for you to change an attitude that is fixed in your mind, even when you have learned that it is not a correct attitude. You prefer familiar attitudes, just as you prefer familiar objects.

When you have money, you spend it very conservatively, except on things that you really like. You hold onto money, and you try to find ways of earning more, not because you are selfish, but because you like security.

Moon in Gemini

Your emotions change very rapidly, and you are quite restless. You get bored rather quickly, and your attention tends to wander if you have to keep it fixed on one object too long. But you are very curious and eager to try out every new experience. Instead of keeping your feelings a secret, you talk about them as if they were the most exciting thing in the world. In fact you may have to be careful not to talk too much about yourself, for others may not always want to hear it.

You enjoy traveling as a chance to have new experiences. And you feel the same way about new ideas, wanting to learn everything there is to learn, as long as you don't have to stay with any subject too long. But you will find out as you get older that some subjects require long hard work if you want to get anything worthwhile out of them. If you try to do too many things, you won't do any of them well.

One very good feature of this Moon position is that you will probably learn to let your intellect control your emotions. In situations where others act wildly and emotionally, you can keep your cool and see what is really happening. On such occasions, your judgment is better than other people's.

Moon in Cancer

Because Cancer is the sign most closely connected with the Moon, you can be very strong and secure emotionally.

Being close to your mother is especially important, and you need a lot of love and affection from her as well as from others in your family. When you're older, you'll be very good at giving the same kind of support to others and taking care of people in need. Even now you may do this with your friends or younger brothers and sisters. You probably like to play games in which you pretend to be the mother or father. Later on in life you may play the role of parent to many people.

Feelings are more important to you than logical thinking, which seems cold or boring. You get very attached to certain ideas, points of view and even objects, for reasons which others don't always understand. They don't realize that if the things you care about are not worth it, you will find out for yourself soon enough.

You are easily hurt by criticism, especially if you feel that someone is criticizing *you* rather than your actions. It's not that you are weak or fragile, but that you are unusually sensitive to other people's feelings. You often know how they feel before they say anything, and you care very much how they feel.

Moon in Leo

You consider yourself important and want to do things that will make other people proud of you. But most of all you must be proud of yourself, and you will avoid any situation that would make you look bad to yourself.

You like to be the center of attention and will often act in a way that attracts attention. In a group, you try to be the outstanding person one way or another. You take your feelings very seriously and are inclined to emphasize or exaggerate them when talking to others. You also may exaggerate other things, which you should be careful of, because the result may be that people will not take you seriously when you want them to.

Above all, you feel the need to be yourself, and you do not easily act as other people want you to. You can be quite stubborn, which is perfectly well and good, but others also have the right to be themselves, and you may not allow them to.

You are emotionally very warm, and if you like someone you let him or her know it. But you need love and affection too, and above all, reassurance. The better you feel about yourself, the less you feel the need to show off.

You are very fond of playing games, either athletics or indoor games. Often you prefer to play rather than work.

Moon in Virgo

You are a rather serious but usually cheerful person. When you realize that you have to do something, you are willing to go out and do it. You are happiest with tasks that engage both your mind and your hands. You like to make things, which you may become quite good at, because you are a careful worker and want to do the best possible job.

You are neat and like order around you at all times. If you are in a messy room, you want to rearrange and clean everything up immediately. It bothers you to have anything out of place. You are concerned with your health, and you follow the best health habits you know.

When you are with others, you keep to yourself, for you are somewhat shy. You may feel that people do not like you very much, or that others will always be more popular. That is not true, and the sooner you realize it, the better. Even though you may not want to be the center of attention, you should at least learn to recognize your own merits and not be so self-critical. Others are not necessarily better than you, they are only less critical of themselves.

You like to be useful and to help other people, because it makes you feel more worthwhile. But make sure that you really want to do those favors, because if you do them unwillingly, people won't get much out of them. Do what you want to do for people, not what you feel you must, except those things that you really *have* to do for others.

Moon in Libra

You like life to be beautiful and prefer not to think about things that aren't pleasant. You are affectionate, warm and friendly, but you may overlook other people's faults that you should keep in mind. Your strong need to be agreeable may cause you to give in when you shouldn't. You are a peace-loving person and do not like to start fights with others.

You very much like to be with a group of friends so that you can talk and be friendly with everyone. But it is harder to be part of a crowd because most of the people are strangers.

You enjoy a good time with music or dancing or just a good get-together. But when there is work to be done, you may find it difficult to get down to business. You may try to use sweet talk to get out of work or to get someone else to do it. In fact you will use such tricks to get out of many difficult or unpleasant situations. But people will like you anyway, not for the charm you use to get out of trouble, but for your real charms. Really you are a friendly and loving person, and you should try to develop that side of yourself.

Moon in Scorpio

You have very intense feelings, which can be a strong force in your life. But you may find it hard to understand your feelings, because they are so complicated and deep. You are either very angry or extremely sad or totally happy. You never feel lukewarm. And you want your whole life to be intense and very deep. Others may not be able to understand your moods, because you do not understand them yourself.

When a friend seems to be paying more attention to someone else, you may become jealous. If you don't get a great deal of reassurance from the people who are close to you, you will feel lonely and misunderstood. But remember that a friend can like someone else and also like you.

You are very fond of anything secret and mysterious, such as stories about the supernatural. And you like to learn about the secrets of the world around you, which makes you a good investigator of nature or of people. Your need to learn about yourself will help you understand others as well, and as you get older, you will know more about human nature than most people.

Try not to get so wrapped up in your emotions, however. It would be better not to take them so seriously.

Moon in Sagittarius

You are an idealist who wants the world to be grand and good and beautiful. You want people to be good and noble and are very disappointed when they are not. Unless you learn to take people as they come, you will always be disappointed.

You are so concerned with the important things in life that sometimes you forget about little matters that really have to be done. On the other hand, you may get interested in many far-reaching subjects as you try to learn more about the world. You are very curious and want to know the answer to every question. This same curiosity makes you want to travel and see foreign places that are very different from the world you live in now.

You are very independent and resent anyone who tries to keep you from doing what you want. Even if you really like someone, it's all right with you if that person likes others as well, and you want others to let you do the same.

You are optimistic and cheerful, and you can't stay sad for very long. Usually you feel good about life, and you try to make others around you feel that way also. People will like you for this.

As you get older, you may become more concerned with religion, and even while young, you may ask deep questions about God and other such matters. When you are an adult, you will be interested in any subject that teaches you more about the universe and your place in it.

Moon in Capricorn

You are serious and somewhat shy. Even while you are young, people will think you are older than you are, because you don't like to do the silly things that many other young people do. You like to achieve and get work done, because it makes you feel good to know that you have done something worthwhile.

However, you are somewhat uncomfortable with your feelings. They almost seem out of place inside you, a source of difficulty instead of pleasure. You don't show your loving feelings very readily, but you need love as much as anyone else. Your relationships with your parents are especially important, because you need parents whom you can look up to and model yourself after. If you can't look up to your parents, you will find another older person to play that role.

You are very practical and ambitious. When you are older, you will want to have an important position in the world, and you will work hard to get it. If you do not get a really good job or respected position, you will judge yourself rather harshly. This is one of the lessons you must learn, not to be so hard on yourself. You will get more done if you worry less.

When your emotional needs conflict with practical needs, you take care of the practical needs first. But remember that your needs for comfort, security and love are real needs, and you will not be really happy if you always deny them.

Moon in Aquarius

You value your freedom very highly and demand the right to do whatever you want at all times. When others try to force you to take a certain path, you can be extremely stubborn. You want to be free to try out any new idea or way of doing things that you come across. You are fond of experimenting with your life, but on your own terms.

You like to be with a group of people, especially your friends, because your own ways and desires have more meaning if you can share them with others. This doesn't mean that you are a follower but that you take the trouble to find people whom you fit in with. You can be quite an exciting person, and you enjoy being with other people who, like you, are ready to try anything.

You feel that you can control your own feelings, and you don't like to be around those who can't. Great displays of emotion bother you. You like to believe that you rely on your brain to solve problems rather than on moods, feelings and impulses. This does not mean that you suppress your feelings, however. Once you get to the point of feeling at ease with your emotions, you will reveal them quite spontaneously to others, and you may even get impatient with those who try to hide their feelings. However, other people's emotions are often much more powerful than your own. They find it that much harder to control their feelings and therefore are more reluctant to display them. You must learn to be tolerant of these and other emotional differences between yourself and other people.

Moon in Pisces

You are a very sensitive person with strong feelings. If someone makes a harsh remark, you take it very hard. In fact, one of your tasks in life will be to develop a thicker skin. Not everyone is so sensitive as you or so considerate of people's feelings. But your sensitivity is good in some ways because it makes you kinder and more considerate of others and less likely to hurt anyone. You like to take care of people and animals, especially if they are sick or hurt. But you should stay away from people who are always negative, because you pick up and react to their feelings very quickly.

You have a rich and lively imagination, which can make you very creative. But you may spend too much time in your own private fantasy world and avoid dealing with the important matters of the world around you. It is much easier for you to daydream than to face up to the real world.

As you get older, you may develop an interest in the occult and supernatural, not in the horrible aspects such as witches and vampires, but in subjects such as ESP and clairvoyance. You are very interested in the mysterious aspects of the world around you.

As you get older, you should learn how to stand up for yourself and resist people who are more aggressive. You are very likely to avoid conflicts, even when you should defend your own ideas. If you do not stand up for yourself, you may attract people who will exploit you and take advantage of you.

Moon in the First House

You get along well with others and are able to win people over to you. Even those who disagree with you have to admit that you are likable, which will always be a useful trait. As an adult you may be successful in public relations or sales. However, while you are young, this position of the Moon will be most useful if you are aware of some of its meanings.

First of all, you may be too emotional in your way of dealing with others, so that you see only your own point of view and not the other person's. Also you should be careful not to judge people just by your feelings unless they are backed up by real observation.

Another difficulty is that others may think you are very changeable and fickle. One day you seem to be one thing, and another day, something else. People may feel that they can't rely on you, unless you try to be more consistent.

You easily pick up impressions from other people and reflect their moods. In fact, sometimes you seem to be just a reflection of those around you, which is a sign that you have to put more effort into being your own person. But strangely enough, this is one reason for your popularity; you are so sensitive to people's feelings that you quickly convince everyone you meet that you are one of them, and people like that.

Moon in the Second House

You have a strong need for emotional security, which is reflected by your desire to own things. Possessions give you a sense of security. But you should be careful not to attach too much importance to what you own, because you may become selfish and possessive, especially if you feel insecure and afraid. You like to keep things a long time so that they become familiar and friendly, and for this reason you may be more attached to objects that are old.

Your feelings affect your possessions in other ways too. If you feel very positive and secure, you may be generous and giving, but when you feel rash and impulsive, you tend to waste money or whatever else you have. Because of this, before you buy anything, be very sure that you really want or need it. However, your interest in money and possessions can enable you to handle them wisely, if you control your impulses. But this can go either way, depending on other areas of your horoscope.

In relationships you form strong attachments to other people, which may make you feel possessive of them, especially if you are insecure about their feelings toward you. However, even if you are not sure how a friend feels about you, do not try to restrict that person or control what he or she does. That kind of attitude drives people away. But if you are willing to run the risk of losing your friends, you will actually find it easier to keep them.

Moon in the Third House

Your feelings influence your decisions so much that it may be impossible to be objective, unless you make a great effort to be. It is not a good idea to base your decisions purely on feelings and moods, because they change so rapidly. Yet you have a good understanding of what is right for you and what isn't, and as you grow up you will learn the difference between judging something on emotional whim and judging by real intuition.

On the other hand, you are good at talking about your feelings. If you feel unhappy about something, you can describe the problem well enough so that somebody can help. At least you can get it off your chest; you don't hide your innermost emotions.

Your habits have a very strong effect on how you think and act. If you answer someone without thinking about what you are saying, you tend to say things that don't fit the situation. Be careful of prejudices and beliefs that others have taught you.

You will have a strong emotional attachment to your brothers and sisters, if you have any. Even though you fight with them at times, you will learn that you need them very much, and you will miss them when they are not around.

Moon in the Fourth House

You are very attached to your home and family. To be at your best, you need to have a peaceful home life, for that means emotional security to you. When you feel strong and secure, you are very kind and sensitive to other people's feelings. You will work to cheer up a friend who feels discouraged, and even while young, you may act like a parent to someone who is younger or less mature. But if you feel depressed or insecure, you tend to withdraw into your own private world. Then you find it hard to give of yourself to others, because you are afraid of losing what you have.

Your mother is very important to you, and you need to be close to her. When you are not, you are lonely and depressed. You also feel the need to belong to a solid, close family.

You are interested in the past, and you may become an eager student of history, especially the history of your own family origins and background. You like to know that you come from a long line of people like yourself. Also the community in which you grow up will always be important to you; in fact you may live there all your life. Even if you leave, you will always have a strong feeling about it.

As you grow up, you will become interested in land and will probably want to own your own land, where you can make a home and perhaps have a garden or farm.

Moon in the Fifth House

You express yourself through your feelings, which are very strong and vigorous. You want others to know how you feel about everything, and you talk about your inner moods and thoughts quite openly. There is little secretiveness about you.

You really love good times, and for entertainment you enjoy plays, stories and television programs that appeal to your emotions. When you get involved in any kind of play or amusement, you give it everything you've got, or else you don't get involved at all. When you are older and are attracted to a person of the opposite sex, you will act the same way.

You don't make any pretense about your strong dislikes and likes. It is important to you to be honest about your emotions.

As you get older, you may find that you really like young children, and even while you are still quite young, you probably enjoy taking care of them.

Sometimes, in a mood of joyous high spirits, you may take risks that are really quite foolish. Be careful of this, because when it happens, your judgment isn't very good, and you may get into trouble. Also you may sometimes get carried away by your feelings, which can be difficult for others to handle.

Moon in the Sixth House

There is a strong connection between your moods and your physical health. If you feel unhappy or depressed for any length of time, you are likely to become sick as a result. That doesn't mean that your sickness is imaginary, but you don't take very good care of yourself when you are depressed, and that leaves you open to illness. Be particularly careful about catching colds, flu or sicknesses caused by an unhealthy diet or poor digestion.

It may be hard for you to work in a planned and disciplined way. If the work appeals to your imagination, you will work enthusiastically, but otherwise you may not be very thorough. But you enjoy work that keeps your own world neat and orderly, such as cleaning the house. To feel secure, you need to have your personal world in order.

Usually you prefer to work for others, because you would rather be directed by a stronger will. But in this regard you should try to be as self-sufficient as possible.

When you are an adult, you are likely to be interested in a career in some field involving home services or products, health care, food service or agriculture.

Moon in the Seventh House

You choose your closest personal friends by your emotional reaction to them. Unless people appeal strongly to your emotions and offer emotional support and security, you are not attracted to them. The people you do choose will be more than friends, they will be extremely close to you. When you get older, this house will indicate the kind of person you would like to marry or have as a partner. Even in a business, you will choose a partner who can give you emotional support and security.

You attract people whose emotions are strong and close to the surface, because you like to be aware of your friends. You may think that everyone around you is far more emotional than you are, but this is not true. The reason you attract such people is that they help you understand your own feelings. You need to see your emotions through other people.

As you get older, you will want someone to share your personal life, so it is likely that you will marry or form a close partnership early in your life. You need the security and emotional closeness of such a relationship.

Moon in the Eighth House

Your emotions are very powerful, and your moods go through regular cycles of change, so that you are always growing and evolving internally. Growth may sometimes be a difficult process for you, but you will emerge with a greater understanding of yourself and of human nature in general. You feel every emotion very intensely, and you can't understand how some people can be so lukewarm in their feelings. However, you are inclined to keep your feelings to yourself, even when you ought to discuss them with someone. It isn't good to bottle up your angry feelings.

Women will be very important in changing your life and you may "inherit" something from a woman—probably knowledge or experience rather than possessions or money.

You must learn to handle money and possessions carefully, because you will probably have to take care of other people's property. In handling money, you cannot afford to get carried away by your emotions. Try not to buy things on an impulse, for you may get stuck with something you don't really want or need.

You love anything mysterious, such as detective stories and crime novels, or possibly stories about the occult or supernatural. This is a reflection of your even greater love of secrets and hidden knowledge.

Moon in the Ninth House

You are always restless and looking for new experiences. Unless you are learning or doing something new, you tend to get bored quickly. Later in your life you may travel a lot just to experience as much of the world as possible. You would hate to be bogged down forever in one place, knowing only one point of view about the world.

However, your view of the world is colored strongly by your emotions, and your thinking may not be objective and clear. An idea that is presented logically will leave you cold unless it appeals to your emotions. For example, you have to get emotionally involved in what you read, so you prefer novels and poetry to nonfiction, unless the subject is heroic and stirring.

The Moon indicates that you really hold on to whatever you learn, so you must be very careful about what you do learn. It will be very hard for you to change the attitudes that you learn early in life, even if you want to. Think carefully about the attitudes that you have learned from your parents and family, for bad habits may persist without your knowing it. If you want to see the world, try not to be limited by the ideas you bring with you from earliest childhood.

Moon in the Tenth House

Your mother will have a great influence upon your life, shaping your basic attitudes and, even more important, your ideas of what values are significant and what is worth doing in life. Thus your mother will have a strong hand in your decision about a career. And if your mother is not with you, another person will take that role.

Your mother will also influence you to be very sensitive to your own and other people's feelings, and you may use this sensitivity in your career later in life. Because you understand how other people feel and how they react, you can be successful in any field involving public relations and sales, in fact, any career that puts you before the public. This position is very good for a career in politics, for example, because you can win people over and get them to agree with your ideas.

This position also means that you may be interested in farming, food services, shop-keeping or some other career that involves supplies and services for the home. You may travel quite a bit in your profession.

You should be careful of your tendency to reflect other people's feelings, because it keeps you from being yourself. If you want to be successful, you will have to find out who you really are, so you don't become what others think you are or want you to be.

Moon in the Eleventh House

You have a strong need for friends who support you in whatever you do and who make you feel better about yourself. You want to be able to trust your friends completely, which sometimes means that you prefer to choose your friends from the people whom you have known a long time and are used to. All your life you may make new friends among the people you know now.

Your moods will have a strong effect on the course of your friendships. Some days you'll really like someone, but on another day, you'll feel cool. But be careful not to act inconsistently toward your friends and make them feel confused about your feelings for them. Often this position of the Moon signifies that you prefer to have girls as friends.

The goals you set for your life will be enormously influenced by the attitudes you have learned while you are young. Be very careful not to get too set in your beliefs, because that could prevent you from taking advantage of opportunities when you are older. As you get older, you will have to make a special effort to adapt your beliefs and ideals to new experiences. Otherwise you will be an adult with the beliefs and ideals of a child.

Moon in the Twelfth House

You are rather unwilling to talk about your feelings with others, because you feel that they won't understand you or won't think well of you. Often you feel that no one should see the real you, but that is not true. You are perfectly all right inside, and your only real problem is that you don't realize it. You may think that your emotions keep you from being what you want to be, but again that is because you won't accept yourself as you really are.

You have a great need for emotional security, but you often feel you won't get it. You feel strongly that the people you depend on will let you down when you need them most, whether or not this is true. But even though it is difficult for you to trust people on an emotional level, you do like to help others. You may pretend that you are not really generous and helpful, but in fact you are. You are very sensitive and can put yourself in someone else's position quite easily, and when you know how someone feels, you are not willing to hurt them. You go out of your way to avoid unpleasant emotional scenes.

Often this position means that you like to fantasize and daydream. The world inside your head is very large and interesting, and you may prefer to spend all your time there instead of in the outside world where everyone else is.

Moon Conjunct Mercury

How well you think depends very much upon your feelings. If you are at all emotionally involved in a situation, as you often are, you can't think about it clearly. Subjects that require detached, objective thinking seem dead and lifeless, and you don't enjoy studying them. In school, you will be more attracted to subjects such as literature and art rather than science or math. When you get older, however, you might be quite attracted to psychology, because you are interested in ideas that you can apply to yourself and theories about how you operate inside. You probably think about your emotions and feelings a great deal, and you can describe what you feel to others quite easily. You are open about your feelings, for you see no reason to hide them.

This aspect means that your emotions and your rational thinking are unusually close, but you pay a price for this. As has been said, your thinking may be less clear, but also your emotions may lose some depth. You don't like people who are extremely emotional, especially if they make heavy emotional demands. You don't like to be possessed by anyone. You are emotionally restless and changeable, and anyone who tries to possess you through love or some other tie is a threat to your need for freedom. You don't want to commit yourself today, because you know you may feel quite different tomorrow.

Moon Sextile Mercury

This aspect means that your feelings and thinking are very nicely balanced. You are able to think clearly and logically about any matter, but you are always aware of how a situation will affect both yourself and other people emotionally. In anything you say, you take others' feelings into consideration.

You always know how you feel—not denying your feelings, but not being overcome by them. You can put your emotions in their proper place in your life and keep them there. This enables you to get along very well with others, because you are sensitive to what people need from each other. Also you work very well in a group because you sense what the group needs and can express it so that everyone understands. Later in life this will be very useful. You will be able to talk convincingly before a large group.

You like to be around people who are interesting and lively, and you want lots of mental stimulation from your friends. As you get older you may be friendly with younger people, because they make you feel fresh and young.

This aspect can mean that you have a talent for writing. You think so clearly about emotional matters that you are able to describe accurately what others can only feel. This helps people understand themselves better through you.

Moon Square Mercury

Your emotions and your thinking influence each other so strongly that it is difficult for you to separate them. In an argument with someone, you often make little sense, because you are arguing totally from feelings, not logic. Your thinking is mostly based on early childhood attitudes, so it is important to learn how to think in broad terms while you are still young. Any narrow ideas that you learn now will remain part of your thinking for the rest of your life, unless you make a tremendous effort to change later on. And then it will be very difficult.

In general your habits will take shape early in life and will have an unusually strong effect on you. So it is very important that you form good habits.

Because you are very subjective, you become too involved in your personal life. Little affairs and problems may get blown up out of all proportion to their real meaning. When you get upset, try to cool off and calm down before making any decisions. An impulsive decision made in anger will usually work against you. Try to move slowly and decide what to do only when you have thought about the problem and realized how important it really is. Also, if someone disagrees with you, do not take it too personally. People can have a different opinion without necessarily disliking you. You could lose many valuable friends if you keep on thinking that way.

Moon Trine Mercury

You are always trying to express your emotions and inner, personal feelings to others, because it is very important to you that people really understand you. Fortunately you are willing to work at showing them what you are like—you don't try to keep yourself a mystery. As a result you may develop some writing talent. You are also very sensitive to other people's feelings, and you can be a very receptive listener when friends come to you with problems. This also means that you are reluctant to hurt anyone, because you sense how that person would feel.

You consider your personal viewpoint very important, and you want to be taken seriously by adults and friends. As you get older you will become less sensitive about this, but now it is better for adults to reason with you than to ignore your opinions. You want to learn, and discussion is one way that you can. Also, because you can understand others so well, you will learn how to handle groups of people, and when you are older you should have the ability to speak before large groups. You sense the needs of a group and are willing to respond to them. This aspect would help in a political career, for example.

One of your strongest points is that along with understanding and handling your emotions very effectively, you are able to keep them from running your life. Your mind balances reason and feeling and prevents either one from controlling the other.

Moon Inconjunct Mercury

As you grow older, you will have to learn to make your feelings and your reason work together. The problem is not so much that they come into conflict with each other, but that your reason and feelings represent two very different sides of your personality. When you are calm and collected and able to reflect carefully, you make decisions in one way. But when you are emotionally involved in a situation, you are likely to make up your mind very differently, which could cause you to seem inconsistent to others and make it difficult for them to understand you.

For the same reasons, it may be hard for you to put your feelings into words, because your emotions are so different from your intellect. Of course, there is nothing really strange about your feelings, but that part of your mind is quite different from the reasoning part. In fact it would be very unfortunate if you decided to listen only to your reason, because your intuition and imagination, both of which are more related to the Moon, can be of great assistance to you. They can tell you much about the world that your reasoning mind cannot.

On the other hand, you shouldn't allow your feelings to overrun your reason. The best thing to do whenever there seems to be a conflict between these two areas is to not make a decision immediately. Reflect and wait for further information that might help you make up your mind. As you get older, this problem should lessen considerably, and you should be able to make decisions more and more rapidly.

Moon Opposition Mercury

You have some difficulty in getting your emotions and your mind to work together. You often feel that they are opposed, that what your reason says is right feels wrong emotionally and vice versa. The challenge is to reach some kind of balance between them. If either your mind or your emotions take control, the results will be disastrous. If you let your feelings guide you all the time, you will act without thinking carefully and without regard for the truth. You will be unable to see beyond your own point of view, which can lead to terrible mistakes. Also you will be isolated from friends who try to understand you.

But if you disregard your feelings and let your reason rule your life, you will feel more and more that nothing in your life has any meaning. The world will seem gray and colorless, as if it doesn't care whether or not you exist. Also the emotions you don't express may begin to work against you, causing strange moods and compulsive feelings. You may have sudden urges to do things that make no sense, or you may feel extremely nervous and irritable.

But it is possible to strike the proper balance and make your feelings work with your mind rather than against it. When you learn to do this, you will be able to get what you want out of life and still respect the truth and other people's needs.

Moon Conjunct Venus

You can be described as a "soft" person who enjoys comfort and pleasure, being with people and having a good time. But beyond this you also have a great capacity for affection. You like people, and you want them to like you. Basically you are even-tempered and kind and cannot bear seeing others suffer or feel pain. Also you can't stand very much pain yourself. You like taking care of other people or animals, and you may enjoy gardening and raising flowers, because you appreciate the earth and the good things that come from it.

Most people will like you, but probably you won't be very ambitious, unless that energy comes from another area of your chart. You are too fond of pleasure and ease to make a great effort if you can avoid it, and you may not enjoy work very much. You can't see why others work so hard when it seems as if they could relax, sit back and enjoy what they already have. To you, that is enough.

But you have your wants too; you like buying elegant and expensive things, beautiful clothes, especially, and you will even work to get them. Just be careful not to get too wrapped up in your own vanity, for in the long run that could make you a shallow person. However, that is not too great a danger with this position.

Your home is very important to you, and the chances are good that your childhood has been emotionally rich. Your mother will be especially important to you and has probably made you feel quite good about yourself, which will make it easier for you to love others.

Moon Sextile Venus

You prefer to be with your friends and loved ones as much as possible. A fun-loving person, you don't like being alone very much, and you feel that to really have a good time you need other people around you.

You are very sensitive to beauty and need to have beautiful things around you at all times. You dislike ugliness so much that you quickly become depressed if you have to live in an ugly or unpleasant place.

You aren't emotionally shy and don't mind having others see your private emotions. As a result, you come across to others as very soft, warm and affectionate. The people whom you like will never be in doubt about your feelings for them.

This aspect does not make you a very dynamic person; in fact, you may be inclined to laziness. You simply do not see the point of vigorous activity and hard work, since you already feel that you have what you need—ease, pleasant surroundings and good friends.

In dealing with others, you win them over with charm, so you have no need to use force. You can even charm people into doing things that they don't especially want to do. If you want something from your parents, you will wheedle and beg until they give in. In the long run, however, you will be better off if your parents take a firm stand on important matters, so that you develop some sense of discipline. Charm is very useful, but you shouldn't get in the habit of using it as a substitute for strong character.

Moon Square Venus

You need affection very much, and you will go out of your way to get it. You are so afraid of being disliked that you give in to others to avoid getting into a fight or making an enemy. By being very friendly and charming, you make others like you, but if you do this too much, you will not develop a very strong character. You tend to think that the more people like you, the better you are. On another level, this can lead you to become vain and overly concerned with your own looks and attractiveness. You may judge people and things by their appearance or style. You must learn that your merits and flaws exist independently of what others see in you. You are not the product of what other people see, but of your own inner energies.

On the other hand, part of you is really very loving, affectionate and kind. You can make the people around you feel very good. If you take the trouble to develop your inner character, people will like you for what you really are. And if you can stop depending on other people's approval, you will be able to relate to them freely and appreciate them for themselves.

You will also have to develop some self-discipline about giving in to all your desires for pleasure. You may overeat and gain weight easily, although some persons with this aspect quickly burn off energy and don't gain. But you could damage your health by drinking and eating for pleasure without considering good nutrition.

Moon Trine Venus

Your emotions are rich and beautiful, and you express them to others so that people like you for what you really are. Even when you act in ways that might anger others, they don't get angry, because they see that your intentions are good. You have an amazing ability to get along with people; you like them, and they like you.

If the people around you start fighting with each other, you try to make peace between them. You hate arguments, and you are a very fair person, so you can see where each one needs to change his or her thinking to get along with the other.

You like to be around beauty, and as you get older, you will have a great appreciation of art, literature and music. Even if you are not especially artistic, you will see and appreciate other people's talent. And you will always look for artistic and beautiful objects for your home.

The only serious flaw indicated by this aspect is that you may not be inclined to work or even play very hard. You prefer ease and comfort to strenuous activity. And you may tend to make peace between others or between yourself and others by backing down, even when you should not. Also you should avoid overeating, because this aspect can contribute to gaining weight.

However, with your ability to sincerely charm people and make them feel at ease simply by being yourself, you will always be surrounded by friends who really like you.

Moon Inconjunct Venus

You need to be loved, even more than most people, particularly by your mother or another woman who takes the place of your mother. This need for love will be the force behind many of your actions. If you don't find the love you are looking for, you will develop an insecure hunger for love from everyone you meet. However, you may express this in very strange ways, such as a desire for food, especially sweets, which unconsciously represent love to you.

There is also the danger that if you spend so much time and effort trying to get what you need, you will not be able to give love to others. Thus this aspect can mean that you indulge yourself and expect others to do everything for you. Of course, if people think that you are looking at things this way, they will not be inclined to help you. That will drive you to seek love even more and make the pattern even stronger.

On the other hand, if you are given all of the love you need while you are young, that is, if you are loved totally for yourself as you are, you will develop confidence in that love. Then you will be able to love others, and the more love you give to others, the more you will get in return. However, there is a catch. You cannot give love solely because you expect to get it back, for people sense this and are put off by it.

Moon Opposition Venus

You very much need affection from others, and you will go to great lengths to get it. You are a very warm and loving person, and you will be liked by many people. The problem here is that you may attach yourself to people who are not good for you in some way simply because they seem loving. You must learn to stand by yourself, not so much because you will have to later, but because you won't feel so dependent on others for your own sense of worth.

You don't like turbulent and heavy displays of emotion very much, preferring to keep your loving feelings light and happy. But it is possible that you may feel too possessive of those you love and won't allow them enough freedom. This could be the case if you are afraid of losing them or even if you are trying too hard to prevent them from being hurt in some way.

This aspect can also be a sign that your mother has been overly possessive at some point. Her intentions are good, but you need to break away from her a bit so that you can stand on your own as you get older. Being too dependent upon loved ones is the greatest danger of this aspect. If you can get past this problem, then your relationships with people should be very pleasant and good. People really like you, and you really like them, which will be clear to them.

Moon Conjunct Mars

You are likely to have quite a temper and fly off the handle easily. However, if you are allowed to express your anger completely, you get over it very soon. You can be very angry at one minute, but as soon as your mood has passed, you are quite calm. However, if you get into the habit of holding in your angry feelings, they can build up to quite a fierce level and even become destructive in your life later on. Suppressed anger can be the source of many nervous disorders and mental problems when you are an adult.

You are a fighter, and once you have made up your mind about something, you fight very hard to get your way. Others have to prove that they are stronger than you are, or you won't give in to them. At least you fight out in the open and reasonably fairly, so no one can complain that you are sneaky and underhanded.

The major problem to watch out for is that you may fight for ideas or causes that you haven't thought out at all carefully. You may react to threats that are more imagined than real if an innocent remark or action triggers off any angry reaction in your mind. You tend to get angry without really knowing why. When that happens, try to see if the reasons justify your anger. A tendency to get angry for no reason or to act without thinking is the greatest problem with this aspect.

Moon Sextile Mars

You are quite courageous and daring, and you will stand up for what you believe is right. Although you won't go out and pick a fight with someone, you won't run from a fight either. You have developed a strong understanding of your rights very early in life.

You like to be free to act on your own without waiting for others. But you also enjoy being the leader or setting the work pace for others, and the pace you set is likely to be quite fast. You have a great deal of energy—enough for several people—and you need to use it up. For the most part, this will attract other people to you.

When you do get angry or provoked, you react very emotionally. If someone says something unpleasant, you tend to take it very personally. However, this tendency is not so strong that you cannot control it. Usually it just has the positive effect of making other people unwilling to tease you.

It is important that the adults in your life give you some freedom to express your personality. It is unlikely that you could ever be made over into the quiet, well-behaved little person that adults seem to prefer. You have your own ways and your own style of acting. You may be a bit noisy and uncontrollable at times, but if you are allowed to express these energies, you will be able to handle them. But if you are held back, you will become extremely irritable and restless and much more difficult to live with in the long run.

Moon Square Mars

You may have quite a bit of trouble controlling your temper, for you usually react very emotionally to any kind of upset. Also, when you are angry, you act without thinking through what you are doing, which often makes matters worse. As you grow up, your greatest task will be learning to control your anger to the point where you can clearly see what is happening around you and can tell whether a threat or challenge is real or imagined. Unfortunately you are very sensitive to teasing remarks from others, and you may react with anger before you have a chance to find out whether the other person is only kidding.

If your family life is turbulent, it will make this problem worse. You need to be around reasonably tranquil people, so that your emotional storminess doesn't develop beyond control. Your relationship with your mother is especially important, because difficulties in that relationship could make it hard, as you get older, to deal with your anger or hostility toward others, especially women. However, at the same time you must be encouraged to vent your inner feelings of anger and resentment, but in a way that communicates your feelings to others without being destructive.

On the positive side, you are an excellent fighter for anything you believe in. Just be careful not to become inflexible about your beliefs, because being wrong is not the worst thing in the world. And when you are justly right, you will strive and fight for what you believe in, with more inner conviction as well as more convincingly to others.

If you can learn to think clearly without letting your feelings overwhelm you, the energies signified by this aspect should cease to be a problem.

Moon Trine Mars

You have a very great need to be yourself and to express your emotions exactly as you feel them without holding anything back. If you feel happy, you express it joyously to everyone, and if you feel sad or angry, you express that very clearly as well. You are honest about your feelings, and you don't keep people in the dark about your reactions to anything. Actually this honesty will make people respect you, because they know that in this way they can trust you.

You will also be known as someone who fights for the people and ideas you believe in. Whenever you believe in something or someone, you make it part of your inner self and defend it as you would defend yourself. And you certainly stand up for your own interests.

You are best off working alone at your own pace because you get impatient with the way others work. You are not particularly interested in being in charge of other people, but you have to be free to do what you want. You can be a good leader if you choose to be, and even when you aren't the leader you are usually the one who thinks up new things to do. You often feel that you could lead the group better.

You are attracted to people who are as strong willed as you are, but you must make sure that your will and your friend's are similar. Otherwise there will be considerable conflict between you.

Moon Inconjunct Mars

Until you learn to handle your feelings, you are likely to get angry easily, have temper tantrums and be touchy about what is yours and what is not. You may feel you have to defend yourself against imagined threats. The problem here is that you are likely to become too emotionally involved with ideas, opinions or even objects without knowing it until someone threatens them. Then you react as if you were being personally threatened or attacked. You have to realize that it is possible to change your opinions and attitudes without damaging your worth as a person.

Your relationship with your mother is especially important. If you and she don't get along in some important way, you will have similar problems with other women when you get older. If you are a girl, you may prefer the company of boys now and men later. If you are a boy, you may have serious problems getting along with women when you are older. In either case, you are likely to be very aggressive and unpleasant when you are emotionally upset.

However, if you have a good relationship with your mother, you will develop self-confidence and the ability to stand up for your rights against any obstacle. You will be courageous, and your strength will inspire others to follow where you lead. You will be independent and able to go your own way, even if others do not choose to follow. But this will happen only if you have healthy emotional experiences as a child.

Moon Opposition Mars

You are likely to be a very competitive person, who sees almost anything that someone else does as a challenge to either outdo that person or work against him or her. This can be a serious problem in your life unless you learn to control it. It is almost impossible for you to have a neutral, in-between relationship with anyone. You either work against the person you are with, or you cooperate perfectly. In most cases it is probably a good idea to work by yourself and avoid conflicts; however, you are best off with one of those few people whom you can have a perfect partnership with. For this to happen, the two of you must be very compatible, and you both must have enough work to keep you completely involved. It is when you are bored or have too little to do that you feel most argumentative.

You must learn to recognize what really matters most to you and what is relatively unimportant. If you do not see the difference, you will spend just as much energy fighting for unimportant causes as for the important ones. You tend to attach yourself to a number of issues and persons and then respond to every little challenge as if your life depended upon it. Part of you is terribly afraid to be wrong or to make a mistake, but remember that everyone makes mistakes sometimes.

If you can learn to control your aggressiveness, you will be a hard worker and a very energetic person who can accomplish a great deal. Just don't waste too much time in needless battles.

Moon Conjunct Jupiter

This aspect is very easy to live with. You are probably well liked, because your optimistic attitude warms people up. You can even make others feel good when they are depressed. And when you are depressed, you don't spread it around. Even in your worst mood you can look at the situation with humor and laugh at yourself, which eases your depression and makes the people around you feel good.

You are quite a generous person who likes to help others and protect those who need it. But you aren't overly possessive either. You won't take advantage of anyone who is in trouble. You are tolerant of the ways in which others are different from yourself, in fact, you are pleased to find them because they help you learn more about the world.

You are a fun-loving person who enjoys good times. And the only negative side of this aspect is that you probably prefer having fun to working, so it may be hard to settle down and do what has to be done. Or you may carry your good times so far that you get physically exhausted.

Your mother is very important to you, and your relationship with her is likely to be very good. She will have a strong influence on your attitudes and on your life as a whole.

Moon Sextile Jupiter

You are a very positive and cheerful person, and you make everyone around you feel better. Even when you get depressed, you don't stay that way for very long. Your ability to not take yourself or life too seriously helps you snap out of bad moods easily.

You are quite generous and willing to give of yourself to others. They in turn feel good about you and offer favors in return. People may think you are lucky, but it is not luck so much as good will and optimism that carries you through every problem.

Your mother and your home are very important to you, especially that part of your home that you feel belongs to you alone. When you are older, your past and the place you grew up in will always be an important source of strength to you. Yet you aren't overly cautious. Probably the happy experiences of your childhood will give you enough confidence and strength to go forth and try new things. You know you always have something to come back to, a solid center either within yourself or in the form of a good home and family that you can rely on forever.

Moon Square Jupiter

This is a very positive aspect, but it can have some drawbacks. You are a very positive and cheerful person who likes others and is generally well liked. Your high energy level makes people feel good in your presence and even cheers up those who are depressed. You feel good about yourself as well.

But you must learn to control yourself somewhat, for you tend to overdo whatever you get involved in, even to the point of physical exhaustion. This may affect your digestion, causing discomfort and irritation. Even when you are totally worn out by some activity, you may feel that you have to go on, so learn to relax.

Also you will have to learn to be less extravagant about spending money. You are likely to buy things on the spur of the moment, then not care about them very much afterward. You may have to control your eating and later your drinking habits, because this aspect indicates a tendency to gain weight.

You really enjoy good times, but again you must learn self-control. You can have too much, even of a good time, but you may not recognize that when you should.

In everything you do, you get involved totally or not at all. You see no reason to do anything halfway. But you are impulsive and change your mind easily, so after getting involved in a project, you often drop it before it is finished.

But you will get along easily with other people, for they will enjoy your energies even when they are somewhat out of control.

Moon Trine Jupiter

This is one of the most pleasant of all aspects. It indicates that you are an outgoing person with a great deal of self-confidence and emotional security. You aren't afraid of being yourself in any situation. Even people who don't approve of something you are doing will admire the spirit in which you do it. You should be popular and be able to make others feel good. One reason is that even when you feel sad, you have a way of laughing at your sadness, which makes you and others feel better very quickly.

This aspect means that you are usually generous and giving toward others. You want to take care of people and animals, helping those in trouble and protecting the weak. However, you do not like others to limit your freedom too much, which limits your desire to help.

Your mother or some other woman will probably help you a great deal while you are young. Because of this strong relationship, you will feel good about yourself without being arrogant or conceited.

As you get older, you will have great respect for honor and honesty, and you may develop a fairly strong interest in religion. Your faith will not be a limited, puritanical kind, but one based on kindness and the desire to help people grow and move forward in their lives.

Moon Inconjunct Jupiter

This aspect indicates that you have a positive, optimistic outlook on life, and you enjoy socializing with good friends. However, there are some dangers with this aspect. First, it can be a sign that you are self-indulgent and possibly even selfish, although this is not likely to happen if you have a good, strong relationship with your mother. You have a great need to be cared for and supported, to be accepted for what you are with no strings attached. If this need is fulfilled, the positive side of this aspect will flourish. But if your mother does not support your needs fully, you will feel insecure and will look elsewhere for support and fulfillment. In this case your concern will be totally for yourself with little thought for other people's needs.

This problem may show up in several different ways. For instance, you might simply have a desire to eat too much, as if food were love. Or you may always be wanting things that other people own. You might be afraid of the world and be reluctant to leave your comfortable and safe surroundings. Some people with this aspect stay tied too closely to their mother.

On the other hand, if you feel emotionally secure and accepted, then you will be able to give others the support that you would otherwise have been seeking for yourself. You will help others in their times of need, share what you have with those who have less, and find great satisfaction in taking care of people and animals.

Moon Opposition Jupiter

This is a positive aspect, but for best results you must learn to have some self-control, for you tend to go overboard in everything you do. You enjoy having strong emotions, but in relationships with other people you may find it difficult to control your feelings. However, this will not create serious problems, because you are such a cheerful person that others will like you even when they think that you have gone too far or done something to excess. When you act like that, you damage only yourself. You will have to curb your desire to do just what you want, because you might overeat and gain too much weight or have other problems because of overdoing it.

You have a kind of frantic nervous energy that never knows when to stop. When you get older, you will want to party all night and even through the next day. Very often you will stop only when you are totally worn out, which is all right while you are young, but later on it could cause illnesses, especially problems with digestion. And continual partying simply wastes a lot of energy that could be used for more important projects.

At the very least, you will cover a lot of ground in your life, not so much by being thorough, but by being fast. Others may find the tempo of your life much too fast and frantic, but it is the only way for you.

Oddly enough, this aspect makes some people lazy. This effect comes about if other areas in your chart indicate low energy level and self-indulgence. In that case, this aspect reinforces those tendencies.

Moon Conjunct Saturn

This is a very important aspect, and its effects depend heavily on how your parents feel about you. Unless you have a great deal of emotional support from your parents, especially your mother, you will grow up feeling unworthy, doubting your abilities and being unable to live easily with your emotions. Unfortunately, this aspect indicates that you are very sensitive to any coldness from your mother. If you do not have a close rapport with her, or if she is physically absent, as may be the case with this aspect, you should find another person who can take her place in your life.

You may have an unusual ability to control yourself very strictly, to sit on your feelings and make decisions according to reason alone. You can be very objective and see a situation as it really is, uncolored by emotion. Just be sure to take your feelings about matters seriously as well, because they are important.

With this aspect you tend to refuse emotional help from others. You may feel that your own inner feelings are not important because they belong only to you. Even while you are young, you have a very "old" idea of self-control and self-discipline. And when you don't live up to it, you feel guilty. You find it hard to accept the fact that you are not grown up, that your emotions are still those of a young person. You may also feel that the adults in your life are impatient with your being young, and that is why you try to hold back your feelings. But if you do this, you are mistreating yourself, and you will feel depressed, lonely and unhappy. You should control your feelings somewhat, but you should also express them.

Moon Sextile Saturn

You are rather reserved about showing your feelings, and you try to look serious and sober most of the time. You find it rather difficult to act young, because you already feel that you are much older. It may also be difficult to accept affection from other people, because it seems "mushy" or overly demonstrative. You prefer situations that don't involve feelings so much.

But this attitude has its strong points. In situations that would upset most young people, you can keep control of yourself and remain calm. You always see what should be done, and you accept responsibility for your actions more easily than most people of your age.

You like to keep busy and involved in some activity. A very practical person, you like to see concrete, visible results in everything you do. You can't see the point of studying ideas or techniques that aren't practical or useful to your own life. This may cause some difficulties in school when you have to study subjects that seem useless, but you are self-disciplined enough to work at something just because someone says you should.

In fact you are very concerned with what others think of you, and you will work hard to win their approval. Just don't carry this too far, because you have to fulfill your own inner needs and not live only for what others think is important. Eventually you will learn to do what is important for yourself and be less concerned with being "good."

Moon Square Saturn

This aspect can be quite difficult at times. You often feel that the people around you or even life itself prevents you from expressing your emotions. You may feel lonely and unsupported by your friends, brothers and sisters and even your parents. To overcome this feeling of aloneness, you must have a great deal of emotional support from your family and friends. Others have to keep assuring you that you really are one of the gang, that you belong. Even so, you often feel like an oddball whom no one understands.

Your mother, especially, must accept and support you, or else you are likely to become emotionally distant from her. This can have two very different effects. Either you will dislike your mother, or you will idealize her as some impossibly perfect person. In either case you won't understand your mother as she really is, unless you make a great effort to. Sometimes with this aspect, your mother may not live with you.

Also, if your mother does not give you emotional support, you are likely to blame yourself, feeling that you are unworthy of being loved. This will make it hard for you to love other people, which can be the cause of the loneliness described above. You probably try too hard to control your emotions so that others won't know how you feel, as if you were ashamed of your feelings. You shouldn't be ashamed of them. If you can learn to express this side of yourself, you will find that others will accept them.

Moon Trine Saturn

You may be shy about your feelings and reluctant to express them unless you trust the people you are with completely. Even more likely, you feel that it is not proper to show your feelings. In your mind is the ideal of being calm and cool at all times. As a result you will seem more serious and sober than most young people. In a way, you may never be young in the way you think, although of course you do not yet have the experience of the world that comes with adulthood.

People with any Moon-Saturn combination have a practical turn of mind. You are not interested in fantasies, dreams or abstract ideas that don't seem to have any use in your life. But once you understand the usefulness of a subject, you apply yourself to studying it until you master it completely. You prefer to be with other people who think the same way.

The only problem with this aspect is that you may be much too conservative. In other words, you may pass up an exciting experience or interesting field of study because you don't want to fool with daring or unusual ideas. You prefer to do things the same old safe way that has always worked for you. But thinking this way could limit you too much and cut out a part of life that might be very interesting.

Moon Inconjunct Saturn

This aspect usually means that your need for emotional security conflicts with your need to live with the world's demands. Each of us needs to be accepted and loved for what we are, in order to have enough self-confidence to deal with the world. But we also have to learn to live with our own life situations in order to survive. In other words, we have to realize that we can't have everything we want. With this aspect, these two needs are working against each other. Probably you will satisfy one of them at the expense of the other.

If the Moon, because of environmental conditions, becomes the stronger energy, you may be afraid that you will never get enough love or support from other people, especially your mother. Because of this fear you may become too dependent on your mother. It is important that she or someone else give you plenty of emotional support and at the same time encourage you to go out on your own.

If the Saturn energy becomes stronger, you may learn to distrust your emotions and become rather cold and unfeeling. You may also be suspicious of anyone who tries to touch you emotionally, especially your mother. But when you are emotionally upset, you may get out of control and act in ways that you usually would consider wrong. This problem would be at its worst when you are older. Later in life you might feel that you have no roots, that no one cares for you and that you don't belong anywhere. This is called alienation, and you are likely to feel that way if you do not learn to balance the needs of both planets.

If you are able to balance the two, this aspect can have a positive effect. You will be able to keep a lid on your feelings and control yourself in difficult situations, but at the same time feel and express your emotions when you should.

Moon Opposition Saturn

You are likely to feel very unloved and remote from other people unless your family and friends make a special effort to be very warm and caring. Even so, at a very early age you may decide that relationships with others are unrewarding. You may play down your feelings and concentrate on practical activities. But of course you need emotional support and care just as much as anyone else, although you are unwilling to admit it. You should make a special effort to get out of yourself and relate to others, for otherwise you will feel lonely and depressed much of the time. Don't be afraid that people will reject you; some of them may, but that happens to everyone.

Your mother is very important to you, and your relationship with her will have a great effect on your emotional development. If she isn't motherly enough, the problems described above will be even worse, and when you get older you will have trouble getting along with other women. Your mother might even be physically absent, but it is more likely that she is emotionally distant. You may idealize your mother too much.

You can be a very controlled and practical person. You may resist doing something just for fun when others would hate to pass up a chance for a good time. But this may be because you feel unworthy of having any pleasure. Of course, you aren't unworthy, and you can do something about your negative feelings if you try to.

Moon Conjunct Uranus

You are likely to be an emotionally impulsive person. Feelings sweep over you very quickly, and you may act in hasty, rash ways that you regret later. But you are a free spirit and cannot stand to be confined or restricted. You like life to be exciting, and you may be tempted to stir up action and even trouble if your life seems too dull. Other people may not love you for this, but you will attract those who like to be around an exciting personality who always does everything differently.

This aspect might have quite a different effect, however. Instead of knowing that you need excitement and going out to find it, you might attract people who are exciting but not very stable. Such people can hurt you because they are usually not very sensitive. When you are older, this can affect your relationships with the opposite sex.

Unfortunately this aspect can indicate emotional problems in your early home life. When you were very young, something may have happened that upset your life when it should have been perfectly peaceful. In this case, you may feel anxious and mentally restless much of the time. You may also feel that you can't depend on other people, so it would be a good idea to avoid situations in which you have to depend on others. It isn't that they are so unreliable, it is simply that you have a strong need to be on your own emotionally.

Moon Sextile Uranus

You have a great need to be free to express your feelings in your own way. You will show this very clearly by the kinds of friends you choose, for you insist on your right to choose them yourself. But your parents may find it difficult to accept some of the friends you pick. Nevertheless, if your parents try to stop you from seeing certain people, you will be drawn to them even more strongly.

You need to be emotionally independent as well, for you can't stand the feeling that you belong to someone, that someone has an emotional claim on you. If a friend demands that you do something because you are friends or starts using the relationship to control you, you quickly lose interest in that person.

But you don't believe that you alone need this kind of freedom; you feel that everyone should have it. Everyone should be free to be themselves without having to play stereo-typed roles. You like to play your own kinds of games, and you will change the rules and break away from the usual ways just to make it more interesting. You are attracted to anything new, anything that takes you away from the everyday world or brings excitement and interest into your life.

Your strong sense of fairness urges you to work for the benefit of all. As you get older you will work to change traditions and fight against customs that have outlived their usefulness. You do not believe that the past has any particular value simply because it is old. But remember, other people may not agree with that, and you must give them the same rights you demand for yourself.

Moon Square Uranus

You are a rather excitable person, always looking for ways to bring excitement and change into your life, although you may not be aware that you are doing this. Sometimes the excitement may come from other people who seem to disrupt your life. Often this aspect indicates that at some time when you were quite young, your home life was upset in a way that made you feel unable to depend on others for emotional support. So you have decided not to depend emotionally on anyone and to be free in as many other ways as possible. You don't want to be restricted, and you will rebel against anyone who tries to confine you.

You have a strong need to have experiences that are very unusual, so you are attracted to anything new and different. You will even do something just to shock the stuffy people around you. Or you may be fairly conventional yourself but attract friends who are offbeat.

You are not very comfortable with traditions, unless it is clear to you that they have some real use. Having to stay in a specific place annoys you, because you want to be free to move about as you want. When you are older, your relationships with the opposite sex will be much freer than usual, because you do not want to be emotionally tied to anyone more than you have to be.

When you are upset, you tend to act without thinking, so try not to do anything at all while you are in that mood. Wait until you cool off and can see the situation clearly.

Moon Trine Uranus

You need a great deal of freedom, and you insist on your right to do things in your own way. It is very important to you to be emotionally independent of others and to be free to form friendships or other relationships with anyone who appeals to you. Probably you will be attracted most strongly to people who are quite unusual. You are not actively rebellious yourself, and others may even think you are quite conventional, but inside you are very much an individual.

You will be attracted to anything that seems different or offers a chance for a new experience. But be careful not to get involved in a situation simply because it is different—it should be worthwhile as well.

Even though you may move often in your life, you will soon feel at home wherever you are. But no one place will seem more like "home" than any other. This is because you don't want to be tied down to anything.

This aspect gives you the ability to tolerate and respect offbeat people and unusual situations, even when you aren't personally attracted to them. You will work hard to achieve the sense that you are a unique person, so you are willing to respect other people's uniqueness. You are not likely to dislike someone because of what you hear about him or her; in fact, when you hear rumors about someone you tend to believe the opposite.

Moon Inconjunct Uranus

With this aspect you must learn to control sudden outbursts of emotion that occur at difficult times when you least expect it. Also your present home life may not be a stable situation in which you can grow up emotionally secure and confident. A particular incident when you were very young may have given you the feeling that you can't count on anything or anyone for support. Later in life, you may try very hard to get away from anything that reminds you of your earliest childhood, even if your childhood has not been difficult. You just feel that you have to get away and go somewhere else.

Your relationship with your mother may be rather unstable. She may be very involved in her own interests, which prevent her from being as close to you as she would be otherwise. She may be an unconventional person, a real free spirit. The problem is that your feelings about her are mixed, both loving and unloving. You may secretly resent her. Probably you don't feel that you can express this consciously, but it could come out when you are angry or upset. Certainly this will result in not wanting to form close relationships with other people, especially women. And the people you do choose as close friends are likely to be exciting and different from anyone you have known in the past. However, they may also be rather upsetting.

You should be encouraged to express your inner feelings and release the tensions that build up within you. In this way you will not be hurt by energies that you aren't aware of in yourself.

Moon Opposition Uranus

This aspect may mean that your emotions are very changeable. But it can also mean that you don't really trust the people you rely on for support and care. You may feel that your mother, for example, is emotionally distant, or that she is not there when you need her. Probably she is trying to pursue her own interests in life, which you can't quite accept, feeling perhaps that she does not love you enough. This is not usually the case, but it will affect the way you feel about other people whom you are very fond of. You often feel insecure with them, fearing that they will not be there for support when you need it.

You are most attracted to people who are very exciting and stimulating, who are following their own way of life completely. But you are reluctant to get involved with anyone who tries to limit your freedom or who makes too many demands. You don't want a friend to tell you that you should do certain things because of friendship. As soon as someone starts talking about what you should do for them, you want to get away. To avoid relationships that are too close and emotional, you may attract unstable and unreliable people.

If you feel hurt because someone doesn't want to be close to you all the time, ask yourself if that's what you really want. The chances are you do not. Instead, look for someone who can be free with you and with whom you can be free, without making demands on each other. Then both of you will be much happier.

Moon Conjunct Neptune

You are very sensitive to the emotions of the people you are with. You pick up their moods and make them your own, so it is very important to be with people who are good for you emotionally. If you spend much time with people who are thinking negatively, you will start feeling bad about yourself and find it difficult to do anything, without really knowing why.

You are a dreamer and not very practical, preferring to sit by yourself and play in your private fantasy world. Your vivid imagination makes these daydreams quite real to you. But you should be careful not to retreat into your little world every time you want to avoid the problems of the real world. Also there is the danger that you will confuse what is real with what you have only imagined. Unless you make an effort to separate reality and dreams, you may start telling lies without really meaning to, particularly if you are trying to avoid something unpleasant.

On the other hand, you can be very sensitive to other people's needs. You can put yourself into someone else's shoes and understand how that person feels, which makes you very reluctant to cause pain to anyone. You are especially attracted to people who are not very well thought of by others, particularly if you feel you can help them. You like to recognize and enjoy the hidden worth of such people. You also get real pleasure from caring for people and animals that need care.

Moon Sextile Neptune

Your rich and vivid imagination will serve you well if you manage to keep your imaginary world clearly separate from the world of your dreams. You can imagine yourself in situations that you have never been in and can feel what others feel. This is called empathy, and it is one of your strongest traits.

But your imagination also allows you to see and understand things that no one has ever seen. If you are at all artistic (which this aspect by itself does not indicate), you will have lots of creative ideas to work with. If you are an inventive person, you will be able to think up new worlds and even figure out how to create them. However, you may have one great problem in that you may not enjoy the mathematical and rigorously logical thinking that goes with studying science, which could limit your inventiveness considerably. This is part of a larger problem, namely, that your fantasies may seem much more interesting than anything you could invent with disciplined thinking. But you need discipline to make anything real, even the products of your imagination. Artists must be disciplined as well as inspired.

You enjoy taking care of persons and even animals that need help. It is easy for people to appeal to your sympathy. Later in life you may choose a career that involves taking care of people, such as nursing or medicine. However, in medicine you would want to be directly concerned with taking care of patients, rather than teaching or doing research.

Moon Square Neptune

You are very sensitive and emotional and your feelings are easily hurt by anyone who speaks harshly. But when someone does hurt you, you may rather enjoy thinking of yourself as a victim. Just make sure that you don't exaggerate how much you have really suffered. And when you are depressed, don't wallow in the feeling that you are downtrodden and no one understands you. That is merely a way of escaping the problem you should be trying to solve.

On the other hand, you have a real understanding of the meaning of suffering, even if you haven't suffered greatly yourself, because you can easily put yourself in someone else's place.

A dreamer, you may have trouble staying in touch with reality, especially when it is unpleasant. But remember that although fantasy may be pleasant, it is only fantasy. Some persons with this aspect withdraw into unreality whenever they cannot handle the real world. Don't get into this habit, because the more you try to escape reality, the harder it becomes to live with. Although you are likely to be reasonably honest, lying is more common with this aspect than with others. This is because telling "stories" is another way of escaping, but you are still responsible for what you say, even if you kid yourself that you didn't know you were lying.

Above all else, learn to be open with your feelings and try to share even your fantasies with others. That will help you keep the real world clear in your mind.

Moon Trine Neptune

You have a rich imagination, which you need to express in some way. Even if your artistic ability is not fully developed, you should take lessons in some art form or learn to write, so that you can release this creative drive. It doesn't matter whether or not your work is "good." It only matters that you express your imagination in some concrete form.

Your imagination is so strong it can't be repressed. One way that you express it is by creating your own private fantasy world. This may upset adults who believe that you are getting too involved in daydreams. However, you should express this aspect of your personality; otherwise you will escape more and more into your own private world when you do not want to cope with the real world. You should be encouraged to bring your fantasy world out into the open and, if possible, express it somehow in the real world.

You are very emotionally sensitive to other people's feelings, and unfortunately you make their feelings your own. So it is important for you to be with people who are thinking positive and healthy thoughts; being with negative people will weaken you emotionally. You also like to care for people who need help. When it comes to taking care of someone, you can be completely selfless. You get total satisfaction just from being of service.

Moon Inconjunct Neptune

This aspect indicates that you are very sensitive and that you pick up feelings from the people around you very easily. The danger is that many of these feelings will be difficult to cope with; they may make you afraid of the world and reluctant to go out into it, as you must do when you are older. As a result, you prefer to be alone with your thoughts and let your fancies wander wherever they want to go. When you are older, this may help you use your imagination very creatively, but it won't help you work out your everyday problems. You must learn to stand on your own and not depend upon others. You also have to learn that you are worth as much as anyone else, for you may tend to withdraw when someone acts aggressive. But the adults who help you learn these lessons must be gentle and understanding. Otherwise you will shrink back into yourself. Above all, you must not be made to feel incompetent or inadequate, or you will think of yourself as a loser all your life.

People with this aspect often hide their real feelings and make sacrifices for others that they do not really want to make. Then they resent the person who asked for the sacrifice. You must learn to tell people how you really feel; if you do not, you have only yourself to blame for what happens. You must learn to accept that you are responsible for your own life. Do not act as if you are the victim of strong forces that you can't control, because you can control them.

Moon Opposition Neptune

You are so sensitive and react so strongly to any upset that you find it difficult to keep truth and untruth sorted out. Most persons with this aspect do not mean to tell lies, but whenever they are upset they can't tell the difference between true and false. Throughout your life you will have to work on building up a clear sense of what is real and what is not. Then when you talk with someone, you both will know that you understand each other. Close relationships with others are likely to be a problem, because you often see in people only what you want to see, rather than seeing them clearly for what they are. This makes it easy to misunderstand them unless you make a special effort. Whenever you talk with someone, make sure they really understand what you are saying. If necessary, repeat what you think they have said and ask that they do the same so that you both are sure of your ground.

One problem to watch out for is that because of your confusion about what others are really thinking, you may often be disappointed or hurt. People may do things that make you feel rejected and misunderstood. Don't feel sorry for yourself or blame yourself when this happens, for that won't straighten out the situation. Thinking of yourself as a noble and neglected soul may make you feel better, but it will not help. The only way to clear it up is to stop sulking and find out why the problem has come up between you and the other person. You will discover that most of your defeats are the result of misunderstanding and were not intended to hurt you.

Moon Conjunct Pluto

You have very deep feelings, but sometimes it is difficult for you to talk about them with others. You feel they would misunderstand what you say and probably think badly of you. You may feel that there is a part of you that is so "bad" that you cannot trust anyone with it. This is not usually true, but you will think that it is. You probably have a strong emotional tie to your mother, and it is most important that you have a good relationship with her. If you and she can discuss your emotional problems openly, it will help you a lot, because you often feel guilty and bad about yourself and therefore quite miserable.

Your feelings are very important to you, and you are likely to react emotionally to every situation and person you meet. But when your emotions get in the way, it is difficult to see clearly what is happening. And your moods affect you so much that as they change, your personality changes accordingly. One day you are positive and cheerful, and another day, sad and gloomy. When you love someone, you love very deeply, and your close family and friends are very important to you. Once you have become attached to a person or even a place, it is difficult for you to break away.

As you get older, you will want to live very intensely. You will often look for a new experience just so you can feel the emotions that go with it. Feeling nothing seems worse than feeling a difficult emotion. This may make your life quite different from other people's, but it can be quite rewarding as long as you don't let your emotions run your life completely.

Moon Sextile Pluto

Your feelings are very strong, and you are quite sensitive to other people's feelings as well. You get quite involved in your emotions, playing out dramas in your head in which you are the villain, the hero or whatever role you prefer. You love mysteries and may spend hours reading stories of mystery or the supernatural. You even seek out mysteries in the real world, trying to find out what is going on behind the scenes in the lives of your friends and neighbors.

This curiosity may make you interested in studying the mysteries of the physical world. If you can get away from your emotions enough, you might be quite a good student in science. Later on, sciences such as psychology and medicine would probably interest you more than physics or chemistry.

As you get older you will understand human nature better than most people, and even while you are young, your understanding is quite remarkable. But be careful how you use your knowledge of people, because you may tend to get others to do what you want through what you know about them. You may do this very successfully for a while, but at some point people will discover what you are doing and resent you for it.

Moon Square Pluto

This aspect means that your emotions are often so intense that you seem to be at their mercy. Your feelings even affect your behavior, causing you to act without thinking. The habits you learn early in life will be difficult to break, so it is important to form good habits now. You will also get so attached to places and persons that it will not be easy to break away from them.

When you are with people you like a lot, you easily become jealous and you may try to control those you love for fear of losing them. Of course, that is the fastest way to lose them, so you should try to trust the people you love and let them be.

You also find it hard to trust others with your emotions, because you so often feel misunderstood. One reason for this is that little things you do seem to attract people who are very critical of you. However, this will improve as you get older.

As you grow, you will go through several critical times when you very much need understanding and support from your family and friends. Changes in your life always bring tremendously strong emotions that are difficult to control. These emotional crises may seem to pull you apart, but they are stages in your inner growth that will help you become better, wiser and more mature. Finally you will understand yourself well enough to deal with your feelings creatively.

Moon Trine Pluto

Your feelings are very deep and intense and are an important part of your personality. For this reason, anything concerning your own or other people's emotions is a very serious matter. You won't play games with anyone's feelings, which makes you more considerate of others than many young people.

Although you are completely serious about emotional matters, you like to express your own feelings quite dramatically. Because you want to make it clear to everyone how you feel about something, you may act out a very emotional role. However, in doing so you may make an unimportant situation seem important. Sometimes you act out the drama inside yourself to make an emotional situation more important to you. Be sure to think about the real meaning of such situations and don't blow them up too far.

You enjoy every new emotional experience and often get into strange situations just to feel something different from your everyday emotions. You are willing to run the risk of pain and hurt to learn about a new feeling. As an adult you will look for relationships with others that are very intense emotionally.

You love everything mysterious and unknown and want to learn about all the dark and hidden areas of your mind. Because of this curiosity, you are naturally interested in psychology and human nature.

Moon Inconjunct Pluto

This aspect means that your emotions are very intense and not always easy to deal with. Often your feelings make you want to do or say something without knowing why. Also you may have very intense moods in which you withdraw from those around you into a world of your own. This should not be a very serious problem unless you have been brought up to have all sorts of fears and worries. In that case your actions will be driven by your fears, and you may behave quite strangely. If you do not feel accepted and emotionally supported at home, you may constantly feel guilty for what you think you have done to others, or jealous that people aren't paying enough attention to you, or generally possessive of those around you.

You should talk about your feelings to someone you really trust, for otherwise the pressure of your emotions will build up too much. You must be made to realize that at some time everyone has those dark hidden thoughts that you think are so horrible. You are not alone, and you must learn not to blow these ideas up to be more important than they are.

You probably enjoy exploring the mysterious and probing hidden secrets. Even while you are young, you will understand human nature better than most people, but to use this ability positively, you must be reasonably calm about your feelings.

Moon Opposition Pluto

Your relationships with others will be intensely emotional and quite often difficult until you learn to see others and yourself as you really are, without so much emotion. You tend to see in other people your own fears and doubts. When your feelings are especially strong, you do not think at all clearly, and you may act totally from habit. All your emotions are very intense—when you are sad, you are very sad; when you are happy, you are full of joy. Others may not understand this part of you, but you needn't be ashamed of it. But learn to express your feelings openly instead of hiding them for fear of what others might think. The only people who would be good friends for you are those who can understand your feelings.

Try not to be so fearful, jealous and possessive with your friends and family. You must learn that everyone needs the same emotional freedom that you want for yourself. In fact while you are young, you may be forced to learn this lesson, because this aspect sometimes means that you live with someone who does not give you that freedom. This is likely to be your mother or another female relative. If you have this problem, you will feel guilty and unworthy. But you must learn to have enough self-confidence to challenge your family and assert yourself. You don't always have to agree with those you love.

Moon Conjunct Ascendant

You make an impression on others largely through your emotions. People always know how you feel about something, because you make no effort to hide it. Some may accuse you of wearing your heart on your sleeve, but most people will like you for it. You have the kind of honesty that others appreciate. This aspect means that you understand how people feel, and you can make them see your point of view. You sympathize with others, and in turn they are sympathetic to you. When you are older, you will be able to appeal to the feelings of the public at large, who will feel that you are one of them. Politicians, salespeople and others who appear before the public often have this aspect in their charts.

Regardless of your own sex, you will get along quite well with women, who may bring you great benefits at times. But you must learn to be responsible in the way you use this ability to attract women, or people will consider you false and deceitful.

Even while you are quite young, you enjoy taking care of others and doing favors for them. However, you may become quite emotionally demanding of the people you help, insisting on a great deal of attention in return. Try not to be jealously possessive of your friends.

Your childhood years will be important to you all your life, even more than for most people. It is important that you grow up in a peaceful and serene environment.

Moon Sextile Ascendant

You are very closely involved with your friends and with the people you meet every day. You have a great need to belong to a group and to have them understand you. On the negative side, this can make it difficult for you to go it alone. You can't always be part of a group, unless you give up all your own needs in favor of other people's. And you are not able to do this gracefully, because your own emotional needs are quite strong. On the positive side, you can relate to others, work with groups, and understand the needs of the people you are with. When you are an adult, this aspect may give you skill in public relations or selling. It may also favor political ability.

You like to be with people who have the same opinions as you have. But you should not let this go too far, because it can keep you from learning more about the world through people who are quite different from yourself. However, you can easily rise above this problem. This aspect often makes you want to travel, and you are sure to meet people who feel and think differently, which will help you grow.

Try not to let your feelings and habits of thought guide your relations with others too much. The way you have done things in the past may not be the best way for the future. Try to be as flexible as possible.

Moon Square Ascendant

Your feelings are quite changeable, and they influence how you feel about people. One day you really like someone, but on another day, you feel completely different. You may find it very difficult to treat others the same way all the time. You may also feel that people make demands on you that force you to hide your feelings. You believe that showing your feelings clearly to someone will hurt your relationship. This can make you feel very tense when you are with someone you like.

If your relationships with others do not go smoothly, you often withdraw into your own private world where you feel safe and secure, instead of fighting for your point of view. If you do this all the time, you won't have many friends, so make an effort to stand up for your rights and beliefs. At times, it will be necessary to go back into your own safe place, such as your room, or to your family for consolation. But don't do it every time your life is difficult.

Beliefs that you learned while you were very young may have too much influence on the way you act toward others. You will have to learn that every situation is different and should be handled differently. Even though two situations seem much the same, don't let the similarities overrule the differences in your mind. Treat each day as a new experience.

Moon Trine Ascendant

You relate to others according to your feelings, and you very much want people to understand you emotionally. Fortunately you are not afraid to show others how you feel, so if people decide they like you, you know they have seen the real you. Being very close to others is important to you, because you need friends whom you can talk to when you feel unhappy about something.

You are a very playful person. You enjoy good times and being with people who know how to have fun. You can also make your friends feel that you belong with them. And this is likely to be true of any group that you are with in your life. You have a real need to belong and to feel that others support and like you. Unlike some people who feel this way, however, you are able to be yourself when you are with others.

Your mother is extremely important in your life, and she will have more influence than anyone else on the way you act with others and how you form relationships. You must have her support and love, for without it, you will not be so able to make friends easily. Also when you are older, it will be more difficult to form relationships with the opposite sex. You show how you feel about your loved ones, and to do this well, you need to feel very secure about yourself.

Moon Inconjunct Ascendant

You tend to put your own emotional needs and wants second to whatever you feel has to be done. In other words, you are likely to be more disciplined emotionally than most people your age. But this is not good if you feel that your emotional needs are not important. Your needs must be fulfilled as much as anyone else's, particularly because your feelings are really very powerful within yourself.

This aspect also ties together in you a Moon sign and a rising sign that are very different. This indicates that the image you project to other people does not reveal very much about your real feelings. When you are upset, you surprise people by showing a totally different side of your personality. If you read the descriptions of your Ascendant sign and your Moon sign, you will see the difference between these two aspects of yourself.

It is very likely that while you are young you will attract people who are emotionally difficult to handle. This will continue until you learn to show your emotional side as well as the surface personality that you allow others to see. It is all right for people to see all the energies that make up your personality. Only by accepting yourself completely can you overcome this conflict.

Moon Opposition Ascendant

You are always looking for emotional support from someone else and, if you are really feeling depressed, protection from the difficulties of the world. You are not attracted to anyone who won't give you this support. For this reason also, you are attracted to people who are quite emotional and who show their feelings. You don't enjoy knowing someone only casually; you want to know everything about the people you are close to. You want them to become part of your personal world and to become part of theirs. This may cause some misunderstandings, because your friends may feel that you are interfering too much in their personal affairs, or vice versa. This may or may not be a serious problem for you; it is up to you to find out whether it is.

Your relationship with your mother will have a great deal to do with the kind of person you choose for a lover or marriage partner when you are older. If your relationship with her has been secure, close and warm, you will be supportive and protective toward the one you love, as if you were that person's mother in a way. In that case, your partner may be younger than you.

If your relationship with your mother is difficult, or if she seems distant or is simply not around when you need her, when you are older you will look for a partner who will be a "mother" to you. This can be a problem unless you find someone who is willing to be both partner and mother.

Moon Conjunct Midheaven

Your emotions are very powerful, and you are quite sensitive to the feelings of others as well. What happens while you are young will have a very strong effect on your future life, so that the attitudes and habits that you pick up now will be very hard to change as you get older. It is also likely that the career you choose will be greatly influenced by your present ideas now.

Your mother may have more to do with the career you choose than your father. If your relationship with your mother is not good, it could cause psychological problems throughout your life that would affect your work and your goals in life very badly. You need her emotional support very much.

Be careful not to believe passively that the world will surely take care of you. You probably will receive a great deal of help from others, especially women, but like anyone else, you will have to work to make the best of it. You should be very good at getting along with the public, because you can make people feel that you belong with them. You have genuine sympathy for people, especially those who remind you of people you knew when you were young.

This placement can indicate that in your career you will work with the public or large groups of people. Your profession might involve protecting and taking care of people, or you might be in advertising or public relations.

Moon Sextile Midheaven

You are very sensitive to other people's feelings as well as your own. Your moods and emotions are intense and have a strong influence on how you see yourself and the world. Probably you get along easily with others, because knowing your sensitivity, people trust you with their innermost feelings. Even while you are young, you won't hurt anyone, because you are so aware of how it feels to be hurt emotionally.

As you grow older you will learn a great deal about your psychological makeup, which will help you understand people in general. This will give you the ability to handle others very effectively, so that they help you while you are helping them. You are not likely to use other people selfishly, but you appreciate an honest exchange.

People may come into your life and help you without very much fanfare. Or they may offer help but prefer to give you what you need quietly, behind the scenes. You may keep your own feelings somewhat hidden, or at least not be particularly demonstrative. But others will know that you have strong feelings and will appreciate your quiet strength and sensitivity.

You can learn a lot through your emotions, for you understand by feeling rather than by thinking. It is important to learn to trust your feelings.

Moon Square Midheaven

Your emotions are quite strong and are very important to you, but you will have to resolve certain tensions.

First of all, your needs and feelings may often conflict with what other people seem to expect of you. Or you may feel like going one way even though you know it would be better to go the opposite way. The problem is, there is no one answer as to which way you should go each time. Your feelings are sometimes more correct than rational judgments, which may be based on ideas taught by others with no thought for your individuality. You have to live with others, but at the same time you have to be yourself.

If reason tells you to go one way and emotion says the opposite, think about your choices carefully. If the "reasonable" path helps others but offers you very little, then your emotions may be trying to tell you what your real needs are. On the other hand, your feelings may come from old outdated ideas and silly childish fears. You may be reluctant to face the world of growing up.

You will need the advice of a faithful friend, perhaps one of your parents, who can show you which choice is best for you without having a stake in the result. As you get older, you should be able to make these decisions more easily. Your emotions and ideas about your life should reinforce each other. Take your time growing up, however; you may take longer than others, because you have farther to go.

Moon Trine Midheaven

You become so attached emotionally to objects as well as people that you tend to think of them almost as part of yourself. This will make you a very caring and loving person in relationships, especially as you get older, but you may try to be overprotective and possessive also. Don't try to limit the freedom of those you love, because you could drive them away. While you are young, you probably enjoy taking care of pets and even wild animals that need help.

You like to be surrounded by familiar objects that remind you of the past, which is very important to you. Also you may enjoy owning old things, which could mean that later in life you will collect antiques. Certainly you would prefer a home that has some sense of the past, that seems tied to a tradition. Objects and buildings that are shiny and new do not attract you as much.

When you are older, owning and taking care of land may be very important, because it makes you feel that you have roots, which you need very much. You may be interested in gardening or farming.

This aspect could mean that you tend to collect objects simply for the sake of having things around you. This habit could clutter up your life in more ways than one. Taking care of a lot of extra things could control your life and limit your freedom of movement. It could also distract you from doing things that will help you grow. You need to learn as soon as possible that real security does not come from having material possessions.

Moon Inconjunct Midheaven

With this aspect you must learn to make your emotional needs and desires for pleasure fit in with your growth and development in the world. It is possible that these problems could make it difficult for you to choose a profession or a course that would give your life a sense of purpose. Or you may be unable to follow one path consistently. In other words, your emotional needs may be in conflict with your long-range goals. You may know what you have to do, but not feel much like doing it. Or your feelings may actually color your perception so much that you really do not see what has to be done. Try not to form bad habits, because they are especially likely to create difficulties of this sort.

You need to feel that your family, especially your parents, give you consistent and reliable emotional guidance and support. Without it, you may easily feel that you are being pulled in two directions, which can only result in going nowhere.

Work very hard to develop an objective awareness of what you are doing and where you are going. You will need this understanding to guide your emotions, which might otherwise lead you astray and make it difficult for you to focus on your goals. Even though you won't have to choose a career or a purpose in life for many years, you can learn now to have good perception, which will make it easier to choose later on. Learn to see others' points of view, even if you cannot accept them. Learn to make logical decisions, and do not let passing moods color your attitudes about yourself and your life too much.

Moon Opposition Midheaven

You are strongly attached to your home and your childhood. All your life, you will prefer familiar situations and objects and people you know well. You want to feel that you belong to a place and to someone, because belonging gives you a sense of security. While you are young, it is extremely important that you have a sense of inner strength and security.

If your life is confused and uncertain now, you will find it very difficult to overcome the effects of this problem when you are older. You would be very insecure and possessive of those you love. You would be jealous of anyone around you paying attention to someone else, fearing that they will stop paying attention to you. You would never feel "good" enough, and your inner self would always be in an uproar, with your emotions working against you. Most of all, it would be difficult to get ahead in life, because you would be constantly trying to resolve your childhood problems.

But if your home life is good and secure and your parents are caring and helpful, you will grow into a warm, loving and generous person. You will enjoy taking care of others and seeing that everyone's needs are met. You will be able to express your feelings more powerfully than most people can, and you will have an inner security that can be shared by others wherever you go. Your love of the old and traditional will always be strong, and you will very much want to have a family of your own.

Chapter Seven

Mercury

Mercury in the Chart

The planet Mercury means logic and reason, as well as communication and exchanging ideas with others. However, it does not have anything to do with communicating feelings and emotions, for that is a function of the Moon. The sign that Mercury is in tells how your mind works and how you communicate with others. The house that Mercury is in indicates what you think about most and talk to others about.

Mercury also rules your nervous system, and a badly aspected Mercury may mean nervousness and being unable to relax. Some people express this by talking all the time for no reason. Others are unable to concentrate or focus their attention. A badly aspected Mercury may make it hard to separate your ideas and your feelings, so that you always think very emotionally.

A well-aspected Mercury means you can think logically and express yourself clearly. While you are young, this ability may not be obvious, because even in the best circumstances, it develops with age. But you might show unusual ability in working with your hands while you are young. Mercury also means being fond of playing games, but be careful that your games do not become practical jokes that hurt people. Mercury does not make you very sensitive to people's feelings; that is a function of the Moon.

A strong Mercury can indicate restlessness and wanting to move around, because you are curious to see as much of the world as possible.

Mercury in Aries

You have a very quick mind and enjoy coming up with new ideas before anyone else. And your thinking is very independent. In fact you may even reject an idea simply because everyone else thinks that way. However, you shouldn't do this, because your own ideas are not the only good ones.

You like to argue and debate with people. When someone makes a flat statement, you challenge them to prove they are right. It isn't that you think they are wrong, but that you enjoy a battle of wits.

One danger is that you may leap to a conclusion too quickly, as if you want to be the first one to get there. And once you have made up your mind, you will defend your view against everyone, even when you are clearly wrong. Here again you enjoy the contest more than being right. But making rash and impulsive decisions can leave you with unpleasant results.

It is very important not to take your beliefs and opinions too seriously. Don't consider every question that is asked as a personal challenge. If you do so, it will interfere with really learning anything. On the other hand, you will always stand up for what you really believe. But be very careful that what you believe is right for you.

Mercury in Taurus

You think very slowly and carefully and arrive at conclusions only after much thought. People may think that you are not too bright, but that is not true. It is just that you want to take enough time to be sure that your thinking is solidly based. You like to have ideas presented concretely, with drawings or other visual aids if possible. It is easier for you to think about an idea if you can see it. Many people with Mercury in Taurus have trouble with math, because it is so abstract and hard to bring into your everyday world. You demand to know the practical use of every subject. You are less concerned with whether something is true than with how useful it is.

You think with your feelings a lot, and you will reject a logically correct statement if it doesn't fit in with your feelings. Common sense and experience are very important to you in making decisions. However, you hate to have someone try to talk you into something that you don't agree with. You are very stubborn and slow to change your thinking, but this prevents you from making rash decisions. You are likely to work well with your hands, because you take the trouble to do everything correctly.

Mercury in Gemini

Your mind is very active, restless and fond of change. You may get bored easily, unless something stimulating comes along. Your desire for constant activity may make you appear extremely nervous and unstable, but what is happening is that you mentally process the world around you faster than most people. This should make you a better than average student in school, as long as you receive intellectual stimulation from your parents. No one wants to learn unless encouraged early in life.

One problem stemming from your desire for new knowledge and experience is that you may never really finish anything. Try to be disciplined enough to stay with one train of thought long enough to learn something from it.

You are fond of communicating with others, and in fact, you may be more talkative than grown-ups want you to be. You should learn to speak only when you have something to say instead of chattering merely to keep the airwaves moving, as you often do. On the plus side, you should become a fairly articulate speaker and good at expressing your ideas clearly in writing as well. Again, this talent will develop only in a supportive home environment. You should read a lot while you are young, because your mind can absorb a great deal of information in this way.

You may also be fond of traveling, and certainly you do not like to be tied to one place for very long. Even if you don't travel very far from your immediate circle, you always want to move around, even if it's just getting out of your chair and pacing around.

Mercury in Cancer

You often let your emotions tell you how to think, and you find it difficult to look at things objectively. But your mind is retentive, so that once you have learned something, you aren't likely to forget it. In fact you prefer ideas that you have known and understood a long time because they have become familiar. Certainly you can learn new things, but it isn't easy if they seem threatening or challenging.

It may be hard to drop your bad habits of thinking. Often you aren't aware of how or why you think as you do. Many of your beliefs and opinions come from your family, who are very important to you. As you get older, you may have some difficulty changing any wrong ideas that you learn now, so be sure that the beliefs you adopt really work for you and are of practical use in coping with the world.

When you are emotionally upset, your whole view of the world changes. At such times, don't take your outlook too seriously, because it will change again when you calm down.

Because you are naturally cautious in your views, you are not likely to get carried away by some new enthusiasm that later proves to have no real value. You are bored by fads and much more concerned with proven ideas.

Mercury in Leo

You are very sure that your ideas are right, and you like to make others think the way you do. You can think about new ideas and make them part of your own thinking, as long as no one is pressuring you to do so. You are quite stubborn, and your pride is involved in everything you think or believe. If someone challenges your beliefs, you feel they are challenging you. But at the same time, your pride in your opinions makes you want to get at the truth. You aren't likely to believe something simply because it is pleasant or because everyone else agrees. You consider it very important to be right, which is fine, as long as you make sure that you are.

You like to organize and direct others. You put a lot of energy into planning, so your plans usually work out well. You like to have people come to you for advice, which you are happy to give. Be sure that they really want your opinion, however, and try not to get a reputation for being a "know-it-all," because then nobody will take your ideas seriously. Above all, when you are talking to someone, try not to act arrogant. If you do, the other person will resist your argument, even if you are right.

Whenever you have to solve a problem, you put a great deal of energy into it, and the more important the problem, the more energy you invest. However, you may ignore problems that don't seem important enough, when actually they are quite important.

Mercury in Virgo

You have a good, thorough mind, and you pay attention to details, so you can learn about subjects that require careful thinking and learning complicated techniques. The more intricate the techniques, the better you like them. Also you are likely to be good with your hands, because you work very carefully to reach a high standard of craftsmanship. If you cannot do something well, you are not likely to do it at all. Whatever you learn, you want to put to practical use, for you feel that everything you do should serve as a useful tool to get a job done.

You have a very critical view of the world, but you must be careful to criticize others and yourself in a helpful manner, not merely to tear them and yourself down. You will have to learn not to say anything at all at times.

You should be good at your studies, because you approach all of your work so carefully. The only possible problem is that if you don't see the usefulness of a subject that you are studying, you may not be interested in it. But stay with it anyway, because its use will become clear later in your life.

As you get older, you will become very skillful at working with ideas and information. This is a very useful ability in library work, scholarship or any field that requires organizing and classifying ideas and data. Even while you are young, you may be fond of collecting and classifying things, such as stamps, shells, coins or the like.

Mercury in Libra

You make up your mind very carefully, for you don't like to jump to conclusions. You prefer to spend as much time as possible looking at each choice and weighing every point of view. This can be very useful, but sometimes you take so long that other people get impatient. Every choice looks so good that you find it difficult to choose. Whenever two points of view conflict, you prefer to compromise and combine the two, rather than reject one of them. You are moderate in everything you do and won't ever go to extremes.

You like ideas and objects to be neat and elegant. You have good taste and a sense of balance. Often this position means that you are fond of music and art and perhaps talented in one of those areas. When you talk to people, you avoid harsh and ugly words, and you try to soothe over anyone's ruffled feelings with pleasing phrases. You are a born diplomat, but there are times when you should speak out clearly and forcefully. Then you must not hang back from using strong words just for fear of making someone angry. Sometimes in relationships with others you have to get down to unpleasant emotions. But on the positive side, you are very good at making compromises, either for yourself or for others.

Mercury in Scorpio

You like to get to the bottom of every problem and are fascinated by mysteries and unanswered questions. To you, searching for answers is almost more interesting than the answers themselves. A born investigator, you may be interested in solving crimes and detective work. Or you might want to study the secrets of nature through science. You are also interested in what goes on in people's minds. You like to find out about everyone's secrets, but you can keep a secret if you want to.

When you are emotionally upset, your thinking gets confused by your feelings, so try not to make decisions at those times. When you are angry, you can speak very forcefully, but if you are not careful, your words may hurt someone's feelings. At least you are forthright and say what you mean.

Your sense of humor is rather sharp. When you see someone pretending to be more than he or she is, you are likely to make sarcastic and biting remarks. You may say them quietly, but others will know what you mean.

You must learn to be more open with people. Something about you may make others uneasy, giving them a feeling that you have some deep dark secret, which makes them fearful. You enjoy giving this impression, but it does hurt your relations with others. To prevent this, you should try to build up a reputation for honesty with adults and friends.

Mercury in Sagittarius

Your mind is very curious and you want to know the answers to every question. To learn as much as you can, you ask questions of everyone who might have some new information. You are particularly interested in subjects that study the universe as a whole, such as science, or that cover a broad area of human activity, such as history or social science. You want to understand the patterns of the world around you. Your curiosity can help you greatly in school if you overcome one problem. You don't always think very carefully, and you tend to ignore details that seem too small to notice, although they may really be important. Also you often work too quickly and make mistakes as a result. You have to learn to work and think more patiently.

When you believe you are right, you speak very bluntly. You think it is dishonest to speak indirectly in the way that others consider polite. But you must be careful not to hurt people's feelings by your bluntness. Luckily it is clear to others that you don't mean to hurt them, that you are only trying to be honest, which they can understand. Truth is very important to you.

A particular strength of this position of Mercury is that you are able to handle new ideas and concepts that others find hard to accept. A strange or unfamiliar idea intrigues you rather than bothers you. You view every new idea as a chance to grow and expand your mind. Mercury in Sagittarius is often a sign of great curiosity.

Mercury in Capricorn

You like to think and plan very carefully, for you have a cautious mind, and you don't want to jump to conclusions. Your mind does not work very quickly, but your careful-ness makes up for that. You are good at organizing yourself and others, so you can direct activities if necessary. These talents may be useful in business when you grow up. You are a practical thinker, and you want to learn skills that will be useful in life.

You do not like to study abstract subjects for their own sake. You want to know about life as it really is, and unlike many people of your age, you don't spend time in dreams and fantasies. But be careful not to become too narrow. Many aspects of the world may not seem interesting to you at first, and your practical mind may reject them as unimportant. However, if you ignore these ideas, you may miss out on something.

Inwardly, you are a serious person, and your thoughts are serious. As a result, you may seem older than most people your age, because adults feel they can rely on you. However, even though you are basically serious, you can be quite funny. You take the world so seriously that you have to make jokes about the things that bother you, in order to deal with them. Mercury in this sign is often associated with comedians.

Mercury in Aquarius

You think the way you want, and it is very difficult for anyone to change your mind. Once an idea or opinion is fixed in your mind, you hold on to it stubbornly. However, you look at the world with few already set beliefs, so you can see aspects of it that others overlook. This makes your mind highly original. Also you are attracted to unusual, even fantastic, points of view about the world. You enjoy being unconventional and shocking people with your offbeat opinions. No ordinary standards of what is proper will prevent you from thinking a certan way. You demand lots of mental excitement, so old or traditional ideas are not interesting to you.

Many people with Mercury in Aquarius are very good at science and mathematics, because these subjects require thinking that is quick and original as well as accurate. Your mind is objective and clear, and you do not let your emotions influence you to do something that isn't logical. In fact, you may find it very unpleasant to be around people who get carried away by their feelings. But don't let yourself believe that you have all the correct opinions. You may cling stubbornly to your own viewpoints, but try to see the merit in other people's beliefs as well.

Mercury in Pisces

You have a very rich imagination, and you love to spend time daydreaming and making up fantasies. However, you may have to put more effort into thinking about the real world, because you can't live in dreams all the time. But you can put your imagination to good use in writing stories or poems, for you can see the world in ways that are hidden from many others. Your biggest task is to learn to communicate your ideas clearly to others. Sometimes you find it hard to speak or write clearly, for that requires you to present your ideas one at a time and in order. But your ideas don't come to you in an orderly way—you think with feelings and images.

Sometimes it is difficult for you to be objective, because your emotions influence your thinking so much. This means that making decisions is difficult, but it also means that you are unusually sensitive to other people's feelings. You are able to sense their moods and emotions even before they say anything.

You are not interested in subjects like science and math, and you may find them difficult because they seem cold and unfeeling. Their careful logic is colorless and boring to you.

Sometimes this position means that you are easily influenced by other people. Certainly you pick up their ideas very quickly, even without knowing it. As you get older you will have to be more aware of this tendency, because without knowing it you may be influenced by beliefs that you really do not agree with.

Mercury in the First House

You are very alert, lively and always curious. You want to be in the middle of fast-moving activities, for otherwise you are bored and restless. By nature you are not patient, but you will have to learn to be. People who work more slowly make you uneasy, and you want to push them to move faster.

You like to talk with people and find out how they think. You are always open to new ideas and willing to try anything once. You usually say whatever is on your mind, but try to make sure that others really want to hear about it. Don't be a chatterbox! You should enjoy reading, especially factual books about subjects like history and science.

You enjoy traveling or at least moving around as one way of settling your restlessness. When you are on the move, you feel alive. But you don't have to go far to be happy, as long as you aren't forced to sit still. While you are young, especially, you may enjoy playing jokes on people, as well as solving puzzles.

Your quick mind should be helpful in school if you can learn to discipline yourself and pay attention to your work long enough to learn it.

Mercury in the Second House

Whenever you have money, you plan what you are going to do with it very carefully. You handle money well and get the most out of whatever you have. With this position of Mercury, you may enjoy owning books or other possessions that make use of your mind. You like to learn because you value ideas highly, especially practical ideas.

Mercury in this house can tell how you will make your living when you are older. It could mean earning money through writing, radio or television work, teaching, traveling, or some other field of transportation or communication. It can also mean that you will make money through many different jobs without concentrating on any one career.

It is clear that you will have to go to college or get further training to make the most of any career that you take up. Mercury in the second house means you will make money by using your wits, which usually requires special knowledge or training. Experience on the job will be very important, too, since this placement indicates that you will learn to be clever in your work through personal experience.

Mercury in the Third House

You have a good mind and are eager to learn as much as possible, especially about your own little world, the world of your friends, neighbors and family. To learn more, you ask questions of everyone you meet. You are very fond of getting together with a friend to discuss all the subjects you are interested in. Your mind doesn't stick to any one matter but wanders far and wide over many topics. In fact, there is a danger that you will not concentrate enough on any topic, because your attention span may be rather short. In the long run, it would be better to learn more about fewer subjects.

You don't like to stay in one place for long, and that includes sitting in classrooms as well as staying in one part of the country. The more you can travel around, the better you like it. Even a short trip, such as going to school by bus, makes you feel happier about staying put for the rest of the day. On days when you cannot go out, you feel restless and confined. You want to be outdoors to see what is happening.

Aside from being too restless and impatient, you should be good at school, because you easily handle the ideas that are taught. Literature and writing may especially appeal to you, but you could be quite good at math and science.

Mercury in the Fourth House

This position of Mercury can have two different meanings. On one hand, you like to be surrounded by books, records and other tools to help develop your mind. You are especially interested in subjects such as history that teach you about the past, for you have a great desire to know about past events that have had an effect on your life. Even while you are young, you may be quite interested in your family's history. You may enjoy reliving some of those past events in your mind.

On the other hand, this position of Mercury directs your attention inside your own mind. You think about yourself a lot and try very hard to understand your feelings and emotions. You also like to discuss your feelings with other people, because you want them to understand you too. But be careful not to get too wrapped up in your own point of view. You should learn to get away from your own concerns and to see matters from another point of view. Otherwise you will not be able to understand others very well, and it is just as important to understand them as to understand yourself.

Parents always have an influence on the way their children think, but your parents will have an even stronger effect than most. What you learn when you are young will stay with you forever. Your parents should be very careful about what they teach you, for if it is wrong, you will have a great deal of trouble unlearning it when you are older.

Mercury in the Fifth House

You like to play games that involve your mind, such as puzzles, riddles, and especially as you get older, chess or bridge. And you like to read or study for amusement. Games and reading aren't work for you, they are fun. If you have a hobby, which is very likely with this placement, you will try to learn everything you can about it. The problem comes when mental exercise becomes work, because you like to have fun with your mind, not work with it. Because of this, you should try to make every learning project —in or out of school—a game, something to play with. Then you will do very well at it. Even so, you will have to learn enough self-discipline to study subjects that are necessary but not fun. You are best off in an open learning environment, where you are free to let your mind wander wherever your fancy takes you.

You enjoy expressing yourself through speaking and, when you are older, writing. You may write for fun and even become a professional writer, but only if you can express yourself creatively through your writing. You let people know your opinions about everything, and you find it very unpleasant not to be listened to.

Mercury in the Sixth House

You have a very orderly mind, and you like to learn techniques for doing various kinds of work. You are quite good with tools, of which you may have many, because of your hobbies. In any kind of work, you try to be extremely careful, and you take great pride in making something as nearly perfect as possible. For this reason you are good at any task that requires discipline and skill.

Your critical mind quickly figures out how any situation could be improved. However, be careful not to be so critical that you see only the flaws. Use your critical ability to improve things, not to tear them down.

Mercury in this position often describes the kind of work you will do when you get older. Your high standards and your desire for order would make you good at clerical work, typing or filing. Your job may involve writing or other creative mental skills. You may teach or train others in the skills that you have learned, or your career might be in transportation, traveling or large-scale communications. It is clear that no matter what you do for a living, using your mind will be important. While you are young, you should work to get the training you will need later. You should do quite well in school, because you have a disciplined, orderly mind for learning skills.

Mercury in the Seventh House

You are attracted to people who seem intelligent, because communication with others is very important to you, and you enjoy being among friends with whom you can have good talks. You do your best mental work with someone else, because you know how to cooperate in such a way that the two of you get excellent results.

You understand how to get along with others better than most people of your age, and you use this ability to help the people around you get along. You may become known as a peacemaker, because you are able to understand others' points of view.

Mercury in this house describes the kind of person you will want to marry when you are older. You will be attracted to someone who is lively and intelligent, someone you can share and exchange ideas with. Quite often this placement means you will marry someone who is quite a bit younger than you.

Mercury in this house may mean that you enjoy a good argument, simply as an exercise of wits. You find that arguing with someone sharpens your understanding. Just don't take these arguments too seriously, and be sure to let your opponent know that you don't. Then this can be an excellent way to learn.

Mercury in the Eighth House

You have a deep and inquiring mind and are fascinated by mysteries of all kinds. While you are young you may enjoy reading detective stories and tales of the supernatural. You like to think of the world as deeper and more mysterious than the world described in science courses. You want to believe that supernatural forces are real, and you would like to know everything about them. As an adult, you will study the hidden aspects of human nature, which will make you a natural psychologist, whether or not you study psychology in school. You are fascinated by mysteries in people as much as any other kind.

You may not say much, for you are a quiet person, and when you do speak up, you don't say everything that is on your mind. Very early in life you may have found that others don't always understand what you say, so you tend to keep quiet. This may cause others to misunderstand you and think that you are holding back some deep dark secret, although that is not the case. But your thoughts may be so complex that you can't express them easily to others.

Mercury in the Ninth House

You are very interested in learning more about the world, especially about foreign places and people. You would like to travel all over the globe and see everything there is to see. Spending all your life in one place would make you unhappy, for you are quickly bored by anything that becomes routine and everyday.

The many subjects you are interested in should help you in school, although you are very impatient with studying any subject that doesn't seem important to you. As you get older you will be especially interested in law, philosophy, medicine and possibly religion.

You think about everything you study very reasonably, because you want it to make good logical sense. This is a good approach, which is unusual in a young person, but you shouldn't ignore subjects such as art, literature and music, which can't be treated logically. Those studies are valuable to you also, but you are more likely to understand mathematics and science, because they fit into your view of the world better.

As you get older you may do some writing or work in some area of publishing. Communicating the ideas that are important to you will play a large role in your life. You consider your thoughts important, and you want others to know them.

Mercury in the Tenth House

Learning and education will be very important to you when you select a career later in life. Even now, you think a great deal about careers, and you may be making plans about what you want to do. With Mercury in this house, your life work will certainly involve using your mind, so you will have to get as much training as possible. You will have to go on to college or at least have some specific vocational training beyond high school.

This placement favors careers in mathematics, science or a technical field, because they take the most advantage of your logical mind. Even now you are more logical than most people your age. Such careers also involve learning new techniques, which you enjoy. Any profession that requires you to learn elaborate techniques that demand much skill will interest you. It may even be something that you do with your hands, as long as it is complicated enough. You may also be attracted to a career in traveling, communications or transportation or to a job that involves much public speaking. You are quite good at expressing opinions that you share with others.

Your father will be especially important in forming your ideas and ways of thinking.

Mercury in the Eleventh House

You enjoy being around friends who are clever and interesting. You like people with whom you can test your mind, perhaps with word games, puzzles and games of strategy. You also like to talk and share ideas with your friends. In fact, you think most clearly when you can try out your ideas first on your friends. When you are older, you will be at your best doing mental work with a group of people. It isn't that you are unoriginal, but you are a team person. You are just as concerned about what is good for the group as about what is good for you. You may join clubs with people who are interested in the same things you are.

As you get older, you will think more about the interests and needs of people outside your own little circle. This position of Mercury often means that you are concerned with humanitarian ideals and the good of everyone. You will rise above your own viewpoint and think in terms of the whole world.

You like to get around in the area where you live, and you try to be on friendly terms with everyone in your neighborhood. As a result you will probably become well known to most everyone in your area.

Mercury in the Twelfth House

You are fond of secrets and often keep your thoughts hidden from others, because you feel it is better if they don't know what you're thinking. Just be careful that you don't make this attitude so plain that people start distrusting you, even when there is no reason to. Unfortunately, this position may mean that you are afraid to tell people your ideas because you think they are no good or that everyone will disagree with them. In school you may be very reluctant to speak up, preferring to hide at the back of the class where the teacher won't call on you. This is not good, because your ideas are probably not at all bad. Your mind is as good as anyone else's, but you will not get any credit for your beliefs unless you learn to speak up.

You like to be alone and ponder your own thoughts, even if you don't share them with others. You are especially fond of beautiful and fantastic ideas. Just be careful not to spend so much time in your private fantasy world that you neglect to learn about the real world outside of your head.

Mercury Conjunct Venus

You like to be surrounded by beauty and are depressed by anything ugly or unpleasant. While you are quite young, you may show some definite artistic ability. Also you appreciate other people's artistic talents. You enjoy making things, which could mean that you will work in one of the crafts.

Perhaps the most important effect of this aspect, however, is that it takes your mind away from narrowly logical thinking. You look for form and beauty in ideas as well as in objects. If you study mathematics, for example, you should try to get a mental picture of what is happening and see the beauty in the forms. That will work better for you than working it out as an exercise in logic. Also you may think visually, by seeing images in your head rather than just connecting ideas.

You want everything you see or think about to be related artistically as well as logically. This may cause some problems in school subjects such as mathematics and science, but it will help you with music and literature.

You talk to people in a way that wins them over. You are very good at soothing hurt feelings and at helping people settle a quarrel fairly. You say what has to be said, without being dishonest, but you express yourself so well that everybody feels good about it.

Mercury Sextile Venus

You are a natural diplomat. You express yourself so gracefully that people have no bad feelings even when you have to express something unpleasant. In fact you deal with people mostly by being charming.

You love harmony and beauty and make a great effort to surround yourself with beautiful objects. You may have some artistic talent, but even if you don't, as you get older you will appreciate other people's talents.

You are very sociable and enjoy having a good time with friends. You try to avoid anything unpleasant, even if it is a necessary part of life. As you grow up, you will have to learn to live with some unpleasantness, because life can't always be fun and games. By trying to keep everything light and easy, you may avoid conflicts that are necessary to build real character. Also with this aspect you may tend not to do anything very thoroughly. Your charm and friendliness may prevent you from really experiencing the emotional depths of life, which are not always that pleasant.

However, you are an amusing and witty person, probably quite popular at parties and in groups. You should have little trouble making people like you.

Mercury Conjunct Mars

This aspect usually means that you get into arguments a lot. You decide on your position and jump to a conclusion, and then you will defend your point of view against all comers, whether or not you are right. The problem is that you act as if your beliefs are you; that is, if someone proves you wrong, you feel threatened. You may not always know you are doing this, but whenever you are in an argument, your body reacts as if in self-defense.

This aspect has many strong points. First of all, you think for yourself and don't need to get anyone else's opinion in order to know how you feel. You do not particularly care if anyone else agrees with you, because you are most concerned with being true to yourself. And being an argumentative person, you always stand up for what you believe. But you should think very carefully about every decision and take a stand only when you really have to. You often have strong opinions about matters that do not affect you at all, and the more opinions you have, the more time you spend defending them.

You have a sharp tongue, which you should use carefully, for the way you say things can start many a battle. Do not be overly critical of people unless the situation affects you in a very important way. You must learn to state your case without forcing others to defend themselves against you. If people often react angrily to what you say, think about your words and your tone of voice, because that is what is causing the hostility.

Mercury Sextile Mars

You think for yourself, and you stand up for what you believe. Your mind is very active and should be constantly working on something useful. If you are at all disciplined, you should be able to do more mental work more quickly than other people, because you have a lot of energy.

You enjoy spirited conversation with others, especially a friendly argument or debate, which you prefer to a real conflict. Your mind is probably quite sharp, so you should be able to argue your position well.

You are not at all timid about expressing your thoughts. In fact, you may have to learn to be honest without offending people by your frankness. While you are young, people may find your outspoken manner charming, but later on, it could be a real problem.

You don't follow anyone else in your opinions, being quite happy to be the only one to hold a particular belief. You have no wish to control what others think, but you will not be controlled by anyone else, either. While you are young, adults may resent you for being so independent and for seeming to disobey them. But they can reason with you, for you are not a very impulsive person. If you know you will feel defeated if you agree with someone, you won't budge. You have to feel free to choose the better alternative and know that your choice will be respected. You cannot bear not to be taken seriously in this regard.

Mercury Square Mars

This aspect can be rather difficult, for it indicates that you are rash and impulsive and tend to lose your temper too easily. You are very sensitive to mean remarks by others and may feel offended even when a comment wasn't meant to hurt you. And when you are angry, your anger takes over completely, and you become quite unreasonable. Your problem is to balance your drive to assert yourself, your anger in everyday conflicts, and the need to think about the world in a reasonable way. You can't afford to ignore either the Mercury element (clear reasoning and communication) or the Mars element (action and self-assertion) of this aspect. You must put them together.

If the Mars side always takes over, you will always be fighting with people, losing your temper and acting rather stupidly. But if you try to let Mercury's sense of reason control your aggressive energies, you will lose a great deal of strength, including the strength to stand up for yourself. Also if you sit on the Mars energy, you may become nervous, anxious and irritable in a quiet simmering way.

You will also have to learn that when others disagree with you, they are not attacking you personally. Let everyone have their say, and do not automatically resist their ideas. Only then will you be able to come to an agreement with others.

When you are angry or irritable, you should stay away from dangerous tools or machinery, for you may tend to have accidents at such times.

Mercury Trine Mars

You stand up for yourself and speak your mind. Other people always know where they stand with you, because you always say what you mean, and if you say something nice, you really believe it. You will be better known for honesty than for tactfulness.

You will know your own mind while you are still quite young. In everything you do, you are self-assured and decisive. Although you make up your mind more quickly than most people, you are usually right, at least about your own needs. You are not so good at understanding how your needs relate to those of other people or of groups that you belong to. The people around you usually have to compromise with what you want. If necessary, you will go off by yourself, quite happily, if that is the only route.

You are sure of your ideas and opinions without being too aggressive about them. Others know what you think, even without your spelling it out, because you are so firm and obviously determined.

You are good at debating, and you have quite a sharp tongue, especially while you are young. You know how to tell off anyone who seems to be acting foolishly, and if someone tries to tell you off, you are ready with a quick answer.

You have a great deal of mental energy, and you should always keep your mind busy. If you do, you will get a lot of work done, and you will be able to soften the harshness of this aspect.

Mercury Inconjunct Mars

You often find it difficult to separate yourself from what you believe. You fight very hard for your ideas, even when you suspect you are wrong. You must learn that you are not your ideas, that you have them but are not them. If you do not learn this, it will be difficult even to have a friendly talk with friends, because you are always trying to make a point, defend your opinion or prove somebody else wrong. This also makes you irritable and touchy, so that others prefer not to be around you. Of course, you should not give in about something you seriously believe in, but it is unlikely that you would make that mistake.

On the other hand, with this aspect you might find it hard to complain to others, especially if you are not sure that you are right. In that case, you should learn to speak your mind, but without being unpleasant about it. You should learn to release your resentment or anger to a certain extent, because that energy can turn inward and cause you to become nervous, edgy or irritable, which could be quite difficult. Or you could develop unhealthy habits.

If you can learn to control this aspect, you will be able to spend a long time on mental work, as long as you are interested in what you are doing. But you will have to learn when to stop. You may work too hard or get too wrapped up in some idea that you are studying and not be able to relax. Get into the habit of taking a break before you get too overtired.

Mercury Opposition Mars

You like to compete with others by using your mind, and you can't resist challenging someone who disagrees with you. If you stay cool, you can argue very effectively but only if you remain calm. If you fly off the handle and get angry, you say things that make no sense. In that case your anger, aggressiveness and even hostility completely destroy your ability to think clearly. Try to stay in control, for then you can be a strong fighter for what you believe.

A related problem is that you tend to take everything personally. You can stay calm in an argument only if you separate yourself from it somewhat. If you begin to take the argument really seriously, you lose control. You are not what you think and believe; you must understand that your ideas are not a basic part of you as a person.

Rash and impulsive thinking can also be a problem. Learn to take your time. Even so, you probably size up a situation faster than anyone else. You are always alert to what's happening in the world and you are especially aware of the people who may come into your life. Thus you often know what is coming before it happens.

This aspect can make you feel nervous and irritable or just barely in control, so that anything sets you off into a great rage. This is most likely to happen if you don't let yourself express your rage and anger. Probably you have a hot temper, but you should allow the anger to come out. Then it will only last a short time. If you hold it in, it can even make you physically sick.

Mercury Conjunct Jupiter

As you get older, you will have many interests in life, and you will never let a narrow point of view keep you from fully understanding the world. As an adult, you may enjoy traveling a lot, but even if you don't go far, you will travel in your mind, through books and ideas.

In your studies, you want to understand how each subject works as a whole. You like to cover a large area first and then fill in the details later. Unfortunately with this aspect, you may not have much self-discipline, so that you are impatient with learning anything detailed or exacting. There is a danger that you will work sloppily or do things halfway. Once you have a general understanding of a subject, you may feel that that is enough.

As you get older, you may have abilities in any of the fields that are concerned with the world as a whole, such as law, medicine, philosophy or religion. You could be skillful in mathematics or science, but only if you can develop enough discipline to learn the details thoroughly.

Your personal habits may be sloppy. Your work may not be neatly done, your handwriting may be hard to read, and your room may be quite messy. However, you are optimistic, open-minded and tolerant of other people's differences. These traits will make people like you and should help you be successful as well.

Mercury Sextile Jupiter

You have a questioning and curious mind, and you love to find out everything there is to learn about the world. Probably you will be interested in foreign places and people, and later you may love to travel.

You enjoy being with friends and neighbors and talking about any subject that interests you. And you can always keep the conversation interesting. Also, when you are with a group you can smooth over people's arguments and bring about agreements. This is because you have an unusual ability to see both sides of an argument and put them together in a workable compromise.

You are quite skillful at expressing your own ideas, and when you are older you may have some skill at debating. You think clearly and objectively, and you can keep from getting so emotionally involved in an argument that you lose your train of thought.

You should also be quite good at planning and organizing your affairs ahead of time. You have the ability to take a long view of a situation and see what is coming. But be careful of your tendency to overlook details and to think only of the whole. This can lead to sloppy thinking. Except for that problem, this aspect is useful to careers in law and business, or any job that needs foresight and organization.

Mercury Square Jupiter

This aspect usually means that you have a sharp mind and great ability to understand ideas that aren't obvious to others, but you will need a lot of discipline to make the most of it. Otherwise, your thinking is likely to be rash and sloppy, and you will jump to conclusions without knowing all the facts. Your personal habits—such as handwriting or taking care of your body and your room—may be rather sloppy. Also, in games or studies that require you to concentrate, you may not be able to keep track of what's happening, so you get tripped up by details that you overlook. You need to train yourself to work carefully with some kind of system. When you start a project, make a checklist of the steps that you might overlook and then make sure that you do each one. If you overlook something, don't get upset, just add it to the list.

On the plus side, you are able to put together ideas and understandings that to others seem unrelated. This will be very useful in your studies, but only if you learn to be disciplined. You are generous and optimistic, which will make people like you. But you may be a pushover for anyone who wants sympathy.

Learn to stick to every project you start and to work carefully, slowly and with much thought. Then you will get a great deal out of life.

Mercury Trine Jupiter

This is a very positive aspect, for it means that you are generous, tolerant and optimistic. You always look at the positive side, but you can also see what is wrong and figure out new ways to deal with it. You respect tradition, but you aren't held down by it, and you can rise above your own beliefs and really grow all your life. You are interested in many subjects and want to learn, and the more universal the subject, the more you enjoy it. You try to understand how your studies apply to your own life and to the lives of the people around you. Ideas that do not work in this way, that are good only for playing mental games do not interest you very much. And you know the difference.

You are good at planning and organizing, because you can put all of the pieces together to make a whole. Even while you are young, you will be interested in the future and will work hard to develop your sense of foresight.

As you get older, you will enjoy traveling, because it allows you to expand your mind and encounter new ideas, which you always enjoy. You are also quite skillful at presenting your thoughts to others. When you are older, people will come to you for advice because you understand how to make a compromise between conflicting ideas.

Mercury Inconjunct Jupiter

You like to think big, and you have great ambitions, but you don't always make sure that your thinking is clear or careful. When you make any kind of plan, be careful. Don't try to take on more than you can handle and make sure not to overlook details, for that could hurt what you are trying to do. Careful planning will help you develop disciplined habits in other areas as well. This aspect can mean that you are sloppy in your personal appearance and in your work habits, especially schoolwork.

On the other hand, if you do learn careful mental habits, you can have creative ability with this aspect, because you are able to see and understand all the elements of a situation. You take a broad and far-seeing view of a situation, which is unusual for someone your age. Most of the time you are willing to let other people think what they choose, as long as they leave your ideas alone. However, you may be inclined to preach about morality, because you enjoy being right and letting others know that they do not live up to your "high" standards. But sometimes you fake it; you aren't as "good" as you pretend to be. Be careful of this, for you could be known as a hypocrite. It's fine to set high standards and live up to them, but do not pretend to be better than you are. And let others decide on their own moral standards.

Mercury Opposition Jupiter

This aspect can indicate that you have a very good mind, but in order to get the most out of it, you will have to work out some problems.

First of all, you need to be disciplined. Otherwise you may make up your mind hastily, without knowing all the facts. You may tend to be sloppy in your thinking as well as in your personal habits. For example, your handwriting may be rather hard to read. This kind of sloppiness is the result of going too quickly, trying to take in too much of the world at a time, without digesting any of it. You often see only the general pattern of what's happening around you, without being aware of the details. Because of this, you tend to be very uncritical, both for good and for bad; you are very tolerant and accepting of people, but you do not judge persons or situations carefully enough. Do not make decisions too quickly, especially about people, for you may make a commitment that you later want to break. Basically you are positive and optimistic, but do not be foolish about it. It's easy to be tripped up by flaws that you overlook.

Sometimes this aspect means that you have many disagreements with others. Usually you allow everyone to have their own opinion, but your impulsiveness in making decisions works against that. You may stick to your decision against the wiser judgment of others, simply because you hate to be proved wrong. Always keep an open mind.

Mercury Conjunct Saturn

Something about the quality of your mind makes you seem older than you are. There is a very serious side to your personality, and you are attracted to subjects that are usually of interest only to adults. Whatever you study must seem important to the whole world, not just to you personally. For this reason, you may prefer talking with people who are older, and you may judge yourself by adult standards.

You are slow and careful in your thinking, because you want to know all the facts before making a decision, and even then you take your time. You are conservative, preferring to deal with familiar ideas that you have tested carefully in the past. Before you adopt a new idea you test it against your experience, partly because you are unusually anxious to avoid mistakes. You feel that making an error reflects very badly on you as a person. In fact, you take your mistakes too seriously; at your age, they are not all that important. Fear of making a mistake can keep you from taking any action.

Unfortunately, your seriousness can make you tend toward depression and loneliness. By nature you are more aware of the barriers between people than of the elements that link everyone and everything together. You may feel that you are alone when you are not, and that no one likes you, although it is not true. Try to learn to relax and have fun and to do things merely for the fun of it. Eventually you will learn that living only for what is "important" does not make life rewarding.

Mercury Sextile Saturn

You do everything carefully and thoroughly, for you hate to. overlook any steps. You don't take up new ideas very quickly, but you do learn quite well, and what you learn you remember forever. You are rather reserved and may prefer being with older people and discussing serious matters. Your mind is older than your body, which can help you in school because you study your homework carefully. Also you may be given more responsibility than others of your age.

You are quite good at organizing yourself, your work and the people around you. You are able to construct a plan that others can follow and make sure that the work is done well. This aspect does not usually make you very popular with others; in fact, you aren't interested in that. So you are likely to work as the secretary in an organization or club rather than as an elected officer, such as the president.

You are good at handling money and probably thrifty, unless other elements of your chart indicate the opposite. You feel that the world is a rather difficult place, which requires you to be careful about money.

Your analytical mind very quickly figures out what is wrong with a situation and how to improve it. But be careful not to be so aware of the flaws that you can't see the strong points of the situation.

Most people will respect you for your carefulness and ability to get things done. If you are at all popular, it will be based on your real merits.

Mercury Square Saturn

While you are young, you must learn to handle the energies of this aspect very carefully to bring out their strong points and minimize the weak points. Your parents should encourage you to look at the bright side of life and avoid exposing you to situations that reinforce your feeling that life is difficult and oppressive. You should not be saddled with too much responsibility while you are young, because you have a natural tendency to be overwhelmed and depressed by the seriousness of the world. Depression may be a problem that you will always have to guard against. However, it will help to realize that you usually make things look worse than they are.

You should be exposed to a broad range of ideas at an early age. Otherwise, if you are brought up in the confines of a narrow morality, you will be likely to narrow it still further. With this aspect there is a tendency to focus very narrowly and concentrate all your attention on small details. For this reason, you must be encouraged to spread your attention into larger spheres of interest.

On the plus side, you can think and work with great thoroughness. You are not likely to ever leave a job half done. On the other hand, you may be inclined to overestimate the difficulty of a job, which you should try not to do. Strike a balance between a broadminded attitude and realistic, pragmatic thinking. Idealism has a place even in the most practical minds.

You will learn best in a rather structured environment, but not so structured that you lose your freedom to think and explore.

Mercury Trine Saturn

You are careful and cautious, and you do everything in a very structured and organized way. You have discipline, which you need in order to get anything done. Your only mental limitation, which will become clearer as you get older, is that you have trouble grasping an idea unless it is spelled out quite carefully and in detail. This makes it more difficult to study subjects such as literature, music and art. However, other indications in the chart could change this particular problem.

Your view of life is practical. You want to know what good something is before you get involved with it. For this reason, you can take an idea and make something real of it that others can see and appreciate. You are a good organizer who knows how to arrange elements efficiently. Usually you are able to see the project as a whole, although sometimes you get too bogged down in little details. Be careful of this tendency.

You want to know the objective truth about the world, and you are willing to study hard to find it out. The only problem is that you may not be sensitive enough to the less concrete aspects of the world, such as other people's feelings or vague impressions that do have real meaning. In short, you may be too hardheaded to appreciate the lighter and more subtle side of life.

Mercury Inconjunct Saturn

This aspect can have several different meanings. First of all, you may have hidden fears that are difficult to express, but they cause you to do things that others can't understand. These may include fear of the dark or of certain places or people. Or this aspect can mean that you often feel depressed and sad for no apparent reason. You tend to see the serious side of life, and it weighs on you more than on most people.

It is possible that your thinking will become unnaturally rigid for someone of your age. You may get into routines or habits that you are afraid to break, for you prefer familiar paths of life and known ways of doing things.

A particularly serious problem can be feeling suspicious of others, which later in life will turn into a cynical attitude about people's behavior. True, it is good to be aware of the realities of life and not overidealistic. But you shouldn't look at life in the worst possible light. You need to be surrounded by positive and optimistic people, and your parents should try not to be too negative around you and to make sure that you experience the best and most cheerful aspects of life. You will learn soon enough what to expect of the world without having your nose rubbed in its less desirable features.

On the plus side, this aspect can make you a very careful thinker. You may not attempt anything beyond your abilities as you see them, but whatever you do attempt will be done very well. You are a neat and careful worker.

Mercury Opposition Saturn

You may feel that others always disagree with whatever you say. You have a strong tendency to feel different from others and not understood by them. This is partly because you have difficulty communicating with people, which has little to do with your intelligence. You find it just as difficult to express yourself clearly as to understand what others are saying to you. You can work on this problem by being absolutely clear and precise in what you say and getting others to do the same. It is very important that your words and theirs leave nothing to the imagination. This is not brutal frankness, it is clear language.

With this aspect, you interpret what people say in a negative way, even when that is not meant. And this may lead others to hear what you say the same way. This problem comes about because you talk so seriously and use language that is very heavy and full of meaning. In itself, this is not bad, unless you do not make yourself clear.

You are rather conservative in your thinking and slow to adopt new ideas, preferring to stick with the ones that work for you. Your standards in your work are very high, so you can be a very demanding perfectionist. And you apply this to others as well.

Mercury Conjunct Uranus

Your mind grasps new ideas and concepts very quickly, and you are always on the lookout for anything new and exciting. You are not very patient with following old ways, especially if tradition seems to be the only reason for it.

You also tend to move so fast that your energies get scattered and you never really get anything done. Be careful not to start a lot of projects and then drop them when the thrill of a new experience has worn off. At times your tempo of activity gets so high that you simply exhaust yourself. During such times you will become extremely nervous and irritable, which is the signal to slow down.

You will probably be interested in math and science, for these subjects require the kind of abstract reasoning that you are good at. However, for this talent to develop, your parents and teachers will have to actively encourage you in this direction. Girls, especially, are often driven away from this area of study by lack of encouragement. Both math and science offer a way to use and even change the world and escape from the limitations of nature. Other fields of study that do this will also draw your attention. When you are older you may be interested in astrology and the more technical branches of the occult. You will enjoy any offbeat, exciting field of study.

Mercury Sextile Uranus

You have a very quick mind and love to discover new angles and ways of thinking. Discovery gives you pleasure. Some people find new ideas frightening, but you enjoy them; in fact, you are quickly bored if the same ideas are repeated over and over. This can be a problem in school subjects that require a lot of drill. However, if along with the drill come many new insights, you will remain interested. People with this aspect are often quite good at mathematics, science, and technical and mechanical fields.

You will form your own opinions very early in life, although you will probably change them as you grow older. But you always have to be free to draw your own conclusions. If someone tries to limit your thinking or keep you from thinking about certain ideas, you will be even more attracted by those forbidden areas. The more that people try to hold you back, the more radical and unconventional you will be. You may enjoy startling people with your statements and even playing jokes, but you don't do it to be mean, as most people will understand.

Try not to be a shallow thinker. Your mind can cover a number of subjects very quickly, but you may tend to move on to something new before you have really understood the first subject. Persons who seem to learn slowly may learn more completely and thus have an advantage over you in later life. But if you can learn to discipline yourself and go slowly, you will be able to think extremely well.

Mercury Square Uranus

You are attracted to excitement and exciting ideas, but you may not be a very careful thinker. Also you may speak out impulsively without thinking about your words. You tend to jump to conclusions without having enough experience or knowledge. But if you can learn to control your mental energy, this aspect can help you escape from the limits of everyday thinking. You are able to grasp ideas that others cannot even imagine, because you have an unusual ability to think abstractly. But without self-control you will not carry these ideas far enough; you will go on to a new area before you have thought through the first one. You often find it difficult to concentrate. In fact you can sometimes work yourself into a nervous frenzy, simply because your energies are scattered. That is the time to slow down. But with discipline, you should be able to excel in mathematics, science and mechanical subjects.

You often like to make outrageous remarks to people, for there is something of the prankster in you. You enjoy challenging other people's beliefs, forcing them to look at their ideas in a new way. This can be very constructive, although it may not be the best way to win friends, especially since you are not very sensitive. By doing this you can genuinely hurt people when you don't need to and shouldn't. Sometimes people do have to be jogged out of their stale old beliefs, but many times they should be left alone. Do not hurt people simply because you're feeling playful.

Mercury Trine Uranus

This is a very creative aspect. It indicates that you have a quick mind and can understand ideas that others can't, because you are open to new ways of thinking. You have a good ability to think about abstract ideas, as in math, science and technical studies. And as you grow older you will be able to combine your understanding of such studies with your practical outlook on the world.

You also have intuition, that is, the ability to come to understandings seemingly from nowhere. While you are young, this may startle people, and at first you may find it hard to defend your insights. But as you get older, you will learn how to show people that your insights are true. Whenever you are confronted with a difficult problem or puzzle, you will solve it more quickly than most. This aspect is good for work that requires originality and new ways of doing things.

When you get older, you may be attracted to offbeat subjects such as the occult or psychic studies. Even while you are young, others will consider your views very strange, but you will work with your ideas until you get as much as possible out of them. This is because you are really interested in these ideas, but also because you enjoy surprising and even shocking others.

Mercury Inconjunct Uranus

Your mind moves quickly from topic to topic, often without pausing long enough for you to understand what you have learned. And if there is a lot of excitement or activity around you, your mind may race so fast to keep up with it all that you work yourself into a state of nervous frenzy. Under these circumstances it is almost impossible for you to concentrate or do any useful mental work.

As you get older, you will have to learn to discipline your mind so that you can think things through. It's all right to be somewhat restless, but you must learn to stay put during school and at other times when it is important to concentrate.

On the other hand, you are quite inventive. You can see solutions to problems quicker than most, and you may be good at designing. Model building and other activities that develop your design sense and ability to see in three dimensions would be very useful. Also these exercises would help you learn to concentrate. In school you may excel at mathematics and science, as long as you can learn to sit still long enough to learn the subject.

This aspect might mean that you have nervous problems, such as a tendency to get exhausted or a sensitive disposition that requires a very calm environment in order to prevent further problems. In any case, your parents should keep you away from situations that will make you overexcited.

Mercury Opposition Uranus

You have a very sharp mind, which you enjoy using to stir people up. Anyone who seems self-satisfied or settled in his or her ways is a likely target for your stinging wit. Especially while you are young, you are likely to challenge and play tricks on persons in authority. Your mind has a rebellious side that always wants to take the opposite point of view from anyone else, especially if someone is trying to persuade you in some way. You must learn that just because someone wants you to believe something, that does not mean it is wrong or untrue. Learn to keep your mind open, even under pressure from others.

However, when you are free to explore on your own, you are completely open. But you tend to be attracted to unusual ideas and those that conservative people consider unacceptable. You are also interested in ideas that teach you new insights and understanding of nature and the universe. For this reason, like the other Mercury-Uranus aspects, this one means that you are good in science and mathematics, but only if the adults in your life help you to develop this ability. Also you must learn to be more disciplined, so that you can stay with a subject long enough to get something solid out of it.

You are likely to be quite restless and even nervous, especially with others. When you are alone, you are somewhat quieter. Being with friends brings out the nervously active side of your personality.

Mercury Conjunct Neptune

You have a very rich imagination, but you must learn to control it enough to understand what is real and what is not. That is the challenge of this aspect. It is unlikely that you mean to be a liar, but you may have trouble telling the truth, simply because you don't always know it yourself. You may tell untruths without meaning to.

You have a very rich fantasy world, which seems very real to you, and in a way it is real, but not in a way that most others can accept. However, as you grow older and learn to understand your mind, your fantasy world can become a rich source of ideas for creative writing or art.

You are also very sensitive to what is going on in other people's minds, even when they don't say a word. This may be confusing at first, because you don't know how you know something, and that makes others disbelieve you, even when you are right. Your intuition is very highly developed.

Sometimes this aspect means that you have nervous problems for no clear reason. Even while you are young, you simply have to rest your nerves at times, especially if you are around people who create a lot of excitement and stress. You need peace and quiet.

In school you are not likely to be very good at math and science, not because you are slow, but because you do not think that way. You do not like your mind to be limited by the dry laws of logic.

Mercury Sextile Neptune

This aspect usually means that you have a very creative imagination and a great deal of sensitivity. You are able to see ideas in your head in such a way that they become real to you. This ability is very useful in art or crafts that depend on original design, or in writing. It will not help you in studying math and science, which depend on strict logic. You are likely to be impatient with the rigid rules that you have to follow in math and science, but you should make some effort to study them, because they can teach you mental discipline. This will make your creativity more productive.

You are very sensitive to people around you and often react to what they are thinking before they say anything. Because of this ability, you should avoid people who are negative or who intend to do harm.

When talking with others, you add something extra to the conversation that makes your world seem more interesting and exciting to them and to you. You bring out the beauty that exists in the world, making it easier for you and others to put up with the unpleasant aspects of life. The only problem is that you must be careful not to use this ability to totally escape or help others escape from the real world.

Mercury Square Neptune

Sometimes your fantasies seem so real that you forget they are just fantasies and that they are not real to anyone else. This aspect is likely to bring real confusion into your everyday dealings with others. You will find it difficult to make yourself understood and to understand others, unless you learn to control your mind while you are young. Also you tend to retreat into your fantasy world whenever the real world seems too rough, so that you avoid problems that you really must deal with.

On the other hand, you have a creative mind, and you can produce beautiful works of imagination. Just remember to separate the world of your imagination from reality.

Another reason you are often misunderstood is that you have difficulty putting your very complex ideas into words. For this reason you should learn to communicate your ideas through some kind of artistic medium, if at all possible. In that way your mind can communicate the fullness of your thoughts to others.

As you get older, it is especially important to avoid alcohol and mind-altering drugs, because they will have a very bad effect on you. Such drugs will not solve your problems and will only intensify your feeling of confusion in the world. And you won't even be refreshed by the escape they provide. You may have nervous problems if your world is not truly peaceful and serene. You very much need a stable home life.

Mercury Trine Neptune

Your rich imagination allows you to be very creative. You can see beauty in the world that is hidden from others, and you can express this through writing or art. Also you are an idealist who dreams of a better world in which all the problems of this one have been solved. But you stay in touch with this world enough so that you can handle it.

As you get older, you may be more interested in making your ideals real than in acquiring money or property. Others may consider you very impractical, but people such as you make the world more interesting for everyone.

Like the other Mercury-Neptune aspects, this one is not very favorable for studying math and science, unless you have an unusual amount of mental discipline. But you approach your studies with a fresh creativity that can make up for lack of discipline. If you make an effort now to learn the difference between the world of your imagination and the real world, your creativeness will become even more effective.

Mercury Inconjunct Neptune

The challenge of this aspect is to make your thinking and communication with others more clear. Your rational mind is strongly influenced by your sensitivity, imagination and ideals, although you aren't always sure how this happens. You tend to spend too much time in your own imaginary world that no one else can share, and this confuses your dealings with others. You will have to learn to face reality, so that you can at least communicate with people. Otherwise you will have a very lonely life.

Sometimes this aspect means that you are so nervously sensitive that you pick up all the negative psychological energies around you and react to them very strongly. If this is true for you, the only way to deal with it is to be moved to a peaceful, positive environment. If there is too much noise or too many bad vibrations in your life, you will withdraw more and more and refuse to face reality.

Your self-confidence needs to be built up as much as possible so that you can face people without fear, tell the truth about yourself and be honest in other ways as well.

Even if you do adjust easily to reality, you should always have a quiet place where you can be alone with your thoughts. Here you can let your imagination run free and become a creative force instead of a force that works against you.

In school you are not likely to be at your best in math and science, but you could be quite strong in creative arts, literature and other areas where your sensitivity would be an advantage.

Mercury Opposition Neptune

You may learn to think clearly on your own, but there is a danger that relationships with others will confuse you and upset your thinking. It is sometimes difficult for you to see the truth about people who are close to you, and you may be unpleasantly surprised when someone turns out to be quite different from what you had thought. You are something of a dreamer, and instead of taking people as they are, you may try to work them into your dreams.

You must learn to accept others as they really are, for if you idealize them, you will always be disappointed. And no one is more cynical about the world than a disappointed idealist. Also when you are disappointed, you may withdraw into yourself, which won't help, because you need to find out the truth.

You also must learn how to be truthful. Usually you don't mean to lie, but your confusion about reality may make you follow a rather fanciful version of the truth. If you do not know the difference between the truth and your dreams, you end up confusing everyone around you, which is the same as lying.

If you learn to be more controlled and think clearly, this can be a very useful aspect. Your dreams can be the source of positive creative ideas in the arts or literature. Dreams are not so useful in math and science, which require rigorous logic, but in other areas that require intuition and imaginative insight, you can shine.

Mercury Conjunct Pluto

You have a great deal of curiosity and want to solve every mystery that comes along. You will work patiently to get an answer, often going off by yourself until you have solved the problem. This makes you a born investigator, but it may also make you want to interfere in other people's lives and get involved where you have no business. On a more harmless level, you will probably love reading mystery stories and tales of the supernatural.

Another side of this aspect is that you may be very stubborn about your own beliefs and also try very hard to make others agree with you. You have very strong opinions, and you hate to have people challenge them. But if you can control this tendency to a reasonable degree, it can help you in teaching, public relations, selling or other work in which you mold the ideas of others. But you will have to be careful that the ideas you spread are not harmful.

You must watch out for one problem. If you try to force people to come around to your way of thinking, they may get so angry that they will fight you on any issue that comes up. No matter what you say, they will oppose you. Fortunately you can also influence others' thinking so subtly that they aren't aware of it.

Even while you are young, you are a natural psychologist in your understanding of human nature. You might even become a psychologist when you are older. You love finding out what makes people tick, and you can put that knowledge to good use.

Mercury Sextile Pluto

You get totally involved in each new interest. Because you do not take any subject lightly, you learn a great deal about everything you study. On the other hand, you are not likely to put much effort into a subject that you are not especially interested in, which may cause some problems at school. You will be much better in some subjects than in others.

You enjoy a mystery and will work very hard to arrive at the solution to one. And you think of people's behavior as a mystery to be solved, so you will probably become a student of psychology. Fortunately this aspect helps you look at matters logically as well as feel them out intuitively. Thus you reach a higher level of understanding than most people.

With this aspect you may be interested in machines and mechanical problems. You want to examine things to find out how they work. Even while you are young, you may become quite clever at repairing broken machines, although you may break a few things in the process of learning how they work.

This aspect favors careers in investigation, including criminal investigation and law enforcement; jobs that require ability in mechanics and repairing; and fields that require an understanding of human behavior. This aspect will help your career in another way, because you can convince people of your point of view without making them feel that you are pushing them around.

Mercury Square Pluto

You have to be careful about how you talk to people, because they may feel that you are trying to push them into an opinion or point of view that they don't agree with. You may do this without realizing it until people react to what you say with great hostility, even though your words are innocent. You may feel that others fight you just for the sake of fighting, which may make you quite bitter. You must try very hard to speak in such a way that the other person knows that you respect his or her point of view. Don't dictate or be overly forceful in expressing your opinions. If you can learn to be gentler in your expression, you can sway people to your point of view.

You may attract other people who seem to force their beliefs upon you. They challenge you to get your thinking straight, so that you can stand up to your opponents. If others disagree with you, it does not mean that you are either wrong or right. It only means that you have to look at your own beliefs very carefully.

You are attracted to hidden matters, which may lead to an interest in the occult when you are older. But be very careful about studying such ideas, especially while you are young, because you tend to latch onto some rather wild ideas and try to make them work in your life at any cost.

Mercury Trine Pluto

Your mind is unusually deep for someone of your age, and you are not very interested in the matters that other young people think about. Already you are interested in ideas about the universe, in finding out where you have come from, the purpose of life, and why people act as they do. For this reason you will seem older than you are, although in other ways you are quite happy being young.

You like to get below the surface and study a subject deeply. You want to master any skill you learn as completely as possible. However, no one can push you into learning something that you aren't interested in. With this aspect you should be allowed to study what you want, because you probably know best, although the adults in your life may not believe that at first.

As with other Mercury-Pluto aspects, you enjoy studying people and learning why they act as they do. When you are older, you will put this study to good use. You will be particularly good at convincing people to come around to your opinion, which is very useful in teaching. Your interest in human nature can also help you in studying psychology and psychiatry. When you are older, you may join a group that tries to reform society by reorganizing some parts of it.

Mercury Inconjunct Pluto

You have a rather complicated and sometimes tricky mind. You usually prefer to do things in roundabout and involved ways instead of being simple and direct.

On the positive side, this means that you enjoy solving puzzles, tracking down mysteries and finding out about hidden matters. At school you might do research in science. You have a natural ability to understand how people's minds work, what makes them act as they do, and what they are thinking, which is quite amazing for someone of your age.

On the negative side, however, you might misuse this ability by trying to control people's thoughts and words. Also you may love mysteries so much that you get involved in complicated plots and arrangements with your friends. You may enjoy working in secret and creating an air of mystery about yourself, but this could backfire and make others misunderstand you or even fear what you are doing. It is important to show people that you are honest and that you are not hiding anything. Otherwise they will probably suspect you, even if you are totally innocent. And if you aren't, they will know it for certain.

On another level, this aspect can mean that at certain times in your life you will go through tremendous psychological changes. All your thoughts and opinions will change completely. These stages may seem difficult, but you will be much better off if you let go of the past and welcome the new ideas.

Mercury Opposition Pluto

You may have a hard time getting people to agree with you about the ideas that you hold to be important. Others may seem to you to put your ideas down, threatening your ability to be what you want. Or you may try to impose your opinions on others, which causes them to resist you.

The problem is that even while you are young, your opinions and ideas bring about conflicts with others. This may happen because of the way that you express yourself, or perhaps you are attracted to people who are unpleasantly forceful, although you like them. Whenever you discuss something, you become very serious, and you only want to discuss matters that are serious to you. In fact one of the easiest ways for someone to make you mad is to not take your ideas seriously.

At times in your life your mind gets so intensely involved in some idea or belief that you become quite obsessed with it, which others find upsetting. However, this is only because you are going through some very important psychological changes. At such times you get all caught up in the process and can't see the rest of the world very clearly. You take your ideas too seriously. But eventually the phase passes and you can go back to normal. The people around you will just have to be patient with you. Trying to talk you out of these states is a waste of time until you are ready.

Mercury Conjunct Ascendant

This aspect indicates that even while you are young, talking and exchanging ideas with others is a very important part of your life. Your mind is very active but does not work best when you are alone. You need others to give you ideas and stimulate your thinking, and you do this for others in return. In school this may cause trouble sometimes, because it is hard for you to be quiet once your mind is running full speed ahead. But at the same time you can give your full attention to what is being taught, which helps you learn faster.

You are probably quite restless and always wanting to be on the move. Your mind changes course very quickly, and you go from idea to idea. Be careful, however, because you could become a person who knows a little about many areas, but not enough about any one subject. Avoid being shallow and try to develop enough self-discipline to stay with a subject or project long enough to get something lasting from it.

As you get older, your restlessness will probably lead you to travel a lot, although not necessarily over long distances. You would be better off in a job that does not tie you down to one spot.

You are very curious about nature and the world, so you ask questions of everyone you meet. You enjoy games, especially ones that involve the mind and help you learn something.

This position may also mean that you have some mechanical ability and can do highly skilled work with tools. If you don't spend all your time playing with your mind, you may be very good with your hands.

Mercury Sextile Ascendant

You have a great interest in the lives of people around you, and you enjoy being part of the general social whirl. You like talking and working with people and having interesting friends. At least at first, you are most attracted to people's mental qualities, and you use your mind to attract others as well.

You need to be busy, to keep your mind and your hands occupied. You enjoy games, reading and handcrafts, which you might be very good at, especially if Venus is also strong in your chart. You may also be clever with tools and machinery or have a talent for writing.

You have many interests, but one problem may be that you find it hard to stay with any one interest long enough to learn something real and meaningful from it. You learn faster than most, but that does not make you thorough or persevering. And you may be the same way with people. You may be attracted to someone for shallow reasons but be too impatient to learn what that person really has to offer. You may not enjoy being with people who express themselves emotionally, considering displays of feelngs sloppy and uncalled for. You prefer to express yourself verbally and with your mind.

As you get older you may join clubs or informal groups to pursue common interests which may be quite intellectual, such as art or literature.

Mercury Square Ascendant

This aspect indicates that you have an active mind, and you enjoy talking about ideas with people and sharing their thinking. But you may find it difficult to reach agreements with others, because you state your own opinions so energetically, even forcibly, that you put people off. You must learn to control the way you express yourself somewhat. You may come across with so much nervous energy that others feel confused or unsettled. Also it is important to learn to listen carefully to others, which you can do very well when you choose to, and find out what they have to say.

Be very careful that your friendships and other relationships do not keep you from setting objectives for yourself and making plans to reach them. Sometimes you get so caught up in talking with people that you are distracted from more important matters.

Try to avoid talking simply for the sake of talk, and avoid gossip and rumor. These may seem entertaining, but they can work against your friendships. What you think of as light fun may be very serious to others. Also be careful not to hurt people with practical jokes, because your playful attitude may seem mean to others who do not know that you intend no harm. Be sure that you don't say different things to different people. If they get together to compare notes, they may decide that you are not very straightforward.

Mercury Trine Ascendant

You like to play games that involve thinking and planning your moves, for you enjoy using your mind for fun as well as for useful work. Also you enjoy handcrafts, for you work well with your hands and with tools, and you can master difficult techniques.

You have a curious mind and want to know the answer to every question that comes up. You ask questions of grown-ups, but you also enjoy finding the answers in books.

As you get older, writing may become a favorite pastime. You enjoy putting your thoughts on paper and preserving them for the future. You can express yourself clearly.

You enjoy being with interesting people who can teach you about their wide experience of life. When you are older and more educated, you may have younger friends whom you can teach. You also prefer lively and active people to those who are quiet and more retiring. The reason for this is that you are easily bored and want to be around people who stimulate your mind, especially if they share your interests.

Hobbies may be very important to you, not just for fun but as a way to learn many useful skills. For this reason your parents should not think of your hobbies as silly. Your mind may well grow more through games and playing than through work alone.

Mercury Inconjunct Ascendant

You are likely to have some problems, but not serious ones, in communicating with others. The problem is that people's first impression of you may not fit in with what you say or your manner of thinking and speaking. People tend to hear what they expect to hear, and they may not listen to you as carefully as they should. So you will have to be as clear as possible and insist that others listen to what you are really saying. If others do not understand you, it is up to you to set them straight.

This pattern also works in reverse in that what you say may make people respond in ways that you can't accept. For example, you may be outspoken and frank but dislike it when others are, preferring to be treated gently and sensitively.

This aspect may mean that you enjoy working with your mind, learning new skills and ways to do things. You may also like working with your hands and using tools. You like to make practical use of your skills as well, so you don't enjoy learning something new unless it seems useful for your life.

This aspect can be a sign of nervousness, so it will help to keep every part of your life in order, because clutter and confusion will make you feel even more nervous and scattered. Some persons with this aspect want to have everything organized and are upset by disorder because they intuitively understand that disorder is bad for them. Even if you are not aware of this, it is true for you too.

Mercury Opposition Ascendant

This aspect means that you like to be involved with others and communicate often with your friends, because you need lots of mental excitement. Also you may compete with others by testing your mind against theirs, trying to prove that you are right, mostly because you enjoy arguing and winning. You like to debate, but you may not take the ideas very seriously. But be careful, because your opponents may take the matter more seriously and resent your casual attitude.

You like to be with interesting and stimulating people, but you do not like the responsibility of relationships. Also, a serious involvement might keep you from having a good time. You stay away from people who are overly emotional, because big displays of feeling make you uneasy. You feel you cannot deal with emotions because they don't fit in with the way your mind works.

If you can keep yourself from challenging everyone's ideas, you will work very well with others in planning and carrying out any kind of mental work. Even your homework may be easier if you work with someone else instead of alone.

Mercury Conjunct Midheaven

This aspect means that you have a very sharp mind, which you will use to get ahead. Very early in your life you will learn to look at the world clearly and objectively, and you will learn to communicate in ways that are very advanced for your age. You may or may not become an intellectual when you are older, but you will use your mind continually, always searching for stimulating and exciting experiences. Because you cannot stand boredom, you are sometimes very restless.

Your most important task is to be more disciplined, so that you can stick to a task long enough to get some real benefit from it. There is a real danger that your interest in any subject will be shallow.

Another possible problem, which may seem less serious but is actually greater, is that you prefer to deal with the world through your mind rather than your feelings. This will keep you from really being in touch with some experiences in life—such as love and sensitivity to beauty—for which your mind alone is not enough. Also you cannot really get in touch with other people through your mind alone. Unless you develop your emotions along with your mind, you may feel lonely and cut off from others.

With your lively mind, you may enjoy playing practical jokes on people. This is fine if you are careful not to hurt people who are more sensitive than you.

Mercury Sextile Midheaven

As you go through life you will be in touch with your own and other people's inner feelings and psychological currents. Your rational mind is more influenced than most by feelings and intuitions, which will deepen your understanding of the world. While you are young, however, it may not be easy to tell people about what you see so clearly. People may think of you as somewhat reserved and secretive. You are not trying to be mysterious, but you have already learned that if you don't choose your words carefully, others will misunderstand you, with some unpleasant results. It will take time before your ability to express yourself catches up with what you already know intuitively.

You may be attracted to mysteries and puzzles, because you like to examine secrets. In fact, you may build up your own secret universe to wander around in, not just for idle play but as a way to express your creative insights.

When you are older, you will use your mind to help you understand human nature. You are a natural psychologist, and later you will be able to communicate your ideas to others through speaking or writing.

You will spend much time planning and arranging your future in your head. Instead of falling into a career by accident, you will work out everything you must do to get where you want to go. You will study hard to achieve your ambition, and you should be a good student in any subject related to this interest.

Mercury Square Midheaven

Even while you are quite young, you will spend quite a bit of time thinking about your future, but don't expect to make up your mind for a long time. Your mind is very active, and each new interest you take up will give you a new idea about your future career. In fact the danger here is that you may never really settle on one career; you will get into many projects but never thoroughly enough to know what each one can really offer you. For this reason, you must teach yourself some self-discipline, so that you can stay with a project long enough to understand it.

You are quite restless and need to be mentally active all the time. You need to keep your mind busy, talk with others and feel that life is moving quickly. Otherwise you get bored, and then you may annoy people. Often you get so wrapped up in your own ideas and needs that you forget about anyone else. But with a little effort you can get away from yourself and see other people's points of view. You are able to think very clearly, but only if you come out of yourself.

As you get older, be careful not to say things that work against you. Your mouth could be your own worst enemy unless you make sure of what you are saying before you speak. It is possible to make your point without offending others.

You enjoy games, especially those that involve your mind, so you may be very good at solving puzzles and other activities that require cleverness.

Mercury Trine Midheaven

Very early in your life you will begin to think about what you want to do when you are older. To this end you will work to develop the talents that will help you get ahead. You will do the best you can in school, especially in those subjects that you think will be useful. While you are young, you will discipline yourself to learn the skills you need.

Your parents will influence your opinions very strongly, and they will probably support you in whatever path you choose. Very likely you and your parents agree generally and have similar ideas on most subjects. You believe you can learn from the people who are above you, so that one day you can be in their position. This makes you a hardworking person who tries to master all the skills you study.

Later in your life you may work in some area of communications, science, education or another field that requires mental skill and the ability to communicate clearly.

You are very good at taking care of everything you own, and you prefer possessions that stimulate your mind, such as books and records. You enjoy playing games with others, especially games that teach you something. You may also enjoy writing as a pastime.

Mercury Inconjunct Midheaven

It is very important that you develop your mind and your powers of thought, so that you can use them to attain whatever objectives you set for yourself. However, before you can accomplish this, you may have to solve certain problems. You may feel that there is a tension between your natural spontaneous views and what is taught by your parents and other adults. Even though their teachings seem perfectly reasonable, you want to think matters through for yourself. But while you are young, you may not be able to accept your own ideas as valid if they contradict what you have been taught. Yet you cannot simply suppress your own ways of thinking. If you try, you will create tension and probably create a gap between what you are trying to do and what you say. When you are older you may express this tension by making indiscreet remarks that totally get in the way of your objectives.

Recognize this tension within yourself and try to accept the fact that it exists. At the same time you should look for ways to resolve by learning how to think what you want to think and still accomplish your objectives. Just make sure as you get older that you set your own objectives rather than fulfilling other people's expectations for you. Otherwise the problem of tension could get worse, and you could wind up very confused.

It is very important that you remember not to speak impulsively. If you do, it is very likely that you will put your foot in your mouth. Consider what you are going to say and how your words can further your objectives.

Mercury Opposition Midheaven

You will look deep within yourself for answers to the questions that come up in life. Your inner feelings will strongly influence your view of the world, and you will consider your own point of view the most important factor. But try not to get so wrapped up in your own way of seeing the world that you cannot imagine anyone else's point of view. Being too subjective is a serious danger with this aspect. On the other hand, you will be able to communicate your ideas and feelings to others very easily, even while you are quite young.

Your basic attitudes and opinions will take shape very early in life, and later it will be very difficult to change them. So it is very important for you to be exposed to broad and sophisticated views of the world, because you will keep the ideas you learn now, even if they are narrow and intolerant.

You will think about your past a great deal, and you may spend much time wondering if it could have been different. Do not worry about this, because you have only one past, and it is pointless to think about it, except to help you deal with the present. Because you are in touch with your feelings, you can react to a situation according to your real needs, but only if you concentrate on the present and future, not the past.

It may be difficult, but you should examine your thinking and never take your feelings and ideas solely at face value. Probably your beliefs are based on what your parents and family taught you instead of on your own observations.

Chapter Eight

Venus

Venus in the Chart

Venus is the planet of love, and in many ways it comes into its own when you are older and more concerned with the opposite sex. However, even while you are young, Venus is important, because it shows how you get along with people and make friends, and whether you can be warm and affectionate with others. It also indicates creativity and artistic talents. Mercury has to do with creating according to techniques, but Venus indicates your ability to think of forms, to design and to appreciate beauty.

The sign that Venus is in shows how you express your love and other emotions to people in relationships. It tells you something about the kind of people you attract. It also describes your ideas about beauty. The house that Venus is in indicates the area in which you express your artistic talents and the area in which you are likely to experience beauty.

A well-aspected Venus means that you get along with people and are liked by others, making you popular and fun to be with. A badly aspected Venus can mean loneliness and inability to express your feelings. Artistic creativity is more likely if you have one of the more difficult aspects of Venus rather than the easier ones, because the difficult aspects are energetic and must be expressed. However, any kind of ability requires a number of indications in the chart, not merely one or two.

Later in life the placement of Venus in the signs, houses and aspects will tell a great deal about your relationships with the opposite sex.

Venus in Aries

You are very affectionate toward others, but you hate to be tied down by anyone. Not shy or reserved, you express your loving feelings freely, and you need to be free to love whomever you choose. When you are older and have some kind of romantic life, you may have problems in understanding the balance between your own rights and the rights of your loved one in a relationship. You are unwilling to give in to your partner, because you always want things your own way. The price you pay for this may be difficult relations with the opposite sex. While you are young, this could be a problem in your friendships. However, now is the time when you can learn how to give and how to make compromises with friends, relatives and other people.

With others, you often make no special effort to be popular and well-liked. But people usually like you anyway because you are yourself, not because you are charming. If you like someone you meet, you will not hesitate to say so. You are usually the person who starts a friendship or, later, a love relationship. You know what you want, and you are willing to go after it.

Venus in Taurus

You are a very warm person who forms lasting attachments to others. Your affections don't change easily, and even if you lose respect for a friend, you will continue to like that person in spite of his or her faults. The only problem is that you want the friend you are with to pay attention to you alone and not be with anyone else at the same time. You will have to learn to be less possessive.

You are very fond of beautiful things and luxury. You like a good comfortable chair where you can relax and have a delicious snack. But be careful about snacks, for you probably have a sweet tooth, and too many sweets are not good for you. Also you may tend to put on weight. You may even eat too much of foods that are good for you. Try not to indulge yourself so much, not only in eating but also in buying things. In general, you find it difficult to say no to anything you want, and you often justify this by saying you deserve it. You must realize that you will have to work to get the things you desire, even though they seem to come to you a bit more easily than to others. People like you enough so that they are willing to do favors for you, which may strengthen your tendency to be lazy. But you should act for yourself and not depend upon other people.

Venus in Gemini

You like to meet many people and have as many friends as possible, for you love variety. The more people you know, the less bored you are, so you act quite friendly and open and meet people easily. You are quite tolerant of people's faults, because that is just part of the variety you seek in others. You express yourself in a lively way, and others will probably enjoy your humor and interesting wit. You know how to amuse people, because you know what sparks their interest.

This position of Venus means that you will be interested in art and poetry when you are older, although now you may simply be fond of reading light, pleasant stories. You don't like books with heavy, emotional plots. And you are this way about people also. Although you like to know a lot of different people, you are not interested in getting close to them or involved in their lives, because it puts too many responsibilities upon you. Also you don't like people who are very emotional or who let their feelings control their common sense. It may be hard for you to form a deep attachment to someone, and when you are older you will play the field rather than settle down.

Venus in Cancer

You like to be very close to people, and you need to have an especially affectionate relationship with your parents. You always want to be sure that you can count on someone for emotional support. At the same time, you are willing to give the same support to anyone you love. You may not have lots of friendships or love relationships, but you don't need to. All you want is a few very good ones.

If you decide that no one loves you, you may be desperate to find a friend to give you moral support. The only problem here is that if you feel unloved and insecure, you will be very jealous and possessive of your friends, especially if they pay attention to someone else. This may lead to rivalry with your brothers and sisters for your parents' attention, if you feel unsure about your parents' feelings toward you.

Nevertheless, when you like someone, you like them a lot, and you show it. You are a very faithful friend, and you will never do anything to hurt someone you like unless they hurt you first. Then you are very likely to strike back.

Your relationship with your mother will be especially important, and as you get older, it may be hard to break away from her apron strings, although you won't want to admit it. However, if you have a good relationship with her, your other relationships throughout life will also be good.

Venus in Leo

You like people, and people like you as well. You are very loyal to your friends, and once someone has won your friendship, you will stand behind that person, no matter what. However, if your friend does something that you consider dishonest or unworthy, especially to you, you might turn away from him or her. You have a strong sense of fairness and justice, which you insist on in all your relationships, for your love is very strongly mixed with pride.

Another side of this aspect is that you may pick friends who make you look good in some way, people who are well-known or popular. You like to know the people who are at the center of what's happening. But be careful not to overlook those who are equally worthy but not so well known. And don't ignore the bad qualities of your popular friends. However, you are not the sort of person who gets others to act against their will. Your basic sense of fairness comes through even here.

In relationships, you will have to learn to compromise with other people's desires. You cannot have your own way all the time, and as you get older, you will understand the positive aspect of the give and take. Your basic warmth and friendliness will always make you well liked.

Venus in Virgo

You like to do favors for the people you like, because serving is one of the ways that you express love and friendship. You are less selfish than most people of your age, and you find it quite hard to relate to people whom you can't help. The only problem in relationships is that you may believe that people like you for what you do, rather than for what you are. You may underestimate your own worth and not understand why other people like you. Learn to love yourself as well as others.

You like your surroundings to be neat, and your work is both graceful and neat. Your personal habits and the way you dress show this also. This position favors all kinds of craft work, because you have high standards of perfection, but you don't let them over-rule your sense of grace and form.

But you must learn not to reject everything and everyone that does not live up to your high standards of beauty or of duty in relationships. You tend to be very critical of everything that you or others make. And you may be overly critical of your friends.

You have a good sense of discipline. You are careful about what you eat and don't overdo sweets. You won't buy something that is expensive and frivolous, unless you can justify the purchase at a practical level.

Venus in Libra

You are a friendly, outgoing person who likes to have fun with others. You don't like to be alone, because you feel lonely very easily. Fortunately, people usually like you, so you shouldn't have any trouble finding company. However, you should be careful of one problem. In your efforts to get someone to like you, you should be yourself, not what you think the other person is looking for. That is the only way to win someone's respect and make a lasting relationship.

You like beautiful, graceful objects and fine clothing, and even while you are young, you may take an interest in art, music or poetry. You have an excellent sense of proportion and perhaps some artistic talent, if there are other indications of that in your chart. You want everything around you to be graceful, harmonious and stylish. You dress fashionably, but in a way that is more graceful and elegant than others.

You may not enjoy doing hard work, especially if you have to get dirty. But you will have to overcome this as you grow older, because everyone has to meet life's demands. You may try to get others to do your dirty work for you, but this would be a poor use of this energy. Instead, use your talent to make life beautiful for yourself and the people around you.

Venus in Scorpio

Your feelings about people are very intense; you either like them very much or not at all. And you will want to have your loved ones near as much as possible. But be careful of this possessive tendency, because you may alienate the very people whom you want as friends by not giving them enough freedom while they are around you. On the other hand, you are very faithful to those you like if they are loyal to you.

Only deep relationships have any meaning for you. As a result, you are likely to have a few very close friendships rather than lots of shallow ones. Friendships you form now may well last all of your life. You find it somewhat difficult to tell someone that you like him or her, because you are afraid of being rejected or misunderstood. It is hard to put your feelings into words, because they seem so complicated. And it is true that not everyone will understand you and your feelings, but you will just have to accept that. Only those who can understand you will make good friends anyway, and those friends will be enough.

Venus in Sagittarius

You try to be very fair and just with all of your friends, because you want everything about your relationships to be on a high moral plane. You are as fair as possible with everyone you like and very upset when someone is unfair to a friend of yours. Yet you are tolerant of other people's weaknesses. You prefer to base your opinion of someone on his or her overall personality, ignoring little faults. However, if a friend breaks an important rule, you may end the friendship on the spot.

You are usually very friendly and quite outgoing. You don't hide your feelings for others, for you are open about your emotions. People will probably like this in you, and you should have many friends. However, you do not like possessive people or those who use friendship to tie you down. You want to be free to be friendly with anyone without your friends saying no. Later in life, you may have difficulty settling down to a single relationship with someone of the opposite sex.

You are fond of nature and the outdoors and may study a subject such as botany, geology or bird life just for pleasure. You like natural themes in art, and art and music that is large and impressive.

Venus in Capricorn

You keep your feelings under control, and at times you may find it difficult to make friends. This is because you express your feelings more seriously than most people your age. For this reason, you may prefer being with older people or people who can teach you about how to get along in the world. You very much need to respect the people you like. However, make sure that your relationships are not based solely on what others can do for you, because sometimes people with this placement of Venus use friendship and love to get ahead in the world. If you use your friends in this way, you won't learn what love and friendship are really about.

You are not self-indulgent and you can control your desires quite well, so you are not likely to waste money or other resources. You will plan very carefully how to be rather thrifty. Your eating and drinking habits will also be moderate; in fact, you are at your best doing everything in moderation. And you don't especially like people who go overboard, particularly in expressing their feelings.

Venus in Aquarius

You are friendly with people but sometimes find it difficult to form close relationships. You are afraid that you will lose your freedom if you become too closely attached to others. You prefer friends who are somehow exciting and different, and especially as you get older, you may become involved with people who are considered odd by the rest of society.

You enjoy being popular, as long as you don't have to give up being yourself, and you work well with other people in group projects and team efforts. You understand immediately what is good for the group and can adjust your own goals to fit. But if your goals are too different from the group's, you will join another group.

As you get older and become involved with the opposite sex, you will look for interesting or unusual partners. You will seek out free, nonbinding relationships that may be quite unusual, although not very stable. When a relationship loses its excitement, you are likely to look elsewhere.

Venus in Pisces

A dreamy and fanciful person, you like books that appeal to your romantic sense of adventure, stories set in weird fairylands with beautiful princesses and dashing heroes. Often your private fantasies seem much more interesting and beautiful than reality, but you will have to learn to deal with the real world, too. While you are young, you should develop enough discipline to stay in touch with reality when your dreams are more appealing. The positive side of this is that you have a very creative imagination, which would be very useful in any kind of artistic work or design. If you can learn to communicate the visions in your mind to other people, you may become a creative artist or writer.

You are very unselfish toward the people you like. You want what is best for them and will give of yourself whenever a friend needs help, for helping others makes you feel much better about yourself. Your sensitivity may limit you to friends who are rather quiet or who do not attack your beliefs. However, you can genuinely love people, and others will respect this in you. Your only problem is that you may pour out a great deal of energy and attention on people who are not really worth it. That thought never seems to cross your mind, but it would be good to be a little more careful about choosing your friends and those whom you work hard to help.

Venus in the First House

This is a very favorable position because it enables you to make a good impression on others and to be liked. Even while you are young, you know how to charm people and be agreeable. You concentrate a great deal on your appearance, because you hate to look sloppy or unattractive. For the same reason, you surround yourself with attractive possessions, to keep beauty and grace around you as much as possible. Depending on other factors in your chart, you may develop some artistic talent, which will be furthered by your sense of form and design.

In many cases this placement indicates that you are physically attractive and will stay young-looking even as you get older. Even if you are not especially beautiful or handsome, your physical appearance has a softness that others will find attractive.

You work very hard to get along with others, and you usually try to win arguments with diplomacy and tact rather than force. In general, force is not your way; instead you try to get what you want with coaxing and even flattery. While this can be a very useful tool, you should avoid relying on it too much. You must learn to be self-assertive when necessary and to stand up for your own rights, forcefully if need be. Otherwise people may think that you are weak and pliable, and they will not have much respect for you. You can give the world much beauty, and you will present it most effectively if you learn to combine charm with strength.

Venus in the Second House

You like to own beautiful things and be surrounded by comfort and luxury. As a result, money runs through your fingers, because when you see something you want, you buy it. You may even borrow money in order to buy things, so you may be in debt to others all the time. This is not a great problem now, but when you are an adult you could get over your head in debts. Besides, now is the time when you should form good habits of spending and saving.

On the positive side, if you learn to have good taste and good sense, you will buy only things that are worth the price. You won't lose money on good investments, although that won't become clear until you are older. For example, you might collect art that will increase in value.

Try not to give in to every desire and whim. You are inclined to be self-indulgent, and you may buy things on the spur of the moment that you really won't want in the long run. Also you enjoy food, and you may find it hard not to overeat.

Venus in the Third House

You like to have beauty in your immediate surroundings and even while you are young, you may take a strong interest in the arts, theater or literature. You may already have learned that you have writing ability. But even if you don't have artistic ability, you will always derive great pleasure from being with artistic people.

You may develop an ability to put your thoughts into words with much grace and elegance. You do not like harshness and ugliness in other people's language, and you work to erase it from your own. You may learn how to charm and flatter others, but try not to rely on this ability too much to get ahead. People eventually learn to distrust flatterers, and you should try to be honest even while saying nice things.

You have a good sense of form and color, and in choosing clothing, furniture or decoration you know what goes together. Even with ideas and opinions, you are more likely to make judgments according to ideals of form, grace and elegance than by strict logic.

If you have brothers or sisters, you are probably very close to them and to your other relatives as well, for their love is very important to you. Also you enjoy making friends and talking with people in your neighborhood. You like to feel that there is a great deal of love in your everyday surroundings.

Venus in the Fourth House

You like your surroundings to be comfortable, pleasant, elegant and gracious. You find it very difficult to put up with ugliness and dirt, and if you have to put up with such conditions for long, you get quite depressed. This is not to say that you are always neat, but you never let disorder become real dirtiness. As you get older you may collect art or other objects to beautify your home. Your taste may be quite unusual, but others will agree that you have good taste.

Being loved by your parents is more important to you than to others. Probably you will receive all the warmth and affection that you need from them, and your memories of childhood will be very warm. But if your relationship with either or both of your parents is difficult, you will be more hurt psychologically than most people would. Bad relations with your parents would be especially damaging to your ability to get along with the opposite sex, which should otherwise be very good.

As you get older, you will remember the pleasant times in the past and tend to forget anything that was difficult. Just be careful not to idealize the past, for that would prevent you from living in the present and future.

Venus in the Fifth House

You enjoy amusements and pleasant times, especially if you don't have to use a lot of physical energy. You like activities in which you can indulge your senses and feel good. As you get older, you will be unusually attracted to the opposite sex, and in any kind of pleasurable activity, you will probably prefer to be with persons of the opposite sex.

If other areas of your chart indicate artistic ability, this placement can help you express yourself artistically. Even if you do not have any artistic ability, you appreciate other people's work, and you enjoy art and music as leisure activities. Your tastes tend toward the elegant and beautiful, however, and you will not be attracted to artistic themes that are turbulent, ugly or tragic.

Unless some other element in your chart counteracts this, you may be lazy and self-indulgent, caring more about your own pleasure than about doing anything that requires some effort but provides long-lasting rewards. Also you may be inclined to indulge yourself by eating or drinking too much.

Venus in the Sixth House

This placement of Venus is usually a sign of such good health that you may even be able to abuse your body somewhat and still stay healthy. If you do have problems, they will probably come from eating too much or from too much sugar.

You like to do favors for those you love. You feel that love is a kind of service, and the more you can do for someone you like, the better you feel about it. However, you may not find it so easy to accept favors from your loved ones in return, because you are more comfortable in the role of the giver. If your chart shows difficult aspects to Venus, you may feel that you are unworthy of being liked by others. In that case, you should try very hard to find out in what ways you are good, likable and worthy. Only when you know that you are likable can you accept being liked by others. Until then you may feel lonely and unloved, but remember that your real problem isn't that you aren't liked but that you are unaware of other people's affections.

This placement can mean that as you get older you will choose a career in an area ruled by Venus, such as entertainment, arts or crafts, counseling, or work involving beauty or recreation. You are likely to be creative, and your work should give you some outlet for your creativity.

Venus in the Seventh House

This placement will affect you more strongly when you are older and more involved with the opposite sex. You love to be with persons of the opposite sex, and you will always want to have a steady relationship that gives you a sense of being more complete than you are by yourself.

Even while you are young, you like to be with other people and to work with others rather than alone. You always try to smooth over difficulties between people, and you may even be thought of as a peacemaker. You are far more concerned with harmony than with getting your own way. That is very useful, but you should learn that in some situations you must stand up for your rights in no uncertain terms. You cannot always give in for the sake of peace, because that will take away from your integrity.

You like to be with people who are graceful and attractive or artistic and creative. When you are older, you may marry someone who has these qualities. You yourself are quite a loving and graceful person, but in a relationship you like to experience this through a loving partner. Unless there are very strong indications to the contrary in your chart, you should be generally well liked and not have any real enemies.

Venus in the Eighth House

You enjoy your senses, and you want to experience the world as vividly and totally as possible. You seem to be looking for a hidden dimension of the world that will transform your life completely. Often you will seek this dimension through relationships with others, which will be very intense and full of feeling. For this reason you don't have many casual friendships, and as you get older, your relationships with the opposite sex will be most intense. You want to make every encounter into a meeting between the basic elements of two souls.

Be careful not to be too possessive of your friends, and don't try to control what they do, for they will probably resent it. Also, you shouldn't choose your friends according to the advantages you will gain from their friendship. But even if you do make friends for your own gain, when you get what you want, you are willing to share it with others. You feel that you can do more with your possessions and money by sharing them than you could by yourself.

While you are young, you should begin to take care of your health by not eating or drinking too much and by getting plenty of physical exercise. Indulging too much in Venus's love of fun and pleasure could damage your health in later years, if you do not begin to be careful now.

Venus in the Ninth House

You enjoy any activity that allows you to enlarge your experience. You enjoy traveling to new and different places and learning about ways of thinking that are different from what you know. You may take an interest in art and beautiful objects, especially those that are unusual and different.

This placement influences your way of looking at the world. You like to relate ideas and concepts to each other through a sense of harmony, because they seem to belong together rather than because they are connected logically. For example, the logic of mathematics seems dull and lifeless to you. Although you can understand how it works easily enough, you don't see the point in it. You are attracted only to those ways of thinking that involve human feeling, so you will be much happier with literature, poetry and art than with science and mathematics. For you, beauty is a basic part of the world as it should be, and you can't understand people who do something just because it is useful, with no thought of beauty or art.

Venus in the Tenth House

This usually means that you have a warm relationship with your father, or with your mother if she has taken a fatherly role in your life. In either case, that parent teaches you about the world in such a warm and loving manner that you learn to think of the world as beautiful and friendly. You see it as a place where you can live and enjoy yourself, rather than as a set of obstacles that have to be overcome.

However, if you have difficult aspects to Venus in this house, you may feel frustrated by the world, so that you look endlessly for the beauty that you believe is there but can't find. To feel good about the world, you very much need your parents' support.

When you are older, the career you choose is likely to reflect your lighthearted feeling about the world. You will probably be attracted to entertainment or the arts. If you are a more serious person, your career may involve working with people in some way, such as some kind of counseling or even diplomacy. You should be good at that, for you have the makings of a natural diplomat, particularly if it aids your purpose.

Venus in the Eleventh House

You are a very sociable person who really enjoys good company and good times. When you are alone, you start feeling lonely quite quickly. At the same time you get along very well with others. You are at your best in a group, and you are an excellent team player in any activity you get involved in, whether it is sports or work projects. Your concern with getting along makes you put the interests of the group above your own interests, although you usually feel that they are the same.

You like to be with friends who are warm and sociable. Serious people and those who do not know how to have fun seem boring. But you may be attracted to people who are very creative artistically, and such people can be serious in your eyes without being dull. When you are an adult, your friends may include artists, musicians or writers.

Whoever your friends are, you are likely to enjoy them. Throughout your life, friendship should be a source of pleasure and fun, unless Venus is very badly aspected.

Venus in the Twelfth House

You are likely to be rather shy and reserved about showing your loving feelings. It is not that you are unaffectionate, for you can be quite friendly and loving to others if you trust them. You probably are afraid that people will reject you if you make the first move. So you wait for the other person to show that he or she likes you before you are willing to show that you like them as well. But shyness can keep you from having many rewarding relationships, because you won't be able to get to know others who are shy like yourself. And they may be the only people who can really understand your sensitivity. Try to be a little more outgoing, so that you can start friendships with people you are attracted to. Also you must learn not to take it too personally if someone does reject you. The fact that someone does not like you may have more to do with that person than with you.

On the plus side, this placement means that you can be very giving toward the people you love. Once you have decided that you like and trust a person, you will do anything for him or her. At times you may even give in when you should stand up for your own beliefs, in order, so you think, to maintain the friendship. But except for that possible problem, your relationships with others should be quite good and rewarding. Because you are willing to give, you will probably get as well.

Venus Conjunct Mars

You have very strong emotions and a great need to give and receive affection from others. Your emotions are so intense that you can't take your relations with others lightly; you form either a very strong friendship with someone or none at all. And in all your relationships, with friends or family, your emotions are likely to be more extreme than other people's. When you are angry with a loved one, you are very angry, but when you feel loving, you are very affectionate. Also, you are very concerned about how well your friends get along with each other.

Sometimes you may be unsure whether to assert yourself, give way to the other person's demands, or compromise, although that can be the most difficult choice of the three. Much of the time you may be very demanding of those you love, insisting that they give you, and you alone, a great deal of love and attention. But when you realize that your demands will probably drive the other person away, you will give in.

Your relationship with your parent of the opposite sex is very important in your development. The patterns of your relationship with that parent will be the basis of your relations with persons of the opposite sex as you get older. Unfortunately this aspect often means that you have mixed love-hate feelings for that parent. If that is the case, you will run the risk, as an adult, of being drawn to people whom you know are not very good for you, but who fascinate you.

Venus Sextile Mars

You get along well with others, and you enjoy having many friends. Your friends like you as well, because you make everyone feel good without flattering them and without compromising your beliefs and what you want in life. That is, you are yourself in a way that creates respect and affection, but not conflict. You have a lively approach to life in that you really throw yourself into each new experience. You do not like to do anything halfway, and this energetic approach will fascinate and charm others.

It is quite likely that you will take an early interest in persons of the opposite sex and that they will be interested in you. As a teenager and later, you should be very popular, because you are warm and friendly, and you make the people around you feel good. Your relationships with the opposite sex will be quite intense, and once you start having such relationships, you will always be involved in one affair or another. But you will not be attracted to people who do not share your love of intense experience or who seem afraid of life. Your own vital energies would not stand for that. For this reason, it is important even now to find friends who are as energetic as yourself and who like to maintain the same vigorous pace. You would find less active people quite frustrating.

Venus Square Mars

This aspect indicates that your feeling are very intense, particularly in relationships. It is difficult for you to like someone only a little bit. Either you like a person completely, or you are indifferent or unfriendly to them. And in all your relationships, your feelings are a mixture of love and hate, which can come out as intense anger toward those you love the most, if you have any differences of opinion. However, if you release your anger in an out-and-out fight, you quickly get over it and go back to really liking the other person.

It is very important for you to have a warm and secure relationship with your parent of the opposite sex, especially if you are a girl, although this is true of boys as well. A difficult relationship with that parent will lead to stormy relationships with persons of the opposite sex later on. The problem is that you cannot imagine love without hate and conflict, so you will try to bring those two extremes together in your later love life. There is nothing especially wrong in that, except that it becomes difficult to have long and deep relationships. Either you or your partner will get tired of the emotional and physical bruises and will leave. At worst, your later relationships may involve physical violence, but only if that is a problem in your present relationship with your father, if you are a girl, or with your mother, if you are a boy.

But if that relationship is secure, this simply indicates that you have an intense and passionate nature, and you will become involved with the opposite sex at an early age.

Venus Trine Mars

You have an enthusiasm for life that others will find inspiring and catching. You like to be with others and have good times, but you do not suppress your real self in order to do so. People will like you for being yourself, so you will attract people all your life.

Often this aspect indicates a strong creative drive, although it does not necessarily mean that you have any artistic ability. Creativity is not limited to art, so you should try to find another area in which you can be creative and bring about something that did not exist before. You will feel fulfilled and complete only when you are involved in creating something.

Your passionately intense approach to life may not be clearwhile you are young, but it will show up as you get older, especially when you begin having relationships with the opposite sex. For you, such affairs will not be casual, although you may have opportunities for that, but will be intense and total encounters. Even your friendships will be like that. You need to feel any kind of love totally. People who aren't so committed will not interest you.

Venus Inconjunct Mars

You must learn to control your emotions to some extent, so that your feelings do not prevent you from getting along with others. It is difficult for you to react to someone without emotions, for you tend to either love or hate people quite intensely. Your feelings are often mixed, even toward your friends. One moment you love your friend, and the next moment you hate him or her. Any little problem can set off your anger against someone, but you usually cool off quickly also. Your close relationships will be a bit stormier than most, but this should not be a serious problem in later life. In fact you probably prefer stormy relationships, because it means that you are really involved with the other person.

When you are older, this aspect will be most important in your relationships with the opposite sex, which you will become strongly involved in. For this reason, your relationship with your parent of the opposite sex will be very important, because the patterns you establish with that parent will continue in later sexual relationships. If you have a lot of problems with your father if you are a girl, or with your mother if you are a boy, you won't be able to have smooth relationships with the opposite sex until you can solve those problems.

While you are young, as well as later, you may be attracted to persons who, if you think rationally about it, do not seem very well suited to you. This problem will be greatest if you do not feel good about yourself, for it is a reflection of your own inner turmoil about love and your right to be loved.

Venus Opposition Mars

You have an intense emotional nature, which will affect your relations with others quite a bit. Often your feelings about people are a mixture of love and hate, so that you are uncertain about how you feel. Many times you will have real fights with those you like most, and then you will make up in a very emotional way. As you get older this will happen even more. If you don't care strongly for someone, you won't have this problem, but you will find the relationship boring and quickly lose interest in it.

You need to be around people who understand you and are willing to let you blow off steam a bit. They should recognize that your frequent blow-ups mean that you are very emotionally involved, with love as well as anger, and they should know that you get over your anger very quickly. At least you let everyone know how you feel, both positively and negatively, and you show that your feelings are quite strong.

When you are older, your relations with persons of the opposite sex will often be stormy, because of your mixed feelings of love and hate. Sometimes, however, you may feel quite serene and peaceful about a relationship, but you will attract someone who has strong love-hate feelings, as described above. You attract such persons because you have these traits within you, even though they may not have surfaced.

If your relationship with your parent of the opposite sex has been difficult or stormy, it will be even more difficult to attract people who are good for you. And if there has been any physical violence in your relationship with that parent, you are likely to have similar problems in sexual relationships. Your parent should use psychological, rather than physical, discipline.

Venus Conjunct Jupiter

This is an extremely positive aspect in most ways. It indicates that you are warm, generous and affectionate, and you enjoy receiving affection from others as well. You are faithful to your friends and loved ones, for you understand that liking people gives you a responsibility to do what is right by them. You don't think of this as a burden, but as part of being with people, which you enjoy. You are very social and enjoy parties and good times. Being with others, either singly or in groups, brings out the best in you. You seem to inspire other people and raise their spirits.

You attract other people, but you also attract material goods. This aspect traditionally means that you will have money, although it doesn't guarantee wealth. Instead, you will have whatever you need when you need it. You may very well feel that you don't need much in material goods, because you have a basic inner satisfaction. It must be said, however, that most people with this aspect enjoy comfort and the good things of life, so they like to have enough money to buy them.

The only negative side of-this aspect is that you may not have much self-discipline. You usually try to get whatever you want, even if it is not the best thing for you. But you won't hurt anyone else just to get something, for you are too good-natured for that. But you do like luxury and good food, and you may be lazy or gain weight.

Venus Sextile Jupiter

You are very sociable and enjoy being with friends, and you probably have many of them. You want to spread your feelings of warmth and affection around as much as possible. In fact you share whatever you have with those you love, even when you don't have much. But you do enjoy luxury and comfort whenever they are available. This aspect does not make you a very hard worker, for you prefer to take life easy. You may feel that hard work just isn't worth it, especially because you are often able to charm people into giving you what you want. This does not mean that you are a scheming person, however. You really are warm, and your affection is not phony.

You are quite loyal to your friends, for you believe in being fair to the people you like. As an adult, you will also be fair in your relationships with the opposite sex. You are willing to overlook faults in your loved ones, because you feel that people's faults are not as important as their strengths, so you concentrate on each person's good points. You try to help your friends whenever possible by making them feel better and supporting them in whatever they do.

Your outlook on life is positive, and you won't let yourself get dragged down easily. You are always able to see the bright side of a situation, and you concentrate on that.

Venus Square Jupiter

For most people this is a very positive aspect, but it can present a few problems. On the positive side, you are optimistic, and you love company and good times. A warm and sociable person, you like to make the people around you feel good. Others will generally like you and enjoy your friendship.

However, you need more self-discipline, because you often overdo whatever you enjoy. You may eat too much, or you may spend so much time having fun that you don't get anything done. And often no one will push you to work, because you charm them out of it. And if someone does put the pressure on, it rolls right off your back, because you are not easily stung by criticism. Nevertheless, you will have to learn to cope with the serious side of life. Don't waste all your time on silly and meaningless activities that build nothing for the future. Your optimism is justified, for you can get whatever you want out of life, but you will have to work for it like anyone else.

On the whole, if you learn to put some effort into working, this can be a very positive aspect. You are pleasant to be around and a positive influence on others.

In some cases this aspect means that you have some creative talent, and if you are willing to discipline yourself and develop your talent, you can probably earn your living by it.

Venus Trine Jupiter

This is one of the easiest and most pleasant of all aspects. It indicates that you are a warm and friendly person who can love and show affection for others. You are fond of parties and good times, and you enjoy being comfortable and surrounded by beauty and elegance whenever possible.

However, this aspect is not limited to a love of comfort. You treat the people you like very well, and you are willing to share everything you have with them. You are very loyal to your friends and always try to treat them fairly. This trait will win you the respect and love of many people, and you will receive the good things of life in abundance.

As you get older, you will set very high standards of behavior for yourself in relationships. Honor and integrity are very important to you, and you always try to be honest with your loved ones. The spiritual side to love is as important to you as the physical and emotional aspects of love.

If your chart has any other indications of creativity, this aspect may give you creative ability in one of the fine arts or crafts. You may even make your living in some artistic field.

Venus Inconjunct Jupiter

This can be a positive aspect if you learn to control some of its negative possibilities. You are likely to lack energy and to be rather passive. You may wait for opportunities to come to you, rather than go after them. You may not have enough energy to pursue your ambitions, or you may not have much ambition. Or you may love your comfort so much that you are unwilling to make any effort or put up with any pain that could help you grow and develop. However, if there are any indications of energy in your chart, they should overcome the passivity.

On the plus side, you need love and affection, and you can usually be very warm and affectionate as well. However, it is very important that you choose your close friends carefully, because you may attract people who are difficult to get along with, who order you around or act as if they are better than you. Avoid such people, for they will do you no good.

If you do associate with difficult people, you may be unable to live up to your own standards of behavior. You may do things that you usually wouldn't approve of, because somehow the relationship weakens your resolve to do what is right. But this won't happen if you choose your friends carefully and avoid people who are not good for you.

Venus Opposition Jupiter

You really enjoy the good life and the company of others. This aspect usually indicates that people like you, because you are so positive, optimistic and cheerful. Also you are willing to share whatever you have with others. Other people enjoy your high spirits and energy, although they may not respect you very much. This is because you don't always show good sense in your good times, and you often do not know when to stop. In a difficult situation, you tend to choose the pleasant way out rather than the best way. Also you may be wasteful and spend money even when you cannot afford to.

The only thing that stands between you and total success in life is the need to be more disciplined and restrained. You have the ability to handle people well, if you choose, and you can make yourself liked. But if you waste your time now, you will regret it when you are older. It is your nature to enjoy doing things on a grand scale, but make sure you really have the means to carry out your plans.

This aspect also means that you are warm and affectionate to those you like, but you do not want to be tied down by anyone. This will be more important in relationships with the opposite sex when you are older. Unless someone can continually show you sides of life that you have never seen before and challenge you in a positive way, you lose interest in a relationship with that person.

Venus Conjunct Saturn

This aspect usually means that you don't feel that it is proper to show affection very openly. You feel affectionate, but you don't show it outwardly. Unfortunately, you may think that you are unworthy of being loved, so you hold your feelings in to keep from being hurt by someone who rejects you. It is very important for your growth that your parents be very loving and warm. Even so, you will probably be rather restrained about expressing love, but at least you won't feel that you are not worthy of being loved.

This aspect usually means that you are more serious than other people of your age. It is hard for you to let go and just have a good time. You are quiet, restrained and rather shy, and you may prefer being with older people. Later, when you have relationships with the opposite sex, this pattern may cause you to seek out older persons, as if you are looking for a parent figure.

It is clear that you need a lot of emotional support from your friends to bring out the best aspects of your character. You can be a more steady and reliable friend than most, and you will always be loyal to the people you trust. You may not have many friends and loved ones, but you will always be close to those you have.

Venus Sextile Saturn

You may not have a great many friends, but the ones you do have will be reliable and long-lasting. You are willing to give up some excitement in your relationships for the sake of having friends whom you can count upon. You do not like anyone who doesn't take life seriously or who doesn't seem responsible. Often your preference for serious people means that your friends will be older than yourself. Sometimes, in fact, you are so serious that you find it hard to let go and have a good time.

You are not as outwardly affectionate as others, but you are reliable and steady in your feelings. When you are older, you will probably have only a few relationships with the opposite sex, but those few will be enduring and dependable. Here again you will choose people you can trust, who will always be there when you need them. And you will be just as loyal to your partner. In fact, a married person with this aspect is unusually willing to work hard and make a strong effort to save a difficult marriage. With this aspect, you consider duty as important as love in a relationship. Also your love relationships may be based on practical considerations as much as on romance.

Venus Square Saturn

This aspect is often difficult to handle in that the demands of the world always seem to get in the way of having fun and receiving love and affection from others. You often feel that persons or circumstances are forcing you to do things that you do not want to do. If this happens too often while you are young, you may become cold and indifferent toward the world. This is because it is easier to be detached from people than to have your needs constantly denied. However, you are less likely to be such a cold person if your parents give you plenty of emotional support.

Sometimes this aspect means that you feel lonely, usually because you believe you are not worthy of love. That is not true, but once this idea is fixed in your mind, it is difficult for anyone to talk you out of it. When you are older, you should be aware that your problems in relationships with the opposite sex occur because you feel unlovable, not because you really are.

You may suffer from extreme shyness, because you are afraid of being rejected. You may have difficulty expressing your feelings to the people you like, so they may pass through your life without ever knowing how you feel about them. You must learn not to worry so much about being rejected. Some people will not like you no matter how nice you are, and it does not mean that there is anything wrong with you. That is just the way it is. More than anything else, you need to have confidence in yourself.

Venus Trine Saturn

You are reserved about showing your affections and not very demonstrative. But once you decide that a person is worthwhile, you are totally loyal and loving. You may not have many friends, but the ones you do have will be very long-lasting, especially as you get older. You are more serious than most people your age, and in some ways you seem older than you are. You are attracted to people who take life seriously. As you grow up, you will realize that every relationship must make a balance between romantic attraction and practical considerations. Even while you are young, you will understand that romance alone cannot support a shaky relationship. But once you commit yourself to someone, you are more willing than most to put an effort into saving your relationship.

Sometimes you find it difficult to have fun, especially with other people. In fact, being in a large group makes you feel alone, rather than with company. You are best in a one-to-one relationship with someone. At times you may feel that you are not a very exciting person, that others prefer to be with someone else, especially at parties. You feel this most strongly when you are with a real "life of the party" person. However, those who know you well understand that there is much good in you and that you can provide a deeper and more intense relationship than most. This aspect will be easier to live with when you are older. While you are young the more difficult side seems to dominate.

Venus Inconjunct Saturn

You need and want love, but you may not be able to get it easily. You may feel that your parents, teachers or other persons in authority make demands on you that you must fulfill before they will give you any love and support. If that is true, it is unfortunate, because you deserve respect and love as much as anyone. Although everyone must fulfill certain social demands, this should not be the condition for being loved. If this demand is carried to an extreme in your case, you will become cold-hearted and unable to love others even when you want to. You may also feel that you cannot indulge yourself in any pleasure or even love. When you are older, you may feel that duty and ambition must come before love and human relationships. Unfortunately, if you follow that path, you will become very lonely, and when you realize that you belong to no one and nothing, you will go through a spiritual crisis.

This aspect means that your family may make you feel that you are unworthy of love. Unless you are given a great deal of love while you are young, you will be attracted to cold and unfeeling people when you are an adult. Such people are an outward expression of your inner feeling of unworthiness.

Even without any pressure, you are likely to be more disciplined than most people your age. You don't go overboard in anything, and you feel strongly that your worth depends on what you do and how much you accomplish.

Venus Opposition Saturn

This aspect can mean that you feel extremely lonely and can't seem to get across to other people. Often the outer world seems like a cold and forbidding place that makes great demands but offers little in return. You may feel unworthy of love and affection and unknowingly attract people who make you feel this way even more. If you feel unworthy of being loved, don't ask what is wrong with you, but what kind of people you are attracting. You are unable to see that there are people who love you. Or do you take criticism more seriously than praise? The problem is your view of yourself, not what you really are.

Of course, with this aspect you may be a real loner, someone who truly prefers being alone. If you are this way, you probably won't understand it until you are older. But don't condemn yourself for wanting to be alone and feeling uneasy with others. It is very important for you to get to know yourself very well, so that you can get a better perspective on the negative opinions of critical people whom you may attract.

You will have to work very hard on relationships in general, but you must also get over the feeling that they are nothing but work. Not all relationships are serious and heavy. Look for the lighter side, which is what makes many relationships worthwhile.

Venus Conjunct Uranus

Although you are affectionate and enjoy being loved, you want to be free, emotionally and otherwise. You want to be free to choose your friends and not be tied down by those you love. This is important, because often the friends you choose are quite unusual, at least as your parents see them. You want to be with people who are exciting and stimulating, who can take you away from the normal daily routine.

This aspect is usually more important when you are older. Now it is important to understand that you need freedom in all kinds of relationships. You must learn to understand your other needs also, because otherwise you will have difficulty with relationships with the opposite sex when you are older. The first point is to recognize that it is all right to not want to be tied down. Don't let anyone make you feel guilty because you want to do your own thing, for you allow others the same freedom.

Also, the fact that you want to have exciting people for friends may mean that your relationships will be rather unstable. After all, the best people for you to be with are people like yourself. Have the courage to live by your own rules in a relationship, but also make sure that the other person understands and accepts those rules. If they cannot accept your rules, you may have to find some new friends. Being alone a lot may be the price you pay for your independence. But if you look for people who understand and fit in with your needs, and if you can fit in with theirs as well, you should be quite happy with your friends and loved ones.

Venus Sextile Uranus

You like to be with interesting people, and some of your friends may be quite unusual. Ordinary people bore you very quickly. You need to find friends who fill your own unique needs, and you also need to be free in your relationships.

You are not possessive of your friends. In fact, you enjoy having your friends around, because you like being with many different types of people. You don't demand that people pay constant attention to you, and you won't let anyone else demand your constant attention. If there is anything you cannot stand, it is possessiveness and jealousy among friends.

You may have unusual creative powers also, although this aspect by itself does not indicate artistic ability. However, if you are creative, your designs will be unusual in style and form. Also your tastes in decoration and personal style—clothing and jewelry—will be unique. While you are young, others may think you are odd, but as you get older, your particular style will look good, because it is your very own. Now, however, your parents may give you a lot of trouble about this matter because they want you to look more conventional.

When you are an adult, your relations with the opposite sex will also be unconventional, for you will insist on freedom to create unique relationships. If you have the courage to act out your own style in relationships, they should be quite happy ones.

Venus Square Uranus

Your close personal relationships may be changeable and unstable in that they form and break up quite rapidly. Even while you are young, you are very independent and prefer not to become involved in a close, committed friendship. Or you may attract friends who are rather unusual or very exciting. You want to avoid relationships with people who are dull and conventional. When you choose, you can be quite charming to others, but only on your own terms. As you get older, you may be able to use this charm to advantage by becoming a very interesting and exciting person whom others enjoy being with. Certainly it is better to express your desire for freedom than to make commitments that you cannot keep.

Unfortunately, with this aspect you may be unable to accept your need to be free. We are taught that it is important to feel close and loving toward people, but you may feel smothered by such attitudes. In this case you may attract unreliable people who eventually leave you or break the agreement between you. This effect is especially likely to show up in your sexual relationships when you are grown up. But if you accept your need for freedom and limit your close relationships to those who can understand it also, you will attract people who are similarly inclined. Or you will discover that you can be close and friendly with someone and still have freedom, as long as you give each other enough room to be yourselves.

Venus Trine Uranus

You like to be with people, but on your own terms. You don't want friends who constantly make demands in the name of friendship or love. You are not jealous or possessive of your friends, and you ask that they have the same attitude.

You prefer to be with people who are exciting and different. An ordinary, routine relationship eventually bores you, although you can have a lasting friendship with someone, as long as he or she is an unusual person. This element of your personality will be much more important in relationships with the opposite sex when you are older. Now your friendships are likely to change a lot, anyhow, simply because you are growing and need different types of relationships to meet your emotional needs.

You may be quite creative, but in a style that is very unusual and distinctly your own. You are not one who takes familiar paths when you create. You like to experiment with unusual media and techniques, and you can see possibilities that others cannot.

The main idea that you have to accept is that not everyone can fill your needs. Many people will simply seem too dull for you. And if you like to be at peace in your personal life, which is entirely possible, even with this aspect, your relationships may occasionally be unsettling. But if you look for the kind of people you really need, your relationships will be very satisfying.

Venus Inconjunct Uranus

You feel mixed up about whether you want to be close to others or be free. When you are really close to a loved one, you feel smothered and want to get away by yourself to do what you want. But when you are alone and free to do what you want, you miss your loved ones and want to be with them. It will take you several years to understand yourself enough so that you can strike a balance between these two needs, so be patient.

Your uncertainty about love and freedom will be even greater if one of your parents doesn't seem to really love you steadily, if you feel you cannot count on that parent when you need help. This would make you feel that love is somehow unreliable, that you cannot depend on anyone who loves you. As a result, you won't permit anyone to depend on you either.

This belief may make you irresponsible in relationships, so that you won't fulfill people's expectations even when you have agreed to do so. Don't promise love that you cannot deliver. While you are young this is not a great problem, but when you are older, you will hurt your partner in a relationship by not being dependable or by not being honest about your dependability. You may tell yourself that you want a steady love relationship, but then go after someone whom you know intuitively will not be reliable. But if you are honest about your need for freedom, this will not happen.

Venus Opposition Uranus

It is difficult for you to form close attachments with others, because you quickly begin to feel confined in a relationship, and you want to get away. The exception to this is when the other person is very unusual or even slightly crazy according to ordinary standards. Then you get so caught up in the offbeat nature of the relationship that you forget to feel trapped. But such relationships are not very stable, unfortunately.

While you are young this pattern is not very important, but the basic tendencies of this aspect are clear even now. You have to be shown that having friends can be fun and interesting and that deep emotional relationships can be very rewarding. The problem is that probably you have learned from experience that relationships are often stifling, unrewarding and full of tiresome duties. You won't be pressured into friendship.

However, it is possible for you to have very good relationships, if you look for people who are like yourself. Unfortunately, with this aspect you may want freedom for yourself but are unwilling to give your partner the same freedom. You cannot do this if you want to be happy with others.

Sometimes in relationships with the opposite sex, when you are older, you will attract a very unreliable person who leaves you suddenly, even though you think you don't want that. But inside, you secretly don't want to be tied down, so you unconsciously attract a person who is sure to leave you.

Venus Conjunct Neptune

You are a dreamer and an idealist who is always looking for something or someone to idealize. At best this trait can be the source of much creative activity; at worst, it can bring you heartbreak and disappointment, because each new loved one proves to be less than ideal. Also you may idealize your own capacity to love. You may believe that if you love someone, you must do everything for that person and ask little or nothing in return. If you have any negative feelings that interfere with the "purity" of your love, you feel unworthy and disappointed with yourself. Remember, people who have a good relationship help each other about equally. It should be a two-way street.

Your basic problem is to accept reality as it is, not as you would like it to be. Accept people as they are and look for their own beauty rather than the beauty you want to see. Even more important, accept yourself the same way. Recognize that you have real needs, which must be fulfilled as much as anyone else's. Once you understand that, you can use your creativity to good advantage.

This aspect means that you have a great love of beauty, and if other elements of your chart reinforce it, some artistic ability. Certainly you will appreciate art, even if you don't have talent yourself. You are able to bring into being the products of your imagination and make them real, but only if you understand what is real and what is not real. This is why you need to have a very clear understanding of reality.

Venus Sextile Neptune

This aspect indicates that you have a romantic imagination and possibly some artistic creativity. You certainly have enough imagination and ability to understand beauty and create art. But you will have to learn to master a specific craft, such as painting, sculpture, writing or music, in order to use this energy. It will not happen by itself.

You enjoy playing with beautiful fantasies, making up secret places and creating imaginary worlds. But you are not cut off from the real world. In your relationships with others, you are very sensitive and compassionate. Even while you are young, you can easily put yourself in another person's position and understand the feelings of those who are less fortunate. At times in your life, you may put a great deal of effort into working with underprivileged or downtrodden people. You may even get involved in close personal relationships with troubled people in order to help them out. This is perfectly all right if you can see these people as they really are, not as some beautiful image in your mind. You can help people only if you accept their true nature.

You are very idealistic, and your goals are likely to be quite unselfish. Again, all you need to do is accept life as it is, so that you can create greater beauty in the real world.

Venus Square Neptune

This aspect indicates that you tend to be a romantic and that you prefer to deal with lovely fantasies rather than with real truth. The real world is often disappointing to you, yet you are not very willing to work to change it. Partly this is because you idealize others, and when they turn out to be less than you had imagined, you are disappointed. So you often withdraw from relationships to avoid running the risk of disappointment. When you are older, you may have problems with the opposite sex, especially if you do not feel very good about yourself.

In that case, you will probably react in one of two ways. On the one hand, in relationships with friends and loved ones, you may feel that you have little right to ask for anything, that you are not worthy of love. Because you won't stand up for your rights, you are likely to attract persons who are not very good for you. Sometimes this pattern means that you will look for someone who can solve all your problems, someone "perfect" whom you can look up to. The problem is that the relationship is based on your imagined unworthiness, not on reality.

On the other hand, you may seek out someone who is even worse off, so that you can take care of him or her. Helping someone in a worse situation makes you feel better about yourself by contrast, and it also uses the more positive side of this aspect, which wants to love generously and unselfishly. But again your relationships are based on your feeling of unworthiness.

Venus Trine Neptune

You very much need to express yourself creatively. You have many beautiful ideas, which you would like to convert into something real. However, in order to do this you must master some artistic craft. A trine such as this does not give you the energy to take action; the first step must come from you. However, even if you do not develop any particular artistic ability, you will always want to be surrounded by beauty.

Your relationships with others will be warm and compassionate, but you may not express your love very physically. You idealize love and friendship, but it comes with the opposite sex, this idealism will influence the kind of partner you seek.

When you like someone, you do not ask for much in return, because you feel it is enough to give your love and not be rejected outright. Liking people is very important to you, for you see love as a kind of service, and you are usually willing to do a great deal for those you love.

This aspect has a spiritual side as well, which will develop as you get older. You have an unusual ability to understand the Christian ideal of universal love, even when you cannot actually express it in your behavior. But don't punish yourself if you cannot live up to it, for an ideal is only a goal to be worked toward.

Venus Inconjunct Neptune

This aspect means that your attitudes about love and affection are very idealistic, as will become clearer later in life. Also it can be a sign of creative artistic ability if there are other indications of creativity in your chart. And, of course, you must begin the appropriate training while you are young.

This aspect will work out with the fewest problems if you get a great deal of emotional support from your parents and other loved ones. You are willing to serve, help and assist those you love, but you may honestly feel that you don't deserve to be loved unless you are forced to serve your loved one in some way. This is because you feel that loving someone requires you to make sacrifices and to deny your own needs and that love may not necessarily make you feel good and warm. While you are young, this attitude is likely to show up only as a feeling of unworthiness and shyness toward others, especially those who seem to like you. When you are older, you may have severe problems in love relationships, because you feel that you are only good enough for society's losers, people who badly need help or have severe emotional problems. Or you may find someone who seems to be perfect, who will help you out of your problems, but later turns out to be a disappointment. You must learn to take a clear, objective view of the people you are attracted to and to realize that you deserve a positive love relationship as much as the other person does, for you are as worthwhile as anyone.

Venus Opposition Neptune

The greatest problem of this aspect is that you tend to project what you want to see onto people instead of seeing them as they really are. If you let this tendency get out of control, you are equally blind to what is really good and really bad about someone, for the truth can't come up to the wonderful, magnificent images in your mind. Consequently you may feel that people are always letting you down. But if you can learn to accept the truth about people, you will eventually discover something as beautiful as your fancies. If you decide to deal with the real world, you are capable of being very sensitive and loving.

Often this aspect means that you feel unworthy in relationships. You may feel that your loved one is better than you are or that you should be very sacrificing to those you love. You tend to take on other peoples' burdens that are actually quite difficult to bear, and unless you draw the line, this tendency may mess up your life. You must learn to stand up for your rights to others.

In some cases this aspect can mean that it is very difficult for you to express love and affection. Again, the problem is that you feel unworthy, a feeling that is usually not justified. You may become friends with people who are very hard on you, and you may reject those who would be good for you, simply because you don't believe that you deserve anything good. But if you can overcome the negative tendencies of this aspect, you will have very loving and beautiful relationships.

Venus Conjunct Pluto

You need to be loved very much, but you also need to love others. The attachments you form are very strong, because you don't take relationships casually. On one hand, this can make your life very rich, as long as the people you are attracted to are equally intense emotionally and are good in other ways as well. But with this aspect you may be attracted to people who are not very good for you or who do not have your best interests in mind. This is particularly so if you do not have much self-confidence or self-esteem.

You should be on the watch for jealousy and possessiveness in relationships, either in yourself or in your friends. If you are the possessive and jealous one, you have to learn that your friend may have other friends without lessening the relationship between you. You also must learn to give those you love the same freedom that you want for yourself.

The most important factor signified by this aspect is that you hope to transform the conditions of your life through relationships. Thus you feel that every strong emotional attachment is very important for your future. Just remember that you must pick only the best people as partners in these relationships.

Venus Sextile Pluto

You have very strong feelings and get very emotionally involved with everyone whom you consider a friend. Your relationships aren't usually casual, because you want each one to be important and meaningful for your whole life. This tendency will become clearer as you get older. One of the good effects of this energy is that when you become someone's friend, that person can count on you forever. You are very loyal and concerned about your friends, and you want to make sure that they always get the best in life. In fact, you are so positive about this that you will even put a great deal of pressure on a friend who seems to be taking the wrong course in some matter. It is not that you like to push people around, it is simply that you can't stand to see anyone go wrong whom you are emotionally involved with.

When you begin to have relationships with the opposite sex, this aspect will make them unusually intense. If you cannot be deeply involved with a lover, you do not want to be involved at all. In all relationships, both with friends and loved ones, you want to be so totally committed that your emotional concern will enrich and enliven your life. A life without love and concern for people would depress you very much. You have an unusually great need to give love and support to others and to get it as well.

Venus Square Pluto

You have very strong feelings about people, and your friendships are emotionally intense, a characteristic that will become stronger as you get older. It is very important that you find out as much as possible about yourself, your needs, what you seek from other people and why you form relationships. And it is very important to have a good opinion of yourself. This aspect signifies that you will work out many of your most important psychological problems through your relationships with others. When something goes wrong between you and a loved one, it is because of changes that are occurring within you or mental impulses that you do not yet understand. You tend to act somewhat compulsively and to follow the voice of your unconscious mind rather than your reason. Some of the attachments you form may make little sense to you or anyone else. You may even choose friends who act destructively toward you. If this happens, it is only because you have a destructive attitude toward yourself. Your inner psychological drives may also push you into unpleasant situations that you want to get out of but seem unable to. That is why it is so important to understand yourself and not lose your perspective. You always have the choice of walking away from a situation; you aren't forced to be with anyone.

Some people who master the energies of this aspect turn around and act destructively toward others, just as they were treated badly. You should avoid that course because it will isolate you from others, and eventually you will be alone.

Venus Trine Pluto

You display a great deal of warmth and feeling toward others. And your relationships will transform your life and make it richer. Through each relationship you will learn something important about the world and yourself. Your attitude toward relationships is more serious than most people's, so it is important to choose partners who are equally serious. Otherwise, you may get hurt by someone who takes relationships casually.

You are very concerned about the people you love and find it difficult to leave them alone. Others may think that you are trying to take control or be dominating, but it is simply that when a loved one is hurt, you feel it too. You identify with your loved ones more than most.

You may get into a relationship in which you have rather negative feelings about the other person because of conflicts that continually arise between you. Yet you do not want to get away from the person because you really need those conflicts in order to get at your inner self. You are fascinated by the feeling of aliveness between you and another, which can exist even in hard times. The only kind of relationship that you really cannot stand is a boring one.

These characteristics will become stronger as you get older and are more involved in your emotional development.

Venus Inconjunct Pluto

With this aspect you must learn a great deal about the kinds of friends you want and the kinds of experiences you will have through other people. Even while you are still young, you may meet persons who are quite difficult to get along with, but who seem to be impossible to get away from, even when you want to. You may be fascinated by such persons, or circumstances may force you to stay with them. These people do have a definite role to play in your life, but it may not always be a pleasant one. They will teach you something about life or about yourself.

However, you don't have to put up with difficult or unpleasant relationships, because if you think about it, you will realize that you are drawn to these people in order to fulfill your own hidden emotional needs. Think about what you really want from others so that you can find it in a better relationship. And if you encounter people who won't allow you any freedom, which can happen with this aspect, then avoid them.

This aspect may also mean that you are very possessive and demanding of your loved ones. You may not want to accept the fact that your friends can love other people besides yourself. Let your friends be themselves freely when they are with you, and try not to be too demanding of their time. Love for friends and relatives should be given freely, not used as a way to control them. If you do that, you will lose their love.

Venus Opposition Pluto

Your close, emotional relationships with others may be difficult at times unless you make an effort to do the following. First of all, make sure that you don't try to hold on to your friends too tightly. Let them do what they want when you are together and allow them to have other friends as well. Sometimes you feel threatened if a friend shows more attention to another than to yourself.

You should be careful about the kind of people whom you are attracted to, because sometimes this aspect means that you are attracted to difficult and demanding people. If you have a friend who is very difficult to contend with, do not be afraid to end the friendship and look for another. Be particularly careful to avoid controlling your friends or being controlled by them. You may try the game of saying, "If you won't do what I want to you to do, I won't be your friend anymore," or you may have a friend who does this to you. Either you are friends or you are not, so don't use friendship as a stick to beat somebody with, and don't allow others to do that either.

On the plus side, if you learn to avoid these problems and have mostly healthy relationships, you will eventually find that you can attract the kind of people you want to meet like a magnet. People with this aspect can be very attractive to others, if they are responsible about how they use this ability.

Venus Conjunct Ascendant

You are probably a very appealing person, and you will discover that you can wind adults right around your finger with a smile or a gesture. You will always have this ability to charm people, which can be very useful, but you must learn to use it well.

First of all, you should not turn on the charm when you don't feel positive about someone. People will quickly recognize when you are sincere and when you are only trying to use them. You could be known as a phony or superficial person, unless you develop real warmth. You may also tend to use your charm to get ahead, when you should depend on real ability. Develop your talents instead of smiling your way through life. You will get more real satisfaction out of it.

On the other hand, you are a genuine peacemaker. You hate conflict, so you always look for a way to compromise. You want harmony around you at all times, which is very useful and positive, but you will have to learn not to compromise on issues that are very important to you.

As you get older, you will be very social, enjoying parties and good times or just being with people. When you are an adult, therefore, you will be very good at working with people and making them feel good. People will appreciate your talent for making your surroundings pretty and attractive, and you will probably be very popular.

Venus Sextile Ascendant

You are very sociable and always enjoy being with friends or social groups. With your lighthearted attitude toward life, you probably prefer playing to serious work, which could be a problem in school. But on the whole you should do quite well, because through socializing you will acquire skills in handling and getting along with people, which will be very useful later in life. You may also have friends who will help you out a great deal.

You enjoy pleasant and comfortable surroundings and dislike anything ugly. You will enjoy life most when you live in a pleasant place with comfortable and luxurious surroundings. Probably you keep your room quite attractive, for example, although perhaps not perfectly neat.

In communicating with others, you try to accent the positive. You hate discord and will try to smooth over any conflicts between yourself and others, even those that do not involve you directly. Negative feelings, resentment and hostility disturb you very much, so you always try to minimize them.

You should be very popular with others, because you project warm and friendly feelings. You make it clear that you like people, and they like you also.

Venus Square Ascendant

Usually this is a very positive aspect, indicating that you are popular and that you make a good impression on others and get along easily in social situations. You enjoy people and they enjoy you. But the very positive energies of this aspect may produce negative results if you are not careful.

You should not use your ability to charm and flatter people as a device for getting along in the world. Be sincere, and show people who you really are and how you feel. You can express even unpleasant truths graciously, so you have nothing to lose by being straightforward. Also, don't try to charm people instead of using your natural talents to get ahead. Develop all your abilities, and do not try to sweet-talk your way through life. You will not get much satisfaction out of that.

The problem is that all strong aspects of Venus, such as this one, indicate a tendency to be lazy. Everything comes so easily, especially your relations with others, that you may think you can stop working. But that would really limit your chances for development and would also win you a reputation for being superficial and shallow, which could be true.

On the other hand, if you work to improve yourself and do not depend solely on the energies of Venus to get ahead, you will win the respect and love of just about everyone you meet. Instead of envying your talents, people will recognize that you deserve whatever you have, and they will work to help you even further.

Venus Trine Ascendant

This indicates that you are a pleasure-loving and agreeable person. You should get along well with others, for you make them feel good about you also. You like being with people and in return they like being with you. Unless there is a very strong opposite indication elsewhere in your chart, you should be very popular all your life.

You may also have some artistic talent. Certainly you will have a great appreciation of beauty and will always want to be surrounded by beautiful objects. But you will probably enjoy art as recreation. Even if you are not especially talented, you will try to create in some way.

Your attitude toward life is gentle and peaceful. You like to know that everyone is getting along pleasantly. You hate conflict and cannot see that very much good ever comes from it. Certainly in your own life you do much more by winning people over through friendly persuasion than by fighting. However, at times you will have to stand up for your own views, and you should be prepared to do so. Don't compromise on what you believe in strongly.

By and large, life will probably seem easy to you, as long as you do not take the easiness for granted. If you do take everything for granted, you may expect too much and be bored by what you have, no matter how much that is. If you can experience the beauty of the world and appreciate what you have, you will be very happy.

Venus Inconjunct Ascendant

You often feel that you haven't any right to ask much of those whom you love. You feel that you must do favors for them instead of asking for their help. For you, love is an act of service, not self-gratification. Also, through relationships with others, you try to learn more about your own and other people's inner workings. For this reason your relationships are more deep and profound than most people's. But they are somewhat difficult, too. Your close friends and loved ones discover that you are quite different in a close relationship than you appear at first. It is not that you are dishonest, but that you show a side of yourself to your friends that you usually keep hidden, often because you are not entirely confident in that role. You may feel unsure that others will like you or accept your affection. This is one reason why you express your love by doing nice things for people. You are trying to win them over.

However, you should realize that others will respect you if you stand up for yourself and ask for a reasonable return in a relationship. If you constantly seem to be apologizing for who and what you are, people begin to wonder if they have overlooked something that is wrong with you, and they begin to lose confidence in you. Thus you may bring about the criticism that you are afraid of. You are as good and as worthy of being loved as anyone. Be yourself with others, and many people will love you.

Venus Opposition Ascendant

You work very well with others and should be an excellent team member. However, you are at your best working with one other person, because you like to get to know people one at a time. You prefer to be with warm and friendly people, for you need love and affection from others and will work very hard to get it. Approval is very important to you. But the problem is that if you concentrate on what others think and say, you may not learn to stand on your own two feet.

Nevertheless, you should have no trouble getting along with other people. You don't want to make enemies; in fact, you work very hard to avoid conflict. Even when there is a dispute between two friends of yours that does not involve you at all, you try to make peace. You believe that every conflict can be settled if each person gives a little.

You think a lot about your relationships with others. Even while very young, you have developed a feeling that you aren't complete by yourself, and you do not like to be alone. When you are older and more involved with the opposite sex, you will always manage to have a close relationship with someone. You like loving and feeling loved.

Later in life, your close relationships with the opposite sex should be very positive. You will be able to strike up a conversation with a new friend and make both of you feel at ease. Probably you will attract persons who are good for you, and unless there is a very difficult aspect to Venus in your chart, you will probably marry only once and quite happily.

Venus Conjunct Midheaven

At its best, this placement means that you are full of love and affection for others, but at the same time you can follow your own path and attract only those who are able to go along with you. You will be liked because you can be yourself without feeling that you must live up to other people's ideas of what you should be.

This aspect may also mean that you have considerable artistic ability, although there should be other indications in the chart to confirm that. Certainly you enjoy and appreciate beauty, and you are able to bring beauty into your everyday life.

You enjoy peace and harmony, and you get along very well with others. Wherever you go, you create a peaceful atmosphere. Your relationship with your parents, as well as with other authorities, such as teachers and later employers, should be excellent. The key element in your ability to get along is that you are true to yourself as well as fair to others.

This placement may indicate a career involving either beauty and art or human relations, that is, getting people to work easily together. Or your career might be in entertainment or some other field in which you make people feel good and lighthearted. In any career, your ability to get along easily with people will be an important part of your success.

Venus Sextile Midheaven

This aspect indicates that you are an agreeable and sociable person, who doesn't like conflict with others. You are more willing than most to make compromises, because keeping peace and harmony with those you love is more important to you than getting your own way. In fact, you will give up a great deal in order to stay on good terms with someone.

You like to have the approval of persons in authority over you, and you will work to get it. Most important, your relationship with your parents is likely to be very good. Because of that and because you have good relationships with other authority figures, you will feel secure in yourself and will be able to love and be loved wherever you go. Also you will attract people who can help you as you go through life.

Your home life is also very secure. You should grow up in a peaceful and pleasant atmosphere, surrounded by beauty and comfort. What you learn now will serve you well throughout your life, and you will always have a warm feeling for your childhood home and the places that you associate with it. But you will not feel tied to your past in a way that prevents you from getting ahead in life.

Sometimes this aspect is a sign of artistic ability, especially if other areas of your chart reinforce this theme. Even at worst, you will have a strong sense of beauty and a love of beautiful objects.

Venus Square Midheaven

This is a positive aspect, indicating that you are a very loving and warm person. You should have little difficulty in getting along with people, because being on good terms with others is very important to you. Just make sure that in seeking love and approval, you don't give up an important part of yourself. Above all, be honest and don't try to use flattery and charm to make people like you. Even now your friends won't respect you if they think you do everything just to get people, especially adults, to like you. The only challenge of this aspect is that you must learn to set your own standards and follow your own goals, and not simply be and do what others want.

You have a strong creative drive, and if anything else in your chart indicates artistic talent, this aspect will reinforce it. You should try out various kinds of crafts and artistic studies to find out whether you have such ability. If you do, you will get great satisfaction from it.

Often with this aspect, you feel that the world will take care of you even if you make no effort. In fact you may not have to work as hard as others, but you will have to work. It is not good for your character to be lazy and dependent on others. Probably you will always attract people who will take care of you, but if you depend on this, you will lose the respect of others as well as your own self-respect.

Venus Trine Midheaven

This aspect means that you love working with and owning beautiful things, so that later you may have a career in art, crafts, decorating or another field involving beauty. But it also means that you have a harmonious nature, that you like to have a good time with others. You are not especially aggressive, preferring to give in or smooth over a possible dispute rather than fight. This is not because you lack self-confidence, but because you hate conflict. You are very warmhearted and friendly, and you like your relationships to be smooth.

Your relationship with your parents should be quite positive, and your early life should be very pleasant. When you are older, you will have happy memories of these years. You also get along well with persons in authority over you, such as teachers and later on, employers. If you want, you can easily charm and flatter them, but you shouldn't do this ordinarily, because others will lose respect for you.

You do not like to be alone very much, for you find it difficult to amuse yourself, feeling that nothing is really worth doing unless you share it with someone else. So you always try to have friends around you. When you are older, you will seek out relationships with the opposite sex so that you are never alone for any length of time.

This trait also makes you a good team worker, because you know how to bring together the various interests of people in a group for everyone's benefit.

Venus Inconjunct Midheaven

You have a strong need to be loved and to love others as well, but this may create some problems in your life. You are afraid that if you appear to others as you really are, they won't accept you. This problem can be corrected only by the most careful upbringing, such that your parents correct your behavior in ways that help you feel self-confident rather than undeserving and unworthy.

You are very likely to feel that there is a conflict between what you ought to do in a particular situation and what would be acceptable to the people around you. Often your friendships come into conflict with your parents' intentions for you, which is difficult to resolve. Later in life, you may see your job, career or profession as a part of your life that is quite separate from your personal relationships with loved ones. This may cause you to neglect one area in favor of the other, instead of trying to create a balance between them.

This same pattern of thinking may make you believe that you must sacrifice pleasure and enjoyment in order to achieve anything worthwhile in life. Here again you cannot afford to let either aspect of your life triumph over the other. Especially as you get older, you should make a conscious effort to find ways to enjoy yourself, be with your friends and loved ones and, at the same time, move toward your goals.

Venus Opposition Midheaven

Your present home should be a place of warmth, love and friendliness, and while you are young, your life should be reasonably calm. As a result, you will have an excellent relationship with your parents as you grow up, and you will feel secure within yourself. You will be able to give and receive love very easily and make others feel your personal warmth. Your present family, as well as your own spouse and children when you are older, will always be important to you. Whenever you need help, you know you can turn to your parents.

You enjoy warm and comfortable home surroundings. Wherever you go, you will create a warm, friendly place where you can get away from the cares of the world. You enjoy having friends come to your home, because you like to share your personal world with others and make them feel as good there as you do.

While you are still quite young, but later in life especially, you will enjoy having objects of art in your home. You like to be surrounded by elegance and grace. Now your taste may border on the flashy, but you should tire of this quite quickly, and eventually your ideas about art and decoration will be quite advanced. Also you will prefer rather fancy clothes.

Chapter Nine

Mars

Mars in the Chart

Mars signifies your ability to assert yourself as an individual. It is the energy that says, "I want to be what I am." Along with the Sun, it also has to do with your physical vitality. A strong Mars means that you are able to take care of yourself, that you have a great deal of self-confidence, and that you will eventually demand a fair share of what life has to offer. With a strong Mars, you are not easily threatened, for you believe you can deal with any crises that might come up.

If your Mars is difficult or badly aspected, you may have problems, because your self-assertive energies will not run so smoothly. A difficult Mars may make you extremely aggressive, so that you step on other people's rights just to show your strength, when inwardly you feel weak. On the other hand, you may be very retiring and shy, afraid that you will be hurt if you show your face. If you have a badly aspected Mars, you may be reluctant to assert yourself openly, but instead work behind the scenes where no one can see what you are doing. Or you may tend to act rashly and impulsively, which can result in accidents or at least unexpected situations.

The house position of Mars signifies the areas of life in which you will be most active, as well as those areas in which you could have great difficulty in getting along with others. The sign that Mars is in modifies the way you express your energies according to the tendencies of that sign. A properly developed Mars energy is extremely important because it means you can be yourself and still get along with others.

Mars in Aries

You are a very independent and self-assertive person. Since you have a great deal of physical energy, you should try to get outdoors and let off steam in some active sport fairly often. You get very restless and fidgety if you are cooped up for any length of time.

You prefer to act on your own and set your own pace without waiting for people who work more slowly. Also you like to be the first to take up a new activity. Although you are not at all a follower, you are perfectly willing to let others go their own way. You have no desire to impose your will on your friends, as long as they don't try to force their ways on you. However, you enjoy competition when someone offers a challenge. If pressed, you will fight for your beliefs. You get angry quite quickly, but you also cool off quickly and don't hold a grudge.

Obviously your greatest problem is learning to cooperate with others. It isn't that you want to create a fuss, but if the people you are with won't do something your way, you do it alone. But that is not always the most efficient way to attack a problem. You must learn to give in now and then. Don't worry about having to compromise on anything important, for it isn't in your nature to do so.

You are also inclined to be rash and impulsive and to act without thinking, which can get you into trouble or even accidents. Accidents don't just happen; you create them through being careless. If you take time to be careful, you will have little difficulty.

Mars in Taurus

You work carefully and rather slowly, but your results are almost always good, because your thoroughness makes up for lack of speed. You are also quite stubborn and will resist anyone's efforts to speed you up or change your direction. You are not a quitter and will stick to any task until it is done.

You have a strong desire to own things, and your possessions are very important to you. If you decide you want something, you will work very hard to get it. The only problem is that you may acquire so much stuff that your possessions get in your way. Your room may look like a packrat's nest.

You may have a problem with jealousy, tending to be very possessive of the people you love. You have to allow your friends some independence, or you will lose them. People cannot be owned like objects.

Whenever you work on something creative, you may be rather slow, but your taste and concern with craftsmanship are better than average. Even if you cannot do beautiful work yourself, you will respect others' work.

Anger can be a problem for you, because you have difficulty expressing it until it builds to the point that you lose control. It is all right to express your anger as long as you don't hurt anyone in the process. The problem is that other people may try to take advantage of your apparent patience, not realizing that you are really angry. It is up to you to let them know how you feel.

Mars in Gemini

Your energies get turned on very rapidly, and you work very quickly. However, you may have trouble directing your energy at a single task for any length of time. You are inclined to start several projects at once and never finish any of them, because it's more exciting to move on to something else. This can be a real handicap in school, because you are required to apply yourself for extended periods to tasks that may not be especially interesting. If you cannot overcome this basic tendency to dabble shallowly in many activities, you will not master any skill very completely.

On the other hand, you do have a quick mind, which you enjoy using, especially to debate and argue with others in a spirit of friendly disagreement. You may argue a particular point of view, not because you really believe it, but because it is fun to defend it. You are more likely to disagree with people about ideas than about most anything else.

Try not to be so impulsive in the way you think. If you make decisions too rapidly, you will often be wrong. This is another way in which you are too impatient to take the time to do the job thoroughly.

Your fondness for change may make you want to travel and move around a lot. You probably like to ride around on your bicycle, just finding out what is going on.

Mars in Cancer

What you do depends on your moods to an unusual degree. When you are feeling positive and cheerful, you act confidently and assertively. But when you are depressed, you are more retiring and much more irritable. Slights and harsh words from others hurt you deeply and also make you quite angry, especially if you do not know the person with whom you are dealing very well. Try not to hold your anger in so much. It is much better to express it than to hold it back so that it gradually poisons your whole mood. Also you may keep that anger in to the point that you begin to feel a permanent grudge against the other person. Emotional upsets are very likely to be expressed as physical problems if you do not learn to release the energy.

Sometimes this position of Mars indicates difficulties and disagreements with your family. However, it is more likely that anything concerning your family, your family background and heritage inspires in you feelings of great loyalty. You will work very hard to preserve a value from the past that you respect, because you are conservative in the best sense of the word.

Mars in Leo

You have a great deal of pride, and you enjoy doing things on your own initiative. An appeal to your sense of fairness brings out the best in you, and you will do anything to maintain these qualities. If you know that someone is relying on you, you work very hard to live up to that person's expectations. On the other hand, you are sometimes quite touchy about your sense of dignity. If someone makes fun of you or says something sarcastic, you get very angry and feel that you have to prove your worth to them. At times you may act arrogant and domineering toward others. You can't always be first, but you have such a need to be a leader that it may be difficult for you to accept anyone else in this role.

You demand that others let you be yourself so you can run your life as you want. You are quite stubborn about this; in fact, the harder someone pushes you, the more you resist or persevere on your original course.

You probably have considerable self-confidence and even courage, but you are not especially reckless. At best you have a good understanding of yourself, of your limitations as well as your strengths, which you emphasize, of course. In fact, you may feel uncomfortable with the softer side of your personality, your emotions and weaknesses. You would like to appear strong and self-possessed at all times.

Mars in Virgo

You are careful about what you do, because you feel that every action should be considered thoroughly and every move should have some purpose. This is reflected in the way you work—carefully, systematically and with great attention to detail. You want everything you do to be as nearly perfect as possible, and you want your work to have a practical purpose. You respect tools, and you enjoy working with them to make useful objects. You are willing to take the time to master difficult techniques, so if you have any kind of natural talent, you should become quite a craftsman.

As you grow up, you will develop a strong sense of responsibility. You will learn quite quickly to do the tasks that have to be done before getting into the activities you enjoy. And you will demand that others do the same, for you dislike irresponsibility in others as well as in yourself.

But try not to be too critical of others. Probably you wouldn't push anyone around for your own sake, but you might do it in the name of what you consider your duty. Try to be more tolerant of other people's ways, and don't be so sure that your own notion of perfection is the only one. Others have their own ways of achieving, just as you do.

Mars in Libra

This placement of Mars can have two quite different effects. Probably you prefer to work with another person, for you have a strong sense of cooperation, and you are willing to make compromises to get along. You discover that you can do much more work with someone than each of you could do separately. Your desire to have your own way is modified by your need to get along with others.

But on the other hand, some persons with this placement are very competitive. In that case, you think of every meeting with someone else as a chance to compete, either in a friendly or an unfriendly spirit. That is, you may just enjoy competition without wanting to put the other person down, or you may see the other person as an enemy to be defeated at all costs.

When it is necessary to act, you consider both sides of the matter before doing anything. But you may spend too much time coming to a decision about what to do. You may waver between two choices until it is too late to do anything.

You have a strong sense of fairness and hate to see anyone treated unjustly. When you are aware of injustice, you try to correct it, even when it is not to your advantage.

Mars in Scorpio

You have a strong will, and you let everyone know what you want. But you do not seem especially pushy, just persistent. You apply pressure steadily until you get what you want. If someone makes you angry, instead of blowing up right off, you go into a slow burn. People know you are upset, however, because you are likely to make sarcastic and biting remarks. But this tendency to hold back your anger can work against you, partly because the anger is not released, so you stay angry. You may hold a grudge for quite a long time. But also the intensity of your anger, even though it is held in, may be rather frightening to others whose emotions are not as strong as yours.

But you do not get angry easily. You can be pushed quite far before you get mad, and even then it may not develop right away. But sometimes you remember a past incident when you could have gotten angry but didn't, and suddenly you are just as angry as if the incident had just occurred. If necessary, you are a fighter, although you don't look for fights. But you don't run from them, either, and when you get into it, you fight with body and soul, for your deepest emotions become involved.

You have such strong likes and dislikes that it is hard for you to be neutral about anything. You relate to the world around you very emotionally, and there is very little to which you do not react.

Mars in Sagittarius

Your actions are motivated by your ideals. You are willing to work hard to improve the world according to your ideals and less concerned with getting your own way, at least in a narrow sense. You will work for a cause if you consider it important, but you don't like to waste your energy on something that doesn't matter a lot to you. If you are working with others, you don't like to be the person who handles day-to-day routine matters. You want to be at the forefront, where the action is.

Being outdoors gives you a sense of freedom and a good outlet for your abundant physical energy. This feeling of freedom is very important to you, permeating your energies at every level. You will rebel against any restriction. If left to yourself, you will do whatever needs to be done, but you resist being forced to do it according to someone else's schedule. Often this placement of Mars signifies athletic ability. At the very least, you should be physically active, because you tend to be restless.

You have a strong sense of justice and are not willing to see anyone given an unfair deal. And at your best, you are motivated by high moral standards and ideals.

Mars in Capricorn

For a young person, you are quite ambitious, and you are willing to work very hard for something that is real and important to you. Even while you are young, you will not usually break any rules. You are practical, rather than idealistic, and you like to work for tangible results. You want to be able to point to the results of your work. For your age, you are quite disciplined and can take on considerable responsibility. Adults find that they can rely on you to keep younger, more reckless children in check. You can be quite courageous, but you are not willing to fight for any cause unless you see the point of it very clearly. The one danger that you should try to avoid is measuring people's value according to their income or their social prestige. There are many important values that can't be measured in this way, but you may learn this too late.

You should start planning your career while you are quite young, because you are so concerned with excelling in it, and to do so you must start preparing now. Probably you will begin the training you need very early in life.

Mars in Aquarius

Rather than working according to established patterns, you want to find your own way, which you hope will be better. As a result you are quite inventive and original. But often you do something just because it is different, even when the old way is better. Being original is fine, but it's a waste of time to be different for its own sake. Also you may have difficulty with authorities—parents, teachers or officials—unless they take the trouble to explain why you should do what they ask. You don't follow orders very well.

As you get older you will be concerned with the greater good of society. You are quite capable of directing your efforts to goals that will not benefit you personally but will benefit others. Even while you are young, you resent authority, not so much because you are against society, but because you feel that your ideas are better ideas and would benefit everyone.

If you are convinced of the importance of a cause, you work better with a group than you do alone. You know how to align your own objectives with other people's so that the results are satisfying to all.

Mars in Pisces

You are quite sensitive, and if you aren't feeling cheerful, you don't have much energy. People with Mars in Pisces often require more sleep at night than others do.

The chief problem with this position is that it is difficult for you to be very self-assertive. You may let people take advantage of you because you are unsure that you are right or justified in going ahead with your own plans. You may shrink from people who are overbearing and domineering, which may make you either ignore their actions or try to get around them secretly. This last tendency should be watched very carefully. If you try to get away with acting behind other people's backs, you will gradually undermine their confidence in you. They will not know whether you are actually doing what you appear to be doing.

But there is a better side to this placement of Mars, which will be seen as you get older and more sure of yourself. You will be able to act more unselfishly and do things for others with less consideration for yourself. You don't have a great need to be the best, or on top or terribly successful, so you are able to work for others without your own ambitions getting in the way. This is not to say that you cannot be successful; you have as much potential for success as anyone. In addition, the people you have helped may be so grateful that they will help you in return, as long as you don't imply, either by words or actions, that you expect it. That is very important.

Mars in the First House

You are very energetic and self-assertive, and you never retreat from a conflict. In fact, you may even look for a conflict where there is none. Be careful of this tendency, because people will probably dislike you for it. However, if you can curb that, your courage and daring in many areas of life will win their admiration.

You always like to be the first to do something, whether or not anyone else follows your lead. You just want everyone to know that you are no one's follower. If you are placed in a position of leadership, which will happen, you will lead very energetically, and you may be rather impatient with those who are not as fast or lively as you.

You find it difficult to stay still for very long or to pursue any task that requires patience and thoroughness. You are quite impulsive and extremely restless. However, if you have to work very hard on something that requires a great deal of physical energy, you enjoy it. You are also likely to be quite athletic. Just be careful, because your innate recklessness could cause an accident.

Learn to take the time to understand other people's points of view. You tend to see only your own and to become angry when someone challenges your beliefs. Not only will this get you into needless fights, but it will also prevent you from learning anything about others.

Mars in the Second House

When you see something you would like to own, you want it very much and you work very hard to get it. You insist on having complete control over what you do own, and you are very unhappy if anyone tries to dictate what you can do with it. You feel you should be free to waste your resources or money if you want, or to be frugal and careful if you want. However, because of the compulsive nature of Mars, you are much more likely to be careless in this regard. You should avoid buying anything on a sudden impulse. Plan carefully for what you really need and then buy it only after much consideration. Anything you buy on impulse is not likely to be satisfying in the long run.

You will fight to prevent anyone from taking anything away from you. Anyone who challenges your strong sense of property arouses your anger. It is not that you are selfish, especially, but you want to make your gifts freely, of your own accord. If a brother or sister uses something of yours without asking, you really blow up. Simply make it clear that they should ask you first. Unfortunately, if they expect you to lend your possessions as a matter of course, you probably won't. And you will be especially angry if someone damages something of yours. You may be careless with what you own, but no one else can be.

In the long run you will have to learn to be less possessive of what you own. Otherwise your possessions will bring you more pain than pleasure. You will be so concerned with keeping perfect control that you will not be able to enjoy them.

Mars in the Third House

You have a very aggressive intellect, so that you like to debate and argue with people, usually not to have a serious fight but rather a friendly argument. But you don't like it when someone really disagrees with you, and you fight very hard to bring that person around to your way of thinking. And when someone tries to change your mind, you resist very strongly. In fact, the only way anyone can easily convince you of something is to make you think it is your idea.

Fortunately your mind works quite quickly, and you have a lot of mental energy. You can work on a problem for a long time, although not always steadily. And you actually learn a great deal through arguing. Just don't lose your curiosity about getting answers by concentrating all your energy on winning the argument. That may be useful on a debating team, but not in life.

Especially while you are young, you may have quite a few disagreements with your brothers or sisters, for they and your other relatives seem to make you more angry than anyone else.

When you are talking with people, be careful how you speak, because you tend to express yourself argumentatively even when you have nothing to fight about. Also you may easily hurt someone who is more sensitive, even when you don't intend to.

Mars in the Fourth House

You may have difficulty getting along with one of your parents. It is very important that you discuss openly any problems that you have with each other, so that you can arrive at a real compromise. Even if you find it difficult to get along with them, they are very important to you, and you very much need their approval.

This placement of Mars means that you feel a strong desire to be the person in charge in your home, which is difficult because of your age. But you should learn to get along with the people you live with, because that could be a problem in your adult home as well. One way to ease this situation is to be by yourself as much as possible. This will minimize your conflicts with others and will also make you feel more in control of your personal life, which is what you want.

Your home life is very important to you, and you spend a great deal of energy getting your personal surroundings, such as your room, exactly the way you want them. When you are older, you will want to own land, and you will enjoy working on it.

As you get older, you may have sudden, unexpected surges of energy—anger, resentment or hostility—that have no clear cause. This can be the result of events in your early childhood when you felt anger but did not allow yourself to express it. As you grow older you must learn to be very honest with yourself about your feelings, because that is the only way you will be able to handle them.

Mars in the Fifth House

You have a great need to express yourself and to be yourself openly. It is difficult for you to hide your real feelings from others, and you don't really want to. You say whatever is on your mind and let everyone know your mood. For this reason, you have a reputation for honesty, if not tact.

You put a great deal of energy into all your activities, but especially into whatever you do for fun. You play very hard, and this position often indicates athletic skills. However, it may also give you a kind of recklessness that can lead to accidents, if you are not careful. Your abundant energy requires that you get outside as much as possible. It is difficult for you to remain cooped up for long, because you get restless unless you are really enjoying your work. This may cause some trouble in school until you learn to discipline yourself and buckle down to work. Basically you prefer play to work. As an adult, however, you may succeed by choosing a career that is really "fun" for you. Everyone should do this to some extent, but for you it is a necessity.

When you meet someone you like, you tell the person immediately, and you eagerly take the first step in starting a relationship. This will happen especially in relationships with the opposite sex when you are older.

Mars in the Sixth House

You enjoy hard work, as long as you can control the way you do it. You are quite disciplined in your own work habits, but because you have very high standards, you don't like to work with people who are less disciplined. All your life, but especially while you are young, you may feel that you know more than the persons you work for. That can create problems if you let them know how you feel. But if you respect those who have authority over you, if they have demonstrated that they do know more than you and can teach you something, you will work very hard and be an excellent employee. However, when you are older, your work drive will be expressed most smoothly if you are self-employed.

Mars in this house often suggests that you will choose a profession involving metal-working or cutting instruments. Or it can indicate any occupation that requires a great deal of physical energy. Surgeons often have Mars in this position.

When working with others, especially if you are the leader, try not to be too critical or bossy. This will only create discord and conflict as well as slow down the work. With this placement, it is very important that you learn to express your honest feelings of anger. Repressed resentment can lead to physical ailments or even accidents brought on by carelessness.

Mars in the Seventh House

If you want to get along with people, you will have to learn how to make compromises. You tend to want your own way all the time, which causes disagreements and even fights. Some persons with this placement of Mars actually enjoy fighting with others, but even so you should try to see the other person's point of view as if it were your own. Then try to figure out how you would react from that position. You may find that from the other's point of view, your own position makes you as angry as his did from your point of view.

Try not to always see yourself in opposition to others. If you really feel that you have to give up more than you get when you cooperate with another, it would be better to work alone.

There is a positive side to this placement, however. If you enjoy working with someone, especially on a task that requires great physical energy, you can work harder than almost anyone else. Mars in the seventh house brings out your energy either in opposition to someone or with another. As long as you believe that you can accomplish your objectives through cooperating, you will certainly succeed.

It is important to learn these lessons now, because otherwise this placement could indicate difficulties in marriage caused by your reluctance to compromise.

Mars in the Eighth House

You have such strong desires that it is very difficult for anyone to stop you from doing something you have decided upon. And if you want something, you will do everything in your power to get it, which may lead to conflicts with others if you are not careful. You may not have enough regard for the fact that others have a right to what is theirs. Also it is difficult for you to share anything, because you feel that you are losing it totally, instead of enjoying it with another. This may result in arguments between you and other members of your family over who owns what. You should arrive at a real understanding of what belongs to whom and then stick to it.

You do everything with great intensity, which should be to your advantage most of the time. But you may easily drive yourself too hard physically, which could be a problem when you are older. Learn to be moderate in all your activities now so that you won't have to change later when it will be harder. When you are tired, you should be especially careful of accidents, because you push on without noticing that you are not as sharp as you should be, so it is easy to make a mistake.

Mars in the Ninth House

You are strongly attached to your own point of view, and if challenged, you will fight very hard for your opinions. You are good at arguing and if provoked, you have a rather sharp tongue. When you are older, you may look for a cause that you can defend. You are much more likely to fight for an ideal than for yourself, so you must be careful about the cause you choose. Once you have made up your mind, you will fight hard, no matter what. On one hand, you can be quite self-righteous and narrowly fanatical about your beliefs, but you can also be courageous in defending the rights of those who are downtrodden.

You don't get involved just at the mental level; you act on your beliefs. Probably you identify so strongly with what you believe that you feel your ideas are actually a physical part of you. Obviously this makes it hard to understand anyone else's position about any matter. Try not to get so wrapped up in your own views that you won't even consider someone else's.

This position also indicates that you are quite restless, and as you get older, you may want to travel around and see the world, which would be a good experience.

Mars in the Tenth House

You want to get ahead in life, and you will work very hard to get there. Even while you are young, you plan to get the proper training to achieve what you want. Your career will be very important to you, and the time to plan for it is now.

However, while you are still in the learning stage, you should be careful how you treat authority figures. You don't automatically respect all adults, because you have very high standards for others as well as for yourself. You respect only those people who are clearly successful at whatever they do. Teachers and others whom you see as less than successful will not find you very cooperative, which may get you into trouble at times. When you are older, you may have the same trouble with employers. For this reason you should probably look for a career in which you can be self-employed or else have a great deal of independent authority.

This position of Mars suggests several kinds of jobs, especially those that require a lot of physical energy or hard work. It is appropriate to working with metal or sharp cutting instruments. It also helps in any field requiring independent and original work. Mars here will give you the courage to act on your own, without waiting for someone else to tell you what to do.

Mars in the Eleventh House

You like to be around people who are active, vigorous and independent. Probably you prefer being with boys rather than girls, although many girls fit this description also. You like to work hard and play very actively with your friends. It seems much easier to do your chores and to keep on working when others are with you. It isn't that you lack independence, but you prefer to work with other people.

It is very important for you to be with people whose goals are similar to yours, because you believe in your own opinions strongly and will defend them vigorously against anyone who challenges them. When you come across people whose beliefs are different, there is likely to be conflict.

If Mars is in difficult aspect to other planets, you may experience a more difficult side of this placement and be unable to get along with any group you come in contact with. You may see other people as such a threat to your goals that you cannot accept them for fear that your wants and needs will be lost in the wants and needs of the group you are with, whether it is an organization or just a gathering of friends or classmates. In this case you may find it easier to get along with others on a one-to-one basis rather than in groups. This is also an indication that you should try very hard to find people whom you are compatible with, because you may not be able to get along with just anyone.

Mars in the Twelfth House

You may often be afraid to assert yourself because you feel defeated, and you are sure that any effort is futile. It is quite likely that you will express this by feeling tired all the time. Your attitude may have resulted from being with people who haven't encouraged you very much, especially when you were very young. You must build up your self-confidence and disregard anyone who makes you feel bad about yourself. You tend to work in secret and to act behind people's backs, which you should try to avoid. Your lack of self-confidence makes you so afraid of direct action that you do everything indirectly. Even as an adult, you may prefer to be someone who works behind the scenes.

However, you are really quite a strong individual, and once you overcome your childish fears about yourself, you can be very effective. Surgeons and athletes, who are very effective people, often have Mars in this position.

Another positive point is that you work very well alone. You don't need other people to encourage you or tell you what to do. All you need is for people not to discourage you.

As you get older, you should make a great effort to find out how you affect others. Be very conscious of the impression you are making on people, because it may be very different from what you think, so that they respond to you in ways that you are not prepared for.

Mars Conjunct Jupiter

You are naturally optimistic and buoyant, always wanting to try out new things and have new experiences. You are very active and have a great deal of energy, for which you should find an appropriate outlet. You don't like to be confined or restricted in your actions. Fortunately this aspect often indicates athletic ability and a love of physical exercise. The only problem is that in your exuberance you may take foolish chances, because you feel that nothing can go wrong for you. But you may go one step too far and have an accident. Actually, this aspect usually indicates a lucky streak, so any accidents you do have are the result of indiscretion, not bad luck.

In many areas of life, you are able to time your moves very well. You have an inborn sense of the best time to act, and you do it. Also you easily get people to go along with you, because you can make them believe that your course is best. You can get what you want without having to give in to others very often. It is your responsibility to use this ability wisely and be sure of what you really want, because you will probably get it. And this aspect can't protect you from the wrath of others, if you exploit them.

You like to be the first to do something new. You enjoy every new and exciting activity, and you will try anything. If you are just a little cautious, all your life you will enjoy new discoveries and have a broader and richer experience of life than most people.

Mars Sextile Jupiter

This is traditionally considered a lucky aspect. You will have many more opportunities than most people, and favorable circumstances will seem to occur without any effort on your part. However, this is not just luck. What happens is that your optimism and positive outlook on life make others feel better. In projects with others, you cooperate easily and get as much as possible for yourself without making anyone feel that you are getting too much. As a result, people are willing to help you and give you breaks that they might not give others.

To you, this aspect may not seem very lucky, but others are aware of it. It is just that your luck is so reliable that you don't even notice it. But if you think about your life, you will realize that large areas of your life—as determined by the house positions of Mars and Jupiter—work very easily and effortlessly, even though others have quite a bit of trouble with those areas. You simply take the energy of this aspect for granted.

Friends and neighbors are very important to you, and you should get along well with them. Also they will probably help you in many ways that will benefit you in the future.

Mars Square Jupiter

This is usually a very positive aspect, but you must develop some self-control. Otherwise you will take foolish risks that cannot possibly work out, even physical risks that could lead to an accident. Also you tend to work hastily and sloppily, leaving jobs unfinished.

You are very optimistic and have a lot of energy. You believe that everything will work out all right, which is true, if you are a little careful. Your energy needs an outlet, and you are likely to be physically active, possibly even athletic. However, in athletics you should be especially careful, for your behavior may lead to an accident.

You hate to stand still in life or be restricted. You want to be constantly on the move, having new experiences and seeing new places. This restlessness may create problems in school, because it is so difficult to sit quietly for long. And you find it hard to work patiently on difficult problems in your subjects.

Most people will like to be around you because of your energy and enthusiasm. However, you may be a bit thoughtless toward others and hurt people's feelings because you are honest to the point of tactlessness. Usually others will know that you aren't trying to be mean, and they will forgive you. But your social life will be improved if you think about what you are going to say before you speak.

Mars Trine Jupiter

This aspect is usually regarded as lucky. You will be able to do pretty much what you want with your life in any way you want. You can be yourself, do what you want and still win approval, for people recognize your integrity and honesty as well as your generous attitude toward others. Even when you get angry, you don't stay angry for long, because it seems like a waste of energy. Usually your actions are motivated by principles that are very high-minded, especially for a young person. You have a fierce desire to do what is right.

You are able to work with others and get what you want without taking anything away from them. People appreciate this and will want to help you. It is your ability to be successful without stepping on others' toes that makes you "lucky." Everything you do creates a favorable climate for your further activities.

Of course, you may have some hard times in your life, but in general you always have enough to get along, and usually you have a great deal more.

This aspect means that you love freedom, and you enjoy moving around in large open areas. You may or may not have athletic ability, but you certainly love nature and the outdoors. You do everything in a big way, and you have very little patience with people who take life only in little pieces.

Mars Inconjunct Jupiter

With this aspect you probably are quite active, with abundant energy for anything you want to do. But you must learn to control your energies rather than have them control you. You may be inclined to take excessive risks, to try out things that you are not sure you can do. But be careful, because with this aspect the energies of Mars and Jupiter do not work very smoothly together. If you overextend yourself and try to do more than you are physically capable of, you may have an accident. Also you may be clumsy when you take up a new activity until you learn to control your physical body better.

It is important for you to realize that you are not unlucky. Accidents or mishaps result from going too far too fast rather than from bad luck. If you slow down and learn new skills carefully and slowly, you will do as well as anyone else, perhaps better. However, this may be difficult for you, because you are somewhat impulsive and quite restless. You find it almost impossible to sit still for very long. You are always eager for change and new experiences, even when you are not ready for them yet. The only way to get over this is through self-discipline.

You have a great need for personal freedom also. But while you are young, you may not be very responsible about the way you use your freedom. You may take too many liberties or even interfere with other people's freedom. Here again the problem is rashness and lack of self-control.

Mars Opposition Jupiter

This is a very positive aspect, signifying a great deal of energy and a buoyant, optimistic enthusiasm that attracts others. However, you may have some difficulty getting along with people when you are expected to work cooperatively, because you are naturally competitive rather than cooperative. Your competitiveness is not nasty or abrasive; you simply enjoy a good, spirited contest. This aspect may or may not signify athletic ability, but certainly it means that you must have an outlet for your abundant physical energy.

You are very restless and need a lot of freedom. You do not like anyone to hold you back or place restrictions upon you. When you get older and have close relationships with the opposite sex, this will be a very important factor. Any partner will have to give you a great deal of room to be yourself.

You are likely to be rather rambunctious, and you are not at your best in small or confined spaces. You may be rather clumsy, especially while you are young, because you do not seem to understand your size and your speed, which is quite fast. As you get older this problem will diminish, and if you are careful and willing to submit to training, you may become quite graceful. But when you are under emotional stress you will always tend to move impulsively.

Sometimes this aspect indicates a tendency to be accident prone, which comes about because you get carried away with your energies, not because you are unlucky. Sometimes you simply act without thinking and get yourself into trouble by over-estimating your strength and ability. Being careful is all that is needed.

Mars Conjunct Saturn

You often feel frustrated, as though you think the world has stacked the deck against you. And when you feel very frustrated, you have difficulty expressing your anger; it seems to burn intensely inside you with no way to release it. On the other hand, you have a great ability to make a sustained effort. Once you get into a project, you carry on until it is completely finished. You are capable of great self-discipline.

The greatest danger of this aspect is the likelihood of conflict with your father or someone who plays that role for you. It is important that your father and other authority figures encourage you and support you in what you do. If they are excessively critical and tear you down, you will show the most negative sides of this aspect, including feelings of bitterness, repressed anger, unworthiness and incompetence, and an inability to handle the world. None of these is usually justified.

This aspect often means that your father has taken the position that his children, especially sons, are in competition with him and must be put down. Your father may demand that you prove yourself through very demanding trials, but then he does not acknowledge your success. But if your father does not have this negative influence on you, the more positive effects of this aspect can come out—great self-discipline, concentration and ability to handle very detailed work.

Even at best, you will have much difficulty handling your anger, because you tend to hold it in. Repressing this energy may cause physical ailments, usually inflammations of some sort, a tendency to break bones or to get rheumatism at an early age. Learning to release your emotions will stop this.

Mars Sextile Saturn

You like to proceed cautiously and carefully in everything you do, with the result that your work is always done carefully and thoroughly. You may take longer than others, but your results will be more enduring. You don't believe in luck, and you don't count on it in your efforts. You see every success as the result of hard work and preparation. In fact, it sometimes angers you when people are able to succeed because of luck.

A practical person, you don't like to make an effort unless you know it will have a concrete result. You don't usually work with completely abstract ideas unless you have personally experienced something real in connection with them. You are much more interested in being effective than in making an abstract point.

Because of your sense of discipline and your ability to work hard, you will know what you can and cannot do quite early in life. The only problem is that you may accept limitations too readily and be too cautious. Don't be so careful that you overlook real chances to get ahead. As you get older, this aspect should help you in business, because you are so practical and sensible. Also, you want to achieve and will follow the rules in order to do so.

One real problem is that you may be quite unable to deal with your anger. Instead of blowing up, you hold it in and get quietly more angry, which may lead to lingering bitterness and resentment. You should learn to release your anger by discussing the matters that have caused it, even though you are reluctant to do that.

Mars Square Saturn

With this aspect, life seems hard and unloving to you. And the danger is that you will gradually become hard and unloving toward others. If your family, especially your father, does not give you enough emotional support, you will eventually come to believe that no one else deserves a better break than you got. Most people with this aspect do not become completely hardened, but it is a tendency to watch out for.

Often when you have a burst of energy that makes you want to go forward, something seems to hold you back. That is very frustrating, but what it really means is that you have to be very thoroughly prepared in anything you do. The universe will not let you get away with doing anything in a half-baked way. If you can accept that with patience, this aspect will lose much of its sting.

Anger and irritation are often a problem with this aspect, because the action of Saturn inhibits the action of Mars. Be careful that you do not let your anger build up so far that it takes over. You don't lose your temper easily, but when you do, you do it spectacularly. But bitterness can distort your vision and make the whole world look bad. It also causes you to withdraw from others and become unreachable.

Sometimes the effects of this aspect surface on the physical level as a tendency to break bones easily or have bone infections and even rheumatoid conditions at an early age.

Mars Trine Saturn

A reserved and controlled person, you want to understand any situation thoroughly before making up your mind. And you want your work to have practical results. You will develop a sense of discipline while you are still quite young, and in many ways you seem to be motivated by adult concerns. In fact, one of your main problems, at least as others see it, is that you can't seem to let go and have a good time like other people of your age. Even while quite young, you will be more interested in activities that are important in the adult world, including business and making money. This is only the beginning of your very careful and controlled ambition. You do not seek power so much as the opportunity to do an excellent job.

Do not let your sense of caution cause you to turn down valuable opportunities. You prefer not to take chances, but sometimes in life you have to take some risks. You believe that there is a direct relationship between success and effort, with little room for luck. You want to organize your life to have as much control over it as possible.

You are very good at work that requires meticulous attention to detail. You can concentrate considerable energy on fairly narrow objectives for a long time until you achieve the result you want.

Mars Inconjunct Saturn

This can be a difficult aspect because it signifies a conflict between your sense of responsibility and your desire to fulfill your own needs and do what you want. This leads to a struggle within you that may keep you from acting decisively. Instead of deciding what you will do, you feel caught between these two forces, wondering whether you have the right to do what you want. You may feel that others are trying to frustrate you, but it is only your own indecisiveness that is causing the trouble. Sometimes this conflict makes you very irritable and resentful about nothing in particular. Then, when someone happens to act in a way that is obviously annoying, you focus all your built-up anger on that person.

Sometimes with this aspect there really is someone in your life who discourages you and makes you feel that your efforts are futile. You must learn to avoid negative people who make you feel bad about yourself. Your parents should work very hard to give you self-confidence and show you that you are a valuable and important person.

On the positive side, this aspect can mean that you control your aggressions and energies so that they work out constructively. But make sure that you do work out your aggression instead of keeping it hidden, because that can result in sudden bursts of temper, which may work against you. Also, if you repress these energies, they may turn against you and be expressed as illness or accidents.

Mars Opposition Saturn

You often have the feeling that persons and circumstances are working against you and frustrating what you want to do. As a result you learn to hold in your emotions, especially anger. But eventually your anger builds up so far that you can no longer keep it in, and it spills over as sarcasm and a generally bitter and negative attitude toward anything that upsets you. Also your feelings of anger and hostility hang on in your mind longer than they do for most people. And this can lead to certain psychosomatic problems, such as allergic reactions.

You must learn to release your anger in a normal manner and to express your feelings, knowing that you have the same rights to do so as anyone else. But in this you will need emotional support from your family, particularly your father, because the energies of this aspect often concern your relationship with your father. You very much need emotional support from him and, if possible, a not too demanding attitude. You don't need to be held down and disciplined as much as some young people, because you have a built-in sense of discipline. In fact, your parents should trust you to fulfill adult responsibilities as soon as possible, although they shouldn't leave you to fend for yourself totally. You may feel that there is no one you can turn to in case of trouble, so support from your parents is necessary for this reason as well.

Your natural sense of discipline makes you good at tasks that require close and careful attention to detail.

Mars Conjunct Uranus

As you are growing up, you may be a real handful for your parents and other adults. Part of you likes to disrupt, surprise and unsettle people. You are restless and unconventional, and you respond very badly to pressure, especially from teachers and parents. At your most difficult, you are rash and headstrong, making sudden moves without thinking about the consequences. In some cases, this can cause accidents, so you should learn to be very careful in situations that might be dangerous. If you don't feel entirely in control of yourself, stop doing anything that involves some danger.

You are strongly freedom oriented, but the problem with your attitude toward authority is that you feel that any restriction is a threat to your being. Any kind of limitation brings out the disruptive side of your personality, and you put all your energy into asserting your own way of being. If you want to get along in the world, you must develop some self-discipline, although most people with this aspect manage to get their own way most of the time. These people are definitely eccentrics according to the rest of the world, and you will be also. Fortunately you have the courage to be your own person.

You also must learn that you don't have to be against something just because somebody else is for it. If you do that, you can easily develop a closed mind, which will only cut you off from some possibly good ideas. If you learn to be more willing to hear other people's ideas and then make up your mind slowly and carefully, you should get what you want out of life.

Mars Sextile Uranus

An extremely independent person, you need to be free to go your own way. You will rapidly discover that it is better for you to learn through experience rather than be taught secondhand by others. You like excitement, so you constantly take up new projects to keep your life from getting dull. On the other hand, you find it hard to settle down into a routine. As a result, you may not do anything very thoroughly, because the most important part of any activity is usually routine plodding work. But you have a knack for getting others started on worthwhile projects. With your unconventional streak, you can see possibilities that other people overlook, and you have the courage and even daring to work on a project until others can see its value. At that point, it can be taken over by people who will carry it through the long haul.

You are a very high-energy person who hates to sit still. But in order to stay busy, you may seek out activities that are pointless and maybe even disruptive to others. Try to avoid that.

You are attracted to people who are like you, which may cause some friction between you and your friends, because it is difficult to get such independent people coordinated.

When others try to compel you to follow a certain course, you may become very stubborn. The best way for someone to get you to do something is to make you think it is your own idea. Then you will go along.

Mars Square Uranus

The lesson you must learn is to act more cautiously with better planning. You tend to go off half-cocked and to act rashly and without thinking. And the more someone pressures you to slow down, the more itchy and restless you get. When your parents try to make you conform to their expectations, you rebel in no uncertain terms. You feel that you have to be yourself, and there is nothing wrong with that. But if you always react negatively to pressures from others, you will be as much at their mercy as if you always did what they wanted you to do. You must learn to judge each situation on its merits rather than do whatever will be considered rebellious and nonconforming.

It is hard for you to sit still for very long, because you always want to be on the go. You have a great need for excitement and are quickly bored by activities that become routine. You will fight when you have to, and even sometimes just for the love of it. If you are not careful, others will begin to regard you as a source of disruption and nothing more. You don't have to be what others want you to be; there is plenty of room for rebels in this society. But you do have to get yourself sufficiently under control so you can be effective in whatever you do, whether it is conventional or unconventional.

The impulsiveness of this aspect leads some people to accident-prone behavior, simply because they move too quickly to be safe in a given situation.

Mars Trine Uranus

You are likely to be very independent, and you need to be given great freedom to determine your own destiny. You will decide very early in life that you must be yourself at all costs. Probably you can do this without creating utter havoc in your immediate surroundings and personal life. You will be able to get where you want to go in your own way, and usually you know when to back down in the face of resistance from others without losing very much. But you are a fighter when you have to be, and you will learn to be a very effective one.

You are likely to be a leader, not because you want power, but because you are able to see ways of doing things that others do not see until you show them. Others will follow your lead although you, personally, do not care whether or not anyone follows you. The only problem is that you probably don't enjoy making a sustained effort in any area. After the thrill of beginning a project has worn off, you lose interest. Others may have to take over the projects you start. However, with your fighting ability, you are able to keep something going through a difficult phase when there is a lot of opposition.

Other people will like you for your daring, although they may sometimes question your good sense. They will discover that in the long run you are often right, even though no one else could see it at the time. However, this ability will develop as you get older and have more experience. While you are young, you probably will make quite a few mistakes.

Mars Inconjunct Uranus

You have a tendency to be rash and impulsive, which may get in your way. If matters proceed too slowly, you are likely to make a sudden move that upsets the whole situation and forces you to start over again. You must learn to be patient if you want to achieve your objectives.

This energy may also be expressed as a hot temper, especially when you have to endure restriction or limitation, such as sitting still in a classroom for a long time. You have a rebellious streak that needs to be disciplined, because everyone has to endure some restrictions, and it takes so little to trigger your temper.

Nevertheless, you need to find some outlet for your energy. It would not be good for you to hold it back totally, because if you do, you may be accident prone. Physical activity is a good way to use this potentially disruptive energy. However, because of the possibility of accidents, you should exercise reasonable care in any sport or other physical activity. Never work or play at anything remotely risky when you are angry, for example. Wait until you cool down. In fact, when you are angry it would be a very good policy to go off by yourself and vent your feelings—scream and yell to your heart's content! If you are able to blow off steam right away, you do not stay angry for long.

Sometimes you may make sudden moves that startle people. You may make a decision very quickly and start to act on it immediately, but that is not such a good idea. Make up your mind more slowly, or at least wait for a while until you start to act. If your idea still looks good a couple of days later, it is probably all right to go ahead with it.

Mars Opposition Uranus

This aspect has two distinct sides. Some people experience its energies within themselves, while others experience it primarily through others.

If you experience it in yourself, you see others as a threat to your actions and yourself. You feel that you must constantly fight anyone who tries to keep you in check. But the more you resist people, especially teachers and parents, the harder you will have to fight, because they will clamp down on you even more. Your relationships will be a source of disruption in your life, because you seem to feel obliged to unsettle people. Someone who is settled in his or her ways is a kind of challenge to you. While you are young, you may do this by playing practical jokes, which can be rather disruptive.

If you experience this aspect through other people, you may be someone who appears quite orderly and conventional, but you attract disruptive people who will not leave you in peace. Others seem to constantly challenge you and demand that you prove your worth.

In either case, you must come to terms with other people in some way. Basically you are a fighter who thrives on a certain amount of conflict, but you should learn to recognize when that is appropriate and when it is not.

As with the other aspects of Mars and Uranus, there is a danger that acting impulsively may lead to accidents, so try to be careful in any kind of dangerous situation. Don't let a sudden impulse make you do something foolish.

Mars Conjunct Neptune

The main problem with this aspect is that you tend to get discouraged. You do not have as much energy as other people, usually not because you are physically weak but because you are too easily discouraged by opposition from persons or circumstances. You are not a very aggressive person. It is not that you are especially shy or reluctant to assert yourself, but you feel sure that in a direct confrontation with someone, you will lose. More than most people, you need abundant support and encouragement from your parents. If they are excessively critical or unsupportive, it will have a very negative effect on you.

The danger is that if this tendency to be discouraged is not checked, you may develop a defeatist attitude toward life. Or what is worse, you may assert yourself in underhanded ways so that no one can see what you are doing and try to stop you.

On the other hand, if you are given emotional support and made to feel good about yourself while you are young, you will develop a very giving, unselfish attitude. You will be happy to be of service to others whenever possible. At its highest level of expression, this aspect signifies a willingness to put your own affairs second to higher, more spiritual principles. But this can happen only if you are basically secure.

Occasionally this aspect may be expressed physically, in which case you might be easily fatigued or you may have a lot of minor infections, illnesses or allergies.

Mars Sextile Neptune

You are not terribly self-assertive, and you tend to shy away from direct confrontations with others. Probably you feel all right about yourself, but you can't understand why some people charge out and make such a big issue of themselves and their demands. You believe that if you wait patiently and help people along, you will get whatever you deserve. You are not a very high-energy person, and you do not like to exert yourself greatly, even on your own behalf.

On the other hand, especially as you get older, if you learn about a problem that you consider very important for the world in general, you are capable of working very hard to correct it. You are motivated more by idealism than by practical concerns.

But your actions are often rather impractical, so it is important to find out where your energies can do some good and where they cannot. If you are defeated in some project, you don't usually pick yourself up and start working again right away. You need encouragement from friends, as well as the lift of personal success. Otherwise you could turn into one of those people whom life seems to run over.

You must learn to stand up for yourself, even if you don't understand why. Don't let yourself be a doormat to other people's aggressive drives. You have as much right to be as anyone else. It is fine to deny your needs in favor of others or of some good cause, but do not carry it too far.

Mars Square Neptune

Your problem in life will be discouragement, which you will always have to fight. At times you feel that everything works to defeat you and make you lose. Everyone feels that way on occasion, but you seem to take it more seriously, as a sign of your own unworthiness. Instead of just chalking up a defeat to experience, you condemn yourself. Unfortunately your feelings of discouragement may lead to underhanded actions. For example, you may talk about people behind their backs instead of confronting them directly. This can create a very poisonous climate in which nobody in your immediate circle trusts anybody else. Others may not be able to pin the problem on you right away, but eventually they will put two and two together, and your position in the group will be weakened.

Sometimes this aspect signifies a desire to escape from this world altogether, perhaps through drugs, perhaps through strange cults and religions. You are easily persuaded that your individuality is not worth much and that you should give it up to some higher power. This may be desirable at some point in your life, but only after you have found yourself and have an understanding of your own worth. You have to be a real individual before you can give up your individuality to a higher power.

Some people experience this aspect as basic physical weaknesses in the form of allergies or a tendency to minor infections and illnesses. All your life you should be careful about the kinds of drugs you take, even under a doctor's care. You may be more sensitive to drugs than others, so don't take them unless you know that they are safe for you.

Mars Trine Neptune

You may be a bit shy and reluctant to commit yourself or even assert yourself, but at heart you are an idealist who wants to do what is best for the world. Especially as you get older, you may not want anything for yourself. You may decide that personal advancement is a very unworthy motive. Be careful not to apply this standard to others, however, because most people are more interested in advancement than you are, which may cause you to be disappointed in them.

Within reason, it is perfectly all right for a person to want to get ahead. Your self-denial is due at least in part to a lack of energy, a feeling that you wouldn't get ahead even if you tried. That is the main problem with this and other Mars-Neptune combinations. Sometimes your inability to stand up for your own best interests may make you less effective at helping other persons or working for worthy causes.

Your sympathy is always aroused by people who seem helpless or animals in trouble. You are a soft touch for any hard-luck stories. While it is fine to be so sympathetic, you should always make sure that your efforts will really be helpful. Unfortunately, you sometimes help people in a way that makes them remain dependent on your help, rather than becoming independent. Make sure that you really want to be useful, that you aren't helping them just to make yourself feel better.

Mars Inconjunct Neptune

With this aspect you must learn to stand up for yourself and demand your rights forthrightly and directly. Often you feel that you don't have enough energy to assert yourself or that any such effort would be futile. Unfortunately, some people with this aspect learn to work behind the scenes or dishonestly. Others simply give up or take a defeatist attitude toward life.

236

Sometimes this aspect operates on the physical plane as well. You may have a generally low energy level and feel tired all the time but not able to sleep because of nervousness. You may actually need more sleep than others, and if so, you should try to get it. This aspect may also indicate that you tend to have allergies and infections.

Obviously you will have to work to develop your energy, both physical and mental. Your parents should give you a great deal of encouragement and always deal with you honestly. They should encourage you to discuss all your problems openly and let you know that you can always expect fair treatment from them. You should also learn to tell the difference between being really discouraged and being just physically tired. You are not likely to feel very positive and optimistic when your health is not at its best. If you feel defeated and want to give up on some matter, simply rest for a while or wait until another day before making a final decision.

You should get regular exercise to build up your body. Watch your diet carefully and get enough sleep. Stay away from any foods that your body does not handle well.

Mars Opposition Neptune

This aspect can indicate that you have little self-confidence and a low sense of self-esteem, unless your parents and loved ones give you as much support as possible. You have an insecure streak that will always be there, even under the best conditions, but it can be minimized. The worst thing for you is to be surrounded by negative or excessively critical persons, but with this aspect you are likely to attract people who always tear you down. If this is not stopped, you will have a very bad image of yourself, and you may become very fearful of others, suspecting that people are always working against you. In this situation, even if you stand up and assert yourself, you fully expect to lose. Some persons with this aspect decide that the only way they can accomplish anything is to do it on the sly. Dishonesty is a possibility with this configuration, but it is not the most common expression.

Obviously, it is very important that your parents give you lots of reinforcement and encouragement. Feeling good about yourself will bring out the positive side of this aspect, which is your ability to put service to the world before your own interests.

In some cases this aspect creates physical problems, such as allergies and bad reactions to some drugs. Mind-altering drugs would have an especially serious effect on you and should be avoided.

Mars Conjunct Pluto

You have a very strong will, although you may express it in subtle ways. If you don't get your way, you may lose your temper, but when you see that that will get you nowhere, you change your tactics. The greatest problem with this aspect is that you may decide that getting your own way is the most important thing in life and that the only way to get it is by controlling others. Unless you are taught to have a high regard for other people's rights, you may trample upon them. But in that case people are likely to gang up on you and try to stop you at every turn, which will make you feel very frustrated and even farther from attaining your objectives. Instead of manipulating people, you must learn how to handle others creatively, so that they benefit from whatever happens as much as you do.

Regardless of your sex, with this aspect you may have considerable difficulty with men. It is particularly important that your relationship with your father be close and warm, with as little conflict as possible and no physical punishment.

On the plus side, this aspect can signify that you have a great deal of positive drive and ambition. You will want to accomplish a lot in life, and you will enjoy having power over others and using it responsibly. You will want to make changes in the world, which you see as a stage where you can make the greatest possible impression. But while you are young, you must bide your time and learn everything that you will need to know to fulfill your ambitions. Then you should go far in life.

Mars Sextile Pluto

You have a great deal of energy, but you express it in subtle ways, through endurance, persistence and stubbornness. You may not always move quickly, but once you start, it is very hard to stop you or change your direction. You have a great need to be in control of your life and to set your own course. Gradually you will decide on your life objectives, and you will begin to learn and do whatever is necessary to achieve them. Because you have a definite idea of what you want to do while you are still young, you may choose to become a leader so you can get others to join you. But you do not usually like to take orders from someone else, and if working with others means doing that, you would be better off working alone. While you are young, this attitude can create some problems, because you are not yet in a position to really control your own life. However, even now you resist and put your foot down if you definitely do not want to do something.

Your determined attitude has many positive results. If you are convinced that a project is worth doing, you will do it completely. You get into every activity so deeply that sometimes you seem to be compulsive. While you are young it is important to learn to relax and not get so totally wrapped up in your activities. Otherwise, when you are older, you could get overtired or strain yourself quite badly. That is not a danger now, but this is the time to establish your lifelong work habits.

Mars Square Pluto

This aspect can create some problems in your life if you do not learn how to handle it, but it can be extremely useful if you do.

You have very strong self-assertive energies, and you want to be in control of every situation you are in, which can create problems while you are young. If you do not get your way, you tend to lose your temper and strike out in a blind rage. You may succeed in holding this energy in, but that isn't a good response, either, because suppressed Mars-Pluto energy is quite violent and can attract violence to you even when you don't consciously look for it. You must learn to use this energy in a controlled way without suppressing it. This is done through ceaseless activity and staying involved in work that really interests you and seems important.

You have great ambitions for your life, and you are able to work very hard. While you are still young, you will decide that you want to get ahead and attain a position of power in the world. But be very careful not to take shortcuts, break rules or seriously violate your own and others' standards of behavior. You can easily convince yourself that your goals justify any means, so you resort to underhanded, even unethical, tactics to reach them. But in the long run that will guarantee your failure, because it will force other people to work against you. Even if you are stronger and more effective than most other individuals, you cannot defeat a well-organized group that sets out to stop you. Also be very careful how you assert yourself, because without meaning to, you may make people uneasy about your intentions, so that they work against you. If you follow the rules and work hard, you should succeed.

Mars Trine Pluto

You have a great deal of energy for accomplishing your purposes. An ambitious person, you will want to get ahead and achieve something important in your life. You have a great deal of self-confidence and can present yourself to others as a leader whenever you choose. Any project that you get involved in, you try to mold according to your own ideas, but you can usually do this in a way that wins the cooperation of friends and fellow workers. You do not tire easily and can keep on going after everyone else has gotten weary. Just make sure that you do not overdo it.

You do not usually start fights, but you won't back down from one either. Others will find you a formidable opponent, but you always fight fairly. You have a great deal of courage and will stand up for your beliefs all your life.

As you encounter the inevitable frustrations of growing up, you will face the obstacles and deal with them directly, rather than try to avoid problems or difficulties. You are quite stubborn and not easily deterred. Normally you control your anger quite well, but when you do lose your temper, it can be quite spectacular. It usually takes a while to regain your composure.

You respect strength and will choose friends who are independent and self-reliant, because that is your ideal for yourself. You are not attracted to people who seem weak. But try to have compassion for people who are trying to cope with serious problems, because you can never really be in their shoes.

Mars Inconjunct Pluto

You have a strong will and always want to have your own way. But very often it seems as if tremendous forces are working to prevent you from getting what you want. If you have this problem, it is because of the way you go about trying to achieve your ends. If .you put too much force into your desire to get something, you may unknowingly alienate people because your aggressive manner shows that you will let nothing stop you from getting what you want. Even if that isn't the way you really feel about it, you should recognize that your forcefulness creates this impression.

On the other hand, this aspect sometimes means that you are the victim of such energies in someone else, that you always seem to attract forceful persons who give you a hard time. Either they never let you have your own way, or they may be rather brutal, physically and psychologically. Learn to recognize such persons in advance and avoid them. Also think about why you are attracted to them, since in fact you may be quite fascinated by their forcefulness.

At certain times in your life, when there are great changes taking place within you and in your environment, you will have to work very hard to make your affairs turn out right. There is nothing to be done at those times except do the work that must be done. Fortunately you have plenty of energy and enough endurance to pull through anything that you will encounter in life. You are basically tough and persistent. These changes are an integral part of your growth, and even if everything seems to go wrong they are necessary to your full development.

Mars Opposition Pluto

You sometimes find it difficult to get along with others. You may feel picked on, as if people were working against you for no particular reason. However, that is not usually true. But without being aware of it, you may be doing things that set others against you. You are very intense about yourself, and you may give the impression unknowingly that you will do whatever you want and that nothing and no one will stand in your way. This can scare people, even when you have no intention of doing so. And sometimes you do get an idea in your head that you pursue relentlessly. At times you feel that no one has the right to get in your way, and you will fight tooth and nail to overcome any obstacle. You are quite a fighter, and your temper may not always be under control. You need to expend that energy in hard work.

Your relationship with your father is very important, for regardless of your own sex, if you resent him you will have trouble getting along with men in general. You will see every man as a potential threat or competitor.

As you get older, you will become very ambitious, and you must make a great effort not to become ruthless. Always maintain high ethical standards, for otherwise you could create powerful enemies who will frustrate your plans, no matter how good your intentions are. And it must be said that even if you act honorably, this aspect sometimes signifies serious conflicts with others that you seem to have no part in causing. But acting morally and responsibly should minimize this.

Mars Conjunct Ascendant

You are strong-willed, and people quickly realize that you are not someone to trifle with. You have all the classic qualities of Mars—self-reliance, courage and daring, personal aggressiveness and independence. You need to have complete control over your own life, but there is a danger that you will be too quarrelsome and domineering.

All of these qualities make it difficult for you to cooperate with others, so you are at your best working by yourself. Usually you are willing to take responsibility for what you do, and you are dependable. Your strong sense of personal integrity and pride makes you somewhat sensitive to comments by others that seem to indicate that they do not take you very seriously. You are easily prodded into defending yourself, even when there is nothing at stake. Try not to fly into a rage over nothing.

You are very competitive in every area of life. You enjoy sports immensely, especially individual rather than team competition, and this gives you a good outlet for your abundant physical energy. Your aggressive energies have caused you, even while young, to dislike anything that seems soft and weak. Even if you are a girl, you do not like to be cuddled and babied by your parents. You want to grow up very quickly, or at least become independent at an early age. You don't like to think that you need anybody, although you can certainly be affectionate in your own way. You just don't like to get "sappy."

Mars Sextile Ascendant

You are independent and self-assertive, but you can work with people who share your goals and ideals. However, it is important to note that you are not very good at giving in on what you want in order to get along with others. You need to work with people who truly share your interests. The groups you belong to are really associations of individuals working independently along parallel lines.

You state your ideas strongly and demand that others take your statements seriously. Occasionally this may create problems with adults who insist on treating you like a child. Even though you are young, your parents should treat you with respect and take your ideas seriously, even when they are off base. The best way for grown-ups to deal with you is to explain each situation very carefully and let you draw your own conclusions. They should not try to convince you and make you feel you have lost the argument, for you do not give in easily.

You enjoy being with friends who are very active, energetic and independent, like yourself. As a rule you prefer being with men and boys rather than women and girls. You choose friends who will not make demands on you and will let you go your own way when you feel like it. But you have a strong standard of fairness, and you will not usually let your friends down. In fact you will fight to defend someone you personally believe in, even if you suspect that he or she may be wrong.

You also like to be free to come and go as you wish, which can be a problem in school, if you are forced to stay in one place for a long time. But you should be able to discipline yourself enough to do what has to be done and not create problems.

Mars Square Ascendant

This aspect may cause some problems because you feel that you can fulfill your own needs only at the expense of getting along with others. This leads either to frequent disputes and disagreements with people or to feeling frustrated and futile if you try to hold in your anger and resentment in everyday contacts. Especially while you are young, you may lose your temper frequently when you don't get your way. When you are older this can lead to feeling that it is you against the world, unless you can find out what you have in common with others and how you can cooperate with them.

You do have a lot of energy, and there is a side of you that enjoys competing, but you should do it in a friendly way rather than with a hostile attitude that you must beat your opponent at all costs. Learning how to get along without feeling held back is the major challenge of this aspect.

Also you must learn to avoid acting rashly when you are feeling angry or emotional. In the first place, you often do things that you regret later when you have cooled down. In the second place, accidents can occur when you move suddenly or impulsively in an already dangerous situation. At the time, your actions may seem innocent and inconsequential. Learn to be careful and to stop doing anything that is remotely dangerous unless you feel that you are in complete control of yourself.

Mars Trine Ascendant

You are strong-willed and have a great need to be yourself. Fortunately, however, you are likely to have enough courage to stand on your own and to uphold your position. You are independent, and your opinion of yourself doesn't depend on what others think of you. So you can work by yourself if necessary, or you can work with others as an independent equal. But you do not like working under anyone else, unless you really respect that person. Then you are willing to take orders from him or her. But anyone who would win your respect should be aware that your standards are very high and that you are easily disillusioned by weakness or inconsistency.

You throw yourself into every activity with wholehearted enthusiasm, and you devote all of your considerable energies to whatever you get involved in. Sports are particularly interesting to you, and it should be said that you are more easily involved in anything that seems like play rather than work. But try not to get carried away and become reckless, particularly when you are feeling exuberant.

You will defend your beliefs and the people you believe in to the very end. You are not one to start a fight, but you will not back down unless defeated by someone else's superior strength. Your ideals and beliefs are very important to you and are a large part of your image of yourself.

Mars Inconjunct Ascendant

The difficulty with this aspect is to find a balance between getting what you want in life and getting along with others. More than most people, you will have to learn the necessity of compromising to get along with people, especially because you often seem more aggressive than you are. While you are young, the need to compromise may be frustrating, because youth is a time when your own needs seem especially urgent and demanding. At times you may feel that nothing is going your way, that you continually have to give in to others and put your own wishes aside. However, it is not really this bad. You do not actually have to compromise any more than anyone else, but you are more reluctant to do so.

Learn to work for the good of others by making their objectives your objectives, whenever possible. This aspect can signify the ability to accomplish a great deal, as long as you do not spend all your time and energy feeling angry or resentful about seemingly undeserved defeats. When you have a real goal to work toward that you can share with others, you will be able to attain that goal.

In close relationships you also have to learn to compromise. Initially you may come on very strong and act very aggressively toward someone you are interested in. But that approach only provokes conflict because the other person feels threatened. If you learn to take a softer approach, you will be able to get what you want, within reason, without having to fight for it.

One of the more difficult sides of this aspect is that you must learn to understand whether or not someone has violated your rights. You may think that this is the case even when it isn't. Learn to discriminate.

Mars Opposition Ascendant

This aspect can signify real problems in getting along with other people. You may be either the obvious cause of these problems or the apparent victim of them through other people.

In the first instance, the problem is your own aggressiveness and competitiveness. You see others as a challenge to prove yourself, and you may act very defensively, taking offense at the slightest unfavorable remark. And then you demand that the other person fight back, which may startle your opponent, who probably didn't mean anything bad at all. Learn to tell whether someone is really trying to goad you before you respond to the challenge, and even then don't respond unless absolutely necessary. Others can control you, which is just what you are trying to avoid, by manipulating your anger.

On the other hand, you may not consciously seek fights, but you seem to attract people who are very strong-willed and aggressive, often at your expense. Actually, these are the only people you respect, even though they give you a hard time. You are not interested in milder people who would be easier to get along with, perhaps because you sense that they would make more demands on you. True, the independent and dominant people whom you are attracted to are self-reliant and free, but they may not be willing to give you any freedom. As a result, you could have serious disputes with such persons.

Mars Conjunct Midheaven

Very early in life, you will develop a firm determination to do everything your own way. You decide upon a course of action quite quickly, and you usually know just what you want to accomplish. If someone tries to stop you, you get very angry, feeling that you are the only one who really knows what is right for you and what isn't. Eventually this will be true, but while you are young you should be a little less headstrong and listen to what others say. You won't always follow their advice, but at least give it a hearing.

However, you are not merely strong-willed, you also identify yourself very strongly with whatever you intend to do. If someone questions your moves, you take it very personally. You must realize that you are more than the sum of your actions and that when someone challenges your decisions, they aren't challenging you personally.

This aspect indicates that when you are older you should choose a career in which you can have a great deal of independence and expend a lot of physical energy. If you work for someone else, you will frequently feel more like a competitor than an employee, and if you don't like the pace set by your employer, you will feel very angry and hostile. You would not be at your best working in a team situation, with the possible exception of an athletic team. This placement of Mars is very common among athletes, but even in a team sport you need to have opportunities to shine on your own in order to be happy.

Mars Sextile Midheaven

You are very independent and self-reliant, but you are able to balance your own energies with other people's and work in a group, as long as you know what you personally will get out of the effort. You have the ability to work for others unselfishly, but in the end you will always defend your own needs.

You may express your will in subtle ways, but you do express it. You know what you want, and you already have some understanding of your inner self as well. This aspect is usually a sign of self-confidence. But even more important, you will learn very early in life how to capitalize on your strengths and minimize your weaknesses. Also you will choose your life course while you are quite young, and for the most part you will stick to it.

Purpose is very important in your life. You do not like to do anything that doesn't fit into some higher scheme relating to your long-range plans. For this reason, you may be less fond of fooling around than most people your age.

Your relationships with your father and with other male authority figures should be quite good. They will teach you to stand up for yourself and be your own person. Probably they will encourage you, and it is very important that they do, because if they choose, the men in your life have more power than anyone else to tear you down and make you feel bad about yourself. Fortunately, that is not likely to happen.

Mars Square Midheaven

You will tend to work against yourself until you really understand who you are and what you are doing. Your immediate desires, especially if they are compulsive and urgent, may actually prevent you from getting where you want to go in the long run. Try not to be shortsighted, and do not assume that people who warn you of this are simply trying to hold you back. You may be rather suspicious of such people and assume that they are just trying to dominate you. This is because you sometimes try to dominate others for no particular reason. Also you sometimes pick a fight just because you are suspicious of someone. You try to seem confident and self-assured, and probably you will be when you are older, but now your aggressiveness comes from a lack of self-assurance, from a fear that others will see your inner weakness and take advantage of you. Actually most people don't want to bother; the aggressiveness you see in others is really a reflection of your own.

Your relationships with male authority figures may be quite difficult, because you see them as challenging rather than trying to help you grow up. It is difficult for you to acknowledge that someone has a right to be above you. Later on, this could be a serious source of trouble with employers.

Basically the challenge of this aspect is to learn about yourself and your limitations, so that you can have self-confidence. Then you will no longer need to challenge others for no reason, and you won't fear challenges from them.

Mars Trine Midheaven

You have a strong sense of self, that is, you know who you are and what your rights are with regard to other people. You have considerable self-confidence and will fight for what you believe to be yours. On the other hand, you are less likely to try to dominate people than those with other Mars-Midheaven combinations. You do have a great deal of physical energy, however, especially in activities that you want to be involved in. As you get older, you will pour out energy in your work and career, and you will be known as a very hard worker. But you may not feel that you are working hard, because the energy comes so spontaneously that you do not regard it as work. For this reason you should look for a task or purpose that your life can revolve around, that you can identify closely with. While you are young, this may simply be a hobby, but later on it will be your career or life work. Fortunately, with this aspect you won't have much trouble finding a purpose in life.

You are not especially competitive, but you are independent. You do not like to be dependent on other people, nor do you like anyone to interfere with the schedule you have set for yourself. Consequently you may find it easier to work and play alone than with others.

When you have to make a choice, you are usually able to do so quickly and easily, because you know pretty much what you want, and you go after it. If you don't know which of two choices to take, you may make an arbitrary decision, feeling that making some choice is better than going nowhere.

Mars Inconjunct Midheaven

This aspect can mean that you have mixed feelings about all authority figures, including your parents. You may feel that you have to violate the rules laid down by your parents in order to get your way. This is a significant problem, because if it continues into adulthood, you will have great difficulties with employers. Therefore it is very important that your parents teach you how to express your self-assertive drives without going against their teachings. Unfortunately it is impossible to state how that should be done, because the conflict between self-will, on one hand, and self-denial and work, on the other, is different for each person.

Clearly you should spend a lot of time releasing your great energy in vigorous play. The more energy you use up in this way, the less you will need to assert yourself destructively. You must learn what society demands, such as going to school and doing schoolwork, learning to obey instructions for your own good and so forth.

Another way to solve this kind of conflict is to learn that you can say what needs to be said and not be forced to remain quiet. You can't expect your elders to always go along with your ideas, but you should be able to feel confident of your right to say it. The exception to this, of course, is that you do not have any right to say something just to hurt others.

Mars Opposition Midheaven

This position can have two quite different effects. On one hand you may be subject to compulsive desires, wanting to do things without any special reason except willfulness. Such actions are usually rash and sudden and may be caused by an inner emotional upheaval. Sometimes this happens because you have had such a stormy and turbulent home life as a young child that all your resentment comes out in sudden aggressive energies. To counter this, your parents should provide you with a reasonably stable and supportive home life, where you can feel that you are accepted for yourself.

On the other hand, if you feel confident that your family loves and accepts you, you will experience the energies of this aspect quite differently. You will determine the course of your life very directly, according to your own inner needs and impulses. You will be conscious of these needs, so that you can gratify them in a controlled way instead of being at the mercy of your inner drives. In general you will succeed by creating a satisfying inner life more than by achieving in ways that the outer world can easily recognize. You may or may not be successful in your career, but that will not be as important to you as inner satisfaction. While you are young, your parents should understand this and help you discover your own needs rather than make you conform to other people's expectations.

Chapter Ten

Jupiter

Jupiter in the Chart

Jupiter is a slower moving planet that stays in the same sign for about a year. Its sign has a direct personal effect on you only if Jupiter is close to opposition or conjunction with the Ascendant or Midheaven, or if it forms a strong aspect with one of the more personal planets, such as the Sun, Moon, Venus, Mercury or Mars. Otherwise it affects you largely as part of the generation you belong to.

The house position of Jupiter tells about the areas of life in which you seek to grow and attain the most freedom. Jupiter increases the range of experience in the areas of your life that it affects and helps you grow beyond the limited world of your youth. The sign that Jupiter is in modifies your manner of growth and tells what methods you will use in trying to grow.

The aspects to Jupiter also have a strong influence on the way it works. When Jupiter is favorably situated, you are positive, optimistic and cheerful, feeling confident and in control of your life. In the affected parts of your life, you have high ideas and strong ethical standards. Jupiter is closely connected to religious and spiritual concerns as well as to wisdom and higher kinds of knowledge.

A poorly aspected Jupiter indicates problems in adjusting to the demands of the universe. You may be arrogant and overly proud or simply a smug know-it-all. Sometimes a weak Jupiter indicates fear and timidity, not because Jupiter is so weak but because its energies cannot adequately balance the energies of Saturn.

Jupiter in Aries

You will grow by finding out who you are, being yourself and letting all of your latent talents and possibilities come into being. Although you must learn to discipline yourself, accept limitations and fulfill the duties and obligations of living with others, you cannot let these factors overwhelm your need for self-expression.

If the energies of this placement are given adequate expression, it indicates that through being an uncompromising individualist, you can benefit others as well, far more than if you always try to live up to other people's expectations. By doing everything in your own way, you are able to show others the way. In the process you will develop enormous self-confidence, justifiable pride and the ability to stand alone against all odds when necessary.

On the other hand, if you deny your need for individual fulfillment, because of inhibitions or pressure from parents and other adults, you will begin to feel that it is you against the world. You would be forced to assert yourself and fulfill your needs at the expense of fulfilling your obligations to others. As a result you would be much more selfish because you would see no way to satisfy the demands of your own life. Or if you give in to others' demands, you would feel unfulfilled, smothered and deprived and finally unworthy of any regard.

Jupiter in Taurus

You will grow by finding a stable foundation for your existence, by learning what elements of life you can depend upon and what you cannot. You have a strong need to be secure and know what tomorrow will bring. As protection against the unpredictable universe, you may tend to accumulate many material possessions.

You need lots of physical affection, plenty of hugging and physical contact with your family. If you don't get this kind of affection, you may project this need onto physical objects, substituting comfortable surroundings and beautiful, soft objects for actual affection. You will always prefer comfort to self-denial and pleasure to work, but the degree of this trait will depend to a great extent upon how secure you feel.

If you feel secure in the world and know that your needs will be met, you are able to give and share with others. Basically you are a warm person, and you should have enough emotional confidence to express that warmth. You will develop a kind of practical sensitivity that will enable you to find immediate, practical solutions to your everyday problems. You will help others by giving them the tools to improve their lives.

However, if you do not feel basically secure, you are likely to be more possessive and grasping, both of persons and of objects. Also you would use luxurious possessions, food, and other self-indulgences to fulfill your emotional needs and give you a sense of emotional gratification. Needless to say, that would severely retard your development.

Jupiter in Gemini

This is traditionally considered one of the less beneficial placements of Jupiter, in part because you tend to use your mind as the sole tool to get ahead in the world, neglecting to grow spiritually and emotionally. Unfortunately the rational, analytical and logical mind has limitations; many aspects of the world can be felt emotionally, but not understood logically. But with this placement you may exclude everything from your life that cannot be reduced to an intellectual statement or principle.

Obviously Jupiter in this sign helps the development of the rational mind and should be useful in school. But it is very important that your parents and family help you develop your feelings and emotions along with your intuitive faculties, so that you will not try to work exclusively with your mind.

There is a strong danger of emotional insensitivity. You may enjoy playing jokes on others that actually hurt their feelings, even though you don't mean to. And when they try to tell you why they feel hurt, you pay no attention.

Fortunately, there are many other factors in the chart that can compensate for this one, so there is no excuse for letting the negative side of this placement become dominant. And there is a very real positive side to it, that is, the ability to examine life with logical detachment, to be objective and to see every possible point of view. Also you understand the larger, more important issues of life, and you can communicate your understanding to others.

Jupiter in Cancer

Your personal path to growth and understanding will come through two different sources that are actually closely related: emotional security and knowing that you are loved and cared for, on one hand, and taking care of and protecting people, on the other. In both of these areas, the emotional experiences of your earliest childhood are extremely important.

You need to have a deep belief in the dependability of those whom you depend on emotionally. You need to know that your family, especially your parents, loves and supports you. The community you live in now will also be important to you, conditioning many of your attitudes about life. You are easily damaged emotionally if your family fails to meet your emotional needs. In that case you might spend most of your life looking for someone whom you can depend on, but you probably wouldn't find that person, because inside, you don't believe that such a person exists.

If you are given adequate security in childhood, you will enjoy taking care of others, working with less fortunate people and making others feel good about themselves. Even as a young person, you enjoy being the host, the source of warmth and hospitality for others. Community and home will always be very important to you.

You respect tradition and prefer anything old and tried rather than the new and untried. You feel that age gives objects a pleasant, friendly cast that new things lack. Even while you are young, you may collect old objects and, later, real antiques. Feeling that you belong and have roots will give you confidence and security to face any trial.

Jupiter in Leo

You need to take pride in everything you do, to feel that all of your dealings with others are honest and aboveboard. The more you can feel right about yourself in this way, the better your life will work. The problem is to avoid seeming overly pleased with yourself, especially at those times when you do not really feel very good about yourself. You are inclined to boast and show off before others precisely when you feel most empty inside. When you are feeling better, you are content to let your real abilities and achievements speak for themselves.

You want everything to be big, for you consider smallness demeaning. You enjoy a spectacle and have a great love of grand and glorious fun. But sometimes it may be necessary to keep from going to extremes in this regard, for biggest is not always best.

While you are young, you try to identify with adults whom you respect, such as teachers, parents or other older persons. You want your peers to look up to you, so you try to gain their respect by acting grown up. As you get older, you will try to gain the kind of position of power and authority that you now respect. You will succeed to the extent that you can get along and make others respect you for what you really are. If you are just an empty show, you will not get very far. Also it is important that you learn to have a sense of responsibility for others and not seek to get ahead just for yourself alone. If you do, others will see it and have less respect for you.

Jupiter in Virgo

You will grow and achieve maturity by developing a constructive sense of duty, by knowing that what you do is useful to the world and by living up to your responsibilities. In some respects, your attitude about the world and other people is very mature for someone your age. But to get the most out of life, you must overcome your timidity, for that affects your expectations for yourself. You are inclined to accept too little and not demand enough of life. You see reality so clearly that you let it get you down. The danger is that you may seriously underestimate your abilities and the possibilities of what can be done in your life. Being practical is fine, but a little idealism wouldn't hurt. Don't always accept matters as they are, either about yourself and others or about circumstances in general.

On the other hand, you can be very helpful to others, and you feel best when you have something important to do. You respect work, even if you do not enjoy it, and when you neglect to do something you are supposed to do you feel guilty. In fact you often tend to feel guilty about indulging yourself. You have to justify your activities by knowing that they are important on a larger scale, apart from yourself. You cannot justify doing something simply because you want to. But this may lead you to become very good at rationalizing, believing that some activity is socially useful, when you are really doing it only because you want to. It is better to recognize that you do want it for yourself and not blame your actions on some "higher purpose."

Jupiter in Libra

You will do best in life if you can keep a perfect balance between extremes. Don't do anything to excess, and examine both sides of every issue before making a decision. On the other hand, when you have considered both sides, make up your mind firmly and decisively. One of the great problems of Libra is that it indicates difficulty in deciding which side to take on an issue.

Beauty is very important to you as an indication of order in the universe, although you are not likely to think about that at this stage of your life. But you are aware of an intense feeling of well-being when you see any kind of beauty. You will always enjoy elegance, the more spectacular the better. At a very early age you will learn to see beauty in every possible situation. By itself, this placement is not enough to indicate artistic talent, but if you have such talent, this will make it larger and more elegant.

Your relationships with others will be very important to your inner spiritual growth. You will discover more about yourself through the people you attract and your relationships with them than through any other means. Therefore, it is important to think about your relationships and not simply take them for granted. It will be particularly important for you to understand the problems you have in relationships, especially recurring ones, because you can learn a lot about yourself from them.

With your highly developed sense of justice, you do not like to see anyone get the short end of the stick. And you are willing to defend other people's rights, even if you are not personally involved.

Jupiter in Scorpio

An important element of your life will be thinking beyond the surface appearance of a situation to understand what is really happening. You love mysteries, and by solving the mysteries, you will develop a great understanding of life. While you are young, you ask a lot of questions, and you keep asking and searching until you get answers. In this regard you are more persistent than most people. Any school subject that interests you will draw all your energies, but you won't give much attention to the subjects that seem dull.

Sometimes this placement indicates an interest in the supernatural, and when you are older, you will be attracted to spiritual and mystical views of the universe. You are not satisfied with appearances at any level, which means you should be a good researcher, if your mind is at all scientific. You have a great interest in people's psychological makeup, which you express now as intuitive insights. However, as you get older, you will understand what your intuitions are based on, and you may even choose a career in which psychology is an important part of your work.

The only problem here is that you may sometimes be reluctant to share your insights with others, for two reasons. First of all, especially while you are young, you have trouble communicating what you know. Later on you may be reluctant to discuss these matters because you know how difficult it is for others to understand them, even when expressed clearly. Also you may just enjoy being secretive, although it is not good to indulge this. Whatever you discover in life, your feelings and emotions will always be an important means to greater understanding.

Jupiter in Sagittarius

Traditionally this has been considered the sign in which Jupiter is most at home, because the sign and the planet are very similar in nature. This placement indicates that very early in life you will develop strong ethical and moral principles, although they may be quite unorthodox. However, those who interpret your unorthodox beliefs as a lack of morality will be very mistaken indeed. In your own way you can be very self-righteous about what you believe is right, and you may even preach to people about it when your morals are challenged. Otherwise you are very tolerant, knowing that a variety of viewpoints and lifestyles is necessary and even desirable.

You have a strong desire to be free to experience life in your own way. Probably you resent any attempts by your parents to warn you away from doing certain things, even though you know that they mean well. You need to have a great deal of direct experience in as many different areas of life as possible. You don't want to be confined to one place or one way of living. When you settle down, it will be after trying out as many alternatives as possible.

A very idealistic person, you will develop a strong spiritual sense very early in life. You need to look up to something or someone, to know that there is something higher than yourself in the universe.

After a period in your youth of being very unconventional and free, however, you are likely to settle down and identify with the established order. Then you must remember how much you needed freedom when you were young, and grant it to those who follow after you.

Jupiter in Capricorn

Your growth in life will come through concrete achievement in the world. You feel that ideals are all very well, and it is good to be moral and ethical, but you want to translate your ideals into action. You want to see real results that others can point to as yours. With your fine organizational skills, you will be good at putting other people's ideas into practice, and you will understand what can and cannot be done. You are, or should be, a practical person and a realist, because if you are not, your life will not work out very well. Capricorn planets must deal with reality. With this placement, you may feel that the universe will not meet your needs unless you work to justify your existence. This has the effect of dampening the normal exuberance of youth to some extent, although you should have plenty left. Most of the characteristics of this placement will be expressed more clearly as you get older.

You are quite concerned about being right, and you will argue very hard for your point of view. Anything that is not right, you condemn as weakness, and you may be very hard on yourself when you make a mistake. Also you are likely to be hard on others when they make mistakes. You must work to develop a sense of compassion for your own and others' weaknesses, for otherwise you will gradually become cold and unfeeling. In that case, people would begin to avoid you.

You enjoy taking responsibility and being in a position of authority. You work hard to gain the approval of authority figures, such as teachers and parents, and you may identify with them rather than with people of your own age. This could alienate you from your peers, however, if you carry it too far.

Jupiter in Aquarius

This is an indication that you will grow through being free to find new ways of living and new methods for accomplishing old purposes. You should not be confined or forced to follow old ways. There is a side of you that is quite inventive, which can really benefit from looking at life from a new angle.

However, although you are in many ways an individualist, you do not think just of yourself. Even while you are young, you are very aware of the groups that you belong to. You are not selfish. You understand that your friends have needs, and you look for ways in which you and your friends can benefit together.

You are usually very fair, believing that everyone should get what is due them. Your sense of justice is strong, and as you get older, you will fight hard to ensure that the people who are close to you are treated well, especially by persons in authority. You have no special awe of authority figures; in fact, you ignore the traditional notion that anyone in authority should be respected. These people must prove their worth as far as you're concerned. You don't respect tradition very much, unless you can see clearly that it has a real purpose here and now.

As you get older, your social consciousness will evolve further, and you may become involved in some mass movement to spread the ideals you believe in. Even while you are young you recognize that you are more effective as part of a larger movement than as an individual. You have a good sense of organization, and you know how to make sure that every part of a group is effectively contributing to the whole.

Jupiter in Pisces

This is a sign that you should serve others and in some way put others' interests before your own. However, there are some difficulties in finding the proper balance, because at the same time you should not deny your own satisfaction and gratification. What you give to others must be given willingly. If it is given in a spirit of martyrdom and self-sacrifice, it will not be much help to those who receive it. When you can honestly give of yourself and what you have, you feel good and you enjoy doing it. This is what you must try to attain.

An idealist, you are easily disappointed when reality does not live up to your expectations. You must learn that you can't assume that the universe will live up to your ideals. You will have to create these ideals in your own life by making them real for yourself and others.

As you get older, you will develop a strong spiritual awareness, which may or may not surface as an interest in traditional religion. However, it will influence your perception of the world very strongly. Even if you do not actively believe in a particular religion, you will be concerned with an aspect of the universe that is higher than everyday material reality.

It is a good idea to go off by yourself now and then and be alone with your thoughts, because the confusion and hustle of the everyday world can make you lose your perspective. You need a quiet atmosphere to find out what is really important to you. When you are alone you may have some of the most important experiences of your life.

Jupiter in the First House

With this placement you are able to make a favorable impression on others because of what you really are, that is, someone who enjoys life, who does everything in a big way, who is generous and helps others. This position frequently means that you are physically large, either having a large frame or being overweight. In fact, you should be careful not to eat too much.

You enjoy being free to have as many kinds of experiences as possible. You want your own world to be large, and you want to see as many different parts of the world as possible. It is unlikely that you will spend your life at home, and even if you always live in the same place, you will see quite a bit of the world.

The main difficulty with this aspect is that you tend to do things to excess. You don't like anything to be small, including your own actions, so it is easy to overindulge in just about anything, which increases the danger of becoming overweight. Sometimes this position indicates personal sloppiness. Your lack of neatness means a lack of discipline, which you should deal with.

There is also a danger that you may take a lordly attitude toward the world, feeling that you are so grand and wonderful that others should bow down to you. This does not happen with most people who have Jupiter in this house, but you should be aware of the possibility, for that is the only thing that would keep you from being well liked.

You like to take care of people and protect your loved ones, because it makes you feel good about yourself and reinforces your self-image. You want to be known as someone who can be depended upon to help in times of need.

Jupiter in the Second House

You are likely to collect material possessions beyond your practical needs, because they signify security and protection to you. And the more insecure you feel, the more extreme this trait will become. But if you feel secure and confident about yourself, this will not be so much of a problem, and in fact, you will share your possessions with others and give generously to those who need it.

You will arrange to get whatever will give you the most opportunities to live more elegantly and to expand the world in which you live. When you are older you may work to earn a lot of money so you can travel and get to know a great many people in as many different places as possible. On the other hand, you may spend money recklessly to get what you want for some particular purpose, since the only value of money, to you, is what you can do with it. All you can count on with this placement is that however you handle your money, you will do it in a big way. Everything you buy has to be large and elegant. Particularly while you are young, your purchases may be quite tasteless and a waste of money, but as you get older your taste and discretion in buying will improve.

Jupiter in the Third House

You are very curious, and you take a deep interest in a wide variety of subjects. While you are young, you may go through an unusually intense period of asking questions of every adult you meet, but later on you will read and find the answers for yourself. You are most attracted to subjects that explain how much of the universe works, such as science or even literature, if it is philosophically oriented. Now, of course, you are limited by your age and mental skills, but later on you will probably read and study widely in religion, metaphysics, law and philosophy.

Quite frequently this position signifies a great love of travel. And if you cannot actually travel to foreign places, you may enjoy reading about them.

Throughout your life, you will want to be free to make up your own mind. This is not because you are especially stubborn, but your view of the world is quite expansive and tolerant, and you do not want to be limited by other people's narrow prejudices.

You should have good relations with the people in your immediate surroundings, such as neighbors and relatives. As you grow up, you are likely to receive considerable support from these people, and in the future you will think kindly of those who helped you when you were young. A brother or a sister may also be very helpful in your development, possibly providing a role model for you to pattern yourself on.

Jupiter in the Fourth House

Your childhood environment and home should be very positive, since this placement indicates that you will receive a great deal of emotional support from your parents and family. In general your early life should provide a solid basis for your adult existence, giving you a great deal of self-confidence and assurance. In particular, one of your parents is likely to be a very positive and outgoing individual with liberal tastes and a great deal of generosity, especially toward you.

Probably, even if your family is not well-to-do, your home is comfortable and pleasant, which will give you a lifelong taste for comfortable and elegant surroundings. You may always choose to live in a dwelling that is much larger than you really need, but if so you will share it with others, because this placement usually indicates that you like to extend hospitality to others.

One possible drawback to this position, but not a serious one, is that you may become very fond of collecting things, and as a result you may live in a clutter that is almost impossible to organize. Unless you adopt some kind of organizational scheme, your possessions will own you, rather than you owning them.

When you are older, you may want to own a great deal of land. Real estate transactions may be very successful for you, although you are unlikely to speculate in land, because you take its value too seriously to play with.

Jupiter in the Fifth House

This is a sign of an optimistic and cheerful temperament. You like to play and have good times in ways that are good for others as well as for yourself. You feel that by giving of yourself you have more than you would otherwise. You are cheerful with people, and you like to be with others who are the same way.

You need to be free to find your own way in life. You do not like anyone to try to restrict you, because you want to encounter as much of the world as possible.

You may enjoy sports very much, either as a participant or as an observer. You prefer outdoor games because they seem more free and open.

You may be quite creative in many ways, although this placement does not necessarily denote artistic creativity, and you will benefit from what you create. Whatever you do or create for amusement, you will do on a grand scale. You don't like to do anything halfway, and you may become well known for your habit of getting carried away by your current enthusiasm. But don't let people talk you out of this, for you will gain more through pursuing your amusements than others will through hard work. Every activity you get into expands your world and gives you valuable experience and knowledge. It is quite possible that what most people consider play will have a more important role in your life than conventional kinds of work. Certainly your hobbies and other recreations will be very important all of your life.

Jupiter in the Sixth House

This is a very useful placement, because it enables you to learn through working. You are able to put off getting something you want at the moment in favor of a goal that is more distant and usually more meaningful in the long run. By doing this, you grow in maturity and understanding. You will gain a great deal by giving to and working for others, which may not pay off immediately, but eventually it will bring you more than you can imagine.

You need to find work that is meaningful for you. Dull, repetitive and seemingly pointless tasks will turn you off very quickly, for you do not have as much patience as some people. But if you know that your duties are important, you will carry them out.

As you get older, you will try to understand the world and people through work and service to others. You will be most attracted to fields that expose you to as many different kinds of people and situations as possible. You may work in a foreign country or with foreign people, or your work may concern travel and other countries. This placement can also signify working in law, religion, medicine or philosophy.

Usually this placement means that you will have good health as long as you don't over-indulge in anything, but you must develop disciplined health habits. Otherwise you could gain too much weight or have illnesses connected with overindulgence.

Jupiter in the Seventh House

You seek to understand as much of the world as possible through close encounters with others. You want to be with people who can teach you things that you don't already know and who can expose you to new experiences. You prefer being with people who do not try to restrict you or prevent you from having any experiences you want to have. Often the people whom you like best are somewhat older and are already established in an area that you are interested in.

You work very well in small groups, and you can cooperate with another person in such a way that the two of you are an effective team. Even when you compete with others, you do so in a constructive way so that everyone gains, not just you.

When you get older, this placement will indicate the kind of person you choose for a lover. In general, you will be attracted to the same kinds of people that you enjoy being with now. But you will be reluctant to tie yourself down to one person right away, preferring to play the field and experience as many kinds of partners as possible. Eventually you might be attracted most strongly to someone whose background is quite different from yours.

Jupiter in the Eighth House

You are able to share what you have with others, and in turn they will share with you. In general you will benefit most from what you do and what you own in common with others. You need to be cooperative and to feel that others share your beliefs and values.

On another level, this placement indicates that you will go through many major, but positive and far-reaching, psychological changes in your life. Each of these major changes will take you to new levels of understanding, experience and knowledge. When you look back on your life, you will see it clearly divided into phases separated by periods of change. Usually at these times you will be assisted by someone who is older and more experienced than you.

As you get older and involved in relationships with the opposite sex, you may gain money or other material benefit from such a relationship. Even though others always seem to provide what you need, don't waste your own resources or value them less. You have to be as careful as anyone else to conserve what you have. Sometimes with this placement, you may tend to waste your resources.

You may develop an interest in medicine and healing, especially psychological healing, because you have a great interest in the process of healing and how it can be promoted. For a young person, you have an unusually good understanding of human nature.

Jupiter in the Ninth House

You are fascinated by anything new or foreign, anything that exposes you to some new aspect of the world. Your curiosity is very deep, and you want to know and understand as much as possible of the world. It is unlikely that you will remain involved with the people and environment of your early years throughout your life, but you will probably stay on good terms and in touch with them. But you have a great need to get out into the world and travel, which will probably happen when you are older, although sometimes this placement indicates travel while you are still young.

This placement also often indicates an unusual interest in ideas that help you understand and deal with the world. As you get older, you will develop an interest in philosophy or religion and possibly law or medicine, although these may be outside interests rather than your career.

You are very tolerant of the ways in which others differ from you; in fact you are even attracted to people because of their differences. You are not especially critical, and even while young you accept others for what they are. If you cannot accept them at all, you simply leave them alone.

You are of a liberal temperament, wanting to see that everyone gets their fair and honest due. With this placement, it is unlikely that you could ever lie or cheat, because those tactics simply don't accord with what you believe to be right. As you get older, this trait will be even stronger.

The only negative characteristic that may come with this placement is a tendency to be self-righteous. Always remain humble about what you believe to be right, and let others have their ideas.

Jupiter in the Tenth House

This can indicate considerable professional success later in life, if Jupiter is otherwise well placed. The reason for your future success is that one or both of your parents has instilled in you a basic confidence in yourself and in your ability to deal with the outer world. Very early in life you will seek experiences through which you can learn all you need to know about getting along in the world. You want to achieve something that is significant both to you and to others. But as you get older, you will especially want your life to deal with matters of the greatest concern to humanity. Many people with this placement are attracted to careers involving social reform, justice, higher consciousness, healing and religion. You will want to feel that your work embodies a higher order of being than your own self and the people around you.

But this placement does create one problem. If you achieve these goals in your life, you will have to keep your sense of humility about your accomplishments. If you become arrogant and self-righteous, all the good you could do will be undone, and instead of honoring you, people will envy you but feel somewhat contemptuous too.

At its best, this placement signifies that your life will revolve around caring for and protecting others and giving them greater knowledge and wisdom. You don't want to care for people by smothering them, because it is important to you to know that they are learning to take care of themselves while they are with you as well as gaining knowledge. Obviously this can be fulfilled very well if you are a teacher of some kind.

Jupiter in the Eleventh House

This indicates that you should have good luck with friends throughout your life and that you like being with others and having a good time. Especially later in life, your friends may be socially prominent people who can do favors for you. However, the danger in this is that you might choose only those friends who you think can help you get ahead socially or professionally. In that case you would be seeking out people for superficial reasons rather than for a real emotional bond. This would be unfortunate, because if you do choose friends for the right reasons, that is, for personal compatibility and mutual emotional support and affection, you will probably find people who are very good for you at all levels.

Also you are likely to seek friends who will show you new aspects of life, who can expose you to what you would never have seen otherwise. For this reason, your friends are often somewhat older and more experienced than you are, and as you get older, you are likely to play this same role for younger people.

Probably you are an idealist with high hopes and wishes for yourself. This does not mean that you are impractical but that you have set high goals for yourself. In fact, if you work hard and remain optimistic, you can probably achieve what you want, especially if you seek out friends who make you feel more confident about yourself. As you go through life, you will grow and mature most rapidly through your friends and the groups you associate with. Don't try to go it alone.

Jupiter in the Twelfth House

This placement indicates that even while young you will be very kind and generous toward less fortunate people. You see that your own growth and advancement in life depend on the advancement of everyone as a group, and you would like to help in that process. Unless there are strong indications to the contrary, you should be a very gentle person who cannot stand to see others hurt and who always takes the side of the underdog. You are more unselfish than most people of your age, and you don't worry so much about getting ahead personally. As a result, people whom you don't even know may help you during your life, and in the same way you will probably help others anonymously.

In some cases this placement may work out less easily, especially if Jupiter in this house receives difficult aspects. In that case, you would have to watch out for errors of omission or sloppiness, possibly extravagance and wastefulness, as sources of difficulty in your life. But if you are careful and pay attention to what you are doing, this should not be so much of a problem.

Unless this placement is contradicted by a strong Sun aspect, you probably do not enjoy being in the limelight very much. You prefer to remain humble and quiet, feeling that if you make a big issue of yourself, it will work against you. And when you are alone, you find comfort in the peace and quiet of your own inner world, a world that should sustain you even in difficulty.

Jupiter Conjunct Saturn

Throughout your life you will make plans and try to organize your affairs with care and discipline. You do not want to go too far too fast, and you want to have a structure that will regulate your life and keep it moving forward in the best possible manner. However, the discipline structure that you adopt must not keep you from growing, because you will develop a strong sense of objectives early in life, and you will rebel against anything that interferes with your progress toward your goals. When your life is working well, you can do everything carefully and in an orderly manner. When you take up a task, you follow it through systematically and thoroughly. You can stick to a job longer than most others, and you can keep track of many details at once.

Problems arise when something or someone stops you or gets in the way of your objectives. Unlike some people, you do not immediately fight back. Instead, you try to go on as before, but you get increasingly restless and irritable. Eventually you cannot stand it anymore, and you try to get away from the restriction. There will be many times in your life when, after getting away from some repressive energy, you will suddenly feel relief from a tension that you hadn't even known was there. This can be a problem in that when things go wrong you may often wait too long to assert yourself, and it may be more difficult to correct a problem if you have put up with it too long.

Jupiter Sextile Saturn

You are very patient and willing to work hard to attain any objective that you respect. And when you decide on your objectives, you always try to achieve a proper balance between idealism and practicality. You are willing to take some chances to bring about something new and innovative, but you are very careful about doing so. You are a hard worker and a good organizer, because you know how to relate ideas to practical human needs. While you are young, you will be interested in acquiring skills that will be useful later on. You want to achieve something of significance with your life, and even while young, you have a strong sense of duty and responsibility. You can be depended on even now, and as a result you may be given responsibilities much sooner than most. These will be an aid to your growth and advancement rather than a barrier, because you will learn how to be an adult sooner than most. You will understand your own capabilities and limitations quite early and be able to work with self-confidence.

When you are older, this aspect may signify ability in business, because you have the unusual combination of ambition, patience, perseverance, conservatism and willingness to experiment within reason.

Very often you prefer to be alone, especially while working. You are quite capable of working with others, but you are self-motivated enough to work alone.

Jupiter Square Saturn

This aspect often signifies that you are mentally restless and find it difficult to accept the world as it is. Very often you may feel that circumstances or persons limit you unnecessarily, and you work very hard to get around any limitations imposed by others. Even your internal discipline is hard to maintain at times, because you tend to get restless very easily, always looking for something better and not being satisfied with whatever you have now.

This aspect is quite common among people who have made a great deal of money, as well as those who have lost a lot of money, because it indicates that you cannot stand still; that is, you must always be moving either forward or backward. As you get older, having money may or may not be a major objective in your life, but having the power to change the world around you will be important. You want to be a person of some significance in the world. However, your restlessness and impatience may cause you to lose out on many opportunities. You must calm down and be a bit more accepting of life as it is.

Try not to constantly change your activities and objectives. Many persons with this aspect continually move from place to place, changing jobs and careers but accomplishing very little each time. You can accomplish a great deal more if you stick to one objective for some time, because you do have many skills and abilities. The problem is that if your expectations are too high, nothing can ever live up to them. Life can give you quite a bit, but you must learn to live within its limitations.

Jupiter Trine Saturn

Patience, perseverance and the desire to accomplish something significant in the world are all characteristics of this aspect. Also you are able to maintain an excellent balance of idealism, innovativeness and practicality. Even while you are young you will be able to see a situation as a whole as well as in detail. This gives you a high degree of organizing skill. Even now you can see the relationship between your present preparation and the goals you wish to achieve later in life. You are likely to succeed in school because you are willing to stick to your studies even when they are not very exciting, as long as you know that eventually they will be useful. Subjects that are totally abstract or academic do not hold much interest for you.

The abilities you develop now will be put to good use later on. You want to be useful, so you learn useful skills. When you are older you may choose a career in business. With your organizational ability and your cautious but not narrow conservatism, you would be very good in an executive or decision-making position.

Even if you do not have many exciting talents, you will be able to stick to a task, so even if you take longer, you will be so thorough and complete that the results will be worth waiting for.

Jupiter Inconjunct Saturn

This aspect may signify great restlessness and unease, so that it is difficult for you to achieve a state of balance or feel calm and at ease. Often you have contradictory impulses; you want to plunge ahead into some relatively risky activity, but you are held back by feelings of caution or inhibition. It is often difficult to decide whether you want to act on your own or in a situation that is very structured and regulated. If your situation is too structured, you will feel closed in and repressed; you will want to break free and go off by yourself and do things your way. But when you get that freedom, you feel rather lost and at loose ends, and you find it difficult to set your own pace.

You may have mixed feelings about authority as well. On one hand you respect and admire your parents, teachers and other adults who guide your growth, but at the same time you resist their teachings. At times you resent these people very much, because they seem to limit you so.

The best solution is to learn how to discipline yourself and structure your activities so that you do not have to contend with regulation by others. Then you will discover that your problems with authority come from within, not from the people who are trying to give you discipline and self-control from without. Perhaps the best way to handle this problem in your life is to make a reasonable evaluation of any situation, make up your mind rather quickly and stick to it until you have completed the activity.

Jupiter Opposition Saturn

You will have to learn to balance the tension that exists between yourself and others. This aspect can work out in one of two ways. You may be a rather cautious and conservative person who is constantly being urged to move faster and more decisively, either by persons or by circumstances. Or you may be too fast and careless, so that you are under pressure to slow down and be more careful. Perhaps you even alternate between the two positions, sometimes acting hastily, sometimes too slowly. If you do not overcome this problem, your progress in life will be halting and uneven, with many reversals and many times when you have to go back over ground that you have already covered.

Very often you feel restless and itchy, dissatisfied with what you are doing and eager to try something new, even if you haven't been working on your current project very long. This means a long string of unfinished projects and half-learned lessons.

If you can curb your natural restlessness and learn to be more patient, you will be able to go far. This aspect makes it possible for you to work in a disciplined and thorough manner, so that anything you build or do will be long lasting. Your standards are quite high, and you will pressure yourself to live up to them. In fact, this is one of the causes of your restlessness, because you often jump to the conclusion that the situation doesn't allow for you to be effective or accomplish what you want.

Jupiter Conjunct Uranus

You have a great need to be free, and you hate to be restricted in any way. This can create problems in school if you don't want to go by the required program. At the same time, you have an advantage in that your mind is quick and eager for new knowledge and a greater range of experience. However, you don't adapt easily to the more tedious and repetitive drill work that school subjects so often require.

Probably you are quite inventive, and you are often the first to see all the possibilities in a new situation. You may invent little gadgets and games, or you may organize an entirely new activity for all your friends to get involved in. And you don't mind going off in a new direction by yourself if no one else wants to follow you. You can be quite independent of other people's opinions if you are doing what you want.

At the same time you are quite willing to let others do what they want, as long as they do not try to control you. In fact, as you get older, you will be unusually tolerant of points of view that are different from your own. According to your liberal temperament, everyone should be allowed to be themselves.

As you get older, you will become interested in problems of social reform, and you may even get involved in politics somehow, but certainly not on the side of the establishment.

Jupiter Sextile Uranus

Your life will be very free, without the limitations that others have to contend with. This is because your view of life is so exciting and alive that it keeps you, as well as the circumstances around you, from falling into a rut. You can always look at a situation from a fresh viewpoint and see angles that others miss. Consequently you are able to take advantage of opportunities that others would be afraid of or would not even see.

An optimist, you have a fundamental faith that everything in your life will work out all right, as long as it stays interesting. However, you tend to get bored rather quickly by routine tasks or repetitive jobs, and these may discourage you faster than anything else. You like a lot of change and activity in your life, and you always want to be with interesting people. Fortunately you are probably quite interesting yourself, so you shouldn't have any difficulty attracting such persons.

Sometimes with this aspect, chances just seem to come to you out of the blue, but that is because you are not fully aware of the energies that you set in motion. You may be lucky, but only because you project such positive energies.

You are quite creative, and you may even be something of an inventor. You enjoy tinkering with gadgets and working on them until they are perfect. You may do this with machinery or even with a handcraft, but you are not likely to be quite so good at any craft or job that requires exacting work and great patience.

Jupiter Square Uranus

A restless person, you want everything to be better than it is immediately. As you get older, you will be willing to work to make the world better, but now you are quite impatient. Also you are unwilling to put up with any restriction or discipline, because you feel that total freedom will work out much better for you, that restrictions only prevent you from having fun. An adult may not agree, but there is some truth to your belief. You need to be given more room to find your way than most young people; otherwise, you are likely to be a disruptive discipline problem. Fortunately it is obvious to most adults that your intentions are positive, that at worst you are playful, and you do not mean any harm. But if you are held back too much, you may develop a resentment of authority that will last all your life and cause problems with bosses, officials, and anyone else in power over you.

As you get older, you will become interested in social reform because you will see traditional ways as obstacles to constructive change and growth. But you must realize that you would see traditions as harmful even if they were constructive, because you believe that new is good and old is bad. You will have to overcome this immature attitude, and you will have to learn to think more about other people's feelings and beliefs. You tend to get carried away by every interesting new idea and want to cram it down everyone's throat. If you get interested in a new philosophy of morals or ethics you may deny that any other philosophy is at all valid. Tolerance is an important lesson for you to learn.

Jupiter Trine Uranus

You love freedom and you want to see everyone get a fair break. If you believe that someone is not getting a fair deal, you will work very hard to help them and fight for their rights. You are also a questioner, always wanting to know why a situation is as it is, especially concerning rules and laws. You are not one to break rules indiscriminately, but each one has to be justified to you. Custom and tradition are not adequate explanations. In fact, you feel that these ideas are barriers to progress put up by people who are afraid of the new, which you are not. All your life you will be eager to have new and fascinating experiences, see new places and encounter new ideas. Very often mere newness, whether of ideas or objects, is enough to sell you, which means you may get stuck with some pretty worthless items. You should make sure that something has proved itself before you decide you must have it.

You are tolerant and are willing to let everyone believe what they wish. Your own philosophy of life will become quite strongly developed while you are still young, but you will not try to shove it down anyone's throat. You like to be around people who are different from you, and in fact you are attracted by their differences. All your life you will be attracted to exciting people and situations because they make you feel more alive and interesting, although you aren't likely to be a dull person. In some people's eyes you may seem eccentric and strange, but that will not bother you as long as you are doing what you want.

Jupiter Inconjunct Uranus

With this aspect, especially if either of the planets is in conjunction or opposition with the Ascendant or Midheaven, you may be unable to decide whether you should act alone in total freedom or with others in group or social situations. Also you may not trust any ideas, values and concepts that you share with the people around you. For example, you may feel that instead of believing something that others believe, you have to establish your own ideas and values. You may try to be a nonconformist simply for its own sake, which obviously is a waste. The validity of an idea is totally independent of how many people believe it, and it is as bad to automatically reject what others believe as to accept it blindly.

You will always need freedom, but you will also discover that what you do with your life will have meaning only if it means something to others. This is not an artificial rule but a truth that you will discover within yourself. When you do, you may become heavily involved in some social movement that advocates unusual ideas or ways of thinking. When you are an adult, you may join a movement for social reform and change. However, even in a group that embodies your own thinking, you will find it hard to adjust to the group's demands on your own time and freedom. Consequently you will probably leave that group and join another, until that one also becomes oppressive. While you are young, you may have a similar problem with your friends as well. When they start to expect too much of your time and energy, you will break away from them.

Jupiter Opposition Uranus

You are a nonconformist and a rebel, and you will spend much of your life finding your own path. You will have to define most of your ideas for yourself, because you won't be satisfied with the beliefs handed to you by others. As you get older, you may live by new standards that are very upsetting to the older generation, so you will have to contend with quite a bit of resistance from others. However, a factor in your favor is that you are clearly not trying to dominate anyone else, and also you are not acting purely for your own benefit. Even while you are young, you have a strong ideal of social order, and you will work to change the existing order rather than escape it.

The greatest danger with this aspect is that you may become rigid or self-righteous about your beliefs and try to force others to agree with them. You may believe that you are doing this for the benefit of those around you, but some part of you is trying to compel others to agree with you so you can feel better about your own ideas.

Think twice before you upset tradition. Many traditions exist for good reason, even though those who believe in them can't always defend them. But you will understand the value of that tradition after it has been destroyed, when it cannot be brought back. Be as free as you have to be, but let others be free in their own way, even if it does not seem like freedom to you.

Jupiter Conjunct Neptune

Your ideals are very high, and you are a bit of a dreamer, who sees visions of a more pleasant and beautiful world than this one. Also you are an optimist, believing that somehow everything in your life will work out just fine. In fact, no matter how often matters go badly, it does not seem to disturb you. This has the positive value of helping you stay cheerful in the face of adversity, but it can also result in being blind to the need for change in your life. You may delude yourself that a situation is marvelous, when actually it is not.

Often this aspect signifies a desire to take risks in the foolish belief that you cannot fail. Gamblers and speculators may have this aspect, which by itself does not tell whether or not you wil be lucky. It can go either way. But even if you are not lucky, you may think that you are. If you really lose out whenever you take risks, come down out of your cloud and realize that you are losing. Learn to be more cautious. While you are young it is easy to change your habits, but as you get older you might become quite addicted to gambling and be unable to change.

On a higher level, this aspect can indicate, even in a young person, a strong concern with spirituality and religion. You need to believe in some higher power in the universe that relates to your life and gives it meaning. As you get older, this belief can blossom into quite a beautiful trait of being very loving, generous and compassionate to everyone. Also you may have a strong mystical streak, a desire to be personally close to God.

Jupiter Sextile Neptune

You are sensitive to the needs of others and willing to help those in need. You have very high ideals, one of which is making life better for others, even if you have to sacrifice something of your own. But you are not a "cockeyed optimist." You can tell the difference between what is true and what is not, and you are willing to accept reality, although you will work to change it.

Even while you are young, you will be interested in religious and spiritual ways of thinking. You need to feel that you are in tune with a higher, more universal being than yourself. You may also enjoy hearing or reading tales of wonderful fantasy realms where magic is real and strange beings still exist.

You may be a bit of a gambler, but you keep it under control, so that it amounts to an intuition about where to look for opportunities, which you often see before anyone else does. But you won't take foolish chances very often.

With your excellent imagination, you can bring creativity to such areas as art and literature, if you take the trouble to study them. However, by itself this aspect will not signify concrete achievements unless you work to develop your talent. You could simply drift through life in a very pleasant world of your own, which would be a waste of the very real creative talent signified by this aspect.

Jupiter Square Neptune

This is not likely to be a very difficult aspect, but you should watch out for some of its negative characteristics so that you can avoid them, and you should also learn to take advantage of its positive side.

On the negative side, this aspect may indicate that you are very dreamy, living in a fantasy world that has little relationship to reality. You tend to be foolishly optimistic, never taking into account the real risks in any venture. Because of this, you may lose material possessions and even friends.

You like to see the best in people, ignoring anything bad even when it is hurting you. On the other hand, this is a strong point in a way, because you are nonjudgmental and willing to accept people with all their flaws. Just make sure that you are realistic about their flaws, without pretending that they don't exist.

Sometimes you may set your ideals too high or have grossly inflated expectations in some situation. Of course you will be disappointed, and then you will become disillusioned and see nothing good in the world. But that is just the other side of the same coin. In either case you are refusing to accept reality, which is usually not as ideal as you would like to think.

The positive side of this aspect is that if you are reasonably in tune with reality, you will take risks that may have quite magnificent results. You refuse to let fear of losing keep you from trying out new things, so your life may be richer than the lives of those who are more cautious.

Jupiter Trine Neptune

With this aspect you are likely to be very interested in religion, metaphysics and spiritual matters—unusually profound subjects for a person of your age. At this time you are not able to deal with these ideas in a very sophisticated way, but you want to know about God, the relation of man to God, and what God means to you in particular. You use your own language and your own imagery in thinking about this, but you are definitely concerned with these ideas quite early in life.

Also you are more of an idealist than most, although you will soon understand the world as it really is. Sometimes you are quite impractical, but only because you have such a deep desire to make the world a better place than it is.

Many people with this aspect are quite unselfish. You are able to see that what benefits others benefits you as well, which is true, but most young people are not able to see that. Even while you are quite young, you may become involved in charitable projects, such as taking care of sick, disabled or disadvantaged people. Or you may enjoy taking care of sick or wounded animals.

Basically you are an optimist. You recognize that the world has its faults, but you feel that on the whole it is all right. Also you are willing to take considerable chances if you feel the goal is worthwhile. Others may think of you as a gambler, but you don't usually gamble for frivolous reasons.

Jupiter Inconjunct Neptune

You are an idealist with very vivid dreams about how you want your life to be, and at certain times in your life you will follow those dreams with all your energy. But sometimes these idealistic dreams will let you down, because you are not concerned enough with what is real and possible. Your parents and other adults may pressure you to be more practical in your thinking, but you think they are just throwing cold water on your aspirations. Yet learning to handle the real world is a very important part of your development, because it is the only way you can avoid becoming bitter and disillusioned when your more impractical ideas have led you into disappointment.

Probably you should not gamble or take excessive risks at any time in your life. Your dreams in this area also will probably go far beyond reality, and you will take chances that can't possibly be realized.

By itself, this aspect does not guarantee that you will have such problems, but if it is reinforced by other, similar aspects in your chart, you should certainly be careful of a tendency toward escapism. It is always easier to create an ideal reality within your mind than in the world, but the world is where you must work. Escapism can include using drugs or alcohol or following strange and delusive religious beliefs. As you get older, you may fall into the trap of guru worship and deny your own vitality.

Your idealism can be the source of much creative imagination, leading to profound insights and realizations, but only if you remain connected with the actual day-to-day universe in which the rest of the human race lives.

Jupiter Opposition Neptune

This can be a positive aspect, in that you have high ideals of a better world for yourself and others, but you are sometimes foolish in believing that everything and everyone is much better than they really are. You may often have serious delusions about people, and when you discover that the people you idealize have feet of clay, you are very disappointed and reject them totally. You demand that the people who are close to you live up to very high standards, but you must learn to accept their limitations. Everyone is human and has human flaws, although it may take you a while to realize that.

Sometimes you are much too trusting, especially of people who propose that you join in wild and impossible schemes. If you are not careful, you are very likely to be swindled. Also avoid risky gambles, because your gambling instincts are not all that good. This is especially important to follow as you get older. While you are young, it isn't such a risk. But even now you shouldn't get into the habit of trusting those who are not worthy of it and distrusting those who really can be trusted.

However, if you take suitable precautions and use your reason as well as your instincts in making decisions, you can take some realistic chances that will bring you opportunities that others would overlook. With your basic optimism, tempered with realism, you will have a very happy and rewarding life.

Jupiter Conjunct Pluto

You have a strong drive to achieve something of significance, and you want to have the power to make positive and creative changes in your world. Most people with this aspect find that it provides considerable help in pursuing a career, getting along with others—except as indicated below—and making a name for themselves. This aspect does not guarantee fame, because it affects so many people at once, but it usually indicates that you will achieve something in your own way.

However, there are some pitfalls with this aspect. If you push too hard to get ahead, you may create enemies who will try to stop you. Especially while you are young, you must remember to consider other people's interests and give them room to achieve along with you. If your personal success can carry others to success as well, you win helpful friends instead of making enemies. This is especially important in dealing with parents, teachers and other authority figures, because otherwise you may make these people think that you are a threat to their ways of doing things. Instead of trying so hard to get ahead, bide your time and learn what you need while you are young. Save your ambitious energies for when you are older. But even then, if you work for someone else, don't act as if you are trying to displace your superiors, or they will displace you. This aspect can be an enormous aid to personal success, but only if you follow this advice.

Jupiter Sextile Pluto

You will strive to improve conditions in any group that you are part of, not only for your own benefit, but for the others as well. You will be quite good at coordinating the aims and ambitions of several persons at once, creating a group that can act quite effectively. Thus you will be a catalyst for a great deal of the action that goes on around you, even though it will usually be difficult to trace what happens to anything particular that you have done.

Your peers, however, will probably recognize your ability and give you the opportunity to be their leader. As you get older, your understanding of what must be done and how to do it will get sharper, so you should be able to accomplish a great deal for yourself and others.

As you get older, but even now while you are young, you are aware of the need for spiritual understanding and concern in life. Very early, you will develop a strong code of ethics and morality, which you will follow all your life. You recognize the power of goodness, and whenever you break that code, you will regret it very strongly.

The only warning here is to maintain a sense of humility. Do not take a position of righteousness toward others, and be tolerant of their weaknesses as well as your own. No one can be perfect, and you should be careful not to think that you are.

Jupiter Square Pluto

This aspect means that you have a strong will to succeed, and you want to have the power to influence people. But you may not have the patience and tolerance of others that makes success easy to achieve. You are likely to be impatient and unwilling to let anyone else have their way. In that case, others will see you as a threat that they will resist strongly. If you are not careful, you will have to contend with one group of people after another trying to keep you from getting what you want. Especially while you are young, you will have trouble with authority figures, unless you learn to restrain your strong will. They will see you as an upstart who has to be put in your place. In some cases this aspect may even mean trouble with the law, if you don't restrain its energies.

Ideas are very important to you, but you must learn to keep them in perspective. It is fine to believe in something very deeply, but you tend to let your beliefs gain control over you and run your life. When you are older, you may be obsessed with some rather fanatical ideas. You must always be careful that your beliefs serve you and reinforce the quality of your life. Do not become a slave to them.

If you can follow this advice, you will achieve a great deal in your life, and you have an excellent chance of becoming a leader within your world.

Jupiter Trine Pluto

You have high standards for your friends as well as for yourself. You want the best, and you are willing to work to make your life better. As a result you will grow and change for the better throughout your life, as long as you do not become so involved in anything that you cannot give it up when the time comes. Usually this aspect indicates a strong sense of morality and ethics. Even while you are young you will try to do whatever is right and honorable in a situation. And you are not likely to allow your friends or anyone around you to do anything that you consider immoral or base. Other young people do this because they want to please adults by being "good." But your behavior is based on a strong inner sense of right and wrong. Consequently you are not likely to sit by when someone hurts another person.

You have the temperament of a reformer, but you are willing to work patiently to bring about reforms. You see no need for hurrying and thus upsetting the apple cart in order to make changes. You are perfectly willing to work through any system that will help bring about change. For this reason you may become quite successful in business or politics when you are older, because you are so good at handling the systems by which society is run. Also you can see, even now, how to get people to work together harmoniously, by coordinating everyone's goals and making it possible to achieve them with a united effort.

Jupiter Inconjunct Pluto

You have a great deal of creative power, and the major challenge of your life will be learning how to handle it. First of all, you must realize that you will get the most out of life if you direct your energies toward helping the people around you and those you love. You will want to change many conditions in the world, which is fine as long as your reasons are not purely selfish ones.

If you use the energies of this aspect selfishly, you will have serious conflicts with authorities, persons in power and adults in general. You may try to make changes before you have learned how to do so creatively, without provoking such resistance that your efforts are blocked. To be effective, you must have the necessary skills.

You may have a natural talent for dominating others, but don't fall in love with this talent and be motivated by it. You can be effective at influencing people only if you use your power to help others and yourself achieve desirable goals together. You must be an agent for betterment at all times, and even so you must listen to others' ideas about betterment to be sure that you aren't just seeking power in a more roundabout manner.

Even at best you will get a certain amount of resistance from others, because they will feel your energy and be afraid of your motives. Unless you show them that your motives are good and that you can be reasoned with, you will run into opponents who are more powerful than you, who will stop you and make your efforts futile.

Jupiter Opposition Pluto

This aspect is extremely useful for many purposes, but you will have to learn how to control its energies. You are very impatient to make immediate changes in your world. You want very much to have the power to control others so that they will do what you think is right. If you are not given this power, you may work behind the scenes to bring about the changes you want, in spite of opposition from everyone. You may be unwilling to let anyone else make suggestions, for you feel that you have all the answers, that you are totally right. Especially when you are older, this aspect can signify fanatical ideals of righteousness, rigid notions of justice, and the feeling that everyone else must be forced to follow whatever you consider right.

Obviously this approach can lead only to intense and furious opposition from others. You may not understand why people oppose you so much; in fact, you may not even be aware that you are putting people off. You must learn to compromise, at least to the extent of letting others have a say in what happens. It is possible to make it clear that you only want what is best for everyone without making them feel threatened.

If you can be somewhat humble about your ideals and respect others' beliefs, this aspect can bring you great success and achievement. Others will be inspired by your strong convictions. But if you do not consider others' rights, you will provoke opposition, which may block all chances of success.

Jupiter Conjunct Ascendant

This aspect usually helps you get along with people, because your generosity and helpfulness make a good impression on them. You are open and honest and prefer to be around other people who are also. Usually you are optimistic and cheerful, and even when you are not very happy inside, you manage to hide it from others. When you are so unhappy that you can't hide your feelings, people are naturally sympathetic and want to help you.

You like to be free to have as many different kinds of experiences as possible. As a result, your life is likely to be more varied than most. With this same energy, you will probably travel or live in many different places during your life, and in each place you will get to know the local customs and habits almost as if they were your own.

You also enjoy traveling in your mind, exploring all kinds of ideas and considering many different ways of thinking. Your range of thought is broader than most people's, and even while you are young, grown-ups will be surprised by your interest in a wide variety of subjects.

For the most part, you are very tolerant of other people's ways, except perhaps concerning ethical behavior. Even as a young person, your ideas of right and wrong are well defined. Your code of ethics may be different from other people's, but it is none-theless strong. As long as people don't break your rules, you let them be. But if someone violates your sense of ethics, you get quite angry and even unforgiving, unless the person in question is extremely apologetic and sorry for his or her actions.

Jupiter Sextile Ascendant

You enjoy being with people and having a lot of friends, and with your pleasant personality, you shouldn't have any trouble attracting people. Also you should have quite good experiences through others, and when you are older, your friends may help you quite a bit.

You are on good terms with your relatives and the people whom you encounter every day. You make an excellent impression on everyone you meet, and when they see that you like to help people, they are willing to help you as well. You are so optimistic and cheerful that you make others feel good even when you are down.

You are quick to take advantage of any opportunity that comes your way, but you are not likely to take advantage of people in a way that would hurt them. You are too idealistic for that.

Your expectations for life are quite high, and you want to go far. Sometimes, however, this aspect signifies a feeling that the world owes you a living, so that you don't work as hard as you ought to. This aspect can bring you opportunities, but you must be willing to develop the skills that will enable you to take advantage of them.

In general, you are attracted to those who are generous, optimistic, reasonably wise and mature. You cannot stand people who are petty and narrow, because you are not that way yourself. However, you are quite willing to overlook other faults, for you are generally tolerant of people's human flaws. You prefer to look at their good side rather than dwell on the bad.

Jupiter Square Ascendant

This aspect usually works out very well, for it enables you to make a favorable impression on others and to benefit through others all your life. However, sometimes you may get so wrapped up in your own personal needs and desires that you demand more from others than you give back in return. If this tendency goes too far, it would negate most of the good effects of this aspect. You must remember that life is a kind of transaction and that in order to receive, you have to give. Fortunately, if you feel secure and confident about yourself, it won't be hard to remember this. It is only when you feel that your personal life is in trouble that you are likely to become selfish.

Especially as you get older, you will want to do everything in a big way, both in your personal life and in your career. You like to live in a large house in elegant surroundings, and you like to have plenty of room outdoors as well. When you are an adult you may very well own a lot of real estate. You will want to choose a career in a field that offers a variety of experiences in many different worlds. If possible, you would like to travel in your work.

One of your parents will make an enormous impression upon you; in fact, you may spend a large part of your life trying to emulate that parent or live up to his or her expectations. This is fine as long as you don't frustrate your own desires in the process. Ultimately you must live according to your own expectations, not someone else's.

Jupiter Trine Ascendant

You are a fun-loving and gregarious person who enjoys good humor and likes to play an occasional joke, although not to hurt anyone. You like to go to parties and other friendly gatherings, and you enjoy being the life of the party whenever possible. In fact, you sometimes find it difficult to face the serious side of life, when you have to. You are so optimistic that you never expect life to come out wrong.

In school this can create some problems if your ideas of fun don't fit in with your teacher's system of discipline. But even so, you will get along all right in school because you are able to charm and win over your teachers as well as your fellow students. Also, you really do·have an interest in learning. You like to learn about new facts and view the world from as broad a perspective as possible. Ideas are fascinating to you because they help you make sense of the world.

All your life you will be very curious, wanting to know the answers to as many questions as possible. While you are young you will probably ask your parents a million questions. As you get older, you will be interested in subjects that have a great social impact, such as philosophy, religion, medicine, law and other fields that affect society as a whole and deal with larger issues. Also you may want to travel widely in the world as well as in your mind. Certainly you will not want to be tied down in one place doing one thing all your life.

Jupiter Inconjunct Ascendant

With this aspect, you may discover that in order to grow and get ahead in life, you will have to put aside your own needs and do whatever the situation or other people require. At times you will go through tremendous and possibly painful creative changes in your life, in which everything that you are is replaced by a new order. Your environment may change radically, or you may lose all your old friends and find a whole set of new ones. During these times you will arrive at new understandings and realizations that make it impossible for your life to continue as before. You must always be open to new ideas and be willing to change your outlook on life.

Probably you will accomplish the most if you direct your energies to tasks that benefit others as well as yourself. It may be that much of your work will not benefit you directly, but in the long run you will gain from it. Even while you are young you need to make a useful contribution to society, and in doing this you will learn and grow as an individual. This is not merely a plea for you to be unselfish, but an assertion that you will achieve your own goals most quickly by doing work that helps others.

On the other hand, if you try to get what you want for yourself alone, especially at other people's expense, you will find it hard to get anywhere. Also you will have difficulty maintaining your friendships and other relationships. With this aspect, being selfish could have very negative results for your eventual happiness. Do not try to selfishly hold on to what you have. If you give of yourself freely, you will have more.

Jupiter Opposition Ascendant

You seek out people who can help you grow and enlarge your personal world. You enjoy learning from others, and you don't mind admitting your inadequacies to anyone who can help you become wiser and more understanding. You may idealize those whom you are close to, but probably not to the extent that you will be hurt or disillusioned when you discover their flaws. You also enjoy being with people whose backgrounds are very different from yours, because they expose you to new ideas and ways of living.

Usually this aspect denotes good relationships with others, but sometimes in a close relationship you may be so restless that you are unable to make a close emotional commitment. While you are young, this is not important, but it can be a source of trouble when you are older and have relationships with possessive, jealous people who try to limit your freedom. You will always want freedom to be with anyone who strikes your fancy.

Often you feel closest to people who are older and seem more mature. When you are grown up, you may marry or have a close sexual relationship with someone who is five to ten years older than you.

Generally speaking, you have a strong sense of honor about those whom you are close to. You want to do the best you can by them, and you want the same in return. Most of your close relationships will be very positive growth experiences that benefit both you and the other person.

Jupiter Conjunct Midheaven

You are an ambitious person who wants to get ahead, not just for yourself, but for the benefit of the larger world to which you belong. While you are young, you will express this as an interest in issues that are usually of concern only to older people. Your wide-ranging interests may include such topics as religion, geography, and even politics and government. In school you may get involved in student government and become quite a leader among your classmates. But they will respect you for this, because while you make it clear that you expect to benefit personally from what you do, you also feel responsible to those around you.

If you receive any kind of religious education while you are young, it will have a tremendous impact, and you will carry those teachings with you all your life. As a result, your standards of ethics and morality will be higher than most people's. You will always be concerned with doing what is right for its own sake, not for what you can get from it. In fact, this position is often found in the charts of those who enter the ministry or priesthood. If you don't receive any religious training while you are young, you will develop your own religious views anyway, which will be as important to you as if they had been taught from earliest childhood. You will always want your life to stand for the highest and best values—honor, integrity, respect and truth. Even when you cannot uphold these principles as you would like, you will respect them. And if you violate your principles, you will hurt yourself more than anyone else.

Jupiter Sextile Midheaven

You will always be able to bring people into your life who can help you move forward in pursuit of your life goals. And you will help them in return. You know how to make a group of people work harmoniously so that everyone can get some part of what they want.

You are psychologically and emotionally sound, and you do not have neurotic habits that work against you. Even if, like most people, you have some emotional problems, they will not constitute a major barrier to your progress. In fact they may even help you out in ways that you do not understand.

Often other people will put their resources at your disposal, because they realize that you can do more with what they have than they can. They see that you have a great sense of responsibility for the people whom you are close to.

While you are young, this aspect will bring you sudden opportunities that will help you get where you want to go in life. You will get along easily with superiors and authority figures, because you make it clear to them that you want to learn and are willing to put aside your own ideas and desires until you are wiser and more mature. In this respect you are more mature than most people of your age. Some people with this aspect know what career they want to pursue very early in life. But even if that is not true for you, everything that you study or do will help you in the long run and support the course you eventually take in life.

Jupiter Square Midheaven

You have a lot of energy, and you want to accomplish something in life, but you will have to learn how to balance your own interests with the interests of other people in your life. If you do that, you can have good relations with others and achieve what you want as well. Sometimes this aspect indicates a selfish attitude, a feeling that you are the only one who counts in this world. If you carry this too far, you will find that everyone you meet works against you because you seem so selfish and arrogant or just because you come on too strong.

Sometimes this aspect means you have conflicts with authority figures, because they feel that you are trying to get above your proper place or that you are a threat to them. While you are young, you should avoid getting a reputation as a smart-aleck, because such people do not get many breaks from others, especially those above them.

You have a very strong belief in right and wrong, but you must learn to have more compassion for those who are on the wrong track. You are strongly tempted to preach to people who are in error, and you may do this at times. But then everyone will watch you to see what kinds of mistakes you make. If you can be more humble and realize that you do not have all the answers, you can convert the negative elements of this aspect to a very positive energy. Others will feel very good about you, knowing they can trust you to do whatever is right and necessary in a situation.

Jupiter Trine Midheaven

This aspect will be extremely useful, first by helping you find the right direction to take in your life and, second, by enabling you to make others feel positive about you and eager to help if you need it. You are able to pursue your goals without making people feel that if you succeed you will take something away from them. You have a strong sense of social responsibility, a feeling that you should give your life over to a purpose that is useful to the world. It isn't that you are totally unselfish or self-sacrificing, but that nothing seems worth doing unless it is of use to others.

You will always get along easily with authorities, and while you are young that usually means people who are older. You know that they have something to teach you, and you are willing to learn from them. You don't feel you have to show everyone how smart you are, even though you believe that you are rather special. You are willing to take your time and let the world find out how much you can do.

You will always have a project to work on, because you hate to be idle, either in mind or body. Usually you are busy with some consuming interest, which may mean more to you than being with others. You feel that you are self-sufficient, that your activities are enough to give you a sense of fulfillment in life. You don't feel an urgent need to be with others all the time.

Jupiter Inconjunct Midheaven

This aspect can mean that you have mixed feelings toward adults and persons in authority over you. Although you know that they have your best interests at heart and that they want you to succeed at your own objectives, it often seems as if their demands are keeping you from doing what you want. When you want to go off and have fun, for example, you are told to finish your work first. At times you want to break free of this restricting influence and go off by yourself.

The problem with this aspect is to find a balance between, on the one hand, expressing yourself creatively, perhaps artistically, and having a good time and, on the other hand, getting ahead in life, learning the ways of the world and finding an acceptable role in society. You know you will have to make sacrifices in order to accomplish anything of value.

Later in life, you will enter a critical period when your need for personal satisfaction and freedom force you to change jobs or even careers. When you have learned more about the world, you will understand how to make changes intelligently, but now you should discipline your Jupiterian drive for freedom and learn what you need to know to take over your own destiny. You should learn as much as possible about any subject or skill that will make you more aware of the larger world. Travel or foreign study would be beneficial, if that is possible. The more you know about how you fit into the larger scheme of life, the easier it will be to make the right decision when you have to change to a more rewarding and personally satisfying course.

Jupiter Opposition Midheaven

Your home and family are very important to you as a refuge that you can retreat to when the outer world is too harsh. You will always remember your childhood as one of the best times of your life, and you will have great respect for your parents, especially the one who gave you the most emotional support.

As you get older, you will remember what you had when you were younger, and you will love anything that reminds you of home. Wherever you go, you will try to find a community like the one you grew up in. And if you can't find such a community, you will seek one in which people are as close as they were where you grew up. All your life you will have great respect for traditions and customs, even if they are very different from your own, not because you are narrowly conservative, but because you know they give people positive emotional support. Temperamentally you are quite liberal, and you enjoy the experience of new places and different worlds.

All of your life you will prefer rather large and elegant homes surrounded by lots of open space. You hate to be cramped, physically or emotionally, so you avoid close relationships with people who are very jealous or possessive, because they would restrict your inner freedom.

Normally this aspect signifies a high degree of emotional security, which enables you to withstand any difficult times and even offer help to others when they are in trouble.

Chapter Eleven

Saturn

Saturn in the Chart

Saturn represents the rules and limitations of your life, the things you cannot do and the places you cannot go. That may seem like a negative function, but it is extremely valuable, because no one has the resources or energies to do everything, even though your Mars and Jupiter energies may make you want to. Thus Saturn gives form to your life and a sense of discipline so that you can be more effective in the areas you concentrate on. Without this energy you would spread yourself too thin.

The effect of Saturn's placement in the signs is generational and therefore not very personal, unless it is near conjunction or opposition to the Ascendant or Midheaven or in close aspect to the Sun, Moon or an inner planet. Its sign position describes characteristics of whole groups of people. But Saturn's house position signifies the area of your life in which the limitations seem most severe or discipline is most called for. It also represents the area where you can direct the most concentrated energies.

Saturn's aspects are very important, especially if it aspects the Sun, Moon, Midheaven or Ascendant. It has a quieting effect on any area it touches and gives discipline and form to the energy of the planet it is aspecting. If the two planets are in a favorable combination, the Saturn aspect can signify your most effective energies. However, a difficult aspect can signify your worst problems, because Saturn in harsh aspect tends to repress the energy of the other planet. Then that energy goes into your unconscious mind and creates psychological or even physical problems until you can release it. Saturn is often related to one's father, and difficult aspects with Saturn often indicate problems in your relationship with your father.

Saturn in Aries

This sign placement of your natal Saturn is important for you personally if Saturn is near conjunction or opposition with your Midheaven or Ascendant or is aspecting the Sun or Moon. It indicates that you have difficulty thinking of yourself in easy, constructive relationships with other people. You are afraid that people will inhibit you and keep you from getting what you want, or that they will try to control you in ways that you don't like. Thus you try to remain alone and independent of others, and yet you are rather lonely, because you still need human contact. The best solution is to seek out people who will allow you to be yourself and avoid critical persons, unless you really believe that their criticism is constructive and well-meant. Your relationship with your father is extremely important; if it is not positive, you may have a greater feeling of frustration and even more difficulty getting along with people.

Obviously, then, this placement is constructive in that it can help you become an independent person. You can learn how to stand on your own and take positions on issues without relying on others for support. You do not feel that it is necessary to either reject or follow anyone else's advice. You will make up your mind according to your own criteria. Just be careful not to let your independence make it impossible to love and be friends with others.

This placement also makes you cautious and careful. You do not like to let your energies flow without following some kind of structure. You prefer orderly activities in which you have a definite feeling for what is wrong and what is right.

Saturn in Taurus

This placement is most important to you personally if Saturn is near opposition or conjunction with the Ascendant or Midheaven or closely aspecting the Sun or Moon. You have a great need to establish a firm foundation in your life. When you have total freedom to do what you want, you feel uneasy. You need a secure center in your life, a place or set of conditions that you can count on as long as you live. However, this drive for security may make you become rigid and fearful about approaching anything new in your life. Even at best, it is sometimes difficult for you to change and adapt. On the other hand, you are incredibly resistant to adversity and hard times.

You may find it difficult to share with others, not because you are selfish, especially, but because you are afraid that there may not be enough to go around. Consequently you hold on to your share for dear life. You should trust the world to take care of you a bit more. It is important that your parents make you feel that their support and your resources are not likely to be taken away. And they shouldn't make you feel that you have to work terrifically hard to get what you need. Of course, you will have to work, but if you do so from fear, it will be all the harder. Everything will work out for you if you believe that it will.

All through your youth, you need lots of support and love from your parents. You need to know that you are loved and that you have a right to be here. Don't be jealous of your friends or afraid that someone will take a friend away from you. There is plenty of love and enough material resources to go around.

Saturn in Gemini

This placement of Saturn is significant only if Saturn is near conjunction or opposition with your Ascendant or Midheaven or in close aspect to the Sun or Moon. Throughout your life you will have to approach learning with discipline and order. You find it difficult to think about intangible or undefined ideas or those that are not well organized. At best this means that you express yourself to others very clearly. But it is also a limitation in that some important ideas or bits of knowledge cannot be expressed in clear logical terms. You will need to work on developing your intuition and emotional responsiveness, or your ability to understand will be limited.

You also need to be more flexible in your thinking and more relaxed in communication. You may believe that you have to know everything about a subject before you can say anything about it. You may be too cautious in advancing your own opinions for fear of being wrong. But it's no sin to be wrong, and you must learn to have the courage to state your beliefs, right or wrong. The only way you can really learn from others is to enter into discussions, say what you believe, and risk making an error. Each time you make a mistake, you will learn from it, but even more important, every time you are right you learn something about yourself and your strengths.

On another level, you will understand better than most how to turn abstract ideas into practical realities. You will be good at applying other people's thoughts to solve real problems. And you are not bad at abstract thinking, either, although your ultimate test for any idea will always be its usefulness.

Saturn in Cancer

This placement of Saturn is important only if Saturn is near conjunction or opposition with the Ascendant or Midheaven or in close aspect with the Sun or Moon.

You need a great deal of emotional security. You must believe that you are loved and that you can rely on your home and family as a refuge in times of personal trouble. Basically you are afraid that your family may not be reliable, that they may abandon you when you most need help.

It is especially important for you to know that you will be loved and supported no matter what you do and who you are. Otherwise, with this Saturn position, your deep-rooted insecurity will be expressed as distrust of others and hiding your feelings from everyone. You may pretend that you are unfeeling and have no concern for others, when really you are very much in need of warmth and affection from them. As an adult, you might get to the point of being totally out of touch with your feelings, not understanding your reactions to persons and situations and thus constantly doing violence to your inner self. Your emotional insecurity can also make you feel that you don't belong anywhere or to anyone, that you are isolated and alone in an unfriendly world. This won't happen if you get lots of unconditional love while you are young.

On the plus side, with this placement you are able to discipline your feelings and remain in control at times when others are completely at the mercy of their emotions. You know how to feel without losing track of yourself and your objectives, but only if you are basically confident of yourself and of your place in others' lives.

Saturn in Leo

This placement will have the strongest effect if your natal Saturn is near conjunction or opposition with the Ascendant or Midheaven or in close aspect to the Sun or Moon. It indicates that you have an unusually strong feeling of isolation from others. You tend to remain alone and separate, especially if you think that the people around you are not as good as you. But you shouldn't cultivate this attitude, if only because it will make you feel very lonely, and you will lose any chance to really understand how other people work.

Sometimes you find it very difficult to express yourself, but you should be encouraged to do so as much as possible when it is appropriate. If you are allowed to follow your tendency to be extremely reserved, you will be further cut off from others.

The standards you set for yourself are probably very high, but you will adhere to them even if those around you do not. Your ideals of what is and is not worthwhile come largely from within yourself, and you feel that this should be the case with everyone. You are more of an individualist than most people your age, and if encouraged and given plenty of emotional support, you can become very self-reliant. But don't be too hard upon yourself as you grow up.

More than most young people, you need a strongly knit family. Your father is especially important, because you will look to him in particular for your standards of behavior. If he is not present, does not pay much attention to you, or does not set sufficiently high standards, you will have difficulty setting a course for yourself.

Saturn in Virgo

This placement is strong only if Saturn is near conjunction or opposition to your Ascendant or Midheaven or in close aspect to the Sun or Moon. You will quickly develop a fondness for everything that is clear, precise, practical and definite. You demand orderliness, which you should be surrounded by if you are to develop properly. At the same time, you should not be encouraged to think that order is the only worthwhile aspect of life. Like everyone else, you must learn more human values, for otherwise you could be quite unfeeling toward other people's weaknesses.

You should be given opportunities to perform useful tasks and do good work. You have great respect for such activity, and later in life your self-esteem will come from knowing that you are a useful person who can perform functions that others can't or won't. In this, you are a very practical person. You do not like spending your energies unless you know exactly how the effort will pay off in practical results. But you should try to avoid a totally practical outlook on life, because ideals are important, too.

Very early in life you will develop a strong critical sense, but you must be careful not to turn it against yourself. Persons with a strong Virgo are likely to be very self-deprecating, and with Saturn in Virgo you are particularly likely to condemn yourself for mediocre work or performance. Probably your standards are very high, which is fine, but also let yourself and others fail now and then without condemnation.

Saturn in Libra

This placement is strong only when Saturn is near conjunction or opposition with the Ascendant or Midheaven or in close aspect to the Sun or Moon. It indicates that you need plenty of time to make decisions and that you always want to know everything about the subject before making up your mind. Others may think you are indecisive at times, but they will find that when you finally make a decision, it is usually right.

You may be somewhat reserved in relations with others, but once you commit yourself, you will stay with that person—friend or lover—for a long time. Your strong sense of fairness is evident in your relationships as well as in every other area of your life. You are conscious of rules and duty toward your friends, and you are not likely to break an agreement that you have made with someone. You take relationships so seriously that you would never make an agreement lightly. While you are young, this trait might not be very obvious, but it will be clearer as you get older.

You are very concerned that everyone has what they deserve, and your sense of justice is outraged when someone takes advantage of someone else.

If you are not encouraged to encounter other people and to believe in yourself, you may prefer to be alone, unburdened by the necessity of relating to others. Or you may feel that others do not understand you. As you get older, this should diminish.

Saturn in Scorpio

This placement is strong only if Saturn is near conjunction or opposition with the Midheaven or Ascendant or in close aspect to the Sun or Moon. Deep and intense psychological change may be very difficult for you to withstand. You may try to ignore it or to repress the energies that come from deep inside you. But this tendency should not be allowed to develop further, because if it does, your emotional impulses will force you to do things that you really do not want to do. Also you may have trouble with other forms of compulsive behavior. For example, you might work on a project until you are dead tired, just because something inside tells you to go on, even though you consciously see no reason for it. While you are young and strong, this is not a problem, but when you are older you could ruin your health. You must try very hard to understand what is motivating you and to accept it, whatever it is. In fact, you must work very hard to accept all aspects of your character no matter how strange they seem. They probably would not seem particularly strange to others, but your reluctance to communicate about such things may lead you to think that you are very different from everyone else. This is not usually the case.

Also, you may be reluctant to express your true feelings, because you prefer to keep an outward appearance of calm and control. But this is not always good for you, because everyone needs to release their feelings from time to time, especially while you are young. On the plus side, when you are under intense pressure, you can show your emotions and still be more in control of them than most people. That can be very helpful when the going gets rough.

Saturn in Sagittarius

This placement is important only if Saturn is near conjunction or opposition with the Ascendant or Midheaven or in close aspect to the Sun or Moon. It indicates that you approach new experiences and new knowledge with care and interest. Throughout your life you will hesitate to accept a new idea until you have become very thoroughly acquainted with it and really feel that you understand it. You will learn new material best by going over it slowly and carefully, so that you see every facet of it,

In many areas of life you are quite conservative, believing in principles that have been proven over a long time. For this reason, you aren't likely to be very rebellious or unconventional in your early years. Probably you respect your teachers and grown-ups generally, unless they do not live up to your high standards.

You have strong ideals, to be sure, but you won't let yourself be carried away by them. You always look for ways to put your beliefs and ideals into practice. Later in life, you should have a good talent for organization, because you can pay attention to all of the little details in a project and keep the overall objectives in mind at the same time. When you formulate a belief or an ideal, you find it very easy to put it into practice; your thoughts are so structured and orderly that it is easy to make them concrete.

Saturn in Capricorn

This effect will be strong only if Saturn is near conjunction or opposition with the Ascendant or Midheaven or in close aspect to the Sun or Moon. Saturn is especially at home in this sign, the sign of its rulership, so it is particularly easy to express Saturn's positive traits here, namely, practicality, thrift, orderliness, attention, organization and a strong drive for significant achievements. If Saturn in this sign is strongly placed in your chart, you may seem much older than your years, although not in a negative way. To be sure, you are serious and adult, but you are still able to have fun. But when someone makes serious demands on you or requires you to fulfill important duties or responsibilities, you do so. However, it is extremely important that your parents not require too much of you, because if you are forced to be too grown up too soon, it could eventually take away the element of joy in your life. You need youth too.

Your standards are very high, and you may tend to be rather hard on yourself when you don't live up to your expectations. Instead of condemning your weaknesses, you will be able to capitalize on your strengths and use your energies more efficiently.

Common sense will always be very important for you, and because you have such a practical mind, you can accomplish a great deal, because you don't spend all your time chasing impossible dreams.

Saturn in Aquarius

This effect will be important only if Saturn is near conjunction or opposition with the Ascendant or Midheaven or in close aspect to the Sun or Moon. You will be yourself most strongly when working with others toward some collective purpose, because you derive your own ideas of significance from what is significant for the people around you. While you are young, you are influenced by your friends, but when you are older, it will be the greater society around you. But be careful not to accept the values of those around you uncritically. It is not that you are a conformist, for you can stand up for your own beliefs when necessary, but you may not pay enough attention to your personal needs. It is important to develop your sense of values from inside yourself.

You don't automatically reject new ideas or go along unthinkingly with the status quo. In fact you are very interested in knowledge and skills that would enable you to change the world around you. But your ideal of change is of a systematic and orderly process. You may put a great deal of effort into studying subjects that can bring about orderly change, such as science, technology and mathematics. But you are not likely to get involved in a new or revolutionary cause until it has demonstrated its usefulness.

It is very important that you keep your eyes open to the subtler aspects of life. While you are young, you are more in touch with your imagination and feelings than you ever will be again. Do not sacrifice these to some ideal of adult reasonableness. Keep your mind open to every aspect of living, and even if you are not a poet or artist, learn to respect what they do.

Saturn in Pisces

This effect will be strong only if Saturn is near conjunction or opposition with the Ascendant or Midheaven or in close aspect to the Sun or Moon. This can be one of the more difficult placements of Saturn, because the energy of Saturn wants to make everything orderly, neat, concrete and predictable, which doesn't combine easily with the fantasy-prone and idealistic nature of Pisces. For one thing, you may feel that you cannot do much in life, that you are more limited than you really are. You may also feel obliged to satisfy other people's needs before your own so that you never achieve satisfaction. And you may deny yourself in many other ways as well, because you believe that having too many material possessions interferes with your life. Above all else you need simplicity.

Finding a balance between the rigidity of Saturn and the vagueness, flexibility and idealism of Pisces may cause some difficulties in developing beliefs by which to govern your behavior. You may be too idealistic about the people who serve as your guides, those whom you pattern yourself after, so that you can't accept any kind of weakness or frailty in them. When you discover their weaknesses, you may be disappointed, and eventually you won't believe in anyone. Scale down your expectations and realize that you can learn something useful from everyone, even those who appear very flawed.

Don't let yourself fall into the habit of thinking that your life is not under your control. You shape your own life, and you must take responsibility for yourself.

Saturn in the First House

Even while young you seem older than you are. In one sense you will never be a child in the same way that other young people are, for even now you see the world as a very serious place where there is no room for childish games. You need to be loved by the people around you very much, because otherwise you will withdraw into yourself and begin to think of the world as a hostile place. You will have to face many obstacles while growing up, but this is not so bad, however it may seem at the time. If you master the tasks that life presents without becoming withdrawn or bitter, even though you have to work harder than others, you will have the power and self-discipline to go farther and higher than almost anyone else.

You are rather reserved, and at first you may find it difficult to get to know people. Even while you are young, you prefer the company of older people, because they seem more worthy of respect. The fact that you want to learn from older people partly accounts for your seeming older than you are. But as an adult you will not age very rapidly, and as you get older, life will become more and more easy, because your body will catch up with the rest of you. The later years of your life will have much joy and interest, which may be lacking in your youth, as you struggle with being young.

Saturn in the Second House

You are quite cautious about spending money or any other resource, because you are afraid that there won't be enough. So you conserve and save wherever possible, in order to prevent an unexpected shortage of money or other resources. In some cases you may not have enough money, but it is more likely that you are motivated by fear of not having enough. On the positive side, this makes you a thrifty and careful planner in using money. But it can also make you overly cautious so that you hold on to your money too tightly. And this kind of fear may set up vibrations in your world that attract situations in which you are actually deprived of money or possessions against your will.

You will work hard to get what you want, because for you that is a basic part of the value of anything. You do not respect or value anything that comes into your life too easily, so you work for it. You may envy people who seem to get what they want more readily, but if you think about it, you will realize that you prefer it this way.

As an adult, you will have to watch out for a tendency to get so wrapped up in financial and property matters that they take over your life. Think of money and property as means to an end, not as ends in themselves.

Saturn in the Third House

You try to think everything through very carefully. Not one to shoot off your mouth, you plan your speech quite carefully and work out your ideas in detail.

When you are learning something new, the teaching has to be structured very carefully to make it understandable. It is not that you are at all slow witted, but ideas have to be orderly for you to understand them. Similarly, abstract ideas or those that have no obvious practical application hold little fascination for you. You ask each new idea what good it is.

When you are older, this trait will be very useful in business, but it can also cause trouble, unless you learn to be more flexible in your thinking. Often the best ideas and innovations are very loose and hazy at first, developing a firm structure later on. But unless you loosen up, you may not give such ideas much credit.

In general, you are likely to be very conservative in your thinking, or at least to hold on all your life to ideas and beliefs acquired in childhood. You may also be more serious than most people of your age, at least in your point of view. But when you are middle-aged, you may have to make some major readjustments in your thinking, because by then the world will have changed enough to force you to change your ideas.

This placement may indicate that you have difficulty in getting along with your brothers or sisters, if you have any.

Saturn in the Fourth House

You need more warmth and support from your parents than most people, and often you may feel that you are not getting it. Your parents may seem too strict, too conservative and cautious, or they may impose too much responsibility on you. Whether or not this is true, you will see it that way. Often this placement of Saturn makes you feel that the people who are closest to you do not give you enough emotional support. Believing this, you may feel empty inside and lacking in self-confidence. An important lesson in life is to learn that you are as good as everyone else and as worthy of love as anyone.

As a result of your feelings about your parents, when you get older you will want to get away from the place where you lived as a child, perhaps to a very different world. But if you have not resolved your relationship with your parents, you will never be able to get away from those feelings of loneliness. You will carry along the idea that no one can ever reach you. Either you must get your parents to approve of you as you are, or you must find some other way to give yourself a sense of self-esteem. It is important to realize that your parents may be warm and loving people, but that for some reason you are just not tuned into receiving their affection. However, if your parents really are not supportive, you should find someone outside your family—a teacher or older friend, for example—who will provide reinforcement.

Saturn in the Fifth House

You are more reserved about expressing yourself than most people. This may be because you are afraid of making a bad impression or because you feel you should live up to very high standards of behavior. It is difficult for you to play like other young people, because you feel that you are wasting your time. You prefer games that teach you something or train you in a useful skill.

You prefer to be around serious people, especially those who are older and, you believe, wiser than yourself. Unconsciously you think of such relationships as learning experiences, and you seek from them the same energies that you seek from your parents. However, your reserve and shyness may lead to misunderstandings with people your own age, and you may find it difficult to form friendships with them. However, you will probably have a few relationships that are quite good, so you shouldn't feel especially lonely.

When you are older, these patterns will continue in your relationships with the opposite sex. Again, you will look for older or more serious partners. And when you decide to have children, you will consider them an enormous responsibility, which might prevent you from enjoying them as you should. Some people with this position either decide not to have children or do not have them for some other reason.

Saturn in the Sixth House

While you are young, you may have to be careful about your health. However, as you get older you should become stronger, but only if you take care of yourself.

For a person of your age, you have a very serious attitude toward work and responsibility. Also you may have more responsibilities than other young people, which may cause you to lose out on some of the fun of being young. But you should learn to accept your lot, because the discipline you learn now will help you out later in life and may bring you considerable success. If you do nothing but complain and resent your situation, you will develop such a negative attitude that you will have difficulty with jobs all your life. Either you will find it hard to keep a job yourself or, if you employ others, you will have trouble with them.

But if you can accept this placement of Saturn as a positive lesson to be learned, you will eventually get great satisfaction from your work, which you will do very carefully. You will gain recognition for the thoroughness and quality of your work, which will give you a head start on those who have a more frivolous attitude. You will have to work hard to get what you want, but you will get it, along with the satisfaction of knowing that your success is the result of your efforts rather than luck.

Saturn in the Seventh House

This position has two distinct effects, and you may experience one or the other. The first of these effects is a definite problem in getting along with people at close range in situations where you and another person must work together and act as partners in some way. You find it difficult to express yourself to the other person. You feel somewhat threatened and are unwilling to put your whole self into making the partnership work, because you are afraid of losing something, usually your freedom. The problem is that you think of a relationship as a responsibility that has very few compensating pleasures. Even though you feel quite lonely at times, you prefer to be alone. Your problem is that in a relationship you concentrate on what you have to give up, losing sight of what you gain. Try to change your way of looking at the situation.

If you experience the other effect of this placement, you still view relationships as a responsibility, but that only makes you more conscientious about living up to your end of the bargain rather than fearful of entering into one. Also you are careful to choose partners who are worth your while, people who can do something for you or teach you something. Thus you often prefer to be with older people. When you are older, this energy will probably result in your marrying late, because you want to be really ready for it. Or you may marry a considerably older person who acts almost like a parent to you. On the other hand, if you never overcome the difficult side of this placement, it is unlikely that you will ever marry at all.

Saturn in the Eighth House

You may have to learn some important lessons about money, property and other material resources. In particular, you may have to decide while quite young what rights you and others have to each other's possessions. You may have to learn to share your possessions instead of holding on to what you believe is yours alone. Do not be afraid that in sharing you will lose what is yours, because you will get back at least as much from those whom you share with. All of us have to depend on other people's resources to get along in life, but that may be particularly difficult for you to learn while you are young.

You may prefer not to borrow possessions, either, fearing the responsibility of caring for someone else's belongings. But as you grow older you will learn to be unusually responsible in handling other people's property.

A quite different expression of this position is a curious fear of change. It may be difficult for you to face the larger transformations that we all have to deal with, such as moving to a new home or losing a friend. Or you may have periods when it is psychologically very difficult to adjust to your situation. At times you may even get into complicated fantasies about death. Your approach to life should be looser, for life always changes, and you should learn to flow with it. Unconsciously you may be reacting to and fearing all changes as if they were death. But changes are really births, and if you can approach them that way, you will be much better off.

Saturn in the Ninth House

Your outlook on life is cautious and conservative, and you prefer not to try anything new until it is tested very thoroughly. When planning for the future, you make a great effort to consider every angle. You may believe that the world is such a demanding place that you must plan very carefully and thoroughly or you will be tripped up.

At best, with this attitude you will be a careful person who attains success by diligent preparation and hard work. You approach every problem in life systematically, looking for practical solutions. You like to have ideas and knowledge presented in a very structured way. You are more at home with science and mathematics, especially in their practical applications, than with writing, literature and art.

You tend to change your opinions quite slowly, not because you are dull-witted but because you are so cautious. The only problem is that you may be unable to adapt to sudden unexpected emergencies unless you have anticipated them in advance and worked out a strategy.

The worst side of this position can be an excessive narrowness of thought, so that you are comfortable only with what is familiar, objects that can be touched and ideas that have immediate practical value.

Saturn in the Tenth House

Even while you are young, you are very concerned about what is important in the greater world. You want to understand the meaning of the world and find out how to make your mark upon it. Even now you recognize the need for hard work and careful planning to find a career that will be satisfying to you and gain respect from others. But at the same time you may feel that the adult world is a cold forbidding place that will show you little mercy and not forgive your mistakes readily. If you feel this way, you should recognize that this is an attitude about yourself that you have imposed on the world. You must learn to be less of a perfectionist and less demanding of yourself.

It is very important that you have a good relationship with your father. Otherwise you may grow up feeling very insecure and believing that the world is against you.

When you do grow up, this position of Saturn means that you will work very hard in any career that you choose. If you do not succeed, it may be because of some carelessness. Above all, do not take any shortcuts. Do your work as best you can to prepare for your future, and follow the rules that apply to what you are doing.

When you are an adult, you may be a teacher, either in school or simply in your everyday interactions with others. You may be quite successful in business, if you follow the advice given above. Your work may involve metal, stone or other hard objects.

Saturn in the Eleventh House

It may be difficult for you to get along with groups of people your own age. You tend to be a loner who prefers to be by yourself. You feel that other people's interests are opposed to yours or that others demand of you far more than you get from them.

But you benefit from associations with older people, often quite a bit older. Your serious attitude makes it easier for you to understand older people than people your own age. Although you have ideals, they are very much suppressed by your need to be practical and realistic.

You may not have many friendships in your life, but the ones you do have will be deep and long-lasting. Not especially social, you are much happier with a small group of close friends than in a large group. In fact, in a crowd you are likely to feel much more lonely than when you are really alone. You tend to view the people in crowds as possibly hostile strangers.

When you are older you may act as a teacher to your friends. This can be very constructive, but you should be sure that it is not merely a way of putting some distance between yourself and others. It is difficult for you to be intimate with people on an equal level, but you need that kind of exchange very much, and when you get it, it does you a great deal of good. Seek to overcome your feeling of distance by finding out what you and others have in common and emphasizing that.

Saturn in the Twelfth House

You often feel discouraged about yourself for no particular reason, even believing that you aren't as good as the people you know, without any justification whatsoever. You may feel that others do not like you, and you won't take their praise seriously.

Also you may have the sense that your personal world isn't very stable, that at any minute sweeping changes could occur that would upset everything. Along with feelings of inferiority, this makes it difficult for you to act decisively when you should. You spend a great deal of time trying to make sure that conditions are safe for you to act without being defeated in your efforts.

The important lesson to learn is that most of your fears about yourself and your world are imaginary. Probably if you could remember your earliest childhood, you would be able to trace these fears back to some deep discouragement or major upset that occurred in your family at that time. Those events are past, but the effects remain, and you must realize that many of your problems are left over from the past and have no real meaning for your life now. As you get older, these problems will lessen and you will become more secure and self-confident.

Saturn Conjunct Uranus

This aspect occurs only once every forty-five years; the last time was in 1942. It signifies a heavy internal tension that can have both creative and difficult results. At its most difficult, it may make you feel restless and irritable, not knowing whether to go forward or backward. This in turn creates tension, and you try to get away from whatever is causing the conflict. If this process goes too far, you may suddenly make a rash and impulsive move simply to get away from the tension by any means at all. When you are older, you may suddenly break away from a relationship or quit your job or suddenly have an emotional outburst with little or no warning to those around you. You find it difficult to release tension slowly, which would be the better way.

On the other hand, if you can keep this tension within reasonable limits, it can make you very alert and attentive to any task that you are involved in. And because you can hold in your tenseness, you can persist in the face of difficulty longer than most people and thereby get a lot done. Just be sure you know when the tension has built up enough and do not hold it in until the pressure becomes unbearable.

Also you are able to maintain a balance between caution and change in your life. You can go through very major changes in a careful and orderly manner without blowing everything apart, as long as you don't wait too long to do so. The changes that you bring about in this manner are more lasting than those that are done with less care.

Saturn Sextile Uranus

This aspect signifies that you are able to pursue a task with persistence and endurance, even when conditions get really tough. Your approach to life is disciplined, and you have no desire to upset the apple cart with impulsive behavior or sudden moves. Yet you don't simply accept your life as it is; you recognize the need to make changes and grow, and you are willing to work hard to do it. Idealism and practicality are well balanced in your mind. You recognize the limits of freedom, but you are willing to exploit your freedom to the full within those limits.

You can learn subjects that are difficult if you feel that they provide a tool with which to master life. You are less attracted to very abstract subjects that have no obvious purpose. But difficult techniques intrigue you because they give you a chance to demonstrate your ability to persevere with precise, demanding work.

As you get older, you may be in the position of having to teach others. A teacher has to be able to revolutionize people's minds in a disciplined manner, and that is exactly what this sextile signifies.

There will be some difficult times in your life, as in everyone else's, but you will come through better than most, because this aspect signifies unusual toughness and durability. However, this could be a problem at times, because you may persist in something long after you should have gotten out. Persistence may become a point of pride, or you may just not realize how difficult the situation has gotten.

Saturn Square Uranus

This aspect indicates considerable tension within you, which you can usually keep under control. However, it will occasionally burst out in the form of sudden, unpredictable acts, such as breaking away from relationships, bursts of temper and such. You will not be easily driven to this point, but you may unconsciously construct the conditions that bring you to it. You must make an effort to learn how to relax and release your tensions gradually. It is particularly important not to hold in all outward expressions of tension, because psychosomatic illnesses can result if you do.

This aspect may be expressed in another way, as a tension in your life between personal freedom and authority or sense of duty. One part of you is always trying to toe the line set by others, while another part wants to break free. Usually you feel that you can fulfill your obligations only by giving up personal freedom. It is difficult for you to be yourself, do what you want to do, and at the same time do what you have to do. Rebellious behavior and grudging acceptance of your duties typify this aspect.

All of this may lead you to take a very negative view of persons in authority, such as parents, teachers, police and officials. And if you do not learn to handle the tension in your life, you could have serious collisions with such persons, which you are not likely to win. Learn to stand up for your rights without being negative and difficult. If you can build discipline into your own life, it will not have to be imposed from outside.

Saturn Trine Uranus

This indicates a creative balance between the old and the new in your life, between authority and discipline, on one hand, and personal freedom, on the other. You are able to be yourself and do what you want in a very careful and controlled manner, so that others do not have to keep watch over you. At the same time you are capable of fulfilling your duties and obligations without feeling that you are giving up your rights.

You are able to carry out demanding work very effectively, with great attention to detail and complete command of the technique. In fact you enjoy complex techniques and are willing to spend a great deal of time learning to master them. With this talent you may be good at teaching others your skills. You learn everything so thoroughly that you are able to show others how something is done step by step. As you get older, you will be a careful and rigorous thinker, who can effectively combine innovative ideas with structure and discipline. You realize that in order to change a situation, you must have a well-worked-out program of change. With your organizational ability, you can deal with groups that want change as well as those that do not.

Even while you are young, you are very persistent and tough-minded and able to endure considerable strain. But be careful not to take on more than you can handle, because you will try even when it is impossible to succeed. When you are older, your tendency to exceed your physical limits may result in injuries to your system.

Saturn Inconjunct Uranus

If either of these planets is near conjunction or opposition with the Ascendant or Mid-heaven, this aspect indicates a serious tension in your life between freedom and restriction. Many people have this conflict, but in your case the tensions may be so severe that you express them physically as muscle tension and possibly nervousness. You feel that somehow you must keep everything in your life under tight control, that if you let go, the whole structure will fall apart. In a very real and direct sense, even while you are young, you must learn to relax.

On the positive side, if you can learn to live with this tension a bit and express your feelings and emotions before they reach the breaking point, you can be extremely patient and persistent. You will be able to accomplish many tasks that others would give up on, if you do not hold in all your feelings and desires for freedom.

Your parents should understand that sometimes you have to let go and act in an undisciplined manner. Otherwise you will go through periods of great turmoil when you become extremely nervous and tense, so that you have to suddenly release all of the built-up emotional tension. This can be quite a difficult experience. And if this pattern of sudden disruptive emotional release continues into adulthood, it could be very disruptive in your career as well as in your personal life. If you have a problem, try to express it and talk to others about it instead of being stoical and keeping it to yourself. You can do this very well, but there are times when you need other people. Learning to handle people and the tensions that arise in relationships is important.

Saturn Opposition Uranus

Relationships may be difficult for you. When you have to work closely or just be with someone, you feel a constant tension between what you want and what the other person wants. In a group, you may be the only one who wants to keep matters as they are when everyone else wants changes, or vice versa. You may feel that the people around you want to limit your personal freedom, or they continually remind you of your duties or of unpleasant events that you would prefer to forget.

Often in close relationships you contain your sense of frustration and keep on plugging to make the relationship work. But eventually the tension becomes unbearable, and you lose your temper or take an unexpected and hostile action against the other person. Such sudden flare-ups can do great damage, because they make people afraid of your unpredictability. The answer is to learn to release your tensions gradually and not hold on to them. Don't wait until a situation has become intolerable before you break loose. This means you must get to know yourself better. When you encounter someone, consider your reactions as well as the other person's reactions. Note immediately anything that makes you tense, and if possible, point it out nicely or else avoid that person.

Many times people try to hold you in check in order to teach you something, and then you must keep the lid on for your own good. Examine your own attitudes to find out just what makes you want to blow up, and find a way to change that part of yourself.

Saturn Conjunct Neptune

This aspect occurs once every thirty-five years, the last time in 1953. The strength of its effects varies, depending upon what houses are involved. Some persons feel the effects very strongly, while others hardly notice it.

Wherever this aspect affects the chart, it brings about a feeling of insecurity, as if reality itself were not quite dependable. You are fearful and tend toward depression. However, if you master its energies, you can learn to live with very little. This aspect does not necessarily mean that you won't have physical resources, it merely means that they are less essential to you than to others. Many persons with this aspect choose to be unencumbered by material possessions, preferring to live ascetically, with few comforts. And the psychological effect is similar, in that you may have a very great capacity to sacrifice yourself for others or for your beliefs.

Basically you must learn to trust, not only other people, but the universe as well. You must believe that circumstances in your life will work out in your favor, because life should be no harder for you than for anyone else. However, if you succumb to the fear that can accompany this aspect, you will be subject to sudden losses of confidence, fits of anxiety and possibly fear of others.

The more you want a situation to proceed in a particular way, especially if it is not the best way for you, the more difficult the energy of this aspect will be. The best solution is to wait for the situation to work itself out, which should work well for you.

Saturn Sextile Neptune

This aspect signifies that you are able to do without immediate pleasures when you are pursuing a higher purpose or helping someone else. Your needs and tastes are rather simple, and your attitude toward life is more sober than that of many young people, especially in your studies. But your greatest talent is your ability to keep an excellent balance in your mind between ideals and practical considerations. Even while you are young, you will know what life demands of you and what you can accomplish, but at the same time you have strong ideals that you will work toward all your life. Being well grounded in reality, you can work harder to achieve your hopes and ideals, which are very important to you. You will succeed, because you don't plod along without demanding anything of life.

If you believe in something or someone, you will do anything for them, because your own needs are not as important to you as other people and ideals. In fact you seem to need less in life than most people. You can take a very detached attitude about a situation and simply make the most of whatever happens, especially as you get older. While you are young, this detachment may not be so obvious. Later on in your life, you may be involved in a spiritual discipline that emphasizes denial of physical possessions and comfort. For you, this would be a way of getting past the barriers of the physical world to a happier and more spiritual place.

Saturn Square Neptune

This aspect can signify a serious conflict in your mind between ideals and reality, so that as you get older, you may feel that the universe or other people are out to deprive you of something that you want very much. This aspect alone does not tell what that something is. If you experience this difficulty, it is either because your expectations are unrealistic or because you haven't properly considered the circumstances that prove difficult for you. You can get as much out of life as anyone else, but only if you think through each situation. Do not be led astray by either pessimism or idealism.

Sometimes this aspect indicates free-floating fear or anxiety about some aspect of your life that you feel you can't depend on. Someone may have hurt you psychologically without even realizing it, so you unconsciously distrust that person. Above all, avoid suspecting everyone, just because you have been hurt by someone early in life.

You should avoid all mind-altering drugs, including alcohol, even when prescribed by a physician, if possible. Such drugs can reactivate hidden fears that you had adjusted to, which could cause serious psychological damage. Learn to deal with your unconscious fears and pressures through your conscious mind, where it is easier to stay in control. Drugs may bring issues to consciousness before you are ready for them.

Saturn Trine Neptune

You are more sober and serious than most young people. You will come out of the fantasy and daydreaming stage of life rather early because you understand that you will get what you want in life only by working in the real world. It is not that you don't have ideals, it is just that you know you have to work hard to reach them. And you are able to make do with very little in order to gain what you want.

You have ideals as well as a strong sense of reality, so your philosophy of life will be based on discipline and deferring today's pleasure to achieve distant goals. You are capable of considerable self-sacrifice when necessary. But you may find it hard to let go and have a good time unless it has some purpose in the larger scheme of things.

Later in life you may develop very strong religious and spiritual principles based on renouncing the pleasures and comforts of life in favor of hard work and discipline. Just remember that although this may be your way, it isn't the right way for everyone. Avoid being self-righteous about your path, and remember that love and compassion are as much a part of spirituality as discipline and self-denial. Even if you don't consciously follow a spiritual path, part of you is very puritanical, so you may not be able to enjoy the comforts and pleasures that you will achieve at times.

Saturn Inconjunct Neptune

This aspect is strongest when either of these planets is also conjunct or opposition the Ascendant or Midheaven. It can have a variety of effects, one of which may be difficulty in relating fantasy and imagination, on one hand, to reality, duty, obligation and work, on the other. Usually the reality, duty and work aspect of the combination is dominant, at least at first. Your imaginative side tends to be transformed into nervousness, fear and irrational anxieties. The most negative manifestation of this aspect is a feeling that you have to keep a tight lid on yourself and that if you look inside yourself too closely, you will find only emptiness and disintegration. It is difficult for you to realize that this is not the truth about your inner self.

If you do not learn to confront your inner fears now, they may surface as chronic physical ailments, although that is not likely to be apparent early in life. If you can learn to release your creativity, you can avoid negative physical effects.

On a more everyday level, this aspect can signify that even as a young child you did not indulge yourself very much, preferring simple food and unpretentious surroundings. You feel that anything more elaborate would be wasteful and wrong. This attitude is likely to be even stronger when you are an adult, especially if your parents now instill in you a very puritanical attitude toward material enjoyment. Another danger of this kind of teaching by your parents is that it can lead to feelings of guilt and inner unworthiness, which could really make it difficult for you to succeed in life.

Saturn Opposition Neptune

This aspect occurs only once every thirty-five years, the last time in 1971. It signifies some confusion about relationships with others or about your individual relationship to the exterior universe. You may express this as problems in determining where your rights and and other people's begin or as problems in understanding the demands of the physical world. You may really be afraid that you cannot live up to what the world expects of you or that the world is somehow vaguely frightening and spooky. Often you project your internal fear, anxiety or nervousness onto other people, so that you act afraid of others or of situations, when the only problem is fear within yourself. You must try very hard not to develop a suspicious attitude toward others because that might attract the very people whom you fear. If you do not learn to trust others, you will probably, by a twisted kind of reasoning, fear the people you should trust and trust those whom you ought to be more suspicious of. And when your trust is not upheld, you will be disappointed and even more suspicious.

On the plus side, you should be able to develop a strong sense of self-reliance and discipline with the help of people who act as your teachers. You will learn that your life will be simpler if you avoid materialistic concerns. Do not encumber yourself with too many possessions, and don't let your life become too complex, for that will lead only to confusion, which in turn will lead to fear.

Saturn Conjunct Pluto

This aspect occurs only once every thirty-three years, the last time in 1947. It signifies that you can endure very difficult times, if you have to, and that you have an unusual degree of tenacity. But it doesn't mean that you will necessarily have difficult times.

There may be a scarcity of some element or experience in your life, as indicated by the house that this aspect is in. If this is the case, you will have to work very hard in an organized and disciplined way to make up for it. In the area of your life that is thus affected, simple good luck will not help you much, but hard work will.

Some persons with this aspect respond to the changes that must come in life with fierce resistance. You will have to cultivate the attitude of letting nature take its course, instead of building up structures to prevent change. If you do resist changes, it will only delay the inevitable and make the changes much more painful when they happen, even resulting in very severe deprivations. But if you allow changes to take place in your life, your inner fortitude will help you through any difficult times.

Whenever you are defeated, which won't happen to you any more than to anyone else, avoid feeling bitter about it. You may develop a cold, hard attitude toward the world if your experiences are rough, but such an attitude only cuts you off from others and makes it more likely that your fears will be realized.

Saturn Sextile Pluto

This signifies that you are able to grow and experience change in your life in an orderly way, without the periods of total chaos and disruption that some people go through when circumstances demand change. It also means that you can endure hard times and emerge in good shape. Even if you feel as though you cannot hold out much longer during some difficulty, you will survive and be better off than most.

If you have to, you can get along with very little, although this aspect does not indicate that you will have to necessarily. You are able to discipline yourself to make do with whatever resources are available. In good times you may be as inclined to overspend as anyone, but in hard times you are very careful. Although it may be hard to believe, you are ultimately better off if you do have to go through some hard times, because you will have a greater appreciation for the good things in life. You will learn that you are quite tough, both psychologically and physically.

Whatever happens to you as you grow older, you will never have the feeling that the world owes you a living. You will always appreciate how much effort it takes to make your life work well, and you will do it.

Saturn Square Pluto

This can be a difficult aspect, in that it often indicates that you resist psychological changes in your life very strongly, which makes the changes very unpleasant when they do happen. You must learn to be quite flexible to prevent this aspect from being excessively difficult. It may also mean that at several times in your life you will have to work very hard against seemingly insuperable obstacles in order to get ahead.

Fortunately, with this aspect you can probably triumph against those obstacles, although as a result you may develop a cold, relentless, and calculating attitude toward life. You may become ruthless, refusing to let anything stand in your way. But you must not respond this way, because it will dull your sensitivity to the real beauty of life and harden you to human sentiment and feeling. This in turn will cut you off from other people, because they will fear you and not want to have anything to do with you.

Most people do not experience such an extreme effect with this aspect, but in some area of your life you may tend to have this cold, calculating attitude toward others, and you should work very hard to stop such tendencies. Let everyone follow their own life course and avoid trying to dominate others just for the sake of having power. Of course, you should stick up for your own rights. Let yourself feel emotional pain from time to time, because it keeps you human, and no one's life can be without pain. Above all, be flexible and willing to undergo change.

Saturn Trine Pluto

This aspect signifies that you are capable of very controlled self-expression. You can monitor your thoughts and emotions at just about any time and prevent yourself from getting carried away by sudden rushes of feeling. However, do not let this control turn into an attitude of coldness. It is possible to be tough without being insensitive.

When great demands are made upon you, you respond very well. Even under the most difficult circumstances, you can dig in and produce, because you have a great ability to discipline yourself. Also you know how to make the most of limited resources.

Your personal psychological development may be slow, but because of that, you can develop into a very complex and effective adult, which takes time. Yet even while you are young, your serious attitude toward life will show a certain maturity that is not usually characteristic of young people. Often you prefer to be alone, because interacting with others sometimes confuses rather than aids you. Also you learn better from your own experience than from what others tell you or show you. When you are older, you will be able to say that you have learned in the practical school of real life, not merely in the rarified atmosphere of the classroom. What you learn, you really understand and apply on a practical level.

Major changes in your life may take place very slowly, because your intrinsic toughness means you are less affected by pressures around you, but nevertheless, the changes in your life will be very deep and far-reaching.

Saturn Inconjunct Pluto

If either of these planets is close to conjunction or opposition with the Ascendant or Midheaven, its effects can be quite strong. It signifies a feeling that you must work extremely hard merely to keep your life running smoothly on a day-to-day level. Often this aspect is associated with quite a bit of tension, especially in your muscles, but also in your emotional approach to life. You need to learn that the world is not always a place of struggle and that occasionally it is good to let go and relax. If your home life has been harsh or difficult, it will bring out the worst side of this aspect, and in time you will develop a cynical attitude toward the world in general. You will become intolerant of your own and others' weaknesses, and you will take advantage of every opportunity, even if it means hurting someone else. But this is likely to happen only if you have not been given a reasonable break or if you haven't been allowed to be a child, to be weak and make mistakes.

Even under favorable circumstances, this aspect usually means that you are resistant to change, that you hold on to any situation, no matter how bad, until it is totally intolerable. Then when change does take place, it has to create a revolution and a total breakdown of everything that came before it. You must learn to adapt to circumstances a bit more gracefully and not be afraid of occasional compromise.

This aspect usually does mean that you are tough and can contend with a great deal of adversity, but don't develop an attitude that makes adversity inevitable.

You may find it difficult to get along with others, because you are unnecessarily afraid of what they want from you. Learn to associate only with people whom you can trust.

Saturn Opposition Pluto

This aspect occurs only once every thirty-three years, the last time in 1965. Its effects depend upon which houses are affected; however, everyone who has this aspect should be aware of certain general principles and watch for certain problems.

The main problem signified by this aspect is in your relationships with other people or with external circumstances. You may feel that the external world demands that you change when you do not want to change, or that it forces you to stay where you are when you do want to change. Because of this feeling, you may become antagonistic toward others or toward the world in general, because it does not seem to want to let you be yourself. You may adopt a cold or hostile attitude toward others.

Some people with this aspect feel that the only solution is to try to control the world, or at least their piece of it, and to be dominant. If this feeling gets too strong, you won't let anything stop you in your pursuit of power or authority. However, in the process you could set in motion such opposition from others that you would not stand a chance of success. In this way the energy of the aspect feeds on itself by producing the frustration that led to the problem in the first place. Obviously the only cure is learning to compromise and being willing to let others alone if they will let you alone. Watch very carefully to see whether some subtle attitude on your part is setting others against you when you don't intend any harm. Make sure that others understand your position.

Saturn Conjunct Ascendant

Even while you are quite young, you will have a very serious attitude toward life, and as a result, youth will not mean as much to you as it does to others. Either you will take on responsibilities very early in life, or they will be thrust upon you. You may find it hard to simply relax and have a good time, but even if life seems hard sometimes, you should try to relax and enjoy yourself when you can. Otherwise, with this aspect you might become the type of person who always seems to put a damper on other people's good spirits. You get so wrapped up in your own worries and responsibilities that you remind others of their own problems, even when they want to escape from them.

It may not be easy for you to reach out to other people emotionally while you are young, and therefore you may have only a few friends and acquaintances. Don't worry about this situation, for it will improve in time, as will your whole attitude toward life. People who get to know you really well will discover that you are a very reliable person who always lives up to your commitments. They can always count on you to help out when they need it most. However, if you begin to feel lonely, which, strangely enough, will probably happen when you are in a large group, simply concentrate on what you do have. If you feel bad, get involved in some kind of work to take your mind off your loneliness. Your situation is not a real problem, although you may feel rather unhappy while you are young. It is just that you are older than your years, and it will be a while until your friends catch up with you.

Saturn Sextile Ascendant

This aspect suggests that early in life you will develop a more serious temperament than most young people and that you will learn to handle responsibility sooner than most. At the same time you are loyal to your friends and reliable in any relationship, especially if you and someone else have to keep some sort of agreement.

You may not have a lot of friends, but the ones you do have will be as reliable and loyal to you as you are to them. Many of them may be older than yourself, which reflects the fact that you act and appear older than you are.

You may not feel very comfortable in a group, preferring to deal with people on a one-to-one basis, so that you and the other person can have each other's complete attention. If you have to relate to several people at a time, you probably don't want to relate to any of them.

You like to learn new disciplines, and when you have a new subject in school, you try to find the most systematic approach. You have a harder time with ideas and subjects that cannot be structured and arranged in a logical orderly way. For this reason you may be better in math and science than in art or literature.

Your hopes for life are practical, for you see no point in trying to live up to impossibly high standards, so you set realistic goals that you know you can attain.

Saturn Square Ascendant

You may have quite a bit of difficulty learning to relate to other people as friends or loved ones, even within your immediate family. This problem usually stems from the fact that you feel somehow unworthy of being loved or attended to. To overcome this, you need a great deal of emotional support in your early years from both of your parents. Neither of them should demand too much of you, and whenever you do not achieve a desired goal, they should be right there to give you needed moral support. If your parents can help you in this way, you may achieve far more than anyone dreamed possible. Certainly you are not incompetent, but you tend to feel that the demands of life, specifically those made by other people, are so high that you cannot live up to them. Rather than let people know that you have failed to achieve perfection, you withdraw from them.

If your friends are critical of you, ask yourself whether you need those friends. Do not accept criticism as the main part of a relationship, for it is not. Mutual love, respect and reinforcement should be the main components of any relationship.

This square can signify two different kinds of retreat. Some persons with this aspect, feeling that the outer world demands too much, withdraw from social contact by going inside themselves. Others feel that there is only a great void within, so they work furiously in the outer world of friends and other contacts to escape from that inner emptiness. You should avoid trying to escape from yourself.

Saturn Trine Ascendant

This denotes that even while you are young, you are a realist. You probably stopped believing in fairy tales and Santa Claus sooner than most, and you were one of the first to try to find out about the meaning of the outer world. As you grow older, you will develop a personal philosophy of life based on getting results. If something works, you do it. At the same time, you aren't sure of the worth of anything that is purely decorative or abstract. In school you are likely to do well in subjects that teach useful skills in a disciplined manner rather than in art, poetry, music or literature. You might be good at math and science if you can see practical uses for these disciplines.

If you are not careful, you could become a dull but practical person, but if you don't get bogged down in practicality, you could be quite effective at dealing with people and getting useful results. This would make you a good organizer, and later on an effective executive and business person.

Even while quite young, you are able to discipline yourself. You are willing to put off temporary gratification in favor of more enduring and significant results later, and you have the foresight to see future possibilities that are hidden from most people. You enjoy working hard; in fact it may not be easy for you to just relax and have a good time, because you cannot see any point in it. But relaxation helps restore you in body and spirit so you can work more effectively and efficiently later on.

Saturn Inconjunct Ascendant

With this aspect you probably have a rather serious attitude toward life and other people. It may be quite difficult for you to simply go out and have a good time. You want to be serious and to spend all your time performing significant tasks. This attitude may have developed because you were discouraged from enjoying yourself when you were younger. You may have been made to feel that only work is important, that play serves no useful purpose. This is not true, however, because playing has a positive and useful function in the development of the adult mind and body. Not only does it serve to release tensions, but it also actually helps train you in social and physical skills that will be useful in any work you do later.

You need to be encouraged to believe in yourself and to recognize your personal strength. You have to be helped to realize that you as an individual are worth a lot and that you need to get some satisfaction from life as much as the next person does.

On occasion this aspect indicates frail physical health, which can be corrected only by paying a great deal of attention to hygiene, personal health habits and proper diet. However, this aspect may also signify that you worry too much about your health. Try not to be so concerned about it unless a physician has diagnosed a definite problem.

You may find it rather difficult to express yourself to other people. This is another expression of your lack of self-confidence, which will change if you get positive emotional support from the people around you.

Saturn Opposition Ascendant

Forming close relationships with people your own age will not be easy for you. The guidance and wisdom you are looking for can't be found among your peers until you and they are much older. For this reason, other people in your age group may think of you as a loner. However, while older people can help you in many ways, try to get to know younger people as well and relate to them as a friend. Otherwise you will always have trouble working or playing closely with your peers, which will make it difficult to form relationships of any kind when you are older.

The relationship that is most affected by this placement is marriage. You may be too young to think about that now, but your present close relationships, even friendships with people of your own sex, will teach you much that you should know about getting along. Otherwise you may build up a wall between yourself and everyone else.

Often the people who are close to you seem to demand too much or don't permit you to simply be yourself. If you feel that people are being too critical of you, reexamine your friendships. You may be unconsciously seeking out harsh and critical people, feeling that anyone who accepts you as you are is not discriminating enough. But that is probably not true; more likely they are just nicer people.

Try to avoid an early marriage, especially with someone your own age. An early marriage with someone much older might work out, but it would be better to wait until you are older, at least twenty-nine, and totally mature.

Saturn Conjunct Midheaven

At a very early age you will learn that life requires hard work and ceaseless activity if you want to get ahead. Also you want to be a person of significance when you are older, so you will start working while quite young to get where you want to go. Since you have so much internal discipline, your parents won't have to impose it from the outside, nor should they make unrealistically high demands, because you will try very hard to fulfill them. Whenever you fail, you condemn yourself strongly, and if you decide you are a loser, it would be very difficult to change that belief. This placement of Saturn can signify that you will be very successful or very unsuccessful, depending on how you experience success while you are young.

You respect those in authority even when you feel they are giving you a hard time. You understand that they have earned the right to their position and that to challenge them you must earn that right as well. Only if you have very negative experiences with authority while you are young—and your parents will have a lot to do with this—will you be negative about it when you are older.

No matter what career you choose, you will be a teacher and a guide for others. You may be a teacher in the literal sense in some kind of school. In any case, others will look to you for guidance when you achieve the goals that you set for yourself now.

As you work to get ahead in life, however, be very careful not to neglect your friendships and other relationships. Otherwise you may be very lonely later on.

Saturn Sextile Midheaven

This signifies that you have a strong sense of inner discipline and that you can work toward the goals you set for yourself steadily and without wavering. It may also indicate that you work mostly alone, without much help from people of your own age. They will not hinder you, but you work best by yourself.

Whatever task you undertake, you work at patiently, with thorough organization and method, leaving no stone unturned. You may take on responsibilities that most young people would be reluctant to attempt. You may seem older than you are.

You are independent, even a loner, because having other people around may seem to distract you from your purposes. For this reason you may not have many friends while you are young, but that will be because you have chosen it, not because no one can get along with you. When you are older, you will be a very dependable person, because you have worked out your own methods and have proved to everyone that they work.

As you grow, you will have the aid and assistance of those in authority, such as teachers and parents. They will approve of your early maturity and will help you find your course. When you are older and working for a living, your relations with employers should also be good, because they will know you can be trusted to do a job well and take responsibility.

Saturn Square Midheaven

You will have to learn how to cooperate and how to establish emotional bonds with others. While you are young, especially, you may feel that other people get in the way of what you want to do and resist your efforts. Consequently you may withdraw and cut yourself off from others, or you may feel that they have withdrawn from you. Often you feel that you are very much alone and that no one really cares about you. This is not usually true, but by withdrawing emotionally, you have made it impossible for them to feel affection for you.

It is also possible that you are surrounded by people who are not very friendly. Perhaps it is your own family that seems to judge you harshly or make too many demands, but you can still go out into the world and find people who are willing to be your friends. But for your future it is important not to simply retreat into yourself, because when you are older, it will be harder to meet people and establish connections, unless you learn the habit now. And later on, your attacks of loneliness will be much more severe. In addition, when you are older, inadequate contact with others could lead you to feel empty and meaningless. These feelings could emerge even if you are highly regarded by others, because they arise from your own sense of distance from people.

In any case you may be more of a loner than most, which is perfectly all right within reason. If you have only a few friends, those you do have may be close and enduring.

Saturn Trine Midheaven

As you grow older, you will get ahead by doing everything in a very systematic and orderly manner. You try to take good care of your possessions, and you like to have them arranged neatly about you. Also you try to use your possessions in the best way possible. As you get older, you will be fascinated by the tools and techniques of any subject that interests you, and you will become very proficient in those techniques.

Even at an early age you will feel that very little that is worth having comes for nothing in this world, but you are willing to work. As a result of this understanding, you may seem older than your age, and you may prefer the company of older people.

Although you can work with others if necessary, you probably prefer activities that you can pursue by yourself, because then you do not have to worry about whether someone else's standards are as high as your own. You are very exacting in your work and find it frustrating to deal with anyone who is less exacting. This same energy may also cause you to feel a bit different from other people, even sometimes as if you don't belong with them. However, this will not bother you greatly, because you are confident enough to be yourself. It is more important to you to be right than to be popular. This attitude will win you the respect of your elders, and all your life you will get along well with persons in authority. Eventually you will probably be in a position of authority yourself.

Saturn Inconjunct Midheaven

This aspect indicates that you very much need a positive relationship with your parents, especially your father. You should not be disciplined sternly unless you are given lots of love at the same time. Otherwise, giving and receiving love from others will be a real problem for the rest of your life. Unless you are truly supported by your family and friends, you will begin to feel lonely and isolated from others and inferior to them. Also you are likely to have very serious difficulties with authority figures, because you are afraid of how they will treat you, not expecting that anyone will ever give you the loving guidance you need. You will see all authorities only as potential threats to your freedom and as sources of pain and trouble.

On the plus side, if you get adequate reinforcement from your parents and other adults, you can become a very conscientious person who understands at an early age what is expected of you. Even while you are young, you prefer work or a serious activity to play. As a result, you may prefer the company of older people. You also like structured situations in which you must do certain things at certain times, with your duties and time limits clearly spelled out for you. Later in life you are likely to adopt a rather strict routine of daily living, because the structure itself gives you confidence.

In any case it is good to associate with people your own age, to avoid becoming so isolated that you cannot deal with people. This also helps to counter your loneliness.

Saturn Opposition Midheaven

This can be a difficult placement, indicating that you feel so lonely and so different from others that it is hard to relate to them. Also you may sometimes feel that there is nothing inside you, that if others could look at your soul they would see only emptiness. This belief is not based on fact, but it can seem very real when you are feeling unhappy. It indicates that you need a great deal of emotional support from your family. Your mother, especially, and possibly your father as well, may demand a great deal and expect you to live up to very high standards, without giving you very much emotional reinforcement. Even if they do support you, you will not feel the helpful effects as much as others would.

One possible effect of this placement is that you will be very active socially, almost as if you could not stand to be by yourself, even though you feel alone when you are with others as well. This is an especially likely effect if your chart has many planets above the horizon. You are trying to escape from your sense of inadequacy through others. However, the only way that you can really conquer this feeling is by going inside, confronting yourself and accepting what you are.

You prefer to keep your immediate personal surroundings—your room, and later on, your home—neat, with as few obstacles as possible. Others may think that your tastes are rather stark and ascetic, but you prefer not to have to contend with any more material possessions than necessary.

Chapter Twelve

Uranus

General Note on Outer Planets

The sign positions of the outer planets—Uranus, Neptune and Pluto—and the aspects among them are, of course, significant and effective. However, because their influences are so long-lasting and affect so many people at once, it is hard to recognize them in an individual. With the inner planets, aspects and sign positions vary greatly from individual to individual in a given age group, so we can see their effects clearly, but that is not the case with the outer planets. Their effects seem to color whole generations rather than specific individuals.

Therefore this text discusses in depth only the house positions of the outer planets, which do vary significantly for individuals, along with their aspects to the Ascendant and Midheaven. Brief comments on the sign positions indicate their general meaning for a whole generation. The same is true of the aspects among the outer planets, except that some of these have not occurred in recent history nor will they occur again in the next century or so. Also many of these aspects have occurred so few times that we know very little about their effects, although we can create hypothetical delineations according to the general symbolic principles of astrology. Aspects that are in this category are noted, and those that do affect people born in these times are discussed briefly.

Uranus in the Chart

Uranus is a planet of freedom and unconventionality. It represents the aspects of your life that cannot be fitted into the rigid patterns of Saturn, perhaps areas of your personality or behavior that are unpredictable or areas of life in which you refuse to follow the rules that others have set up. Or Uranus can be expressed outside of yourself, in the environment, as circumstances that challenge you and occasionally upset you because you had not planned for them.

The sign that Uranus is in affects you only as a member of a generation, unless it is very near to conjunction or opposition with the Ascendant or Midheaven or in close aspect to the Sun, Moon or an inner planet. The house that Uranus is in designates the areas of your life in which you need the greatest freedom, or where you are most likely to experience sudden surprises, either pleasant or unpleasant. If circumstances in some part of your life continually upset you because of the energy of Uranus, you need to examine that area of your life and think about your need for freedom there, and you need to do things in your own way.

A well-aspected Uranus makes it possible for you to be free and flexible, to face any situation in life without getting upset. Uranus grants the ability to live at a very fast pace. You can handle anything that is new and radical and make positive use of it.

Negatively, Uranus aspects can cause you to be totally unconventional, seemingly just for the sake of being rebellious, and unable to get along with authority figures such as parents and teachers. You may tend to make sudden moves that upset and surprise others, or you may attract others who upset you in this way. On the physical level, a difficult Uranus can signify accidents.

Note: the dates in parentheses are approximate.

Uranus in Aries (1927-1934)

This position will be repeated in the 21st century, beginning about 2011. It seems to indicate a generation of individuals who have an unusually strong drive for self-expression and who may have quite a bit of trouble conforming to society's norms. Certainly, for this generation, intense personal concern with individual freedom is stronger than concern with freedom as an abstract social issue. In other words, these people prefer to seek freedom for themselves on a day-to-day practical level rather than fight for freedom as a social principle. In fact, they might be rather apolitical except about issues that affect them personally.

Uranus in Taurus (1934-1942)

This position will happen again in the 21st century, about 2018. Presumably it has two different effects. Some individuals in this generation might try to rid themselves of concern with material considerations, to become free of property and the duties involved in managing it. Others, however, might become quite concerned with building up a stable financial base in their lives, because they feel insecure about their material resources. They don't feel sure that they will always have whatever they need. Taurus is an earthy, practical sign, very concerned with stability and order, and it does not fit very well with the radical and revolutionary nature of Uranus. One can expect considerable tension in children for whom this placement is prominent.

Uranus in Gemini (1942-1949)

Children born with this sign position can be expected to have very unusual ideas and be interested in new methods of communicating. They would be strongly inclined to think in abstractions, so it might be hard to get them to deal with the practical necessities of life. Nevertheless, a strongly placed Uranus in Gemini indicates considerable cleverness and innovative ability and possibly good understanding of the design of machines and electronic apparatus. Such people would be strongly attracted to revolutionary ideas and new approaches to life.

Uranus in Cancer (1949-1956)

Children born with this placement generally need less security at home and want to be free of old ideas and traditions. But even though they require less emotional support than other children, they may suffer from a home environment that is too unstable to provide a secure sense of well-being. The parents of these children cannot cling to them or be possessive, but they cannot ignore them either. They still need love and attention. When they grow up they will want to be free of entangling relationships.

Uranus in Leo (1956-1962)

These children will find new ways to express themselves and make an impression on the world. In many ways they may be rather eccentric, which makes it difficult for them to fit easily into groups because they are so individualistic. But as a group they should be relatively honest and want others to be honest also. They value individual self-expression far more than self-discipline. In fact it may be quite hard to pin them down to fulfilling commitments, obligations and responsibilities.

Uranus in Virgo (1962-1969)

The conflict here is similar to the problem between Taurus and Uranus, that is, the conflict between the earthy nature of the sign and the eccentric and airy nature of the planet. However, Virgo is more flexible and less rigid than Taurus. These children have some difficulty dealing with matters of duty and responsibility, but they find new ways to get their work done. They are not very good at following a routine, however, unless they have set it up themselves. At any rate, whatever innovations they come up with will be practical ones that can be used in everyday life.

Uranus in Libra (1969-1974)

These children deal with their relationships differently from others. They do not accept traditional patterns, and when they are grown up they will find entirely new kinds of relationships, both sexual and otherwise. They are likely to have rather unusual aesthetic tastes as well, and they may establish new artistic and cultural patterns. As a rule, these children require a great deal of freedom in relationships and do not want to be pinned down to emotional commitments. Their relationships will probably be made and broken at an astonishing rate of speed.

Uranus in Scorpio (1974-1981)

This generation of children may exhibit rather difficult moods and, according to adult standards, seem to act compulsively. It is rather difficult to get them to talk about their feelings, which they can't easily express in words. However, as they get older they will want to make sweeping changes in the world around them. As a generation they aren't likely to do things halfway, and the changes they work for will be extremely important. When they are older they may develop new techniques of therapy and healing for both mind and body. They encounter human needs at a very intimate and feeling level and try very hard to implement whatever measures seem necessary.

Uranus in Sagittarius (1981-1988)

These children are strongly attracted to new philosophies and will question all accepted traditions and ideals. They are interested in new and innovative ideas rather than the tried and true, feeling that the past has outlived its usefulness. They have a strong drive to be free and may be quite eccentric. If the current interest in new religious sects and cults continues, these people are likely to be very much involved in them and will change them tremendously.

Uranus in Capricorn (1988-1996)

These children have difficulty in getting along with established authorities, not because they reject the idea of authority, but because they have so many ideas about how it should be changed. However, unlike children born under the previous sign, they make changes on the practical level, like Virgo, but with a much better grasp of the social significance of change. The changes made by this generation will be real and far-reaching, but while they are young there may be great tension with their elders.

Uranus in Aquarius (1912-1920 and 1996-2004)

Uranus is in its own sign here, which means that these children are very good at initiating constructive changes and making sure that they are for the good of society. However, like other humanitarian types, they may have problems in individual relationships, because they do not consider individuals to be as significant as society and can't understand the demands of one-to-one relationships. They are reformers, but they need to learn about the importance of individual human emotions and needs.

Uranus in Pisces (1920-1928 and 2004-2012)

This generation has very high ideals, but they are not particularly concerned with the here and now. They formulate their goals in more abstract and spiritual terms, as ideals to be brought about in the soul of society rather than in its individual members. Religious and mystical ideals may be rather important to these children, but they run the risk of being impractical dreamers and ineffective idealists. They have to be taught how to deal with the real world, because like it or not, that is where they live.

Uranus in the First House

A very unconventional and restless person, you have a great need for freedom to do things your own way, which is seldom anyone else's way. You are inclined to be rebellious, wanting to do the opposite of what anyone tells you to do, although not in a mean way. Others may consider you a bit strange by their standards, but they probably admire you rather than resent you. Persons in authority, such as parents and teachers, are more bothered by you, because you often don't do as you are told unless you have decided in advance to do so.

When you grow up, this placement of Uranus can be either useful or a problem. On the positive side, it can make you a very creative and innovative person who is always the first to come up with new ideas. Often this position signifies someone who is good at science, mathematics or technical fields, such as electronics and engineering.

Negatively, this placement can make you an erratic, unpredictable and unreliable person whom no one can count on for anything, because you always do just what you want. There are times when it is necessary to rebel against existing circumstances, but you may rebel whether or not it is necessary. You must learn to tame with reason your desire to be different. If you learn to use this drive creatively, you can be a powerful force for change in your world, rather than someone who irritates everyone.

Uranus in the Second House

This placement can have a variety of effects. First of all, as you get older, you may want to be free of the duties and obligations that go with having possessions. This will not affect you very much while you are young, but later, you will come to regard property as more of a problem than a help in your life, and you will try to remain as free of its restrictions as possible. Now you may show this attitude by being careless with possessions or just not wanting any. Also you may spend money impulsively, so that you never have it when you need it, which probably won't bother you.

But this energy can be expressed in another manner also. When you are older, you may earn your living in a way that is quite unexpected, through an unusual occupation in which you move around quite a bit. This placement can also signify earning money through inventions and innovations, scientific work or technology.

Whatever you do with money and possessions, and however you make your living, you will very likely use your earnings for unusual and even startling activities. You may like to own possessions that are distinctly unusual, and you may even enjoy shocking others with them somehow, or playing jokes.

Uranus in the Third House

You have a quick and original mind, and you enjoy dealing with new ideas and concepts, especially ones that others consider too extreme. You can size up a situation quicker than others, and you sometimes use this knowledge to play jokes and pranks on people. You may even enjoy amazing or shocking people with your words. Your beliefs may not be all that different from others, but you like to challenge their opinions. When someone makes a statement that they believe is true, you often argue the opposite just to see their reaction.

At worst your mind is undisciplined, because you don't concentrate on any one subject for very long. Also you are likely to get bored more quickly than most people. For these reasons you tend to scatter your mental energies by trying to do too many things at once. In some cases this placement can be a sign of nervousness.

At your best, you grasp complicated principles quickly and are always open to new experiences. It is very unlikely that you will become set in your ways, mentally at least.

Your relations with your brothers and sisters are very changeable. This placement may indicate a brother or sister who is quite unusual in some way, or you may live in a neighborhood where the people are out of the ordinary.

Uranus in the Fourth House

Your early life may be quite inconsistent and unpredictable, or sudden changes may have occurred that prevent you from having a normal home life. If your parents are very supportive of you, this should not be a problem. The result will be that you may grow up with a sense of not belonging anywhere or to anyone in particular, but not being very upset with it. At best, this is a sign of a free spirit who can be at home anywhere.

But this placement can also indicate insecurity because of the sudden disruptions in your personal life. You may move often and without warning during childhood, or major changes may take place in the family, which are unsettling. In particular, your relationship with one of your parents may be unconventional. Often you are more of a friend to that parent than a child in the usual way. One of your parents may be away much of the time while you are young, or your mother or father may be very eccentric. This probably won't cause problems, although you might occasionally have trouble getting along with your parents because of these eccentricities.

Wherever you live, you will arrange your personal surroundings in a way that is peculiarly your own. Others may have trouble getting used to it, but you enjoy doing it. When you are older you probably won't want to own land or a house because you feel that they tie you down too much.

Uranus in the Fifth House

You want the freedom to be yourself and to be as unusual or different as you choose. Many of your tastes are unconventional, especially in what you do for fun. You look for activities that are exciting and provide a break from everyday life, and you enjoy being with people who are exciting and unconventional. People with this placement are often quite conventional in their way of living, but they have unusual friends.

It is difficult for you to do anything that seems like work, although you can work hard if you can do it your own way and make a game out of it. Following other people's rules it is not very easy for you, which certainly might cause some problems in school, unless you attend an experimental school that is relatively unstructured.

This position of Uranus has an important effect on your relationships, which will be more relevant when you are older. You do not like to be tied down by any relationship, because it is too much of a limitation on your freedom of self-expression. However, you may not admit that this is true, because we are generally taught to fulfill obligations and duties in our relationships. As a result you may attract very unpredictable friends or lovers with whom you can only have an unstable relationship. Thus you get what you want without taking any responsibility for it. But that is not a very good solution, because when such relationships break up, you are still hurt emotionally. You need to intentionally build freedom of self-expression into your relationships, especially those with the opposite sex.

Uranus in the Sixth House

You may be quite restless and find it hard to settle down to any kind of stable working pattern. You may also be very impatient when you have to put off until tomorrow something that you want to do today. And work that requires slow patient effort and attention may not be your strong point. Because of this, you are probably restless in school and possibly a minor discipline problem for your teachers. This is not because you are intrinsically "bad," but just because you can't sit still. You like to attack tasks with new and innovative methods rather than by established procedures. You don't mind work, but you hate to be restricted in the way you go about it. When you get older, you can use this energy quite creatively in science and math or in any work that requires inventiveness.

Some persons with this placement tend toward nervousness and scattered energies. So many things attract your attention that it is difficult to keep your mind on all of them at once, and you may exhaust yourself in the effort. Also you may move rashly and impulsively, which can cause accidents unless you are careful. You must learn some self-discipline in order to suppress the bad side of this energy and bring out the good side. However, as long as you are free to pursue your activities with your own methods, you should not have much trouble.

Uranus in the Seventh House

This placement will affect your life most strongly when you are older. In any kind of partnership you will want to maintain considerable freedom, and you will create a form of marriage according to your own unique scheme. You will rebel against the traditional roles and rules of marriage, and if you try to abide by them, your relationship will not be very stable. In that case, you will probably marry more than once.

Even while you are young, you clearly need a great deal of freedom in all your relationships. When someone tries to tell you about your obligations and restrictions in a relationship, you refuse to listen. And it is very important to find out now exactly what you do want in relationships. Don't accept what others tell you; find it out for yourself. If you try to arrange your relationships according to other people's rules, you will only become increasingly restless and want to escape.

You need to be with people who are very stimulating and challenging, even though they aren't the most stable people in the world. Stability is not what you need; instead, your relationships must be continually exciting. And you should try to give your partner and yourself plenty of freedom to express yourselves. Only then can a relationship be a source of richness and fulfillment in your life.

Uranus in the Eighth House

Changes in your life tend to take place suddenly. You are impatient with slow changes that you cannot see happening before your very eyes, so you do everything in your power to ensure that necessary changes come quickly. On the other hand, you may resist change altogether until the pressures are so great that they have to come suddenly and with great force. Obviously you need to be more patient about change and more willing to let nature take its own course.

You are also interested in the hidden aspects of life, wanting to know the answer to all mysteries and riddles and seeking any understanding you can get from them. When you do this, you have a unique ability to think about new ideas with an open mind and, even more important, to apply them to your everyday life.

When anyone tries to press their ideas and values upon you, you resist strongly. You have to be free to set your own values, and those values must allow you to be free. Often this comes out as a lack of concern with material possessions. You do not want to be bothered with owning a lot of things, especially if it involves you in other people's concerns. However, when you do work with others and share tools or ideas, you use your common resources in ways that are unexpected and quite inventive.

Whatever you do, be careful not to move suddenly or behave rashly, for this could lead to accidents. If you can learn to act carefully and deliberately, this possibility will be minimized.

Uranus in the Ninth House

Even while young, you are a free thinker. You must arrive at your own understanding of the world and be free to see it in your own way. The more others try to control or even influence your thinking, the more you will go your own way. Under pressure, even from parents and teachers, you can be quite stubborn. You automatically question everything you are told.

The positive side of this tendency is that you can think quite originally, which is especially useful in studying science, technology, mathematics or even occult subjects. You are attracted to revolutionary ways of thinking that others may be too timid to get into, because you are free of the limitations that hold back their thinking.

However, if you carry this tendency too far, you may become a very rash and even sloppy thinker. It is as wrong to assume that anything new is necessarily good as to think that the old is necessarily good.

This position does not make your mind very disciplined or careful. You may be inclined to jump to conclusions before all the evidence is in. Also you are likely to get impatient with people who think more slowly even though they are more careful. You haven't the patience to wait around for answers that come slowly, which can cause you to miss out on a great deal of understanding that you might want.

Travel is a source of excitement for you, and you like to get away and escape from the routine of everyday life.

Uranus in the Tenth House

You are a very restless person who wants to do everything in your own way. Because you do not like being told what to do you may have trouble getting along with authority figures such as parents, teachers and other officials. But your aims are not destructive. You just need freedom to find your own path, because that is the only way you can be really successful. If you try to take the same path that everyone else does, your life will be full of disruptions and instability, and you will feel unfulfilled.

One of your parents is likely to be a strong individual also. This parent may not live up to your childhood expectations of what a mother or father should be, but nevertheless he or she is showing you the kind of path you should follow.

Later, in your career, you should try to find your own way of doing your job, your own unorthodox approach. If other indications in the chart concur, this placement may favor work in a technical or scientific field in astrology, social reform or any other field that involves change through originality and insight. You will always be upsetting to people who cannot bear to see change, but those who appreciate inventiveness and individuality will recognize your ability. Just learn to have enough discipline so that you can follow your own path, because without it you will simply dart from one activity to another without making any impact.

Uranus in the Eleventh House

Even if you are a conventional person, you are likely to have very unconventional friends and to associate with groups that are considered offbeat. Some of your friends may belong to very unusual groups or subcultures, or they may be generally unpopular because of their exceptional views. As you get older, you may associate with people who are involved in the occult or astrology.

Your choice of friends reflects the fact that you don't want to be held in by conventional viewpoints and ideals. Nor do you want to be friends with people who try to limit you or make great emotional demands in the name of friendship. You want to associate with people in your own way, but you do want to associate. You are not a loner.

Often this position means that you prefer relationships in which you share similar interests or attitudes with your partner rather than a strong emotional bond. Your friends, through their unusualness, will probably show you different views of life than you would otherwise have, and you may make some really startling discoveries about the world through your friends. Those friends may be quite upsetting to you at times, but if they weren't, you would soon consider them dull.

Uranus in the Twelfth House

You tend to suppress your feelings of individuality in favor of living up to others' expectations. However, you must learn to be yourself as well, because secretly you resent holding yourself back. Part of you wants to be free and different, to live an exciting and unusual life. However, because of certain experiences when you were very young, you are afraid to go out on your own. It is important for you to realize that the only things holding you back are your own fear and reluctance. No one else is stopping you.

When you are alone in your own world of your imagination, or when you go off someplace to be alone, you live out your inner desires to be free and daring. As you get older, you may become interested in very unusual studies that you do entirely on your own with no one else knowing about them. You may become interested in the occult or in studying the inner workings of nature or the human mind. But you probably won't discuss this with anyone except people whom you trust completely.

Some persons with this placement suppress the drive to be a unique and different individual so much that the energy comes out only in compulsive behavior and sudden actions that don't make sense to anyone. If you have this problem, you must learn to get in touch with the part of yourself that yearns to be free. You may be afraid of some aspect of your personality, usually because you are afraid that others would disapprove if they knew you were really like that inside. Don't be afraid to express this side of yourself; it isn't that bad.

Uranus Conjunct Neptune (1993)

This aspect should produce a generation that will have a whole new approach to consciousness and idealism. They won't accept the old view of the material universe, and they may initiate new religious philosophies. The same concern with the occult and mystical philosophy that characterized the generation born in the 1940's (Uranus trine Neptune and Uranus square Neptune) will probably rise up again with this generation. However, these children will make a whole new beginning and will not adopt the forms of the old traditions.

Uranus Sextile Neptune (1966, 1967, 1968)

These children will be rather idealistic on the whole and quite comfortable with new spiritual and religious ideals. It is interesting to note that they are the children of the generation born in the early 1940's (Uranus trine Neptune), which was the vanguard of the counterculture in their experiments with new modes of consciousness and spiritual ideals. Their children with the sextile should follow in their footsteps, although perhaps more cautiously.

Uranus Square Neptune (1953–1956)

This aspect indicates a generation that is very concerned with new ideas and ideals about consciousness, but also very uneasy about them. As a group they feel that their hold on reality is not too strong. They tend to go off the deep end with ideas that others can't accept, or they choose systems of thought that give them some degree of structure and rigidity, so that they won't lose hold of reality.

Uranus Trine Neptune (1939–1943)

This aspect signifies a generation that was willing to experiment with consciousness, in ways that other generations have found rather frightening, but the result has been a rebirth of concern with spiritual matters and human consciousness. This generation challenged the materialistic premises of the older culture and did more to generate the new age of consciousness than any other group. However, as with all Uranus-Neptune aspects, there has been a problem in putting these realizations to work at a practical level.

Uranus Inconjunct Neptune (1893–1896 and 1924–1927)

This aspect indicates a generation that had mixed feelings about its ideals and how to implement them. They often felt very confused about their ideals, and when they found that their ideals failed because they were badly formulated, this group became disillusioned. States of consciousness beyond the ordinary are very confusing to them, and they prefer not to get involved with such matters.

Uranus Opposition Neptune (1906-1910)

Many people of this generation are confused and upset by anything out of the ordinary. This aspect can signify a real fear of confusion, of elements that do not fit into everyday reality. However, a few extraordinary individuals were able to break through this aspect's disruptive effects and come to a new synthesis of consciousness. They were able to bring forth radical new ideals and universal points of view.

Uranus Conjunct Pluto (1965)

This aspect undoubtedly signifies a generation of children who will have very powerful effects upon the rest of the culture, for they will be revolutionaries in the truest sense. They will be very eager and restless for change, but at the same time patient enough to learn how to really bring it about. They will undoubtedly have a very powerful impact on everyone in society. The parents of these children must be patient and instill in them a real respect for human values. There is the danger that some of them could be absolutely ruthless in their desire for change.

Uranus Sextile Pluto (1943-1945 and 1994-1996)

This aspect indicates children who, as they grow older, will bring about creative changes in the world. They will not have to resort to violent or disruptive methods to bring about reform, because as a group they understand how society works. And they can go through considerable changes in their own lives without losing their sense of equilibrium. They can be effective revolutionaries, simply because they have the power to stick to the task until it is accomplished.

Uranus Square Pluto (1932-1934)

This was one of the aspects behind the Great Depression, and it signified a time of great upheaval and change. Under this aspect, Adolf Hitler came to power, an excellent example of the turbulent social forces embodied by it. Children born under this aspect must contend with a great deal of change and unpredictability in their lives, which might lead them to feel uneasy and insecure. Also some children born under this aspect are quite disruptive themselves, when the aspect affects more personal points in their chart, such as the Midheaven, Ascendant, Sun or Moon.

Uranus Trine Pluto (1921-1923)

Tremendous social change occurred under this aspect, as reflected in the "jazz age" of the early 1920s. But the more relevant energies of this aspect were expressed when this generation grew up, for they were the ones who had to fight the Second World War. That war, of course, caused more great changes in the political structure than any event before or since, a pattern that is characteristic of this aspect. But because it was a trine, this generation was able to withstand the crises of change.

Uranus Inconjunct Pluto (1892-1894 and 1911-1912)

This aspect indicates changes in the world of the people who were born at these times, changes that were difficult to understand because they were very revolutionary but subtle in many ways. The people born during the first period experienced the consequences of these changes through having to fight in the First World War. The second group reached maturity at the time of the Great Depression. Both the First World War and the Depression were expressions of the breakdown of the nineteenth-century world order that was dominated by Western Europe.

Uranus Opposition Pluto (1901-1902)

This is another aspect indicating great changes in the lives of children born under it. It signifies impatience with any kind of established order or convention. This generation were the young adults of the 1920s who changed so many of the old habits and customs of nineteenth-century America. This aspect will not occur again in this century.

Uranus Conjunct Ascendant

You are an unconventional person, and your relationships with others will be unconventional as well. A free spirit, you do not like anyone to make claims on you. Persons with this aspect are often regarded as rebels, but for some the rebellion is rather quiet, expressed simply as eccentricity. However, whichever group of people you belong to, your differentness in itself will challenge people's ideas and preconceptions about the world.

You are quite restless and do not like staying put for any length of time, which can cause some problems in school, for example, where you are supposed to sit still. Also, to keep things stirred up, you may enjoy playing practical jokes upon people. By and large, you are easily bored, and you want to be as active as possible.

Sometimes people with this aspect are quite high strung and nervous. If that is the case, it is very important to look for opportunities to be quiet and at rest now and then. You cannot always be on the go, even though you may feel compelled to do so.

You are original and creative in many ways because you can see things in a different light from other people. But unless you learn to stick to your work and complete the tasks you have started, you will not be able to take advantage of your creative ability. Do not scatter your energies.

Later in life you may gravitate to one of the offbeat subcultures that exist in the world today. However, even there you may not be entirely at peace, because the pressure to conform can be as great in such groups as anywhere else.

Uranus Sextile Ascendant

An outspoken and independent person, you have your own ideas about the world, and even while quite young you demand that others respect your point of view. Very often your remarks upset your elders, because you have a strong tendency to say what is on your mind without thinking of the effect it will have on others.

Your mind is very active, and you like to learn new subjects or see the world from a new angle. Because you get tired of old ideas so quickly, you may make the mistake of adopting an attitude or point of view simply because it is new, novelty being an important element in your life. But that is not a good approach, for although age does not make something good, neither does it make it bad.

The people you associate with are likely to be quite free and independent in their views also. You like to be around exciting people who always challenge you in a positive way. If they don't, you will seek new friends frequently. Often your friends are very eccentric and offbeat and later in life they may be considered part of the bohemian element of society.

In general you don't readily identify with a group unless it is made up of exciting people doing projects that are different and stimulating. You do not like to associate with people who demand that you conform in any way to their ideals, even if those ideals are considered offbeat by the rest of society.

Uranus Square Ascendant

This signifies that you are a very independent person, and throughout your life you will value freedom very highly. The only problem is that in some instances you may not be aware of this feeling, because this aspect can be experienced in either of two ways.

On the one hand, you may be an obviously independent sort who demands freedom to do anything you want without being held back by others. You may be quite openly rebellious against authority figures, including your parents. You could be very undisciplined, flitting from interest to interest and scattering your energies in many different activities. However, when you learn to slow down the pace of these energies, you could be quite original and creative. Adults might not consider you particularly cooperative or orderly, but they recognize that you intend no harm. You would even be admired by some for your uncompromising will to be yourself, however eccentric that might be.

The second way of experiencing this aspect is that while seeming to be quite conservative, you attract people who are very independent and rebellious. This usually means that you have buried your conscious drive for freedom and independence and instead seek out others who are this way. Unfortunately this can bring about relationships with people who upset you because you cannot seem to count on them. They may be unreliable or come up with unpleasant surprises and other upsets. You would be better off getting in touch directly with these freedom energies within yourself. Then you would be in more conscious control of your relationships.

Uranus Trine Ascendant

This aspect is a bit more subtle than other Uranus-Ascendant combinations, but it has a definite effect. Even at a very early age, you insist on your right to be yourself. You may or may not be particularly rebellious, but as you grow up you do need a lot of room without restrictions. You like to find things out for yourself instead of being told about them or reading about them in books. The reason for this preference is that you see and experience everything you encounter quite differently from others, which gives you a great creative and inventive drive. You enjoy finding new ways to make things or play games and other activities. The old ways never seem satisfactory to you.

You like to be with other people who share this attitude, rather than with people who are afraid of change or who are totally predictable. You like to be excited by your friends and, within reason, startled by new and exciting ideas. You enjoy being with people who are interested in new ideas and beliefs, some of which may be quite startling to your elders. Even you occasionally try to startle people with your remarks because you enjoy stirring them up a bit, although you are not the least bit malicious.

No matter what comes at you from other people, you can take it. You are very adaptable and can handle changes very quickly. This gives you an unusual ability to survive in a fast-changing environment, especially since you are not particularly attached to the past and to traditional methods.

Uranus Inconjunct Ascendant

Your need to be free and do what you want is often in conflict with what others require of you and even with what you feel you ought to do. Sometimes this conflict can cause considerable physical and emotional tension. The task you face is to organize your life in a disciplined way that will enable you to satisfy your need for freedom through your everyday activities. One way to accomplish this is by figuring out your own methods for doing your work. Or you may choose to do the most interesting and exciting tasks, which are often the most difficult, so that others shy away from them. You need to be challenged by puzzles and problems in all your activities. You are not good at routines and repetitious tasks.

Your need for freedom may also interfere with your close relationships. When you are with others, even those you like, you feel very restless but you can't get up and leave because you want to be with them. This is typical of the ambiguity that comes with this transit. Certainly, the more others try to restrict your freedom of movement, the more you try to get away.

The restless energies of this aspect should be given some kind of release, because otherwise they can turn inward to create the kind of rash and compulsive actions that lead to accidents. If you have accidents, it is not because you are unlucky, but because you are not careful at critical times. Learn to avoid any kind of dangerous activity when you are nervous, upset or feel that your energies are scattered.

Uranus Opposition Ascendant

You may experience this aspect in a number of ways. First of all, you probably prefer to be with people who are very free and even eccentric rather than those who are predictable and "normal." This may cause some problems, however, because such people are likely to disappoint you greatly by not keeping agreements and constantly coming up with unpleasant surprises. However, with more ordinary people you are bored.

The reason you are attracted to independent people is because they do not make demands upon you. They are so interested in preserving their own freedom that they are not likely to interfere with yours. This characteristic will be most strong when you are older and having relationships with the opposite sex. If you always attract people who disappoint you and do not give you the emotional support that you ask for, it is because unconsciously you don't want to be trapped by the obligations of a normal relationship. As a result, you attract people who will not obligate you. This will affect all kinds of partnerships, not just sexual relationships. Any working agreement with another person should be kept loose, and you should give each other a great deal of freedom. Any such partnership should be as close to a non-partnership as possible without actually ceasing to exist.

If your relationships with others are generally unsatisfactory, it may be because your search for exciting relationships attracts people who are not very good for you. Perhaps excitement should not be such an important factor in choosing your friends.

Uranus Conjunct Midheaven

People should be prepared to encounter in you an extreme individualist. Even while you are very young, you insist on doing everything your way, and you strongly resist any pressures to conform. In fact the best way to ensure that you will not do something is to try to force you to do it. You are a rebel, and the established ways of living will not attract you particularly.

On the other hand you can be very creative with this aspect, because you have much originality and can see life in ways that others are blind to. You may be very inventive; in fact, this placement is characteristic of people who make a career in scientific or technological invention.

You may get a great deal of satisfaction from goading others. When you see people who are set in their ways, you cannot resist playing jokes or otherwise outraging them. Obviously if you are going to do this, you can expect to have problems with teachers and other authority figures, even your parents, who would prefer that you conform a bit more and stop rocking the boat. Teachers might find you quite difficult to deal with, not only because you insist on breaking rules, but also because you are very restless and hate to sit still for long. This placement may indicate a nervous disposition as well.

Eventually you should learn when it is worthwhile to rebel and when it is not. However, adults who want to restrain you should not try to do so by force. If they do, you will develop a lifelong negative attitude toward authority.

Uranus Sextile Midheaven

With this aspect, you want to be independent and to find a lifestyle and life work that are unique and yours alone. While you are young, others will consider your interests quite unusual, especially for someone your age. You may be particularly interested in a technical or scientific field, and in fact when you are an adult you may choose a career in such a field. This aspect may also indicate an interest in the occult or in offbeat philosophies. You do not feel obligated or held back by tradition. You seek to carve your own niche in life, and in the course of doing so, you may come up with some rather original and even daring ideas. At some time in your life, you may even make a totally new discovery.

You may prefer to be alone much of the time, not because you can't get along with people, but because you prefer to be free to program your own time. Other people may keep you from doing this, so that you feel you cannot accomplish what you need to.

You are likely to identify yourself as being different from others, because you feel that if you are just like everyone else, you are less of a person. Everyone follows some kind of pattern in order to feel unique, and yours is simply to be different.

You are capable of working with others as long as you feel that you share common goals. In fact, you can work very hard for a belief in something higher than yourself, usually a belief that is radical or unusual.

Uranus Square Midheaven

This aspect can signify that you are rather eccentric and easily excitable. Sometimes your actions are quite unpredictable, which confuses other people and may make them think that you are unreliable and irresponsible. But even though you do not take on the responsibilities that others think you should, you do carry out those duties that you impose on yourself.

Unfortunately you probably don't get along very well with people who try to tell you what to do, including teachers and other officials, and perhaps your parents. You feel that when they discipline you, they are merely forcing you to conform to their expectations rather than letting you be yourself. On the other hand, they consider you stubborn, rebellious and always wanting to do what they don't want you to do.

In this there is some truth, because you tend to be negatively suggestible; that is, you want to do the opposite of whatever someone tells you to do, even if at first you wanted to do it. This is unfortunate, because you can cut yourself off from activities that you might enjoy being involved in. Learn to choose your interests according to what you want to do, not merely to avoid doing what someone else wants. Also, the fact that someone else knows something that you do not does not mean they are wrong. You will always be yourself and usually somewhat eccentric, but when others try to give you some kind of inner discipline, you don't need to worry that they are threatening your integrity as a person.

Uranus Trine Midheaven

Probably your beliefs and ideas are different from those of the people around you, and you put a different value on physical objects as well. You do not like to be tied to possessions that you must take care of. This means that eventually you will prefer to have as few possessions as possible so that you can go wherever you want without any worries. Very early in life you will decide that you have to follow a path that is uniquely your own and does not follow anyone else's ideas about what is good for you. You want to break new ground, but in order to get there you won't have to battle others, especially your parents or other authority figures. You should be sufficiently creative so that you can make them see the desirability of letting you have your way to a reasonable extent.

You may change your mind several times about what you want to do with your life, not so much because your mind is unstable but because it is so difficult to find exactly what you need. Incidently, this can be a sign of an interest in or, later, a career in a technical field, such as electronic, computers, engineering or science. Or you may be interested in the occult and astrology.

You like a certain amount of excitement in your life, to keep from getting bored. You prefer anything new to what is old, so you will not be particularly interested in keeping in touch with your childhood and your past once you are finished with it. You are future oriented, always looking ahead to the next thing to come along.

Uranus Inconjunct Midheaven

You need to express your thoughts and feelings, but you often upset the people around you with your words. You seem to enjoy creating a stir every time you say something, but this can get you into quite a bit of trouble with parents, teachers and other authority figures. The underlying principle of this aspect is the need to balance your individual self-expression and manner of communicating with your need to learn and grow under the guidance of older people.

When you feel rebellious and unwilling to accept anything you are told, you should be allowed, within reason, to have the experience that will help you understand your elders' point of view. If you are lucky enough to have parents who let you do this, you will eventually get over your childhood resentment of being told what to do. Although you may not always agree with what they tell you, at least you will consider the merits of their ideas.

On the other hand, if your movements are restricted and you have few opportunities to experience yourself directly, you will become more resentful of authority and finally disregard whatever you are told, regardless of its merit. Later in life this attitude could make it extremely hard for you to hold down a job, because you will respond to bosses in the same way that you respond now to your parents and other grown-ups.

Certainly you will discover your own routes to what you want in life. Now you need to be given the confidence and encouragement to look for these routes on your own with total freedom.

Uranus Opposition Midheaven

This aspect signifies that you are an individualist and that you should go pretty much your own way in life. You especially need emotional freedom, and you don't enjoy being with people who are jealous or possessive. In fact, as a young child you probably did not like to be coddled by your mother, feeling that such emotions were smothering rather than reinforcing. This attitude probably resulted from an incident or series of incidents in earliest childhood that taught you that you couldn't count on the kind of nurturing children need from a mother. Therefore you understood that you must learn to do without it as much as possible. Quite likely your mother is very independent and has a busy life outside of being a mother. However, this aspect does not usually signal extreme emotional inadequacy or difficulties, unless Uranus is otherwise poorly aspected. It often signifies a parent who, like yourself, is a very free spirit.

As you grow older, tradition and home life will mean relatively little to you, and in fact, you may regard them as elements that hamper your freedom of self-expression. As soon as you are able, you will try to break free of your family and your place of growing up. Even while you are quite young you may enjoy the freedom of having no real roots, of fitting in, more or less, wherever you go. When you are older, you will keep your home simple and sparsely furnished, and you will try to have as few obligations as possible. If you ever have a family of your own, you will teach them to be as independent as possible, because you do not want anyone to depend on you.

Chapter Thirteen

Neptune

Neptune in the Chart

While you are young, Neptune can be a very difficult energy to deal with, but it can also be the source of much beauty and fascination. Neptune, like Uranus, does not follow the established rules, but instead of breaking them by sudden upsets, it makes the rules unclear and vague. Neptune can often be a planet of confusion and mystery.

The sign placement of Neptune affects whole generations and does not have much personal meaning unless Neptune is very near conjunction or opposition with the Ascendant or Midheaven. As Neptune goes through each sign, it denotes the area of life that the generation born then will challenge and alter in subtle ways when it grows up. For example, the whole nature of male-female relationships was changed by the generation born with Neptune in Libra.

The house placement of Neptune indicates areas of your life that you idealize, fantasize or, at worst, are confused about. In these areas also you may have to serve others in some way or give up what you want in order to learn more about life.

A well-aspected Neptune denotes great imagination and creativity. It also means that you can empathize with others and be sensitive to their needs and wants. In fact, a strong Neptune confers the highest kind of sensitivity. To have artistic ability, you must have a strong Neptune as well as a strong Venus.

Neptune poorly aspected denotes problems in accepting reality, which may be seen as confusing and disorienting. It can also mean that you try to confuse or disorient others, which can be a serious problem.

However, in its highest expression, the energy of Neptune puts you in touch with the meaning of existence, and for this reason it should be mastered as much as possible.

Neptune in Aries

This placement will not occur in this century.

Neptune in Taurus (1874-1889)

This placement will not occur again in this century. It indicates that the children born at this time have a very different idea of practical reality. They try to live according to much more abstract and spiritualized beliefs about material resources and their proper uses. Probably these children are much less practical than other generations, and they idealize nature and the things of the earth.

Neptune in Gemini (1889-1902)

This placement will not occur again in this century. It has the effect of introducing spiritual and idealistic themes into literature, art and philosophic writing and thought. The children born under this influence are unusually idealistic in their routine everyday thinking and might be more inclined to study mystical, abstract and impractical subjects than studies that can be put into use in the everyday world. Because of this idealism, they are very open to the kind of disillusionment that followed World War One, which most of this generation either fought in or felt the effects of.

Neptune in Cancer (1902-1916)

This placement will not be repeated in this century. Children born under this influence are inclined to idealize their homes, tradition, the past and all other ideas associated with Cancer. Nevertheless, their personal lives are rather unstable, because it is hard to relate the inherently impractical ideals of Neptune to the practical realities of a home and family. This generation was later at the forefront of the isolationist and America First movements, which were based on idealizing the homeland. In Europe this development was paralleled by the formation of the ultra-nationalistic fascist movements, such as the Nazis in Germany, Mussolini's movement in Italy and similar groups all over Europe and in Japan as well.

Neptune in Leo (1916-1929)

This placement will not be repeated in this century. Leo is often said to parallel the fifth house, and therefore it is considered the sign of speculation. It is interesting to note that while Neptune was in this sign the economy of the United States and Europe boomed, after a rocky start in the early twenties, and that the boom was based on totally illusory premises. This placement suggests an idealization of self-expression and of the rugged individualist who stands alone and becomes self-sufficient. However, at the same time, these people have less self-confidence than others, because of the ego-denying quality of Neptune. The serious conflict between the need for self-expression and the Neptunian ideal of detachment and noninvolvement would lead many of these people to be confused about what they can rightfully expect from the world.

Neptune in Virgo (1929-1943)

This placement will not be repeated in this century. This was the silent generation of the 1950s, whose ideal was to settle down, get good jobs with security and become responsible members of society. They idealized work and duty somewhat, which weakened their desire to protest even when things went wrong in the world around them. The influence of Virgo made them feel that they were too insignificant to protest. Even so, some of them were in the vanguard of the protest movements of the 1960s. However, their approach to large-scale social organization was a great deal more disciplined and in some ways conventional than that of the generation immediately following.

Neptune in Libra (1943-1957)

This placement will not be repeated in this century. One of the main features of this generation, the age group of various countercultures, is their idealization of relationships. However, the individual's commitment to the relationship is less strong. More recently, this group has been at the forefront of the spiritual revival, which has created new kinds of social groupings, such as communes.

Neptune in Scorpio (1957-1970)

This placement will not be repeated in this century. This generation may be characterized by a love of the mysterious and strange. As these children grow older, the current interest in the occult and related subjects will probably continue, but they may use these energies to gain power over others, which could create very dangerous psychological forces. On the other hand, they will be more concerned with individual regeneration and techniques of healing, both psychological and physical. They will have extreme ideas, either very lax or very strict, about personal morality.

Neptune in Sagittarius (1970-1984)

This placement should produce a generation of the most extreme idealists in many years. Even with older people, this energy has brought about a religious revival unparalleled in this century. As is characteristic of both Neptune and Sagittarius, most of these religions are sects from other countries such as India, and their teachings are quite foreign to Western tradition. However, there is also a strong Christian revival, especially among the fundamentalist and pentecostal sects.

Neptune in Capricorn (1984-1998)

This generation should represent quite a reaction against the previous one. These children will probably idealize work, thrift, practicality and duty rather than the abstract spiritual ideals of the preceding generation. However, they may not be very effective in dealing with practical principles, which may decline considerably, simply because this generation does not deal with them in their daily lives.

Neptune in Aquarius and Pisces

These twenty-first-century placements are beyond the scope of this book.

Neptune in the First House

You enjoy acting and putting on different "faces" for others to see. A very sensitive person, you pick up impressions from others very easily. Thus you sense what another person is about and can imitate him or her if you wish. However, this can create some problems, for if you are around someone who feels unhappy or negative, that mood becomes part of you without your realizing it.

Because it is so easy for you to assume different roles and acts, you may be unable to distinguish between what is really you and what you have picked up from someone else. One of the great problems of this placement is to find out who you really are.

But you can be a very kind person. With your sensitivity and awareness of other people's feelings, you can put yourself into someone else's place and understand that person. You are reluctant to hurt anyone because you know why they act as they do.

You enjoy fantasy very much, and you spend a great deal of time in your own private dream world, where others may not be able to reach you. Unfortunately you must learn to live in the real world like everyone else, but you may be reluctant to do so.

Neptune in the Second House

You probably have a lot to learn about the value of money and possessions. You may feel that money is not important to you, that the world will take care of you somehow. Or you may be very impractical about using money, so that others can talk you into buying things that have no real value or are not as they are represented. Learning to use money and other material resources properly is one of the important lessons of life, and the sooner you learn it, the better off you will be. However, you will never be very attached to money and possessions, so you are quite unselfish and willing to give whatever you can to others.

For some people, this placement works out very favorably in that they know instinctively where to find money and how to earn it. This is partly because they have a casual attitude about it. They know how to get money, but it is not a major concern in their lives, so they accept what comes. With this placement, if you are afraid that you will not have enough, that will probably be true. You must learn to relax about money, to use it intelligently and try to get only what you need.

If you ever feel tempted to gamble, be very cautious until you understand your real attitudes about money. If you are relaxed and calm, gambling may be all right for you. If you are not, you should avoid it completely.

Neptune in the Third House

You have an excellent imagination, which you will be able to use creatively in writing, speaking, possibly acting and even in learning about the world. However, this will be true only when you learn to separate truth from fantasy, what you want to believe from what you know to be true. You may be inclined to accept too much on faith and to be too idealistic. Do not believe what others tell you until you see it with your own eyes. You may be inclined to embroider the truth a bit; in fact, some people with this placement can be outright liars. More commonly, it simply means that you distort the truth unintentionally.

Some people with this placement are afraid to talk to others directly for fear that they will be misunderstood or thought badly of. But it is actually this fear that causes the problem. If you learn to talk directly to people without fear, you will discover that you can easily make them understand you. In fact with your rich imagination, you can say a great deal to make others understand you.

Your relations with brothers and sisters may be difficult, largely because of misunderstandings. You may feel that they do not accept you or that they undermine your self-confidence. It is also possible that you do the same to them.

Neptune in the Fourth House

You will feel the effect of this position of Neptune in two different ways. On one hand you will have a very strong intuition about what is happening deep inside other people. However, your feelings about others may not always be clear to you, so what you learn by intuition confuses you. At the same time you have a great need to be alone and think in your private world of imagination.

The other side of this position is that you may idealize one of your parents. It may be difficult for you to accept the fact that your mother or father is an ordinary person like yourself, so you may be very disappointed when this perfect person makes a mistake and reveals that he or she is only human. For this reason, you may be constantly disappointed in this parent, making your relationship quite difficult. This pattern of idealization may affect your home life as well. As an adult you may continually look for the ideal home, a place to which you can withdraw and be at peace with yourself. Even as a child you will try to find your own special place where you alone can go to be calm and peaceful. As you grow up, you will learn that this place of retreat from the demands of the world must be located inside yourself. No place in the material universe is that peaceful, so you may be rather disappointed in the real world.

Neptune in the Fifth House

You like to express yourself through your imagination by playing with beautiful fantasies and dreams. This position can be a sign of great creativity in writing or art, if you can discipline yourself to master the skills involved. As an adult you may become concerned with the entertainment media, such as the theater or television, or you may have some ability as an actor.

However, this placement can signify some problems in relationships. You may see in others what you want to see rather than what they really are. As you get older this will be especially troublesome in love relationships. With your romantic imagination, you tend to imagine your lovers as romantic figures whom you might encounter in fairy tales. Or you might cast yourself in the role of someone who rescues people in trouble and takes care of them. When you are older, you may take in severely troubled or disturbed people and care of them as loved ones.

In its highest expression, this position means that you derive pleasure from helping others. But you have to learn to distinguish between those who are worth helping and those who are not. While you are young you may be very indiscriminating, so that you are continually disappointed in the people you try to help.

Neptune in the Sixth House

This placement can affect you in two ways. First of all it makes your body very sensitive to outside influences, such as temperature, drugs, different kinds of foods and such. It can be a sign of allergy problems, and certainly you need to be very careful about what you eat, drink or take as medicine. Your psychological problems can also bring on physical illnesses or allergic reactions, but it is important to note that these are not imaginary, as is usually thought. However, to cure the illness, you must find the cause in your feelings and emotions as well as in your body.

On the other hand, this placement means that you need to help and be of service to others. At best, this comes from genuine love and sympathy for others. But you may feel that you don't deserve anything for yourself and that helping others is a way of compensating for this. Give yourself credit for your strengths and your individuality. Do not always give in to other people. A strong person who believes in himself can do much more for others than someone who acts like a doormat.

When you have to work at something, this position can cause problems in understanding the nature of the task, or you may feel inadequate to do the job. Here again you must learn to understand your real strengths and not overestimate your weaknesses.

Neptune in the Seventh House

Whenever you have to play a game or work very closely with someone, be sure you understand the task or the rules that you are playing by. You tend to see what you want to see in others, and when you talk with someone, you hear what you want to hear. This creates great problems when you discover the truth. Even while you are young, you may make enemies simply because you fail to make sure that you and the other person really understand each other. You are likely to have conflicts with others over imaginary slights and hurts.

At the same time you idealize some people so much that you cannot bear it when they show normal human faults or flaws. This can be especially troublesome later when you decide to get married, for you may demand that your partner be pure, noble and ideal. Or you may go to the other extreme and choose friends whom you feel superior to in some way, persons who need your help. This is often a way of avoiding your own weaknesses and faults by projecting them onto other people. You see your faults as if they were in others rather than yourself.

You cannot expect someone else to save you from the "cruel world," and you cannot expect to save others from it until you find out who you really are and accept others as ordinary people like yourself.

Neptune in the Eighth House

You are unusually interested in matters of the mind and in finding out what makes people tick. Even while young you may be interested in psychic and spiritual matters, although at this point it is likely to be just a fascination with stories about ghosts and the supernatural. You see mysterious forces at work in ordinary everyday events that others can see only the surface of. But you must be careful, because you can become rather morbidly obsessed and scared by the strange fantasies that you concoct. Don't get so involved in these that you lose your sense of proportion.

Sometimes this position means that you get into very strange moods which you can't bring yourself to discuss with your parents or other grownups. Your fears may make it difficult to go about your daily affairs. It is important to realize that these fears are based on what is happening in your mind rather than on anything that exists in the outside world. Your fantasies may be significant, but they won't hurt you, even though they may scare you sometimes. In particular, you may have an irrational fear of death.

The best solution for all of these problems is to take up some activity that completely involves both your body and mind and absorbs the energy that would otherwise go into these negative emotional states.

Neptune in the Ninth House

You are an idealist and dreamer who looks beyond your everyday world for topics to think and dream about. The normal world that we all live in seems to you a rather dull, uninteresting place. But you are fascinated by faraway worlds and peoples, even though your ideas about them probably don't have much to do with reality. Also you like ideas that are fantastic and otherworldly, such as notions concerning the supernatural, spirits and ghosts. As you get older, you may be concerned with religion, although your religious beliefs are likely to be different from what other people think of as religion. You always look for the hidden aspects of your world, the movements going on behind the scenes and the events that do not quite fit in with ordinary views of the world.

A serious problem that may arise with this placement is that you may be quite impractical. Your head may be so far up in the clouds that you cannot come to grips with the real world down here. Or you may choose your beliefs simply because they are fantastic rather than because they are true. This position indicates faith, in all its good and bad meanings.

On the other hand, your idealism has a positive side also. A compassionate person, you have a feeling of kinship to all life, which you probably express by being kind to other people and to animals. You are able to see that there is very little difference between you and those who are less fortunate than yourself, and thus you are reluctant to hurt or cause pain to others.

Neptune in the Tenth House

At times in your life this placement will cause trouble, because you will find it difficult to decide clearly what you want to do with your life. And you should be careful, because the wrong choice will lead to frustration and disappointment. For now, you probably shouldn't concern yourself too much with this problem, because it is unlikely that you will find your own path until you are quite a bit older. In fact the more effort you put into finding a path for yourself, the more difficult it is likely to be.

Neptune in this house suggests that you will choose a career or profession having to do with service to others, often with little thought of reward, although you may be well rewarded. It can be a sign of a career in religion, nursing or another profession in which you take care of sick, disabled or disadvantaged people. This placement by itself does not indicate medicine, although it can help a physician to be really involved in caring for his patients. Whatever the profession, the major force that directs you will not be ambition but rather a sense of service and dedication.

This position can indicate that you idealize one of your parents too much, or that you want to idealize that parent, but he or she does not live up to your ideals. You must learn to look within yourself for fulfillment of your ideals, not to your parents or other adults.

Neptune in the Eleventh House

This position requires a certain amount of care, because you are likely to have many unrealistic ideas about your friends. You may expect them to be more perfect than they possibly can be, to be without human flaws. Even more difficult is that you may get yourself into situations in which you can be seriously misled by friends, or you may attract friends who are unreliable. You will have to work very hard to develop a realistic attitude toward your friends.

On the other hand, you may attract friends who are very sympathetic and unselfish, people whom you can lean on in times of trouble. Under any circumstances that is something you would like to do. Or you may attract friends who lean on you, so that you have to perform many services for them. This is all right as long as they are worthwhile people, but you may not discriminate very clearly, and your friends may take advantage of you.

You are very idealistic about your goals, and you like to be with groups of people who feel the same way. When you are older you may become involved with spiritual and religious groups.

Neptune in the Twelfth House

This is one of the better twelfth-house placements. Even as a young person you are unusually sympathetic to people's problems, simply because you are able to feel what they feel and thereby understand their suffering. You are very reluctant to cause pain to any living thing, and you are as considerate of animals as of people. A very sensitive person, you immediately pick up impressions from others, which allows you to get to know someone quite well, even without many words. But you should be careful of one problem. Because you are so sensitive, it is unpleasant to be around negative people whose thoughts are evil or sick. You pick up these thoughts very readily, and they have a bad influence on your thinking. You have no problem with people who are trying to get away from such thoughts, but persons who are negative without realizing it can be very bad for you.

As you get older, you are likely to take an interest in religious and spiritual ideals and the supernatural. It seems to you quite obvious that there is more to this world than is apparent, and you need very much to get in touch with those hidden aspects. This position can indicate that you will spend much of your life taking care of less fortunate people, either personally or in institutions.

Aspects of Neptune to Pluto

These aspects are extremely long-lasting and therefore very difficult to understand. In the time period covered by this book, there have been only three—the conjunction of 1891 and 1892, the semisquare of the Great Depression era (and this text does not cover semisquares) and the sextile, which began in the late forties and will continue for the rest of the century. The sextile will last that long because Neptune and Pluto are now moving at almost exactly the same speed. The conjunctions seem to coincide with great historical climaxes, with peaks and valleys of culture. They do not seem to have much impact on individuals. But this is partly because it is so difficult to get an accurate perspective on long time periods. The sextile has been going on for so long that it is hard to separate its effects from those of other elements and indications. Therefore any discussion of its effects would be totally speculative.

Neptune Conjunct Ascendant

You will spend a great deal of your life getting to know who you are and how you impress other people. Especially while you are young, but sometimes continuing well into adulthood, you will have a hard time understanding people's attitudes toward you and your part in creating these attitudes.

Some of your problems stem from the fact that you look to other people's reactions to find out who you are, when you should be looking inside yourself to find that out. Get in touch with your feelings about yourself instead of being confused. Also don't fall into the trap of simply feeling inadequate and unworthy. Those feelings are probably not justified, but you may think they are. Another source of difficulty is that this aspect signifies enormous sensitivity to people and situations around you. But unfortunately you get so much input from the environment that you find it difficult to make sense out of it. When you eventually sort it out, you will discover that you are quite psychic or at least intuitive.

Also learn to stand up for your own rights and not let others take advantage of you. You may feel that it is better to serve others than to be served, but don't waste your efforts on people who are unworthy of being served.

Very often when people with this aspect get in touch with their real feelings, they make the astonishing discovery that they can project themselves to others in many ways, as if they have different personalities for different people and situations. You may or may not be a professional actor, but you will probably do quite a bit of acting in your everyday life. Just try to avoid getting a reputation for being deceptive and untrustworthy. At your core you have to be honest with others, even if you enjoy seeming mysterious and elusive.

Neptune Sextile Ascendant

You are very sensitive to other people's needs and desires, and in many cases you go out of your way to help those whom you love. This reinforces your sense of self-esteem. Also you are able to empathize with others, that is, you can put yourself in their place, which makes you want to ease people's pain whenever you can. These are signs of a highly intuitive and sometimes even psychic mind. You often perceive truths about the world around you that others are blind to.

Especially while you are young, people may disbelieve you, thinking that you are making it all up or indulging in childish fantasies. To make the situation more difficult, while you are young it really is difficult for you to understand the precise meaning of your insights about the world. However, everyone will be far better off if your family and friends try to help you understand what you see and feel, rather than make you distrust your intuition.

Certainly you love anything mysterious or fantastic, for such ideas help you get in touch with that dimension of the world that others cannot see. If you learn to understand yourself, you can become a very creative individual. In itself, this aspect does not designate artistic ability, but it does signify the kind of creative inspiration that is essential to art.

Your friends and the people you encounter every day are likely to be very sensitive and intuitive as well. They may help you, or you may enjoy helping them out. You tend to be idealistic about your friends.

Neptune Square Ascendant

You must learn to be very straightforward and honest in all your contacts with other people. Even harmless pretense—kidding someone or playing a joke—is likely to lead to real misunderstandings and difficulties with others. Your actions are so easily mis-interpreted that any willful act of this type will cause serious trouble. Others may have mistaken ideas about what you really are, or they may not trust you, even if your intentions are perfectly all right. Similarly you may misunderstand your friends. You are very sensitive to unconscious messages from everyone you meet, because you perceive feelings and emotions that everyone has that are not usually perceived. While you are young, you may blow up the significance of these hidden emotions out of all proportion. You may become suspicious and fearful, even of people who really like you, just because they occasionally feel a little anger toward you.

Also be careful not to form your image of yourself entirely through your relationships. At times, difficulties with others will make you feel demoralized and discouraged, especially if you are dependent upon others' reactions for your self-image. You must avoid feeling unworthy, because that will cause others to walk all over you. Sacrificing yourself for someone else is a good idea only when the other person is really worthwhile, which is not that often. You have as many rights as anyone, and you should stand up for them. Also try not to attract people who want to sacrifice themselves to you or who play the role of victim. They can be very confusing and discouraging to be with.

Neptune Trine Ascendant

You are very imaginative and potentially creative. Also you may be quite an idealist about other people. You are very sensitive to what others feel and need, and as you grow older, you will become more so. Throughout your life, you will have the capacity to be unselfish and giving in relationships, even preferring a partner who seems to need you rather than someone who is more self-sufficient. And, especially when you are older, you will seek out people who can teach you about the deeper world within.

This aspect can be a sign of considerable intuition and even psychic ability. Later on in life this will be very useful, but for the present you will have to be patient while you learn to interpret your impressions, for they will be very confusing at first. Eventually this talent will be quite useful and the source of much creative inspiration in your life. Like other Neptune-Ascendant aspects, this one by itself does not signify artistic ability, but it does give you the inspiration needed for true creativity.

While you are young you are attracted to otherworldly and fantastic interests. You enjoy hearing stories of the supernatural, and you probably believe there is some truth to that view of the world, because the known world seems a bit dull and colorless. Later on in life, this may become an interest in the occult or in spiritual studies.

Neptune Inconjunct Ascendant

This aspect can be a sign that you feel you must give way to others in order to get along with them. This can take two forms, both of which will be difficult to handle while you are young. The less positive form is simply yielding to all outside pressure and always giving in to others' desires. This will produce unconscious feelings of resentment that you can't express, but that make your relationships with others rather difficult. And as you get older, if you do not learn to stand up for your rights, this problem will get worse, because you express your unconscious resentment as a martyred attitude, which makes it impossible for others to appreciate or use anything they get from you. Thus the results of your sacrifice are totally negative, because you are not happy with giving and they are not happy with receiving.

But the other, more positive, way of dealing with this energy is by giving freely before others try to take it from you. In order to do this, you have to feel good about yourself and confident that you will always have enough for yourself and others. One side of you likes to help and take care of people and will not feel taken by those whom you give to. In the highest expression of this aspect, what you gain for yourself will not mean as much as what you gain for others, which is the effect you should work for.

On another level entirely, you should be very careful of your health because you are unusually sensitive to certain elements in your environment. You may not be able to handle certain foods or drugs—even prescribed drugs should be handled with care— and you should avoid letting your body become weak.

Neptune Opposition Ascendant

This aspect can create problems in relationships in that you feel deceived or disappointed by your closest friends. Or there may be much misunderstanding and confusion in your relationships. Very often they seem to demoralize you or make you feel inadequate. Often you take on other people's problems that are very hard to manage, especially at your age. When you are older, you may feel like giving up everything you have to help out someone you love, but be very careful to do this only for someone who is worth it, someone who is trying to improve his or her own life. Some people will try to take advantage of your selflessness in relationships by just staying the way they are, feeding off your energies.

There is another way that you may experience this aspect. Instead of looking for people whom you can help, you may seek out teachers, people who are wiser, more mature and evolved than you. Very often you idealize an older person and hang on to his or her every word and gesture. Do not carry this too far, however, because we are all only human, and eventually you will be disappointed by the flaws of even the best and wisest people, and you will feel cheated. However, you should recognize that this person does have something to offer; the only problem is your inflated expectations.

You may be attracted to very creative and sensitive people who see aspects of the world that you do not see. These people can be very rewarding but also confusing.

Neptune Conjunct Midheaven

This aspect presents many opportunities and many challenges. You are very sensitive to whatever happens around you, and you seem to soak up impressions like a sponge. But you do not always know what these impressions mean or what to do with them. Consequently there is a real danger that you will be confused much of the time, especially about who you are and where you are going. Unfortunately, with this aspect you tend to get discouraged and depressed about yourself, feeling that you will never get a real grasp of what is happening in your life. One of your parents, at least, should be able to lovingly but firmly guide you through life and point out the difference between realities and illusions.

This position is often associated with psychic ability, which may be the source of the impressions that seem so confusing and hard to understand. Your parents should accept the fact that your so-called fantasies are actually based on a reality that is not easy to understand. They should help you learn to interpret this reality rather than saying that you are only dreaming or making it all up.

It won't be easy to find the right course to follow in life, but this position provides a few clues. First of all, you should feel that you are working for a cause higher than yourself, whether it is serving or taking care of others in some way or working for an idea or faith. This aspect has a very strongly religious dimension. But it is more mystical than orthodox, and even while you are young you will be attracted to mystical and otherworldly ideals.

Neptune Sextile Midheaven

This aspect signifies that you aren't particularly interested in being self-assertive, that you prefer to live in a quiet and peaceful world of your own making. If you cannot find anyone else who shares your attitude, you don't mind living alone. You do not really care that much about being with other people, because they interfere with your excursions into the private world of your ideas and fantasies. But you don't dislike people; in fact you are very sensitive to their needs and wants, and you feel that you should be of service in some way.

You are very interested in ideas that others of your age usually ignore, such as religious ideals (at a rather simple level of understanding while you are young) and even occult beliefs, a love of the mysterious and supernatural.

Because you are quite sensitive, you need to be with very positive and supportive people. If you are with people who harbor many negative thoughts, you will become a victim of their negativity and feel very unhappy. Also such people would make you feel suspicious of others, when you really want to see their finest, most spiritual side. Your parents should support your efforts to see the good in other people, so that you will grow up to be a loving and unselfish person whose presence makes everyone's lives more beautiful. Without this support, you will be a rather retiring and shy person who avoids contact with others for fear of being hurt.

Neptune Square Midheaven

This aspect can indicate extreme insecurity and self-doubt, unless your parents and other influential adults make a special effort to reinforce your self-confidence. When you meet a difficult person or an obstacle, your first tendency is to run away, because you feel that you cannot overcome it. This is probably not true, and you must learn what you really can do, instead of limiting yourself to the few tasks that you are not afraid to do.

Sometimes you seem to be surrounded by energies that are very weakening, usually from people you are with who give off very negative energies such as resentment, hostility or anger. You don't attract such people to any unusual extent, but you suffer more than others from being around them. As much as possible, you should associate with positive and optimistic persons.

This empathy has a positive side, however, in that you understand other people very well, knowing what is going on in their minds as well as what they say. But it will take you a while to learn how to interpret the signals you get from others. While you are young, you may frequently misinterpret people.

You will feel a need to work for an ideal that is higher than yourself or for a person whom you can idealize and respect. This is fine, but you will probably be taken advantage of by people who are unworthy of your devotion, unless you work very hard to get past your idealizations and see who they really are. Then you can choose intelligently.

Neptune Trine Midheaven

You are very idealistic in your attitudes toward the world, and you want to be as free as possible of values and possessions that limit you or prevent you from encountering the world. You may be less interested in material possessions than most people of your age, feeling that the burden of taking care of them is more trouble than it is worth. Besides, you value emotions, ideals and other immaterial concerns more than possessions.

Very early in life you show how unselfish and giving you are, especially to people in need. You like taking care of people or animals and trying to make them better. As you get older you will have a strong need to be of service to others, putting spiritual and moral ideals above personal gain. Even if you do not always succeed in living up to that ideal, it will be a very powerful force in your life.

You are very sensitive to other people, so you are a bit reserved and shy until you know you can trust them. Your feelings are easily hurt, and a misplaced gruff word can make you very unhappy. Your family should try to understand this and treat you a bit more gently. They should realize that they will be rewarded with your devotion.

Even while quite young, you are fascinated by the mysterious and supernatural. You find the worlds of fantasy stories and fairy tales more interesting and alive than this world, which is so full of dull concerns and mundane preoccupations. Of course, you must learn to relate to this world, anyway, and you should try to see the mystery that is inherent even in the everyday world.

Neptune Inconjunct Midheaven

With this aspect you may have to build up your self-confidence considerably while you are young and learn that you are as worthy as anyone else. Even though these are your learning years, when you must develop a great deal of discipline, you still deserve as much consideration as anyone else. Your natural tendency is to yield to authority, so that those people who are most influential in your life, including your parents, should be very careful about how they exercise their authority over you. If they try to control you too much, or if they make you feel that you just aren't able to manage your own affairs, it will be difficult to correct the effects of this negative influence later in life.

You are very impressionable, in that you pick up the energies around you very quickly. Therefore it is very important that you be surrounded by wholesome influences in your early years, because negative influences will weaken your self-esteem and make it much more difficult to accomplish anything when you are older. On the other hand, your impressionableness may give rise to some psychic ability, or at least a very sharp intuition when you are older.

While you are young, you won't have a clear idea of what you want to do in life. In fact you may never orient your life around a single idea or purpose. But don't worry. Your purpose in life may not be one that is readily defined in terms of a career or profession. More important may be your style of living or your experience of life. Simply learn to always be aware and to learn whatever there is to be learned. With your sensitivity and intuition you can understand much more than other people, especially those who have wrapped their lives around their career or profession.

Neptune Opposition Midheaven

This aspect indicates great sensitivity, but for this energy to work positively, your earliest childhood must be reasonably serene and peaceful. You are very sensitive to the hidden energies in your home and between your parents or other members of your family, and any kind of ongoing negative feelings at home can cause you to become insecure and lacking in self-confidence. Later on, you may feel that you cannot easily cope with life's challenges, because inside you cannot depend upon your emotions and your spontaneous actions to make everything come out right.

Your relationship with one of your parents may be rather difficult. Often this aspect signifies that one of your parents is too weak psychologically to play his or her role in your life. This might lead you later to seek out someone who can be a guide and a loving parent figure for you. The problem is that such a relationship would displace your search for normal adult relationships.

However, even if both parents are strong, you may go to the other extreme and idealize the more influential one. In that case you would compare everyone you meet to that parent, instead of dealing with each person as a unique individual. This is not so bad as the first alternative, because at least you have strong ideals that you can believe in. Later in life this may turn into a strong belief in God. Because you are so sensitive, you may eventually develop a strong psychic and intuitive ability.

Chapter Fourteen
Pluto

Pluto in the Chart

Pluto is the planet of transformation and the powers that cause transformation. The condition of Pluto in your chart describes how you approach the changes that must occur in your life as you grow and develop. It also indicates your ability to use and handle power as it comes to you. This is not likely to be a large issue while you are young, but it will become important later on in life.

The sign placement of Pluto affects whole generations and is important to you individually only if Pluto is close to conjunction or opposition with your Ascendant or Midheaven or in close aspect to the Sun, Moon or inner planets. The house placement of Pluto suggests the areas of your life that will be the sources of greatest change and most intense development. Pluto can also indicate using power or someone else using power to influence you.

A well-aspected Pluto makes you very ambitious and desirous of making a positive impact on the world around you. It also means that you are deeply concerned with truth, which you will seek out in the most obscure and difficult places. Pluto confers persistence and the ability to keep on going through the most difficult times. It often signifies someone who is a natural psychologist as well.

A badly aspected Pluto often signifies power struggles with certain individuals or groups of people. At its worst it can mean a ruthless, willful person who will stop at nothing to get his or her way. If you are even the least bit ruthless, you should learn to curb it, because this type of Plutonian energy causes people to react against you with fierce resistance. Sometimes a difficult Pluto means that you have to contend with others who are this way, and in doing so, you grow into your own strength and power.

Pluto in the Signs

These placements have long-term effects. In the period covered by this book, Pluto has been in only five signs—Gemini, Cancer, Leo, Virgo and Libra. Later in the century it will enter Scorpio and Sagittarius. In general, Pluto signifies breakdowns and new beginnings in the world as symbolized by the sign it is in. The persons who have Pluto in that sign may contribute to these changes.

Pluto in Gemini (1882-1912)

This was a period of rapidly changing beliefs, as old habits of thinking broke down and totally new ones came into being. Some of the people born with this placement tried to create an ideology of power and control of the masses, for example, Adolf Hitler. Others born at this time led the fight against him. Many of the greatest breakthroughs in modern communications took place at this time, and even after Pluto left Gemini, these people were at the forefront of the discoveries in radio and telephone communications.

Pluto in Cancer (1912-1938)

To some extent this placement coincided with the time when Neptune was in this sign. It helped to bring about the rise of dictators who based their power on glorification of the homeland. This period also saw the downfall of the extended family in industrialized countries, especially in America, and the rise of the less stable nuclear family, with its lack of real emotional support for children.

Pluto in Leo (1938-1957)

These are the children who grew up to form the counterculture, with its ambiguities about the individual's relationship to the larger group. On one hand, these people have worked in large groups to create formidable mass movements. But at the same time many of them have returned to an earlier idea of the self-sufficient individual living off the land. They have tried to become independent of the centralized machinery of society by generating their own power, growing their own food and so forth.

Pluto in Virgo (1957-1971)

This passage coincided with the revolutionary fervor of the sixties, and the children of this period will probably have radically new ideas about work and duty. They are likely to be very much involved in ideas about nutrition and new methods of healing the body through food. They will be very concerned with health, but their approach will probably not be orthodox.

Pluto in Libra (1971-1984)

For those who are now adults, this period represents the greatest breakdown in modern history in the relationship of marriage. Many couples live together without getting married, and those that marry often do not stay married. Because of the general instability of their parents' marriages, the children of this era will have a much more fluid but unstable view of relationships and mutual commitments between people. They may be very reluctant to make binding agreements because of their childhood experience of marriage.

Pluto in Scorpio (1984-1995)

Many astrologers believe that this is the sign that is ruled by Pluto. The children of this era should be much more concerned with the forces underlying the surface of reality.

They will put their intelligence to investigating all kinds of phenomena, and it is just possible that they will bring the arts and sciences out of their present stagnation to a new period of dynamic activity. This period will be a time of change that is intense even by twentieth-century standards.

Pluto in Sagittarius (1995 into the twenty-first century)

During this time many more of society's cherished beliefs will be destroyed, and new religious, spiritual and cultural values will take their place. Few of us would be able to deal with these changes comfortably, and the children of this time will probably be quite iconoclastic, even by the standards we have known.

Pluto in the First House

You are a very intense person who takes almost everything seriously. If an activity isn't important enough to warrant throwing your whole self into, you feel it isn't worth doing. You tend to go to extremes, which may make other people uneasy. You have to understand that others are afraid of experiences that you find interesting.

You enjoy having power over people and being in a position to make changes. Sometimes you seem to work behind the scenes, in that other people can see what is happening, but they cannot see who is doing it. It is extremely important that you develop a strong sense of responsibility about using power, because you will probably always use it to some extent, and if you are not careful you can create problems in your life and the lives of those around you. For example, you may be a leader among your friends, but you must be sure that what happens is best for all of you. If it isn't, you will probably be at least partly responsible.

Your life will not stand still, for you need to have changes to keep it interesting—not sudden explosive events, but slower, more gradual changes that will create clearly marked periods in your life.

Other people will either be drawn to you very strongly or will not like you at all. For this reason you will probably have a few strong friendships, and few if any casual ones.

Pluto in the Second House

When you want something, you want it very much, and you will work very hard to get it, whether it is a possession or an important goal. Usually it is a possession. As you grow older you will discover that money is very important to you, not for itself, but because it allows you to get what you want. Not a possessive person, you do not want things simply for the sake of owning them, although you are likely to accumulate a great number of possessions. Instead, you want things because of what you can do with them, which is determined by other elements in the chart.

You are very concerned with having complete control over everything you possess. You resent interference from people who tell you how to use your possessions. While you can be generous in lending things to people, you demand that they return them promptly, and you get quite upset if they do not. Your possessions give you the ability to control your life, and you feel that someone is taking that control away from you if they take away a possession.

The major problem to watch for is that of becoming so loaded down with possessions that you lose your freedom of movement. If you own too many things, taking care of them all becomes more of a burden than they are worth. In such cases you must get rid of the excess baggage.

Pluto in the Third House

When you become interested in something, you try to get as deeply involved as possible. You want to understand its workings at a very profound level and from every point of view. You even try to get inside people's minds to understand how they work. Even while young, you are a better student of human nature than many adults.

You form opinions about what you study only after long and profound thought. Those who disagree with you will find it very hard to change your mind because you analyze ideas so thoroughly before arriving at an opinion. Also you are very resistant to pressure to change your mind, because you feel that you must form your opinions in your own way. You are a born investigator.

You are quite good at getting others to agree with you, as long as you do not try to force them. You often try very hard to make people agree with you, but if you put too much energy into it you will scare them off, and instead of agreeing, they will resist you. But if you state your point of view without trying to convince anyone, others will agree with you quite readily. People with this position make good teachers, because teachers shape others' beliefs.

On another level this placement can indicate an intense relationship with a brother or sister. If such a relationship is bad it will be very bad, or if it is good it will be very good. Either way the relationship will be important.

Pluto in the Fourth House

You feel very strong urges from deep within yourself, particularly whenever something reminds you of your earliest childhood. Even though you are young, much has already happened in your life that has had a tremendous impact upon you, which you probably do not understand. You have already acquired many emotional habits that totally control your behavior when you are upset, making it impossible to do what you know is right.

One of your parents has had an enormous impact upon you, either for good or for bad. You may be very attached to one parent and too dependent upon him or her, which is not a great problem now, but it may become one when you are older. Or you may have great difficulty getting along with one of your parents who makes you feel bad about yourself and undermines your self-confidence. You may feel guilty about acts that you have committed, even though they are actually quite harmless. You must learn not to take your guilty feelings so seriously and to recognize that you are really quite all right. Even if your relationship with this parent is good, you must learn that you take it too seriously and that you have to live your own life. You will probably spend a great deal of your life getting beyond that relationship and learning to live out of your parent's shadow.

Pluto in the Fifth House

You do not play like other young people, because you take any game very seriously, as if it were not really a game at all. You like to play for very high stakes, and whether you win or lose, it is the experience of putting everything on the line that appeals to you. At this point in your life, however, you may not recognize this, and you may wonder why playing with others and winning always seems so important. You must learn not to take everything so seriously, however, because your attitude makes it impossible for you to have fun. Also you and others around you get so stirred up that fights, arguments and disputes break out in situations that should have been just good times. It doesn't matter whether you are right or wrong—in fact, you may be right most of the time—but being right is not the point of an activity that is supposed to be fun.

Whatever you do for fun, you get wrapped up in it completely. Nothing else interests you at that moment, and others may accuse you of having a one-track mind. But your interests will change and you will get involved in other activities.

When you are older, you will approach love affairs as seriously as you approach playing now. Here again, too much seriousness will deprive you of enjoyment and fun.

Pluto in the Sixth House

You approach work with great intensity, and you prefer tasks that involve you completely. You like to shut out everything else and simply be involved in what you are doing. You take your work very seriously, and even while you are young, you prefer work to play. Also, you want to do your tasks your own way, which may create troubles with employers when you are older and have a job.

Also you prefer to work by yourself, and you do not care to have people interfering with the way you do things. Others may consider you secretive about your activities.

You should be careful of your health, for otherwise you will have a number of serious health crises in your life. It isn't that your health is especially weak, but your work will be exhausting and require that you be in good physical and mental health. If you allow yourself to become run down, the consequences could be serious.

Pluto in this position can be a sign that you might work in some area involving investigation, research, psychology or secret projects.

Pluto in the Seventh House

Encounters with others will play a significant role in your life. Most of the major changes that you go through will be the result of your relationships. You will attract people who seem very strong willed and powerful, who may try to change your life. It may seem as if they won't leave you alone, and you may have to struggle against them at times in order to remain yourself. Listen to what these people say, but do not believe everything they tell you. Learn to judge yourself independently of what others say. Of course, this placement can be a sign that you try to change everyone you meet, which is equally wrong. In that case you would have to learn to leave others alone. You and everyone around you has the same right to be themselves.

When you are older, this will have a strong effect on your relationships with the opposite sex. You will always look for relationships that are very intense emotionally, and you may get involved in power struggles about which of you is going to control the other. However, this may result in positive changes as well as negative ones.

This placement may indicate that you are good at counseling others in psychology or related fields.

Pluto in the Eighth House

Your life goes through periods of very intense and deep change. You are always aware of something inside you pushing you to grow and become different from what you were. You are not afraid of these changes, because they seem quite logical, a natural unfolding process within you. However, others may be surprised by your changes and amazed by your easy approach to even the most serious and difficult problems that you face in life.

While you are young, adults may feel that you are overly concerned with death at times. This interest is not morbid, however, it is simply a sign of your general interest in the basic processes of existence. You are equally concerned with birth and the mysteries it signifies. Even now your interests are more serious than those of other young people.

You may express these interests as a great love of investigating, immediately looking for the answers to any question that intrigues you. However, you don't mind spending a great deal of time and energy to find the answers. You may spend many hours looking through books for the answers or asking questions of adults. But this is more than casual curiosity, it is a deep psychological drive within you.

You want to use all the resources, objects, money or other possessions that come your way for whatever purpose is dominating your life at the moment. This may make you unwilling to share with others, because your own intentions seem so important that you don't want to compromise and let others have their way.

Pluto in the Ninth House

You have a strong desire to learn about everything at a very deep level of understanding. Superficial knowledge does not attract you. Consequently, in any subject that you are interested in, you will probe and ask questions and probe further until all mysteries are solved. You like games that are puzzles and puzzling situations that arise in life. You are fascinated by mysterious and deep matters and bored by anything that turns out to be simple and everyday. For this reason you probably enjoy stories concerning the supernatural, ghosts and strange mysteries. You don't even mind being scared a little if the story is good.

On another level, this placement indicates that your opinions are very solid, and once you have made up your mind, it is very difficult for anyone to change it. In fact you probably try at times to make everybody think as you do. But be careful about this, because you have to give others the same freedom to think as they want that you demand for yourself. Later in life you may be very forceful in molding the opinions of people you know, but to do that well, you must learn the art of getting people to see your point of view without making them feel you are pushing them.

As you get older, you will have an increasingly profound understanding of human nature. You may not always be able to put your knowledge into words, but you can feel it deep inside. This is a very useful placement for any field that depends on this kind of understanding, such as psychology or psychiatry, advertising and public relations, or even politics. But you must be sure to avoid using this ability to control other people unnecessarily, for that will make others try to keep you under control.

Pluto in the Tenth House

You have a great need to be a leader among your friends, for you want to make changes and to be a person who others consider important. But in order to be a successful leader, you must learn to be more patient and to work within the rules. While you are young, rules may seem to be an obstacle in the way of getting what you want, but you will learn that following the rules in any activity will actually enable you to enjoy your success in it. If you persist in doing everything your way, without thinking of the rules, you will encounter such opposition from others that you will lose everything you seem to be winning.

Pluto in this position signifies that your life work will involve changing the world around you, perhaps rebuilding and reforming circumstances or repairing things that have become worn out and making them useful again. This placement may also signify work that helps heal and rebuild people, such as medicine or psychiatry. Whatever your later career, you will take your work very seriously and put your whole self into it. This may not be apparent at first, because it may take quite a bit of time to find what you want to do. While you are looking, you will go through several periods of change and development, such that you and others may wonder if you ever will discover your life's work.

Pluto in the Eleventh House

Your friends and the people you associate with will play a very important role in your growth. You may attract friends who are very intense and powerful, who have a strong influence on you. But you will have to be quite careful, especially while young, not to let your friends lead you in directions that you do not want to take or make you do things that you know are bad for you. No matter how much influence your friends have, you are ultimately responsible for what you do, and others will hold you to that if you do something wrong.

The best people for you to be with are those who have a clear purpose in life, some constructive work to do. Such people will help you grow in a positive direction, whereas those who seem to have nothing to do may get you into trouble. When you are older, this placement may signify that you will work with groups that try to make changes in the world.

No matter what you do or whom you associate with, you will learn that your friendships help you understand yourself better. The people you are with are reflections of yourself, and you will learn about yourself by seeing how they affect you. Other people are very important to you even when youre relations with them are not very pleasant. You should not try to work out all your problems by yourself. Find a good friend who will give you sound advice, and follow it.

Pluto in the Twelfth House

At times you feel a very strong desire to do something that doesn't really make sense. You wonder what made you do that, try to figure out what created the drive. The problem is that you do not like certain aspects of yourself, or you think others would not like them. So you try to keep these drives secret from others or from yourself, even though you are aware of their effect on you. Yet because these parts of your personality need to be expressed, they generate strong energies that seem to push you around, as if another person was hiding inside you and forcing you to act.

What you must recognize is that nothing in you is really that bad. You have to look at these hidden aspects of yourself as if you were meeting another person and ask yourself whether they really are that bad. Most people are perfectly all right inside, but they do not realize it. Holding yourself back and trying to hide certain elements of yourself from other people is likely to cause more problems than being totally honest about yourself, because the repressed drives get out of control and demand expression at the worst possible moments.

This placement can also indicate that you are a born investigator with a strong interest in secret and hidden things. You like to solve riddles and search out the answers to obscure and difficult questions. This trait could be very useful later on in science or other fields that involve asking questions about the universe.

Pluto Conjunct Ascendant

This aspect can have a very powerful effect on your life, but unless you learn how to use it responsibly, it could create problems. You approach other people and situations in life with great intensity. It is difficult for you to take anything lightly, for you either get into something totally or not at all. In fact, when you do get wrapped up in some project or activity, you may neglect everything else in your life. This aspect has a compulsive quality that makes it difficult for you to do anything in moderation.

Your emotions are very intense. You go through periods of very dramatic psychological change, and after each of these periods others will feel as if they are seeing a new you. During those phases of change you are very touchy, irritable and subject to outbursts of emotion. But you thrive on the process of change even though it is often painful.

As you get older you will be more concerned with power and control. When you see something wrong or being done poorly, you want to take it over and do it right. This is the most important and difficult side of this aspect. As you grow up you will have to choose between being someone who works for positive change and reform or a person whose drive for power makes you dominate others strictly for personal gain. If you follow the latter course, people will fear your energies and will band together to stop you. Such opposition can render you totally ineffective. But if you work for positive change in society, you will be respected and effective. You must become an agent of change and creativity above and beyond your personal desires.

Pluto Sextile Ascendant

Your relationships with other people are very intense, and many of your friendships, even everyday contacts, will eventually change your life. It is hard for you to have casual relationships, because you want to encounter everyone at a very deep psychological level. This makes your attitude toward life much more serious than that of most people your age. On the other hand, this aspect can make you magnetically attractive to other people.

Whenever you meet a new situation or person, you want to know what makes it tick. You have a very inquiring mind that likes to get inside everything and see its innermost aspects. Later in life you may be very interested in human psychology and even now, at a less mature level, you are interested in how people work. You may become effective at handling other people so that they will do what you want within reason. But you must learn to use this power responsibly; otherwise the people you alienate will watch your moves very carefully and try to keep you under control.

Eventually you may attain a position of influence and leadership over your friends and immediate associates. You want very much to have effective control over the world around you. When you see a situation that needs to be changed, you want to make changes. However, you can be quite subtle about it, and you will quickly learn not to rock the boat unnecessarily. Your efforts will be very practical.

Pluto Square Ascendant

There are some difficulties with this aspect, unless you learn early in life exactly where the dividing line is between your rights with respect to others and their rights with respect to you. With this aspect you may get involved in problems with others because one or the other tries to take control. At times you feel that others are continually trying to take unfair advantage of you. Or you may try to take advantage of them. This is why you must learn the proper balance between your rights and others'.

Also you must be very open and honest with people, because it is very easy to create the wrong impressions in your relationships. This is because you are naturally a very intense person and may seem to be brooding or secretive even when there is nothing weighty on your mind. You should realize while you are quite young that even now you make a strong impression on others, either good or bad.

If you have trouble getting along with others, even when it seems to be totally their fault, think about your own attitudes and actions. Quite unwittingly you may have brought about the situation that has led to conflict. You may have been too stubborn or unwilling to compromise, forcing others to oppose you just to get their way.

It would be good to avoid getting involved with people who seem strange, difficult and emotionally intense about everything. These persons can produce problems if they try to force you into doing things that you do not wish to do.

Pluto Trine Ascendant

You are very intense emotionally, and you take life seriously. Your relationships with others are also intense, and you probably prefer to have a few close friends rather than a lot of casual acquaintances. You want to know your friends in depth and feel that your emotional interaction is very strong. Some people resent what seems like an intrusion into their inner selves, but you don't usually attract such people anyway.

Eventually you will arrive at a philosophy of life that you will hold quite intensely, and when you decide on your position, it will be very difficult for anyone to make you change your mind. However, you will spontaneously change your philosophy several times in your life because of intense experiences with others. In fact, the most intense changes in your life will happen through relationships. However, there is no reason to fear these changes, for most of them will be beneficial, simply stages in growing up.

In turn you will be able to make some very creative changes in the lives of those around you, and to a great extent, your life will revolve around doing so. Your drive to reform and rebuild can range from making creative changes in your world to being fond of repairing and rebuilding broken objects or even possibly broken people. It is very difficult for you to leave matters alone, but you must learn when to leave others' lives as they are. People resent uninvited interference, and their resentment could get in your way, unless you learn this lesson.

Pluto Inconjunct Ascendant

This can be an indication that through experiences with others, you will be forced to undergo many significant changes in life. At times the crises may be quite unpleasant, but for the most part the results will be very positive, although for some people, they may be less constructive. But you must be very careful about the kind of people you get involved with. Choose your friends with great care and try to find people who have a healthy outlook on life and who seem reasonably well balanced. People who are driven to extreme behavior or who act compulsively, as if they could not plan anything in advance, are not very good for you. They will get you into difficult situations that you do not need.

Also watch for compulsiveness or extreme behavior yourself. These qualities could be quite hard for others to handle, and people will probably avoid you if you express them freely.

However, you should not avoid people who force you to observe yourself and the world very clearly. Such people will come into your life at times when changes must occur. While you are young, these people might be your parents or a special teacher.

You probably will resist their influence, because what they show you will be hard to take, but you must accept it, for they have the highest concern for your well-being.

With your friends, you must learn to give in at least as often as you get your way. Don't let either you or your friend become dominant. Winning, losing and compromising in equal measure are all part of getting along, which you may find hard.

Pluto Opposition Ascendant

Your interactions with others are very intense and will cause changes in your life and the lives of those you are close to. The effects can vary, however.

On one hand, you may have very serious conflicts in relationships because you or the other person or both are trying to control each other's actions. Often you see relationships simply as struggles between two people. If you attract people who seem to always start fights with you, think about your own actions and make sure that you have not somehow invited it. Also look at the kind of people to whom you are attracted, to see if perhaps you inadvertently avoid those who would be easier to get along with.

If you are the one who tries to manipulate the relationship, you must learn to be more tolerant, to let people be. This placement can signify very powerful and destructive battles with others unless you learn to lower the level of these energies.

On the other hand, this aspect can indicate that throughout your life, your encounters with others will be opportunities for positive change as well as the negative kind described above. Every close relationship will teach you something about yourself and give you increased self-understanding. Your relationships have an emotional intensity that you may not be aware of now, but later on you will seek it. You will avoid people who cannot respond as intensely as you want. However, in all of your relationships you must try to be completely honest and fair with the other person, even if the other person doesn't seem to be making the same effort. Otherwise the negative side of this aspect will be more prominent.

Pluto Conjunct Midheaven

During your life you will go through many changes, but you will always have the desire to make an impact upon the world and to be regarded as a person of significance. The danger you must face is that you may want to go too far too fast and thereby alienate the people who have authority over you. While you are young, this will mean mostly parents and teachers, but you might occasionally encounter police or government officials.

You are likely to have a very intense relationship with one of your parents, and it is important that this be a good relationship as well. Unless it is constructive, guilt and other forms of emotional bondage may arise from it. You must be able to talk to that parent openly and honestly, and he or she must be able to let go as you become more mature. Unfortunately this placement often indicates that one of your parents tries to arrest your development at some point through being overpossessive and domineering.

Sometimes the method is very subtle, using self-sacrifice and guilt, instead of more open power tactics. But a positive and creative parent relationship will give you self-confidence and the desire to achieve something of great significance in your life.

One thought that you must always keep before you, however, is the necessity of doing everything openly and honestly. Otherwise, at some point in your life, all the negative consequences of your actions will be exposed, thus tearing down whatever good you have done. Nixon is an example of this type of person.

Pluto Sextile Midheaven

This aspect denotes that you are ambitious to succeed and be a person of some significance in later life. But it also suggests that you have certain talents that will be especially useful in this regard. In particular, you enjoy getting to the heart of any mystery and finding out what is really going on. You are very fond of puzzles, and solving puzzles of some kind may be the basis of your profession when you are older. This aspect also indicates a natural ability in psychology, an understanding of people's inner motivations, which will be useful no matter what you do.

On the positive side, you will discover as you get older that you enjoy helping people who need advice or guidance. This will become more pronounced when you are an adult and keep encountering people whose lives need to be reconstructed in some way. You will derive great satisfaction from assisting in this process. While you are young, you will very much enjoy salvaging discarded objects and making something useful out of them, demonstrating the potential of what others regard as waste. Because of this, you may be surrounded by a great deal of clutter, but the results can be quite spectacular.

However, as you get older and begin focusing this pattern on people rather than on objects, a great danger can arise. You gain a great deal of power when you help others, power to influence and to make others live up to what you want. In trying to help someone, always be careful that your main concern is the other person's benefit. Do not manipulate others' lives for trivial reasons.

Pluto Square Midheaven

This aspect indicates that you will have to make a special effort to get along with people. You must make it clear that you will not try to fulfill your goals in life at their expense and that you will not allow them to take advantage of you either. A very ambitious person, you probably picture yourself as being quite important when you are older. This can be a very constructive attitude, but it will be difficult to achieve your ambition unless you are able to get along with others, to give them a constructive part in your goals. Also it is very important that you play the game of life honorably and adhere to high ethical standards. You don't need to worry that doing so will be dull, because whatever you get involved in, you make it exciting and powerful.

You have a strong desire to bring about change in your world, and you may want to be a reformer and rebuilder. However, you should not try to get power simply for its own sake. You have to use the energies of Pluto for a purpose higher than yourself. It is perfectly permissible to be personally rewarded by your work—you do not have to be totally self-denying—but personal gain should not be your principal motivation.

A born psychologist, you should be able to gain great insight into human behavior. But again you must not use this knowledge for personal gain or to manipulate others. Eventually you may choose a profession that will use this knowledge.

Pluto Trine Midheaven

This aspect indicates that you will always want to use your resources and talents to the best of your ability in order to get ahead in life. Even while you are young, long before most people are considering a career, you will begin to learn the best ways of using your talents to get where you want to go. However, some problems may arise in the course of your development that you should be aware of.

For example, although later you will be concerned with resources, now you may simply be interested in owning things, which may result in your having a lot of useless clutter. Also you should not be so possessive that you are unwilling to share at all.

On another level, this aspect can signify that you get very involved in learning various skills. This can be very useful if you concentrate on useful skills and if you do not get so wrapped up in them that you lose track of relationships with others. Do not become too self-involved. Any situation in which you feel compelled to act by some inner compulsion can be bad for you because you are not aware of yourself and what you are doing at the time. As a result, your activities might have totally unexpected consequences. Make sure you understand your reasons for doing whatever you do.

Nevertheless you have a strong drive to get ahead and to succeed, which should be very advantageous in competition with others. Your objectives in life may change several times and as an adult you may change careers, but your work and your outside interests should be enormously satisfying to you.

Pluto Inconjunct Midheaven

You may have trouble with older people who try to teach you how to effectively take control of your life. Even while you are young, you may resent their control over you and resist everything they are trying to teach you. To a great extent, your path in life will be shaped by your early confrontations with authority figures. Your parents would be well advised to give you as much control as possible over your own affairs and as much self-determination as you can handle. They should not try to keep an extremely tight rein on you, for if they do, you will explode and become very difficult to handle. Also your self-esteem would be damaged. Your parents and teachers should be very straightforward with you, because if you feel that people are not being honest with you, you will not be honest with them. You are quite capable of acting behind people's backs if you consider it necessary or if you feel that you never get your own way.

Another problem that can arise if you are not treated properly is that you may withdraw into yourself and become very secretive, as though you have something to hide even when you don't. This can make people distrust you.

Your parents should discipline you in a straightforward manner, and when the punishment is completed, they should leave it at that. You should never be made to feel guilty or remorseful and have no opportunity to make amends for your wrongdoing. With this aspect, feelings of guilt can lead to serious psychological problems.

Pluto Opposition Midheaven

Your early childhood experiences will have an unusually strong effect upon your whole life. One parent in particular will be very important to you, and it is essential that that parent's influence be for the good. The problem is that the energies resulting from your early childhood experiences operate at a very deep inner level, probably unconsciously, so that they affect your life in ways that are difficult to understand. Negative experiences in childhood may give rise to fears, which bring about compulsive behavior patterns and bad habits. You might not even be aware of these fears, but if you understood them consciously, they would be less difficult.

On the other hand, attitudes that you pick up from your elders may seriously limit your ability to make judgments on the basis of your experiences. Be very wary about acquiring any prejudices, and always question your beliefs so that you know they are helping your life rather than hindering it.

One of your parents may try to exert too great an influence over you, even when you have outgrown the need for it. That parent must recognize each new stage of your life and let go of you a bit at each stage. If he or she tries to control you too much for too long, your psychological development will be seriously retarded. Of course, good influences from that parent will also have a very powerful positive effect on your whole life. It is simply that the bond with that parent is very strong, which can have both good and bad long-term effects upon your development.

Chapter Fifteen

Rising Sign

The Ascendant in the Chart

The Ascendant in your horoscope indicates the ways in which you interact with the world around you, the energies you put out and the energies you receive from others. Aspects to the Ascendant indicate what kinds of interaction you experience with others, the impressions you make on people and the areas of your life that most involve other people. Often these aspects tell you about yourself, not directly but through encountering other people. It is very important to realize that any behavior pattern that you constantly experience with others, even when you seem to have nothing to do with it, is a reflection of some part of yourself that you are unaware of. So if you have recurring social problems, look within yourself for the solution.

The sign of the Ascendant is as important as the Sun sign, and its effects are often more obvious to other people, because it represents how your personality appears to others. No sign is better or worse than the others, however. Each sign has its own potential strengths, which you should develop, and weaknesses, which you should minimize. You can be successful in ways that are truly satisfying, no matter what your rising sign.

You may run into problems, however, if your rising sign is quite different in nature from your Sun sign, because there is a conflict between an element of your inner self and the way you appear to others. This is not usually because you are dishonest but because there is a real conflict between different parts of yourself. When you deal with people, you may feel that there are two yous.

Aries Rising

You are a free spirit who likes to do things your own way and to be the first whenever possible. No matter how you are feeling inside, you always try to act energetic, active and self-assertive. Sometimes this is more mask than reality, and if you feel like being calm, gentle and serene, do so, for it is not inappropriate.

You like to compete with others, especially in one-to-one situations. Competitiveness may carry you far in life, if you can accept losing gracefully and if you learn to cooperate when necessary. Cooperating is sometimes a problem because you are so independent.

When you feel depressed or unhappy, you do not like to show it. Instead, you are likely to make a joke about your mood, letting others know that you do not take it seriously. Others will like you for the positive energy that you radiate and for the fact that you don't drag others down when you feel bad. At the same time your lighthearted attitude about your feelings may make it hard to get sympathy when you really need it.

You tend to be rash and impulsive, acting first and thinking later. At your best you are courageous, but at your worst you are reckless. Learn to be a little more thoughtful about your actions.

You will fight for what you believe in, so it is important to think carefully about your beliefs, so that your energies will go to a good cause.

Taurus Rising

You are very calm and deliberate in your actions. You don't like to move too quickly or act hastily. And when you do make a move, you want it to accomplish something, for you are a practical person. As long as you feel sure that your efforts will achieve results, you are willing to work very patiently to complete the task. With this kind of persistence, you can achieve just as much as people who seem to work faster but who are not so steady.

Sometimes you are quite stubborn, and the more that someone applies pressure, the more firmly you resist. Someone who wants to make you do something has to talk you into it very gently without arousing your stubbornness.

Outwardly, you appear quite calm and self-possessed. Because you do not get upset easily, you can calm down those who are more easily upset. Even when you feel considerable turmoil inside, you may not show it. It is not that you suppress your. feelings, but that your exterior does not reveal them very readily. At the same time, you show others an earthy kind of warmth and friendliness, so that they do not think of you as cold. Most people with Taurus rising have a kind of charm that makes them well liked by others.

You enjoy comfort and the good things of life. You may also be rather lazy, preferring to sit around and relax rather than getting up and doing something active or energetic.

Gemini Rising

You are a very active person who likes to get around, meet people and have as many different experiences as possible. Because you are so restless, you find it difficult to stay in one place for any length of time. If you have to be confined, as in school. you begin to feel itchy, and it is hard to keep your mind on the subject. In general you do not stay with one project for very long. You prefer activities that do not demand persistence, that enable you to do a lot in a short time. However, with your quick mind, you can learn a lot despite your lack of persistence.

You like to communicate with others, and in fact you may have difficulty keeping quiet even when you are supposed to. Instead of just sitting back and passively listening, you want to be actively engaged. Sometimes this takes the form of writing ability or a fondness for books, anything that keeps your mind going. Sometimes Gemini rising indicates ability in such fields as journalism, editing, communications or mass media. It can also be an indication of considerable ability with the hands or in science and math.

One of the virtues of this sign is that you will never really grow old. You will always look younger than you are, which may be a bother when you are young, but you will appreciate it when you get older. Even more important, you will always be open to new ideas and experiences, so that you will never grow old in your mind either.

Cancer Rising

You are a very sensitive person and very attached to familiar surroundings. Because of this, you are somewhat cautious and prefer to make changes in your environment rather slowly. When you encounter new people, you are friendly enough, but you won't talk about your inner feelings until you get to know them quite well. However, once you decide to trust someone, you trust him or her completely. As a result, the friends you make while you are young will probably stay with you for the rest of your life.

Where you live while you are young will always be important to you, and even later, when you have grown up and perhaps moved to a new area, you will prefer places that remind you of home.

If you feel secure in yourself and self-confident, you can be a generous person, always willing to give of yourself. You especially enjoy protecting people who have been hurt by the outrages of others. You are sensitive to people's feelings and do not like to hurt them, physically or psychologically. You know how easily your feelings are hurt by harsh words, so even while young you try to be gentle.

In those areas in which you lack self-confidence, you have a serious problem. Your sensitivity makes it difficult for you to take criticism or harsh words from anyone, especially those whom you love. When you feel hurt, you withdraw into yourself and avoid others. Sometimes you may pretend not to care, so that you seem unusually insensitive to people's feelings and words. However, this is not really the case, and it actually will hurt you to act this way.

If your childhood home is not a stable, secure place, you will feel the lack most of your life. Therefore it is important that you have security from the beginning.

Leo Rising

You like to be the center of attention, to appear strong, confident and dominant, even if something is bothering you. Your pride is so important that even when your feelings are hurt badly, you may act as if nothing is wrong.

You like to be the leader, and you can be a good one as long as you remember that leadership is a responsibility as well as power and privilege. If you feel that people are dealing with you fairly, you conduct yourself with dignity and honor. Other young people may do cheap or dishonest things, but ordinarily you will not go along.

Leo is the fixed fire sign. You can be stubborn, especially if your pride is involved. You don't respect grown-ups just because they are older than you. You are idealistic, and people have to prove to you that they have integrity. But when they do, you are very loyal in return.

You like to have rich and elegant things that you can show off to others. But remember that just because something impresses people, it is not necessarily good. You need to learn the difference.

People who have Leo rising are often very impressive looking, which is a powerful asset. Others may or may not see you as beautiful or handsome, but as you grow up you will develop a regal bearing that will make others feel that you are dependable. Many people will like you, and most will also respect you.

Virgo Rising

You may be somewhat shy and not very self-assertive toward others. You may think of yourself as an uninteresting person or as one who appeals to only a few people. This is probably not true, but it is a feeling shared by many persons with Virgo rising. In fact you are a soft-spoken, neat and orderly person who is quite likable. Your only real problem may come from the fact that you are a perfectionist, and you may demand that others live up to the same high standards that you set for yourself. You are quick to point out people's flaws to them, but you should learn to be a bit more tactful. Sometimes correcting someone is not worth the trouble it causes.

You are quite practical, and you do not like to waste time on impractical schemes. If you cannot see the point of some activity, you are not interested in doing it. Often you won't do something for its own sake; it has to have a purpose. But in making objects of one sort or another, you have excellent taste, although very reserved, and you like everything to be both graceful and practical.

If you can be useful to others or find some purpose that you believe in, you will be very happy. You believe in work, and you feel best when you are involved in some project. This attitude will intensify as you get older.

Libra Rising

With this rising sign, you are likely to be attractive to others and probably popular. Because you are very concerned about getting along with people, you take the trouble to learn how. This is not to say that you never get what you want, but instead of using force of character to persuade people to do something your way, you use charm. Even when your actions annoy people, something in your manner prevents them from getting really angry at you.

You dislike unpleasantness in any form, whether it is physical ugliness or angry feelings between people, so you do your best to keep everything peaceful. And when you are confronted with ugliness, you try to make it better or cover it up with something beautiful.

In this same spirit, you like to dress elegantly, perhaps even flashily, although some element in your taste usually prevents you from dressing too gaudily. You also like to be surrounded by beautiful things, and you may develop an early taste for art, music and literature.

In your desire to be agreeable, you must be sure not to compromise something that is important to you. Sometimes it is necessary to fight, and you should learn when and how to do so. Many people with Libra rising actually become quite competitive, once they have gotten over the stage of being agreeable at all costs.

Scorpio Rising

You are rather quiet and reserved, but others see clearly that you have deep emotions and feelings, even though you may not say very much. You seem secretive, although that is not really your intention. But you do find it difficult to make yourself understood to people.

You are quite stubborn, and if necessary you will fight very hard for your position against anyone who opposes you. Your anger is not easily aroused, but when it is, it is a very strong anger that can't be calmed down easily. You want very much for others to take you seriously, and even if they don't at first, they will eventually. With this rising sign, you may not seem very formidable at first, but others will quickly discover how tough and resourceful you are.

You like to experience life with your total being. In fact, others may feel that you go to extremes. You feel that if you approach a new experience cautiously and with moderation, you are watering life down. Thus you may display a kind of courage that others find frightening, although you are not usually reckless. You think out a situation in advance and then take a calculated risk.

In addition, you are quite sensitive to other people's feelings. You are somewhat easily hurt, but instead of pulling back, you often strike out with a cutting remark or biting sarcasm. Anyone who watches you at all carefully will see your anger. Your sensitivity also makes you interested in what makes people tick, and even while quite young, you have an unusual understanding of people's inner selves.

Sagittarius Rising

You are a very open and outgoing person, quite frank and honest; in fact, you may be blunt to the point of indiscretion. But people who are hurt by the frankness of your remarks feel better when they realize that you really do not intend any harm. Your honesty results from a sincere desire to keep life straight and simple. You do not like social niceties, seeing them simply as obstacles to real communication.

You have a great deal of energy, and you enjoy freedom very much. When you have to remain quiet or confined for any length of time, you get extremely restless. If you can't direct your own life as much as you want, you feel trapped. For this reason you are particularly fond of open spaces. Sagittarians usually like mountainous areas, and being outdoors in general is very good for you.

But while you need to run your own life, you do not feel any particular urge to run others' lives. You feel that having control over people is more of a responsibility than you want to take. However, you do not mind informing them of their duties and obligations.

You are likely to be interested in sports and outdoor activities as well as subjects related to the outdoors, such as ecology and nature studies.

Capricorn Rising

A practical person, you are reserved but also ambitious. You want to achieve something of significance in this world, and you are willing to work to achieve it. You respect successful, prominent people, and you try to learn from them, if you can.

While you are young, you appear older than you really are. You are very serious about life, and you view the world as a difficult place in which you must work very hard and get few breaks. It is difficult for you to understand how some people can just breeze through life without putting out much effort. Try to avoid feeling envious or bitter about such people, however, because you need to work for your own good. If you think about your own life, you will realize that. It isn't easy for you to just relax and play, and as you get older, this will be even more of a problem.

Your parents are very important to you, especially your father, and a good relationship with them will bring out the best in you. Without their active support, you will get to feeling lonely and isolated from others, believing that the world is uniquely against you. Oddly enough, people with Capricorn rising have a very good sense of humor, in that they are able to make fun of themselves. The ability to laugh at yourself is a necessary antidote to the seriousness of Capricorn.

Aquarius Rising

You have a good mind, which you like to use, and you are very open to new ideas and experiences. You don't like to do things as they have always been done, preferring to find new ways that might be better. But although you are interested in new things, it is very difficult for anyone to persuade you to take up a new idea. You want to form your own opinions so much that when someone tries to talk you into a point of view, you turn away from it almost automatically.

Aquarius rising is often an indication of interest in science, mathematics and mechanics. But you may also be interested in social problems, and, later in life, in social reform. Even now you have great sympathy for the downtrodden, and you don't like to see anyone get an unfair break. You want everyone to get along on a friendly basis with no one being superior or inferior. For this reason you may have difficulty accepting your elders as authorities, unless you are convinced that they are completely fair.

Usually you are calm and able to control your emotions. Because you learn with your mind rather than your feelings, you have difficulty understanding emotional people who let their feelings run away with them.

Once you are convinced that an idea is true, you try to talk everyone else into agreeing with you. You have some difficulty letting others have views of the world that differ from yours.

Pisces Rising

You are very sensitive and can perceive others' feelings very quickly, but in such a way that they become your feelings. For this reason, it is a good idea to avoid being around negative people, because you will start feeling negative also. You are inclined to be idealistic, so it is important for you to believe in something beyond what you know with your senses. You should avoid people who try to disillusion others as a matter of course, because when you become disillusioned, you feel bitter and depressed.

You like to dream and to retreat to your own little world from time to time. This is fine, but you should not use it as an escape too often. Your imaginative quality may give you talent in art or music, or it may simply emerge as inventiveness and creativity that you can apply in many areas of your life.

You are very sympathetic to others. If someone needs help, you are there to give it. In fact you may gather around yourself people who are dependent upon you in some way. This can create problems later in life, if you start living for such people rather than for yourself.

You are not always very self-assertive, and you may be envious of those who appear to have more energy or who can push to get their own way. Do not envy them, because the world needs your kind of person also, the quieter people who try to make the world better for the rest of us.

PLANETS IN TRANSIT
Life Cycles for Living

Robert Hand

This is *the* definitive work on transiting planets. Its psychological insight and completeness as a reference book have brought Robert Hand recognition as a leading astrologer. Hand takes a humanistic, multi-leveled approach to transits: the events that may happen, the feelings you may experience, and the possibilities of each transit for growth and awareness.

This book covers complete delineations of all the major transits—conjunction, sextile, square, trine and opposition—that occur between transiting Sun, Moon and all planets to each planet in the natal chart and the Ascendant and Midheaven, as well as complete delineations of each planet transiting each house of the natal chart. These 720 lucid delineations are full of insight for both the professional astrologer and the beginner.

ISBN: 0-914918-24-9
544 pages, 6½" x 9¼", paper $29.95

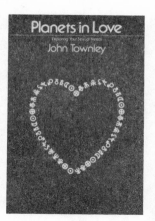

PLANETS IN COMPOSITE

Analyzing Human Relationships

Robert Hand

Robert Hand has written an important reference book that is much needed in the astrological field, a definitive work about human relationships.

After extensive research and professional experience, Hand has concluded that the composite chart technique works more effectively than other techniques as a method of interpreting relationships.

Planets in Composite, contains an introduction to casting and reading the composite chart, five case studies and twelve chapters of delineations. You will find 374 interpretations of composite planetary positions including forty-one delineations of the Moon's nodes.

Planets in Composite is the most authoritative book ever written about the astrology of human relationships.

PLANETS IN LOVE

Exploring Your Emotional and Sexual Needs

John Townley

This is the first major astrological work to take a direct and detailed look at human sexuality. It explores the variety of relationships people form to satisfy their individual emotional and sexual needs.

An intimate analysis of sex and love, *Planets in Love* is not a collection of chatty commentaries on paired Sun signs but 550 in-depth delineations of all planetary positions by sign, house and aspect.

In addition, the book includes numerous case studies illustrating the use of the natal chart in interpreting an individual's unique expression of love.

This is a mature text that takes a sophisticated approach to love, sex and sexuality.

ISBN: 0-914918-22-2
384 pages, 6½" x 9¼", paper $19.95

ISBN: 0-914918-21-4
384 pages, 6½" x 9¼", paper $19.95

PLANETS IN HOUSES

Experiencing Your Environment

Robert Pelletier

This major work brings natal
horoscope interpretation to a new level
of accuracy, concreteness and richness
of detail.

While the fundamental forces at
work in a chart can be found in the
relationships of the planets, signs and
aspects, it is the houses that bring
chart-reading down to earth,
indicating how planetary energies will
work themselves out in daily life.

Pelletier synthesizes the meaning of
each planet in each house—as derived
by counting from each of the houses
and in relation to each of the other
houses with which it forms trines,
sextiles, squares, oppositions,
inconjuncts and semisextiles.

So if you've been waiting for the
definitive work on house meanings, a
book that will both encourage the
beginner and challenge the expert, this
is the book for you.

ISBN: 0-914918-27-3
384 pages, 6½" x 9¼", paper $19.95

PLANETS IN ASPECT

Understanding Your Inner Dynamics

Robert Pelletier

"Robert Pelletier has presented the
world with a mighty volume of
mature, erudite and modern aspect
delineations...Delineations by Pelletier
embrace a large portion of every
aspect's spectrum of potential
manifestation."

—Noel Tyl, *Gnostic News*

There have been many books
written about astrology, but the
subject of aspects has often been
overlooked or treated too lightly.
Planets in Aspect is a book every
astrologer needs: a complete reference
work on planetary aspects.

Pelletier delineates 314 aspects;
every major aspect between planet is
covered: conjunction, sextile, square,
trine, opposition and inconjunct with
300 words devoted to each aspect.

Planets in Aspect is the most thorough
study of aspects ever published.

ISBN: 0-914918-20-6
384 pages, 6½" x 9¼", paper $19.95

WORLD EPHEMERIS
FOR THE 20ᵀᴴ CENTURY

by Para Research

Preface by Robert Hand

The *World Ephemeris for the 20th Century* is the first computer-calculated and computer-typeset ephemeris with letter quality printing. Now ease and clarity in reading is combined with accuracy and precision of data to provide the most complete and convenient ephemeris available for astrological calculation and analysis.

Available in either Midnight or Noon calculations, the *World Ephemeris* presents the Sun's position accurate to the second of arc; the Moon's mean Node and the nine planetary positions are given to the minute of arc.

Positions are reported for every day of the 20th Century. One hundred and one years in all.

Midnight Edition: ISBN 0-914918-60-5
624 pages, 8 x 9¼", paper $29.95

Noon Edition: ISBN 0-914918-61-3
624 pages, 8 x 9¼", paper $29.95

HOROSCOPE SYMBOLS

Robert Hand

Horoscope Symbols, Para Research's latest book by leading astrologer Robert Hand, explores astrological symbolism. Hand, with twenty years experience in the field, analyzes traditional meanings, considers alternatives and uses his own experience to develop and clarify these symbols. He thoroughly explains astrological symbolism—its history as well as its application for modern astrologers. In this new work, Robert Hand continues to build his reputation as the major new voice in humanistic astrology.

The author covers such basics as signs, planets, houses and aspects, illuminating their core meanings. In addition, Hand discusses midpoints, harmonics, the effect of retrograde planets and other often confusing areas for the astrologer.

Previously announced as *Planets in Synthesis, Horoscope Symbols* is the culmination of four years work. If you are new to astrology, this is the book to grow with. If you have already studied the basics, Robert Hand's approach will give you new perspective, insight and wisdom.

To quote the noted astrologer Alan Oken reviewing Robert Hand's *Horoscope Symbols:* "As usual, his writing is very clear, . . . what is most noteworthy is his ability to synthesize his comprehensive understanding of astrology from his basic scientific viewpoint . . . in humanistic prose.

ISBN 0-914918-16-8
400 pages, paper, 6½" x 9¼" $24.95